METHODS in

MICROBIOLOGY

METHODS in

MICROBIOLOGY

Edited by
T. BERGAN

Department of Microbiology, Institute of Pharmacy
Aker Hospital, University of Oslo, Oslo, Norway

J. R. NORRIS

Agricultural Research Council
Meat Research Institute
Bristol, England

Volume 10

 1978

ACADEMIC PRESS
London · New York · San Francisco
A Subsidiary of Harcourt Brace Jovanovich, Publishers

ACADEMIC PRESS INC. (LONDON) LTD
24–28 Oval Road
London NW1

U.S. Edition published by
ACADEMIC PRESS INC.
111 Fifth Avenue
New York, New York 10003

Library of Congress Catalog Card Number: 68–57745
ISBN: 0–12–521510–X

PRINTED IN GREAT BRITAIN BY
ADLARD AND SON LIMITED
DORKING, SURREY

LIST OF CONTRIBUTORS

G. A. J. AYLIFFE, *Hospital Infection Research Laboratory, Summerfield Hospital, Birmingham B18 7QQ, England*

T. BERGAN, *Department of Microbiology, Institute of Pharmacy, and Department of Microbiology, Aker Hospital, University of Oslo, Oslo 13, Norway*

E. L. BIBERSTEIN, *School of Veterinary Medicine, University of California, U.S.A.*

B. WESLEY CATLIN, *Department of Microbiology, Medical College of Wisconsin, Milwaukee, Wisconsin*

DAN DANIELSSON, *The Department of Clinical Bacteriology and Immunology, Central County Hospital, S-701 85 Orebro, Sweden*

J. R. W. GOVAN, *Department of Bacteriology, Medical School, University of Edinburgh, Edinburgh, Scotland*

KARL-AXEL KARLSSON, *Department of Biological Products, National Veterinary Institute, Stockholm, Sweden*

B. LANYI AND T. BERGAN, *National Institute of Hygiene, Budapest, Hungary, Department of Microbiology, Institute of Pharmacy, and Department of Microbiology, Aker Hospital, University of Oslo, Oslo, Norway*

J. MAELAND, *The Department of Medical Microbiology, University of Trondheim, 7000 Trondheim, Norway*

NORMAN B. MCCULLOUGH, *Departments of Microbiology and Public Health and of Medicine, Michigan State University, East Lansing, Michigan 48824, U.S.A.*

T. MEITERT AND EUGENIA MEITERT, *The Cantacuzino Institute, Bucharest 35, Romania*

SMIGEO NAMIOKA, *Faculty of Veterinary Medicine, Hokkaido University, Sapporo, 060, Japan*

TOV OMLAND, *Norwegian Defence Microbiological Laboratory, National Institute of Public Health, Oslo, Norway*

NEYLAN A. VEDROS, *School of Public Health, University of California, Berkeley, California*

v

PREFACE

Growing awareness of the factors controlling the spread of disease-causing bacteria in various environments has led to the proliferation of methods for typing individual isolates of human pathogens. For some organisms these are highly developed, and there is a correspondingly detailed understanding of their epidemiology; in other cases understanding is still rudimentary. Although the main typing techniques, biochemical, serological, phage and bacteriocin typing, are applied across a wide spectrum of bacterial types, the details of the technical modifications needed to adapt them to different genera are important and numerous and we are responding to several suggestions from microbiologists in bringing together the typing techniques and discussion of their results in a series of four Volumes of "Methods in Microbiology" (Volumes 10–13). We hope that the Volumes will thereby contribute to a standardization and optimalization of methods.

The collection of various typing methods for many different species also contributes to the general understanding of the problems involved in typing and interpreting the results. Often, the research worker may think that difficulties with the methods and species with which he is working are unique. Consideration of the Chapters contained in the Volumes shows that many problems are universal. We hope that collecting the information together will serve to demonstrate the areas that might benefit from further attention and inspire development and research.

We have tried, as far as possible, to follow the order of genera as they appear in Bergey's "Manual of Determinative Bacteriology", 8th Edition. Volume 10 opens with two general Chapters dealing with the application of typing methods to epidemic disease in general and to the particular problems involved in studying hospital infections. Other Chapters deal with *Pseudomonas*, *Brucella*, *Francisella*, *Haemophilus*, *Pasturella* and *Neisseria*.

It is a pleasure for us to acknowledge the friendly co-operation and patience of our contributors. As in earlier Volumes we have, as far as possible, allowed individual authors considerable freedom in selecting material for presentation and in choosing the way in which the Chapters are constructed. Nevertheless, we have ensured that methods are described in full detail and that references are adequate for the effective orientation of newcomers to a particular group of organisms. It is our hope that these Volumes will make a significant contribution to an important and rapidly expanding area of microbiology.

T. Bergan
J. R. Norris

November, 1977

CONTENTS

CONTENTS OF PUBLISHED VOLUMES

Usefulness, Applications and Limitations of Epidemiological Typing Methods to Elucidate Nosocomial Infections and the Spread of Communicable Diseases

T. MEITERT and EUGENIA MEITERT

The Cantacuzino Institute, Bucharest, Romania

I. GENERAL INTRODUCTION

The use of modern epidemiological typing methods in the survey of communicable diseases is fully recognized today. A very important place in epidemiological typing methods is held by phage typing. These methods (phage typing, serotyping, bacteriocin (geno) typing, biochemical typing,

typing by antibiogram and R factors) are used either separately or together to obtain a more detailed level of differentiation within bacterial species.

The history of the practical use of these methods runs parallel to the history of the development of phage typing as a supplementary and very necessary approach to epidemiological investigation. The discovery of the bacteriophage by Twort (1915) and d'Herelle (1917) and of lysogeny by Bordet and Ciucă (1921, 1921a) opened up new ways for research in the field of bacterial genetics and into the ecological, pathogenic and epidemiological characteristics of the host–parasite relationships involved in many communicable diseases.

Today, control of many communicable diseases is not possible without an active follow up of the epidemiological process, control of the spread of pathogenic agents, sources of infection, mechanisms of transmission and features of the spread of infection in terms of the susceptible population. Repeated follow up over several years of these factors by modern methods of epidemiological typing within the framework of national and international programmes, is of particular importance in disease control.

The present Chapter describes the study of the applications and limitations of these methods, with examples from current epidemiological practice. We will discuss, from this point of view, the principal methods of epidemiological typing among which phage typing occupies a foremost place. It is designed primarily for the subdivision of microbial species whose serotype has usually been previously determined. Serotyping and the other approaches mentioned above are also applicable to a series of microbial species of medical interest.

II. PHAGE TYPING

A. Introduction

Phage typing is a method of bacterial differentiation based upon the sensitivity of strains to certain bacteriophages.

Bail (1921) seems to have been the first to be interested in the differentiation of bacterial strains with the aid of bacteriophages. Subsequently, attempts were made for some time to determine certain antigens with the help of phages (Burnet, 1927) or to use them for diagnostic purposes (Sonnenschein, 1925, 1928, 1929; Schmidt, 1932), but phage typing actually began with the investigations of Marcuse (1934) concerning the subdivision of *Salmonella typhi* strains.

The methods of phage typing include:

(a) Direct phage typing with:
- empirically found, unadapted phages (e.g. phage typing of *S. typhimurium* according to Lilleengen, 1948);

– adapted phages (e.g. phage typing *S. typhi* according to Craigie and Yen, 1938).

(b) Indirect phage typing (lysogenotyping) based upon the lysogeny of bacteria, i.e. detection and identification of temperate phages present as prophages in bacteria (for instance phage typing of *S. typhimurium* described by Boyd, 1950, and Boyd *et al.*, 1951).

(c) Combined phage typing: The concomitant use of direct and indirect phage typing.

B. Applications and usefulness

The increasingly widespread use of phage typing in various countries throughout the world for the subdivision of different microbial species has shown that the principal applications and possibilities of this method might be summed up as follows:

1. *Determination of the spread of some organisms in time and space*

There are universal or widespread phage types while others are only of regional interest. Among widely disseminated *S. typhi* phage types A, E_1, F_1, D_1 may be cited; phage types such as B, O, 38 are less widespread. Other *S. typhi* phage types occur only in certain regions of the world; such as phage type M occurring especially in the Far East, in Indonesia or Vietnam. Likewise phage type G is seen in the Far East, in Egypt and Congo, phase types L_1 and L_2 are encountered in North Africa, and so forth.

Ziesché and Rische (1973) report in East Germany *Shigella sonnei* phage types spread throughout the whole country, occurring every year, and others which are only of local importance.

For the different *Escherichia coli* serotypes O_{111}: $K_{58}(B_4)$, O_{26}: $K_{60}(B_6)$, O_{55}: $K_{59}(B_5)$ Nicolle *et al.* (1960) also showed the presence of phage types either with a general or a local distribution. Similar remarks were made for the same *E. coli* serotypes according to the phase typing scheme of Eörsi *et al.* (1953, 1957) and Milch and Deak (1961).

Corynebacterium diphtheriae phage type XVI (Saragea and Maximescu, 1966) was identified in a collection of strains isolated in Australia in 1938 (Gibson *et al.*, 1970), and the same phage type was identified later in Europe (Italy, Jugoslavia, Hungary) and Canada (Vancouver). *C. diphtheriae* phage type I "a" was identified first (by the same authors) in the U.S.A. and never in Europe, except incidentally in Hungary where it was introduced by some relatives coming from the U.S.A. (Saragea, 1975). Saragea *et al.* (1973) showed that in a certain geographical area the same *C. diphtheriae* phage type will persist until all healthy carriers are cleared up.

2. Differentiation between endemic and epidemic strains

The existence of a great number of phage types (for instance in *Sh. sonnei* and *Sh. flexneri* (Meitert *et al.*, 1975) within a given territory allows for differentiation of the endemic from the epidemic strains isolated from foci and which, in most cases, belong to only one predominant phage type.

Another example is the differentiation, by phage typing, of ubiquitous *Staphylococcus aureus* strains from epidemic strains with an increased virulence—of real importance from the viewpoint of public health (Meyer, 1966).

3. Spread of epidemic foci from one area to another

For certain phage typing schemes, for instance that used for typing *Vibrio cholerae eltor* biotype, the main usefulness is "in tracing the spread of the epidemic from one place to another, rather than tracing chronic carriers and the spread of infection through individuals" (Mukerjee, 1973). It has thus been possible to demonstrate the spread of an infection from Calcutta to neighbouring districts and states (Mukerjee, 1963).

The original source of the cholera outbreak in Afghanistan, in 1960, was an infection in West Pakistan, likewise confirmed by phage typing of *Vibrio* strains isolated in two areas. Similarly, the 1958 cholera outbreak in Nepal could be linked up with the Bihar outbreaks.

Moreover, by phage typing, it was possible to detect the penetration of new phage types in a region, particularly when strains with these characteristics had not yet been encountered in the area.

4. Determination of the sources of infection in epidemics and epidemic foci

Phage typing fulfils a valuable function when establishing the source of numerous epidemic foci, since it allows us to exclude apparent sources and reveal the real source of infection. Many examples have been reported in this connection showing that in epidemics or epidemic foci with a single source of infection, the same phage type is isolated from all patients and contacts. Phage typing within the focus also makes it possible to establish the extent of the epidemic area, the persistence in the carriers of the pathogenic agent and differentiation of the epidemic strains from those of carriers or sporadic cases unrelated to the local outbreak.

Within an epidemic focus, corroboration of the epidemiological data with the phage typing results, makes it possible to establish the relationship of cases, thus excluding sporadic cases from a chain of epidemic ones. It is known that a phage typing scheme may be considered reliable when all strains of an epidemic focus, with a single source of infection, belong to the same phage type. For instance, the various cholera epidemics in India and in Thailand in 1966 were demonstrated by phage typing to start from a single source of infection (Mukerjee, 1973). Numerous similar examples are also found for phage typing of different other pathogenic agents: *Salmonella, Shigella, E. coli, C. diphtheriae* (Rische, 1973).

Moreover, phage typing also offers the possibility of establishing two or even more sources of infection within certain epidemic foci and the extent of the spread of different phage types by patients and carriers.

5. *The role of carriers in epidemic outbreaks*

Not all carriers initiate epidemic foci. Phage typing not only makes it possible to determine the carrier or carriers that caused an epidemic focus by contact or other mechanisms of transmission, but also permits the exclusion of certain carriers (with different phage types) as sources of an epidemic outbreak.

In the follow up of carriers, especially for *Staphylococcus aureus* (Popovici, 1968), *Pseudomonas aeruginosa* (E. Meitert and T. Meitert, 1973) and *C. diphtheriae* strains (Saragea *et al.*, 1973), phage typing may further contribute to determine:

– Carriage in time of a certain phage type and its disappearance (spontaneous or after treatment);
– Reinfection of carriers with the same or another phage type;
– The appearance of new carriers with identical or different phage types;
– The increased spread by contacts of certain epidemic phage types;
– The existence of a mixed carrier with several phage types;
– The role of carriers in alimentary food poisoning.

Many examples can be found in this connection in the Chapters dealing with specific pathogenic agents. We shall recall only the predominance, at a given moment, of certain *C. diphtheriae* strains (Saragea *et al.*, 1973). Thus, *C. diphtheriae* phage type XIV displayed a quicker spread, but shorter persistence in the community and caused milder clinical cases. Phage type XIV "a" showed a higher infectivity, but shorter persistence (duration of carriage in healthy subjects is about 2–3 years). Phage type IX caused sporadic cases, but the clinical picture has been more severe (Saragea *et al.*, 1973). It is of interest to note that at a given moment, *C. diphtheriae* phage type XIV produced about 20–35 healthy carriers around a patient, whereas with phage type XIV "a" there were only 10–12 carriers. With phage type IX no more than 2–3 carriers occurred around one index case.

6. *Retrospective elucidation of certain epidemiologic processes*

In 1957, in a camp on the Baltic Sea, a number of cases of typhoid fever were not identified as such. From the campers, who returned home to different regions of the country (East Germany), strains with the same phagolytic pattern (uncharacteristic Vi-strains) were isolated. Thus, it was possible to point out the epidemic focus retrospectively by phage typing (Sedlak and Rische, 1968).

By determining the phage type of some strains collected during the years 1927–1947, Blair and Carr (1960) identified 15·6% of 276 *Staphylococcus* strains as phage type 80, the test phage 80 being isolated later.

7. *Characterization and follow up of the spread in hospital of pathogenic and opportunist agents*

(a) *Determination of the epidemiological significance of certain strains of the same microbial species.* By phage typing of *E. coli* O:111, 55, 26 according to Eörsi *et al.* (1953, 1957), Milch and Deak (1961), it was possible to differentiate the following categories of strains:

– strains arising from a concurrent hospital outbreak;
– strains from a previous hospital outbreak;
– strains introduced more recently into the hospital (Milch, 1973).

Numerous examples may also be given for other microbial species.

(b) *The existence of a phage type in specimens from several patients and the increased incidence of the same phage type in a hospital ("hospital strains").* The selection of certain strains with an increased ability to spread and pathogenicity, often resistant to antibiotics in hospital conditions, is more easily followed up by phage typing.

Williams and Jevons (1960) showed that certain *Staph. aureus* staff strains may spread throughout a hospital without causing infections, while others always cause disease. The predominance in hospital of *Staph. aureus* phage type 80 over a certain period is well known (Nestorescu *et al.*, 1956, 1957a; Meyer, 1957; Meyer *et al.*, 1973; Ciucă *et al.*, 1958).

Similar observations have been made for other opportunists. Thus, Meitert and Meitert (1971) observed that *P. aeruginosa* strains belonging to the same phase type, isolated from hospital infections, were associated with increased properties of spread and virulence. Vieu (1969) showed that the diversity of *P. aeruginosa* phase types, which appear endemically in hospitals, contrast with the uniformity and virulence of the phage types isolated in extensive hospital outbreaks.

(c) *The occurrence of hospital strains in the environment.* Meyer *et al.* (1973) noticed that penicillin-resistant, phage group III staphylococci were at first seldom encountered outside hospitals, but were after a while gradually penetrating into the environment.

(d) *Change of phage type in hospital strains.*

(e) *Detection of mixed infections.*

(f) *Detection of autoinfection.*

(g) *The staff as a source of hospital infections.*

(h) *Determination of in-hospital epidemic evolution.*

(i) *Similarity of strains isolated from mother and child.*

(j) *Follow up of predominant phage types in hospital.*

(k) *The role of objects and drugs in dissemination of infections.*

Typing in nosocomial infections is the subject of Chapter 2 of this Volume.

8. *Epidemiological relationships between sporadic cases*

Strains isolated from endemic cases offer a greater variety of phage types than epidemic strains. This fact in many instances discounts the possibility of direct epidemiological relationships. There are, however, certain situations in which sporadic apparently unrelated cases may be correlated by phage typing. Thus, Bercovici *et al.* (1966) reported the same *Sh. boydii* phage type in several cases of acute enteritis occurring in different districts of a town. These followed the consumption of a meat jelly prepared by a chronic carrier from whom the same type was isolated.

9. *Determination of routes of transmission*

(a) *Phage typing in food infections.* In the course of food poisoning, isolation of the same phage type from food, from patients, and sometimes also from people who have prepared the food, may resolve the mechanism of an epidemic outbreak (Allison, 1949; Williams *et al.*, 1953; Ortel, 1957; Kühn *et al.*, 1973; Meyer *et al.*, 1973).

Phage typing may also elucidate the mechanism of occurrence of food poisoning produced by imported foodstuffs. Thus, Kallings *et al.* (1959) reported on food poisoning by frozen veal imported from New Zealand, contaminated with *S. typhimurium*, belonging to the same phage type, lysogenotype and biotype as that isolated from the patients.

A particularly interesting epidemiological situation exists when the distribution of a great number of new phage types within a certain area may be correlated with the wide-scale introduction of a new type of food product, as occurred in the case reported by Rische (1968). Consequent to the import of ducks into East Germany, numerous cases of various *S. typhimurium* phage types were reported.

Phage typing likewise may play an important role in the elucidation of different epidemic foci or epidemics caused by different species, e.g. *Salmonella*, *Shigella*, *E. coli*, transported by contaminated food. Particularly interesting in this connection are epidemics caused by milk or dairy products (Rische, 1968).

(b) *Phage typing in water-borne infections* allows differentiation between water-borne diseases and those originating from other sources. Predominant phage types may also be differentiated from less frequent phage types of the same species (transmitted by the same water source), as sometimes occurs in water-borne epidemics.

An interesting epidemiological situation was reported by Tomasic (1960) who described an aquatic epidemic focus, with 179 bacteriologically diagnosed cases. The causative agents of 163 cases were various phage types of *S. typhi* and *S. schottmuelleri*, discovered in the central water supply system of the area. The epidemiologist's attention was drawn to another 16 cases from a restricted area caused by *S. typhi* phage type A, subtype Duala. The patients had drunk water from a private well contaminated with the same *S. typhi* phage type as that isolated from the owner of the well, who was a carrier.

Phage typing is also increasingly used in water-borne epidemics caused by *Shigella*. Thus, Meitert *et al.* (1969) noticed the net prevalence of a *Sh. sonnei* phage type 6 in the course of a massive water-borne epidemic.

(c) *Phage typing to follow up relationship contact cases* is likewise currently used in epidemiological investigations (Istrati, 1960; Rische, 1973).

(d) *Phage typing in determining the role of fomites in the spread of cross-infections* has been mentioned previously (7.k).

10. *Relationships between virulence and phage types of some microbial strains*

No close correlation has yet been established between phage type and virulence; however, it has been found that more or less virulent epidemic strains belong to certain phage types. Different opinions exist concerning this problem.

Parker and Jevons (1963) noted a higher virulence of *Staph. aureus* phage type 80/81. Fekety *et al.* (1958) observed a clinical symptomatology in 70% of neonates, related to the presence of phage type 80/81. For certain staphylococci Fekety and Bennett (1959) used the term "epidemic virulence", referring to strains that are able not only to produce disease but which may also cause a greater number of infections. Parker and Jevons (1963) even established for different phage types of *Staph. aureus* an "index of epidemic virulence". Nevertheless, Meyer *et al.* (1973) consider that virulence is not a feature linked to the lytic spectrum, but an individual property of the strain, so that a correlation cannot be established between the lytic spectrum and the clinical form of the disease. Nestorescu *et al.* (1958), while investigating the virulence and toxinogeny of *Staph. aureus* phage type 80, which had spread in a hospital environment, did not observe any significant differences from other phage types.

A closer correlation, however, could be observed between enterotoxinogeny and the phase type of *Staph. aureus* strains belonging to groups III and IV, isolated from food poisoning cases (Allison, 1949; Williams *et al.*, 1953; Gullotti and Spano, 1960; Meyer *et al.*, 1973), enterocolitis (Hallander and Laurell, 1966) or other infections (respiratory, burns, wounds, etc.) (Hallander and Laurell, 1966). Popovici *et al.* (1966) showed that while staphylococci of bovine origin belonged to group IV, the enterotoxic staphylococci which produced food poisoning belonged mainly to group III. Bülow (1966) showed that furuncles could be produced by inoculating hair follicles of swine only with Tween-positive staphylococci of phage type I and not with Tween-positive staphylococci of phage group III.

Correlations between lytic spectra and pathogenicity for man and animals have likewise been demonstrated for streptococci (Mihalcu and Vereanu, 1974; Mihalcu *et al.*, 1974).

Vieu and Ducrest (1960) reported a high frequency of *Proteus hauseri* phage type I in human infections.

Certain relationships between phage type and the clinical form of a disease were also established by Saragea *et al.* (1973), who showed that phage type XIV produced milder forms of diphtheria than phage type IX, which caused severe forms.

No obvious relationship was found by Meitert and Meitert (1971) between the virulence of *P. aeruginosa* and its antigenic structure or sensitivity to bacteriophages. A particular aspect, with important epidemiological implications, was the successive occurrence and predominance in certain hospital epidemics of *P. aeruginosa* strains with an increased virulence and an enhanced diffusion capacity. Similarly, phage types 4a and 1a belonging to serotype II, have frequently been isolated from severe infections caused by *P. aeruginosa* (Meitert, 1965; Meitert and Meitert, 1972).

11. *Phage typing in epizootiology and zoonotic infections*

Phage typing is also of particular importance for elucidating the mechanisms of infections caused by pathogenic organisms common to both man and animals.

In infections with *Salmonella typhimurium* and other salmonella it is presently necessary to phage type organisms isolated from man, animals, food products and fodder. The distribution and frequency of various *S.*

typhimurium phage types isolated from humans reflect their overall spread. It is often possible to establish epidemiological relationships between the high incidence of a certain phage type in man and its increased frequency in animals and animal products (Kühn *et al.*, 1973). The relationships established between the phage types isolated from different animal species and human infections may confirm the zoonotic character of the disease (Anderson and Wilson, 1960; Kühn *et al.*, 1973). Phage typing is always of practical importance for determining the mechanism of spread in an epizootic infection (Kühn *et al.*, 1973).

In *E. coli* infections it has likewise proved possible to establish certain relationships between the phage types of strains isolated from children with severe digestive disturbances and the enteritis of certain animal species (Bercovici *et al.*, 1969).

In staphylococcal infections, phage typing is widely applied to characterize the strains isolated from humans and especially those isolated in hospitals or from different animal species (host adapted strains) (Meyer *et al.*, 1973).

Nicolle *et al.* (1969) described the common origin of certain *Yersinia enterocolitica* phage types isolated from different species, i.e. from hares and breeding chinchilla, from hares and man and especially from man and swine (Nicolle, 1973).

Meitert *et al.* (1969), Meitert and Meitert (1972) showed that 98% of the *P. aeruginosa* strains of animal origin may be listed among the phage types isolated from man and that at a given moment, the prevalence of the same phage type may be observed in both humans and animals. Bergan (1972) likewise showed the possibility of phage typing *P. aeruginosa* animal strains with bacteriophages of human origin and reported the isolation of the same serotypes and phage types of *P. aeruginosa* from human infections and cattle.

Finally, Maximescu *et al.* (1974a) found identical *Corynebacterium ulcerans* and *C. ovis* phage types among the strains isolated from humans and animals.

C. Limitations

Parker (1965), referring to phage typing as a classification method based upon sensitivity to certain phages, says: "The one thing it can never do, therefore, is to show that two organisms are 'the same'; what it can do is to establish with varying degrees of certainty that they are 'different'." Meyer *et al.* (1973) showed that phage typing of staphylococci may be important for understanding the epidemiology of an outbreak, but that phages can never prove by themselves the common origin of two staphylococci strains with identical phagolytic spectra. In contrast, staphylococci displaying sufficient phagolytic spectrum differences may be considered as different (Blair and Williams, 1961; Meyer *et al.*, 1973).

The principal limitations of the phage typing method may be summed up as follows:

1. *Too few differences obtained by phage typing within a certain microbial species, serotype or biotype*

Such situations have been reported in the phage typing of *Shigella sonnei* (the Hammarström set) (Ziesché and Rische, 1973; Chanishvili and Chanishvili, 1974) or in *intermedius* and *mitis Corynebacterium diphtheriae* biotypes by means of the original phage typing scheme (Saragea *et al.*, 1973). In this connection it is worth noting that the predominance of a phage type in a particular area may be either real, due to its massive spread, or wrongly interpreted due to the imperfection of the phage typing method used. Consequently, different phage typing schemes have been developed with time to complete and complement the earlier ones. For instance, Quinh (1968) subdivided *Sh. sonnei* phage type 3 with the help of bacteriophages 3 alpha, 3 beta and 3 gamma.

Salmonella typhi phage type A was subdivided by Desranleau (1947), or Nicolle *et al.* (1953a, 1954), *S. typhi* phage type E_1 by Brandis (1955), *S. typhi* phage type C_1 by Nicolle *et al.* (1955), *S. typhi* phages types F_1 and F_4 by Chomiczewski (1961a), Chomiczewski (1965), Hudemann (1965) and Ziesché (1974), non-typable Vi strains $(I + IV)$ by Nicolle and Diverneaux (1961), uncharacteristic strains by Nicolle *et al.* (1953), and so on.

The combined typing systems of Felix and Callow (1943) and of Scholtens (1956) led to the conclusion, after several years of observation, that *S. schottmuelleri* phage types are constant (Rische and Ziesché, 1973a).

The Felix and Callow (1943) phage typing system, completed by the Lilleengen system (1948) for *S. typhimurium* and additional phages for *S. panama* (Szegli *et al.*, 1974), offer supplementary possibilities for subdivision of the strains.

Similarly, supplementary phages for subdivision of staphylococci (Popovici *et al.*, 1974) and an additional set for phage typing of *C. diphtheriae* (Maximescu *et al.*, 1972) have been used.

It is obvious that a series of microbial species, for which an international standardized phage typing system has not been reached (as for example for *Shigella* sp.), can be widely differentiated by combining some phages from different described phage typing schemes.

2. *Existence of a great number of phage types, which have a very rare epidemiological incidence*

Such phage types are sometimes represented by only one strain. Use of the term "lytic spectra" has been recommended until the epidemiologic constancy of such "phage types" is proved.

3. *The existence of a high proportion of non-typable strains or atypical lytic spectra*

Some investigators, however, found methods to render strains typable. For instance, Milch (1967) by exposing non-typable staphylococci to 56°C for 2 min succeeded in rendering 46·3% of them sensitive to typing phages. Witte (1975) showed that in about 50% of *Staph. aureus* strains, non-typability was due to the formation of a capsule. By growing them in a liquid glycerol-minimal salts-medium, he was able to hinder the formation of the capsule in some of the strains and render them typable.

4. *The regional value of some phage typing schemes*

Some phage typing schemes may be reliable for some countries but less useful for other parts of the world. Thus, Scholtens (1960) by his phage typing scheme for *Salmonella typhimurium* succeeded in typing all his strains originating from the Netherlands, West- and East Germany, but only 50% of those from Hungary and Italy. The untypable strains were considered by Scholtens to constitute different subspecies of *S. typhimurium*. Chiracadze and Chanisvili (1974) reported that only 35% of the *S. typhimurium* strains isolated in the U.S.S.R. could be typed with the Felix–Callow set, whereas 98·5% were typable with the phage set of the Tbilisi Institute of Sera and Vaccines.

5. *Difficulties of comparing phage types*

The difficulty in comparing phagotypes is due to the different methodologies used at different centres, to the variability *in vitro* and *in vivo* of the phage types under the influence of various ecological factors, and to changes in the properties of certain typing phages. The diversity of the lytic spectra of staphylococcal phages may make it difficult to compare the data reported from different countries even with the same international set.

6. *The reduced morbidity of some communicable diseases*

The few cases due to *S. paratyphi-A* for instance limits very much the usefulness of phage typing in this species (Buczowski, 1973).

7. *The relative stability of phage types*

Already in 1951, Felix and Anderson showed the possible transformation of certain *Salmonella typhi* phage types into phage type A. Similar findings were subsequently made by other authors (Anderson and Felix, 1953a; Nicolle, 1956; Borecka, 1965; Rische, 1968).

As is already well known, in *S. typhi* phage typing it is necessary to select positive Vi-colonies, because Vi-negative strains are not typable (Craigie and Yen, 1938; Nestorescu *et al.*, 1953).

Bercovici *et al.* (1968), in a study involving the typing of 3703 *S. typhi*, found that the phage type was constant in the same patient and carrier in 89% of the cases, whereas only 11% among the strains exhibited variations in their phage sensitivity related to the variation of their content of Vi-antigen.

According to Rische and Schneider (1960), *S. schottmuelleri* occasionally presents lytic spectra that do not correspond to the epidemiologic data (especially in the Taunton and Dundee phage types). Istrati *et al.* (1962) found changes of the *Sh. flexneri* phage types *in vitro* in 27·2% of isolates in contrast with recently isolated epidemic strains which always pertain to the same phage type. A certain instability of the phage types was reported by Rische (1968) in *Sh. sonnei* (the Hammarström method). The present authors demonstrated the constancy of *Sh. sonnei* phage types only for a limited period of time. Changes in *Sh. sonnei* phage type have also been reported by other authors (Mayr-Harting, 1952; Junghans, 1958, 1958a, 1958b).

Meitert (1965a) observed changes in 16% of the phage types and subtypes of *Pseudomonas aeruginosa* strains *in vitro*. This does not affect the utility of phage typing in epidemiologic practice in connection with *P. aeruginosa* infections.

Some remarks were made by Milch (1973) concerning the *E. coli* phage types of serogroups O: 111, 55 and 26, which prove to be less stable, but significant in epidemiologic investigations.

Meyer *et al.* (1973) reproduced, by experimental investigations, the variability of the lytic spectra of some staphylococci, especially of strains of the 80/81 complex and 83A/84/85 complex.

8. *Modification of phage types by genetic mechanisms*

(a) *Lysogenic conversion.* As is well known, lysogenic conversion means the acquiring by a bacterium, simultaneously with its lysogenization, of a character it did not previously possess. Freeman (1961) and Freeman and Morse (1952) reported the toxinogenic conversion of a non-toxigenic *Corynebacterium diphtheriae*, and Iseki and Sakai (1953) antigenic conversion of *Salmonella anatum* to *S. newington*, by lysogenization. Nicolle and Hamon (1951) showed that lysogenization of *S. schottmuelleri* with homologous phages may lead to changes in lytic sensitivity. In other cases, organisms submitted to lysogenization may acquire the same phage type as that of the host-strain of the lysogenic phage. Such phages were called by these authors "determinant phages" since the lytic picture of the phage type is determined by their presence in the respective organisms as "prophages". Similar lysogenic conversions were performed by Nicolle *et al.* (1969) and Nicolle (1973) in *Yersinia enterocolitica.*

Transformation of *S. typhi* phage type A into phage type D_1 by artificial lysogenization with the temperate phage d_1 was observed for the first time by Craigie (1942, 1946) and subsequently also by other authors (Anderson and Felix, 1952, 1953; Anderson, 1955). By lysogenization with certain phages, non-lysogenic *S. typhi* phage types (Rische, 1968) were transformed into other corresponding phage types, as for instance the transformation of phage type A into type 29 by means of phage f_2; Ciucă *et al.* (1966) obtained modifications in *S. typhi* by lysogenization with heterologous phages.

(b) *Loss of "determinant" phages.* Loss of determinant phages brings about changes in the sensitivity spectra of *S. typhi* and staphylococci (Wahl and Fouace, 1958; Iosub, 1974).

(c) *Phenomenon of semi-resistance.* This phenomenon was described in *Shigella flexneri* by Wahl and Blum-Emmerique (1952, 1952a). They observed that some strains presented a very slight sensitivity to homospecific phages. This weak sensitivity was expressed by very few, small, unequal-sized plaques, of different degrees of opacity, occurring when the organism was grown on nutrient agar. When, however, the same organism was grown on nutrient broth, it permitted good multiplication of the phage. The same phenomenon also influenced the results expected following phage typing of *S. typhi*, which reduced its epidemiological value (Cornelson and Iosub, 1962; Iosub, 1962).

(d) *The transfer of R factors.* Close relationships are known to exist between lytic sensitivity of certain *Enterobacteriaceae* and R factors (Anderson, 1966; Guinée and Willems, 1967a; Lebek, 1967; Anderson, 1968; Watanabe, 1968; Wiedemann and Knothe, 1968).

The acquiring by microbial cells of R plasmids in the course of antibiotic therapy leads to a restrictive effect involving the selection of organisms with a modified phage type. Such phage type variations, occurring either experimentally or naturally, induced by R plasmids, may be found among different microbial species, for instance *S. typhi* (Anderson, 1966; Toucas, 1974; Rusu *et al.*, 1974), *S. schottmuelleri* (Anderson, 1966), *S. panama* (Guinée *et al.*, 1967), and *S. typhimurium* (Anderson and Lewis, 1965; Anderson, 1968; Kühn *et al.*, 1973).

Egler *et al.* (1968) transferred the R factors of some *Sh. flexneri* strains to *E. coli* strains with a different antigenic structure, and observed changes in their lysosensitivity, characterized either by resistance or the occurrence of new phagolytic spectra. Milch *et al.* (1974) proved the possibility of classifying the R factors of *E. coli* on the basis of their restrictive properties.

Tschäpe and Rische (1970, 1970a) and Ziesché and Rische (1973) noted in the course of phage typing *Sh. sonnei* a restrictive capacity of the R plasmids, especially for bacteriophages VII and V.

Meyer *et al.* (1973) observed a diminished capacity of phage typing with the international set of bacteriophages, simultaneous with the occurrence of multiple antibiotic resistant strains of *Staph. aureus*.

9. *Limitations linked to test conditions*

(a) *Strains under test.* A series of microbial species (e.g. *Salmonella, Sh. flexneri, E. coli, P. aeruginosa,* staphylococci) must be typed as soon as possible after isolation and in the "S" form.

For instance, in the case of phage typing of *S. typhi* (Craigie and Felix method) and *S. schottmuelleri* (Felix and Callow method), Rische (1960) showed that phage typing is no longer possible when the strains present negative or atypical reactions with "O" phage or positive reactions with "R" phages, the strains becoming untypable as a consequence of an S-R variation.

In contrast, phage typing in *Sh. sonnei* is possible (Hammarström scheme) only with strains in phase II after their isolation and selection from patients (Ziesché and Rische, 1973).

The various degradations undergone by strains *in vivo* and *in vitro* may be reflected by greater or lesser changes in their lytic spectrum, expressed either in a greater sensitivity to new phages or phage resistance (Nicolle *et al.*, 1957, 1960).

To overcome this difficulty it is sometimes necessary to select colonies in the corresponding forms and to carry out phage typing with several colonies from the same growth (Meitert *et al.*, 1968). Selection is also necessary because of the lack of uniformity in the same, initially isolated, growth. Thus, Schmidt (1962) and Kende (1964) found that several kinds of *S. aureus* may coexist in the nose, throat and wounds, in contrast to what is usually observed in purulent exudates.

In order to obtain adequate *E. coli* strains for phage typing, Nicolle *et al.* (1960) proposed a previous passage in mice by intraperitoneal inoculation.

(b) *Typing bacteriophages.* The increasingly vast problem of the criteria for selection of the most adquate bacteriophage preparations for phage typing schemes, will not be discussed, nor will these criteria be critically appraised; it must, however, be recalled that among the most important conditions for phage typing schemes are the following:

1. Reproducibility of phage spectra.
2. The existence of a sufficient number of typable strains (by the selected bacteriophages).

The phagolytic spectra must be sufficiently differential to permit an unequivocal recognition of epidemiological relationships.

Nakagawa (1960) emphasized the fact that it is not only of importance to select typing bacteriophages, but also to choose adequate propagating strains.

Attention must also be paid to the so-called "inhibition-reactions" that may be confused with bacteriophage lysis and which are often encountered when too high bacteriophage concentrations are used (Meyer *et al.*, 1973).

(c) *Methodology*. Changes in the phagolytic spectrum may also be linked to several conditions, variations of which, even when minimal, may be particularly important for the reproducibility of phage typing. Among these conditions, studied by several authors (Lenk, 1955, 1956; Pöhn, 1957a; Parker, 1965; Bergan, 1972; Meyer *et al.*, 1973), are the following:

– the initial ratio of infectious phages to bacterial cells;
– poorly growing cultures;
– thickness of the growth film;
– the presence of non-lysogenic organisms in the subcultures;
– the development of certain components of the bacterial cells to the detriment of others;
– different physical conditions of the strains and selective influences;
– differences in the composition of the medium, i.e. different batches of ingredients;
– temperature and time of incubation;
– thickness of the agar layer;
– agar concentration;
– degree of humidity;
– the presence of glucose;
– pH;
– the amount of Ca^{++} in tap water;
– the age of the preculture and its quality (the way in which it was prepared);
– physiological state of the bacterial strain, actively multiplying cells being more sensitive.

In order to avoid drawbacks linked to a possible lack of uniformity of such a great number of methodologic conditions, it is recommended (Nicolle *et al.*, 1960; Meitert and Meitert, 1973; Meyer *et al.*, 1973) that strains should be typed as soon as possible after their isolation, always using as controls standard strains and standard batches of medium previously checked for their value in phage typing. Together with phage typing, other biological properties (serotyping, determination of the antibiogram and R factors) should be concomitantly checked.

10. *Difficulties in the interpretation of lytic reactions*

In some situations even minimal lytic reactions must be considered, i.e. when they are reproducible and are the only reactions defining the respective phage type (Meyer *et al.*, 1973).

A skilled laboratory worker will have to consider as different, strains sometimes showing less marked lytic reactions produced by a given bacteriophage preparation, just as he will have to tolerate in other cases greater lytic differences. In these situations, corroboration of the laboratory results with epidemiological findings is of particular importance.

It is also necessary to mention the so-called "observer error", consisting of subjective interpretations of the lytic reactions (variations from one observer to another—inter-observer discrepancy—or errors in the subsequent readings made by the same observer—intra-observer discrepancies) (Bergan, 1972).

III. SEROTYPING

A. Introduction

To characterize different microbial species, serotyping requires specific antisera (anti-somatic, anti-flagellar, anti-capsular or envelope) according to the antigenic structure of each microbial species.

Serotyping is used not only for the diagnosis and routine taxonomic grouping of species, but also for a more analytical differentiation, of particular interest in epidemiological investigations.

B. Possibilities, limitations and use of serotyping

For a series of microbial species (for instance *Salmonella typhi*, *S. paratyphi-A*, *S. schottmuelleri*, *S. typhimurium* and *Shigella* sp.) serotyping represents a very important tool for routine identification; supplementary differentiations are obtained by phage typing. For other microbial species, such as *E. coli*, *P. aeruginosa*, *Klebsiella*, serotyping has become a conventional epidemiological typing method, used for differentiating strains obtained in different epidemiological situations. The epidemiological characteristics of *E. coli* strains, isolated from different epidemic foci, are frequently determined by establishing their serogroups, respectively their H-antigens.

For instance, Milch (1973) remarked the increased frequency of *E. coli* with flagellate antigens H:2 and H:12 and the rare occurrence of *E. coli* strains with flagellate antigens H:4, 21, 27 and 40, of regional importance.

In *P. aeruginosa* infections, serotyping is considered a remarkably reliable epidemiological marker. The *P. aeruginosa* investigations carried out during the latter years by serotyping based upon O-antigens, have shown that useful information may be obtained by this method (Habs, 1957; Kleinmaier, 1957; Kleinmaier *et al.*, 1959; Meitert and Meitert, 1960; Meitert, 1964; Meitert *et al.*, 1974; Sandvik, 1960; Verder and Evans, 1961; Véron, 1961; Wokatsch, 1964; Lányi, 1966/67, 1970; Matsumoto *et al.*, 1968; Fisher *et al.*, 1969; Homma, 1971).

Serotyping as epidemiological marker is now increasingly used for some microbial species (*Klebsiella, Proteus*) while for others, supplementary studies are still necessary (corynebacteria, staphylococci).

Determination of the serotype is particularly important in connection with the existence in some bacterial species (e.g. *P. aeruginosa*) of homologous type immunity. Consequently, for the preparation of certain immunobiological products (for instance, therapeutical antiserum, polyvalent vaccines) it is necessary to choose representative serotypes.

The limitations of the serotyping method are related especially to the possible changes in the structural antigens:lysogenic conversion of *Salmonella* antigens (Iseki and Sakai, 1953, 1953a; Le Minor, 1963; Chomiczewski and Piatkowski, 1969a), structural changes of O-antigen in *Shigella*, especially at the level of the secondary lateral chains of the polysaccharide molecule (Giammanco and Natoli, 1974) changes in the antigenic structure of *P. aeruginosa* (Homma *et al.*, 1972).

IV. BACTERIOCIN (GENO) TYPING

A. Introduction

The bacteriocin typing method is based upon the sensitivity of the strains under test to the bacteriocins produced by a set of selected strains; bacteriocingenotyping uses the sensitivity of certain selected indicator strains to the bacteriocins produced by the strains under test.

The utilization of bacteriocins in different microbial species for bacteriocin typing or bacteriocingenotyping has offered additional possibilities of subdividing and characterizing strains isolated in different epidemiological situations.

B. Possibilities and limitations. Examples

1. *Shigella sonnei*

Using the Abbott–Shannon method (1958), Rische (1968) demonstrated that certain *Sh. sonnei* phage types established by the Hammarström scheme (1949) (for instance phage types 2, 3, 6, 7, 12, 25 and others) can be further differentiated into different colicin types. The same author found no correlation between phage type and colicin types; the same colicin type 2 occurred in various *Sh. sonnei* phage types. Rische (1968), as well as Ziesché and Rische (1973), noted that the strains isolated from an epidemic focus always belonged to the same colicin type.

Whereas Rische (1973) recommends colicin typing for *Sh. sonnei*, especially as a supplement to phage typing, English researchers prefer colicin typing instead of phage typing, since they consider that stable results are not always obtained with the latter.

Cook and Daines (1964) found only one *Sh. sonnei* colicin type in 9 of 11 epidemic foci and in 47 of 50 familial outbreaks.

Ogawa *et al.* (1965) likewise found the predominance of only one colicin type in some epidemics caused by *Sh. sonnei*. In others, however, besides the predominant type, several other colicin types were found. The authors were unable to determine whether these secondary colicin types pertained to other sources of infection or represented only mutants of the predominant colicin type. The "main type" often differed considerably from one epidemic to another, thus making it possible to differentiate between epidemics. Still, the authors demonstrated the stability of colicin types in $91 \cdot 1\%$ of the strains by passage on different nutrient media.

Brandis (1971) showed annual or multiannual changes in *Sh. sonnei* colicin types. Gillies (1965) demonstrated that *Sh. sonnei* colicin types may predominate within a certain region for several years and then may be replaced by other colicin types. On the other hand, Farrant and Tomlinson (1966), following up *Sh. sonnei* colicin types during many years in England, considered that the eventual changes in *Sh. sonnei* colicin types are due to the transfer of the *col* factor from other bacteria in the intestine. This mechanism might also explain the incidence of the same colicin type in different places in the absence of any epidemiologic connection.

Kameda *et al.* (1968), as well as Aoki (1968), found in Japan an increased incidence of colicin type 14 that they attributed to superinfection of the strains with a transmissible *col* factor (i.e. superinfection of colicin type 6 with *col* factor I). Moreover, they were able to establish a relationship between colicin type 14 and multiple resistance to antibiotics.

The epidemiological constancy of colicin types has been noted by different authors. Thus, they observed the same colicin type from epidemic foci with a single source of infection and almost constant excretion of the same colicin type by the carriers.

In contrast, several other observations tend to limit the utility of *Sh. sonnei* colicin typing, such as the findings pointing to the instability of colicin types excreted by carriers. Thus, Filichkin *et al.* (1968) noted that at the beginning of the disease, in some patients, non-colicinogenic strains were isolated, and subsequently colicinogenic strains; the converse situation was also sometimes observed. Davies *et al.* (1968) consider that modifications of colicin types and antibiotic sensitivity in carriers may be due to the transfer of some extrachromosomal factors from the intestinal flora to *Sh. sonnei* cells and not to reinfections.

An important technical consideration necessary for obtaining reproducible data in the course of the colicin typing of *Sh. sonnei* is the need to check periodically the specificity of the indicator strains (McGeachie and McCormick, 1967; Brandis, 1971). As some colicins (particularly types 6 and 7) are influenced by minimal changes in the medium, Abbott and Graham (1961) recommend the use of a standardized medium for colicin typing. According to these authors, colicinogeny and sensitivity to colicins are remarkably stable in *Sh. sonnei*, when the strains are lyophilized or stored in Dorset medium at 4°C.

It was not possible to establish any correlation between the phage type and colicin type, nor between the colicin type and biotype or between the colicin type and phase I and phase II in *Sh. sonnei* (Ogawa *et al.*, 1965; Aoki, 1968; Rische, 1968).

2. *Shigella flexneri*

Colicinogeny is very rare in *Sh. flexneri*. Attempts to test the sensitivity of the strains against the standard colicinogenic strains (Fredericq's series) (Papavassiliou and Huet, 1962; Papavassiliou *et al.*, 1964) presented severa l difficulties discussed in detail by Brandis (1971): colicin typing must be performed only with recently isolated strains; the instability of colicin types after storage in the laboratory; the inconstancy of the colicin types isolated from the same patient; the great number of different spectra. If this method is used in *Sh. sonnei* marked differences may occur, due to the coexistence of phases I and II in the same microbial population (Brandis, 1971).

Moreover, by using 11 selected bacteriocinogenic strains, Meitert *et al.* (1974a) succeeded in sub-dividing different *Sh. flexneri* serotypes (except serotype 6).

3. *Shigella boydi*

Szturm-Rubinstein (1970) showed that types 1 and 8 produced colicin in 100% of cases. Colicinogeny was rare or absent with types 5, 6, 7, 9 and 15. The same author found no relationship between resistance to antibiotics and colicinogeny in the 112 strains investigated.

4. Escherichia coli

Fredericq et al. (1956) observed that E. coli serotypes were often colicinogenic, Hamon and Brault (1958), studying 141 strains isolated from 40 epidemic foci, demonstrated a constancy of the colicin type among different enteropathogenic E. coli serotypes. Shannon (1957) using colicin typing only differentiated 40% of the E. coli O:55 B$_5$ strains investigated. Hamon (1958, 1961) subdivided E. coli serotypes by their sensitivity to standard colicinogenic strains. McGeachie (1965) as well as Papavassiliou and Samaraki-Lyseropopoulou (1965), by combining colicinogeny and colicin sensitivity, succeeded in typing 72·1% of E. coli strains isolated from urinary infections.

Hamon (1960) showed that epidemiological investigations confirm the identity of E. coli colicin types isolated from the same patient or the same source of infection and that colicinogeny of certain phage types isolated in the same locality was identical. The author emphasized the utility of colicinogeny of certain E. coli phage types in epidemiological investigations.

5. Other enterobacteriaceae

Colicin typing in Salmonella has not been widely used (Zaritski, 1968; Chomiczewski and Piatkowski, 1969; Atkinson, 1970). Bacteriocin typing of Klebsiella (Maresz-Babczyszyn et al., 1967, 1967a; Slopek and Maresz-Babczyszyn, 1967), Arizona, Citrobacter (Sedlak et al., 1967a) and Proteus (Cradock-Watson, 1965; Coetze et al., 1968) has been attempted, but the method is not currently used.

6. Corynebacterium diphtheriae

In C. diphtheriae epidemiological investigations, Meitert (1974), using her bacteriocin typing scheme with a set of 20 bacteriocin-producing strains, was able to classify 1150 C. diphtheriae and 21 C. ulcerans strains into various bacteriocin types. The same author noted no correlations between biotype, phage type and bacteriocin type. The same bacteriocin types were found in strains of gravis, mitis and intermedius C. diphtheriae and in C. ulcerans. Certain relationships could, however, be established at a given moment between the predominant bacteriocin type and phage type in some epidemic foci or in carriers of a closed community. It was also possible to subdivide the predominant phage type into several bacteriocin types. Meitert (1974) has shown that even minor reactions in bacteriocin typing of *C. diphtheriae* may be useful in order to establish the common origin of strains.

The stability of *C. diphtheriae* bacteriocin types being relative, Meitert (1974) recommends that bacteriocin typing should be applied simultaneously and under similar working conditions for all strains isolated from one single epidemic focus, in order to obtain the most reliable results.

Other authors, using various bacteriocin typing schemes, have emphasized the utility of the method of bacteriocin typing in tracing the epidemiology of *Corynebacterium* infections (Krylova, 1972; Krylova *et al.*, 1973; Gibson and Colmann, 1973; Zamiri and McEntegart, 1973; Rurka, 1974). Darrel and Wahba (1964) evidenced, by their pyocine typing method, up to 16 times the same pyocine type in 62 patients with *P. aeruginosa* urinary infections and established the existence of certain hospital cross-infections. The authors consider this typing method to be of utility in epidemiological investigations. Wahba (1965a), Zabransky and Day (1967) and Brandis (1971) showed that pyocine typing is limited to a small number of pyocine types. Bergan (1968, 1968a), modifying the Darrel and Wahba method, succeeded in completing the 11 initially described pyocine types up to 27 types.

Pyocine typing was also used with good results by other authors, who pointed out its utility in different epidemiological situations and underlined its high constancy *in vivo* and *in vitro* (Osman, 1965; Gillies and Govan, 1966; Tinne *et al.*, 1967; Phillips *et al.*, 1968; Govan and Gillies, 1969; Tagg and Mushin, 1973).

C. Conclusions

Although colicinogeny is a relatively constant character, loss or acquirement of new colicinogenic properties may occur in the course of an epidemic process (Kudlaj *et al.*, 1970).

Transfer of col factors or R factors may occur both *in vivo* and *in vitro*, between individuals of the same species or between different species (Fredericq, 1963; Kiselev, 1967). This may change the sensitivity to colicins and, in some instances, change the sensitivity to bacteriophages (Hamon, 1957). Loss of colicinogeny may be due to alterations in the correlated replication of chromosome and plasmid, with the subsequent segregation of col⁻ cells.

Particular care should be taken in assessing the results of these methods since an exchange of colicinogenic factors *in vivo* may lead to a change of colicin type.

Notwithstanding possible variations in colicin production and colicin sensitivity, published data demonstrate the utility of bacteriocin typing in epidemiology.

V. BIOCHEMICAL TYPING

A. Introduction

Differentiation within a species by biochemical typing has been used to a lesser extent than other epidemiological typing methods, and may be a valuable adjuvant for epidemiologic investigations.

B. Possibilities and limitations. Examples

1. *Salmonella typhi*

Kristensen and Henriksen (1926) used xylose for subdivision of *S. typhi*. Subsequently, Kristensen (1938), using xylose and arabinose, described three biochemical types to which Meitert (1952) added a fourth, concomitantly described by De Blasi and Buogo (1952). Several authors have applied biochemical typing to *S. typhi* strains (Olitzki *et al.*, 1948; Buczowski and Lachowicz, 1950; Felix and Anderson, 1951a; Brandis and Maurer, 1954; Combiesco and Meitert, 1957; Ciucă *et al.*, 1957; Nicolle and Diverneau, 1961).

Worthy of note is the possible transformation by lysogenization of *S. typhi* phage type D_1, biochemical type 2, into biochemical type 1 (Chomiczewski, 1961).

Le Minor and Pichinoty (1963) and Nicolle and Le Minor (1965) obtained regional differentiation of *S. typhi* by means of tetrathionate reductase.

2. *Salmonella typhimurium*

The biochemical typing of *S. typhimurium* strains (Kühn *et al.*, 1973) offers the possibility of subdividing the same phage type strains isolated from two different epidemic outbreaks. According to Kallings and Laurell (1957) and Rische and Kretschmar (1962), a phage type may be subdivided into more biochemical types. Scholtens (1969) showed that the biochemical properties of *S. typhimurium* may be inconstant and that phage typing and biochemical typing complement each other, the existence, accordingly, of bio-phage types being emphasized.

3. *Salmonella schottmuelleri*

In the typing of *S. schottmuelleri*, rhamnose and/or inositol (Kristensen and Bojlen, 1929; Rische, 1955; Lalko, 1965) were used, as well as the production of arylsulphatase (Köhler *et al.*, 1966). A certain correlation between the phage type and the biochemical type of *S. schottmuelleri* was observed. The use in the same species of phage typing (according to Felix and Callow) together with biochemical typing may avoid errors in phage typing.

4. *Escherichia coli*

Although biochemical typing has been used by several authors (Kauff-mann and Dupont, 1950; Laurell *et al.*, 1951; Le Minor *et al.*, 1954; Kauffmann and Orskov, 1956; Nicolle *et al.*, 1960; Milch and Deak, 1961) to subdivide the enteropathogenic *E. coli* serotypes and phage types, the method is not yet being used routinely. In this connection, the beta-phenyl-propionic-acid reaction of d'Alessandro and Comes and the lysine decar-boxylase reaction of Moeller and Carlquist are the most reliable biochemical methods (Eörsi *et al.*, 1954; Nicolle *et al.*, 1960; Kunin and Halmagy, 1962; Milch, 1973).

5. *Shigella sonnei*

Different schemes have been used for the biochemical typing of *Sh. sonnei* (Bojlén, 1934; Novgorodskaya, 1968; Szturm-Rubinstein, 1964; Gillies, 1965). Ziesché and Rische (1973) described in detail the possibili-ties, limitations and difficulties of the biochemical methods; the difficulties are especially due to the quality of ingredients, the media used and checking the optimum time for reading the reactions. With reference to Bojlén's scheme, the authors consider the stability of the biochemical types *in vivo* as satisfactory, even if in some cases the biochemical type, with regard to the fermentation of maltose, is not precisely determined. The stability of the biochemical types *in vivo* is paralleled by the stability of maltose fermentation. Freshly isolated strains may exhibit delayed maltose fermen-tation and stored strains a more rapid fermentation.

Biochemical typing has been used, particularly in countries with a high incidence of *Sh. sonnei* (Ziesché and Rische, 1973).

C. Conclusions

Owing to these limitations and to the small number of biochemical types in each species, biochemical typing can only be used in epidemio-logical investigations in association with other epidemiologic methods (phage typing, serotyping and colicin typing).

VI. TYPING BY ANTIBIOGRAM AND R FACTORS

Recording the pattern of antibiotic resistance has been used as a sup-plementary typing method, e.g. in *Enterobacteriaceae*.

In *Enterobacteriaceae*, resistance to antibiotics may be linked either to chromosomal genes or to transferable extrachromosomal factors (multiple resistance transfer factors = R factors).

The antibiogram used as a supplementary epidemiologic typing method for *Sh. sonnei* has been recommended by several authors (Ankirskaja, 1965; Zarikova, 1965; Pfeiffer and Krüger, 1968; Stepankovskaja *et al.*, 1968; Stepankovskaja and Brutman, 1969; Fardy and Cross, 1969; Ziesché and Rische, 1973; Levine *et al.*, 1974). Abbott and Graham (1961) subdivided colicin types of *Sh. sonnei* on the basis of sulphonamide resistance. Farrant and Tomlinson (1966) observed that the resistant *Sh. sonnei* strains produce fewer epidemics than the antibiotic-sensitive strains. Ziesché and Rische (1973) noted in epidemic foci a perfect correspondence to antibiotic sensitivity markers.

The limitations of the method are obviously linked to the frequency of resistant strains and the incidence of strains carrying R factors. To these may be added multiple possible changes in the resistance spectra. This also applies to staphylococci (Mitsumashi, 1967).

Tschäpe and Rische (1970a) do not consider the antibiogram an important epidemiologic marker, especially when it is not possible to differentiate R plasmid resistance from that of chromosomal origin.

Milch *et al.* (1974) and Milch and Gyenes (1975) showed that the R factors in *E. coli* could be classified on the basis of their restrictive effect upon phage activity.

VII. COMBINED USE OF EPIDEMIOLOGICAL TYPING METHODS

A. Introduction

The combined use of different typing methods for a number of microbial species avoids the difficulties arising from limitations of the methods used separately.

The previous Sections have expounded not only a wide range of topics concerning the subdivision of certain microbial species or serotypes based upon several epidemiologic markers, but also the correlations between the different epidemiologic typing methods.

B. Usefulness. Examples

1. *Salmonella*

Nicolle and Prunet (1965) showed that in *Salmonella typhi* the association of phage typing with biochemical typing, complementary phage typing (for phage types A and E_1) and the investigation of colicinogeny, is of twofold interest: on the one hand, it permits a detailed knowledge of the *S. typhi* species and, on the other, it yields a more accentuated differentiation within the framework of the epidemiologic investigation.

The use of the bio-phage types in the study of *S. typhimurium* strains (Scholtens, 1969) and the combined use of biochemical and phage typing in *S. typhimurium* and *S. schottmuelleri* have been useful in numerous investigations (Rische and Schneider, 1956; Kallings *et al.*, 1959; Bulling, 1960; Seidel and Eilsberger, 1962; Milch *et al.*, 1963; Beumer and van Oye, 1965; Lalko *et al.*, 1967; Kilesso and Nikityiuk, 1969; Rische and Ziesché, 1973; Kühn *et al.*, 1973).

2. Shigella

In *Shigella* the combined use of phage typing and bacteriocin typing has led to further differentiation within a serotype or a phage type, demonstrating its practical utility in various epidemic bacillary dysentery foci (Ziesché and Rische, 1973; Meitert *et al.*, 1974). Numerous examples of different combined uses of epidemiologic markers in *Shigella* and particularly in *Sh. sonnei*, are cited by Ziesché and Rische (1973).

3. Escherichia coli

The association of different markers for a more detailed characterization of the enteropathogenic *E. coli* serotypes allowed a more easy differentiation of the strains, in contrast to the separate use of markers (Milch, 1973). Similarly, it is likely that an additional subdivision of some *E. coli* serotypes may be obtained by colicin typing, lysogenic properties, haemolytic capacity, and certain biochemical properties (Nicolle *et al.*, 1963; Milch, 1973).

4. Other Enterobacteriaceae

For epidemical *Klebsiella* strains, phage typing was used together with biochemical typing (Sjöberg and Nord, 1975).

The association of serotyping, phage typing and the test of the demarcation line of Dienes (1946) in *Proteus* species can also elucidate the aetiology of food poisonings with this germ (Popovici *et al.*, 1968).

5. P. aeruginosa

In *P. aeruginosa* infections, several authors by combining serotyping and phage typing (Wahba, 1965; Basset *et al.*, 1965; Ayliffe *et al.*, 1965; Shooter *et al.*, 1966; Meitert and Meitert, 1966; Phillips, 1967; Knights *et al.*, 1968), by combining phage typing with serotyping and pyocine typing (Farmer and Herman, 1969) or phage typing with pyocine typing

(Sjöberg and Lindberg, 1968) obtained further subdivisions of the strains isolated from hospital cross-infections.

6. Staphylococcus aureus

Phage typing of *Staph. aureus* may be also combined with the detection of coagulase by plasma from various species (especially human and bovine), sensitivity to crystal violet or sublimate and production of haemolysin and fibrinolysin (Tshäpe and Rische, 1972).

C. Conclusions

It is worthy of notice that the combined use of the different epidemiologic typing methods, whose importance may differ in terms of the different bacterial species, is an efficient working method only when used in correlation with epidemiologic data.

VIII. GENERAL CONCLUSIONS

Epidemiologic practice has demonstrated the usefulness of typing methods. They gradually become further developed, and the sphere of their application becomes extended. Typing procedures are expected to be extended to more pathogenic or opportunist species.

The importance of each of the epidemiologic typing methods discussed may differ from one species to another and many methods still need further improvement, or standardization, both regarding technique and concerning international agreement.

In the course of epidemiologic investigations, account must evidently be taken of a series of limitations to the use of epidemiologic typing methods, because of the various mechanisms and factors that may induce type changes *in vivo* and *in vitro*. In nature, microbial strains undergo constant fluctuations due to associated flora, bacteriophages, bacteriocins and, sometimes, antibiotics. The acceptance of bacteriophages or plasmids, the selection of certain variants and phenotypical or genotypical modifications of the infectious type may occur. It should, however, be emphasized that these changes are infrequent and therefore have little consequence for the usefulness of the methods. It should likewise be borne in mind that closely similar phenotypical characteristics in strains originating from epidemic foci, distant in time and space, may have a different genetic basis. Such strains may be considered to have a common origin only by corroboration of the epidemiologic data and of several typing methods.

The importance of epidemiologic data in analysing typing methods takes on a particular significance in the case of hospital infections. Thus, for instance, in staphylococcal infections, the character of the hospital strain can be determined only by correlation of the phage type from at least three clinical cases, related epidemiologically (Meyer *et al.*, 1973).

In a final analysis of typing results, it is not so much the identity of the strains as a certain type that is important as the exclusion of a possible common identity of strains with different biologic characteristics. It is obvious, that this implies a previous epidemiologic analysis, since the data obtained by typing methods will complete the epidemiologic findings.

A complete investigation also includes, besides the epidemiologic information, data concerning the origin of each strain, the way in which the pathologic specimen was collected and cultivated, and the quantitative and qualitative relationships of the strain in the respective pathologic specimens. Investigation of these matters is the joint responsibility of the epidemiologist, hygienist and the typing centre. In many situations, the co-operation of clinicians and veterinarians will also be necessary; these specialists have to be acquainted with the principles of interpretation of the results offered by epidemiologic typing methods.

Of particular importance is the variety of different epidemiologic situations in terms of the information that can be furnished by the various epidemiologic typing methods.

The utility of epidemiologic typing methods is of major importance in epidemic foci, whereas in sporadic cases it is of more restricted value. In various epidemiologic situations, the utility of these methods depends upon the stability of the types in time. Thus, limitations have been reported, for instance with phage typing, when strains isolated from carriers are followed up. Other studies demonstrate a remarkable stability *in vivo* of the phage types of various microbial species, as well as the utility of the methods for strains from sporadic cases.

Without going into the details of the various conditions necessary for different typing methods (for instance stability, reproducibility, a better differentiation of the strains, possible standardization, epidemiologic constancy, and rapid reporting), the main purpose is to eliminate a great number of the shortcomings. The usefulness of epidemiologic typing methods has been fully proven, even for methods which do not exhibit perfect reproducibility.

In order to perform epidemiologic surveys it is advantageous to have both national reference centres and international co-operation for the centralized distribution of typing preparations and reference strains, as well as for the standardization of new typing methods and further development of different typing systems.

REFERENCES

Abbott, J. D. and Graham, J. M. (1961). *Mon. Bull. Minist. Hlth* **20**, 51–58.
Abbott, J. D. and Shannon, R. (1958). *J. clin. Path.* **11**, 71–77.
Allison, V. D. (1949). *Proc. R. Soc. Med.* **42**, 216–218.
Anderson, E. S. (1955). *Nature* **175**, 171–173.
Anderson, E. S. (1966). *Nature* **212**, 795–799.
Anderson, E. S. (1968). *Ann. Rev. Microbiol.* **22**, 131–180.
Anderson, E. S. and Felix, A. (1952). *Nature* **170**, 492–494.
Anderson, E. S. and Felix, A. (1953a). *J. gen. Microbiol.* **8**, 408.
Anderson, E. S. and Felix, A. (1953b). *J. gen. Microbiol.* **9**, 65–88.
Anderson, E. S. and Lewis, M. J. (1965). *Nature* **208**, 843–849.
Anderson, E. S. and Wilson, E. M. J. (1960). 4. Colloquium über Fragen der Lysotypie, Wernigerode, 32–35.
Ankirskaja, A. S. (1965). *Zh. Mikrobiol.*, (Moscow) **42**, 89–93.
Aoki, Y. (1968). *Archs. Immunol. Therap. Exp.* **16**, 303–313.
Atkinson, N. (1970). *Austr. J. exp. Biol. Med. Sci.* **48**, 199–206.
Ayliffe, G. A. I., Lowbury, E. J. L., Hamilton, J. G., Small, J. M. and Asheshov, E. A. (1965). *Lancet* **2**, 365–368.
Bail, O. (1921). *Wien. klin. Wschr.* **34**, 447–449.
Basset, D. C. J., Thompson, S. A. S. and Page, B. (1965). *Lancet* **1**, 781–783.
Bercovici, G., Popa, S., Beşleagă, V., Sasu, D., Iosub, G., Freund, S., Brebenel, G. Grumăzescu, M., Buzdugan, I. and Oană, C. (1966). *Arch. Roum. Path. exp. Microbiol.* **25**, 343–344.
Bercovici, C., Iosub, C., Beşleagă, V., Popa, S., Brebenel, G., Grumăzescu, M., Sasu, D., Oană, C., Cuciureanu, G. and Boghiţoiu, I. (1968). *Conf. nat. Epidemiol.*, Sept. ,12–13, Bucharest, 166–167.
Bercovici, C., Iosub, C., Beşleagă, V., Greceanu, V., Trifan, G. and Brebenel, G. (1969). *Archs. Roum. Pathol. exp. Microbiol.* **28**, 964–973.
Bergan, T. (1968). *Acta path. microbiol. scand.* **72**, 396–400.
Bergan, T. (1968a). *Acta path. microbiol. scand.* **72**, 401–411.
Bergan, T. (1972). Bacteriophage Typing of *Pseudomonas aeruginosa*. Universitetsforlaget, Oslo.
Beumer, J. and van Oye, E. (1965). 5. Colloquium über Fragen der Lysotypie, Wernigerode, 81–84.
Blair, J. E. and Carr, M. (1960). *Science* **132**, 1247–1248.
Blair, J. E. and Williams, R. E. O. (1961). *Bull. Wld Hlth Org.* **24**, 771–784.
Bojlén, K. (1934). "Dysentery in Denmark," Biacho Luno, Copenhagen.
Bordet, J. and Ciucă, M. (1921). *C. r. Séanc. Soc. Biol.* **84**, 747–748.
Bordet, J. and Ciucă, M. (1921a). *C. r. Séanc. Soc. Biol.* **84**, 748–750.
Borecka, J. (1965). 5. Colloquium über Fragen der Lysotypie, Wernigerode, 52–56.
Boyd, J. S. K. (1950). *J. Path. Bact.* **62**, 501–517.
Boyd, J. S. K., Parker, M. T. and Mair, N. St. (1951). *J. Hyg.* (London) **49**, 442–451.
Brandis, H. (1955). *Zbl. Bakt.*, *Abt.* I. Orig. **162**, 223–224.
Brandis, H. (1971). "Bacteriocine und bacteriocinähnliche Substanzen," VEB G. Fischer Verlag, Jena.
Brandis, H. and Maurer, H. (1954). *Z. Hyg.* **140**, 138–143.
Buczowski, Z. (1973). "*Salmonella paratyphi-A.*" "Lysotypie," VEB G. Fischer Verlag, Jena.
Buczowski, Z. and Lachowicz, K. (1950). *Med. dósw. Mikrobiol.* **2**, 262–266.

Bulling, E. (1960). Proceedings "2nd Symposium of the Intern. Assoc. of Vet. Food Hygienists", Basel.

Bülow, P. (1966). IXth Intern. Congr. Microbiol., Moscow. Abstracts, 420.

Burnet, F. M. (1927). *Br. J. exp. Path.* **8**, 121–129.

Chanishvili, L. G. and Chanishvili, T. G. (1974). IVème Symposium sur "Les bactériophages et les phénomènes de bactériophagie", Bucarest, 47–48.

Chiracadze, Y. G. and Chanishvili, T. G. (1974). IVème Symposium sur "Les bactériophages et les phénomènes de bactériophagie", Bucarest, 45–46.

Chomiczewski, J. (1961). *Zbl. Bakt., Abt. I. Orig.* **181**, 380–384.

Chomiczewski, J. (1961a). *Zbl. Bakt., Abt., I. Orig.* **181**, 388–390.

Chomiczewski, J. (1965). 5. Colloquium über Fragen der Lysotypie, Wernigerode, 62–63.

Chomiczewski, J. and Piatkowski, K. (1969). *Med dósw. Mikrobiol.* **21**, 351–356.

Chomiczewski, J. and Piatkowski, K. (1969a). *Arch. Roum. Path. exp. Microbiol.* **28**, 934–938.

Ciucă, M., Combiescu, C. and Meitert, T. (1957). 3. Colloquium über Fragen der Lysotypie, Wernigerode, 6–12.

Ciucă, M., Nestorescu, N., Popovici, M., Alexenco, E., Novac, S. and Cheptea, A. (1958). *Zbl. Bakt., Abt. I. Orig.*, **171**, 601–605.

Ciucă, M., Popovici, M., Tupa, A. and Coşman, M. (1966). *Arch. Roum. Path. exp. Microbiol.* **25**, 279–287.

Coetzee, H. L., Klerk, H. C. and Coetzee, J. N. (1968). *J. gen. Virol.* **2**, 29–36.

Combiesco, C. and Meitert, T. (1957). *J. Hyg. Epid. Microb. Immunol.* **1**, 329.

Cook, G. T. and Daines, C. F. (1964). *Monthly Bull. Minist. Hlth Lab. Ser.* **23**, 81–85.

Cornelson, D. A. and Iosub, C. (1962). *Arch. Roum. Path. exp. Microbiol.* **21**, 278–283.

Cradock-Watson, J. E. (1965). *Zbl. Bakt., Abt. I. Orig.* **196**, 384–388.

Craigie, J. (1942). *Can. Publ. Hlth. J.* **33**, 41–42.

Craigie, J. (1946). *Bact. Rev.* **10**, 73–88.

Craigie, J. and Yen, Cl. H. (1938). *Can. Publ. Hlth. J.* **29**, 448–463, 484–496.

Darrell, J. H. and Wahba, A. H. (1964). *J. clin. Path.* **17**, 236–242.

Davies, J. R., Farrant, W. N. and Tomlinson, A. J. H. (1968). *J. Hyg.* (Camb.) **66**, 479–487.

De Blasi, R. and Buogu, A. (1952). *Riv. Ital. Igiene* **12**, 16–58.

Desranleau, J. M. (1947). *Can. J. Publ. Hlth.* **36**, 343–351.

D'Herelle, F. D. (1917). *C. r. Séanc. Acad. Sci.* **165**, 373–375.

Dienes, L. (1946). *Proc. Soc. exp. Biol.* **63**, 265–267.

Egler, L., Laszlo, G. V., Milch, H. and Schmidt, M. (1968). Cited by Milch, H. (1973) Chap. E. *coli* "Lysotypie", VEB G. Fischer-Verlag, Jena, 145–214.

Eörsi, M., Jablonszky, L. and Milch, H. (1953). *Nêpegěszégügy* **34**, 220–223.

Eörsi, M., Jablonszky, L. and Milch, H. (1954). *Acta microbiol. Acad. Sci. Hung.* **1**, 1–8.

Eörsi, M., Jablonszky, L., Milch, H. and Barsy, G. (1957). *Acta microbiol. Acad. Sci. Hung.* **4**, 201–215.

Fardy, P. and Cross, R. (1969). *Can. J. Publ. Hlth.* **60**, 39–40.

Farmer, J. J. and Herman, L. G. (1969). *Appl. Microbiol.* **18**, 760–765.

Farrant, W. N. and Tomlinson, A. J. H. (1966). *J. Hyg.* (Camb.) **64**, 287–303.

Fekety, F. R. and Bennett, I. L. (1959). *Yale J. Biol. Med.* **32**, 23–32.

Fekety, F. R., Buchbinder, L., Shaffer, E. L., Goldberg, S., Price, H. P. and Pyle, L. A. (1958). *Am. J. Publ. Hlth N.Y.* **48**, 298–310.

Felix, A. and Anderson, E. S. (1951). *J. Hyg.* (Camb.) **49**, 349–364.

Felix, A. and Anderson, E. S. (1951a). *J. Hyg.* (Camb.) **49**, 409.

Felix, A. and Callow, B. R. (1943). *Br. med. J.* **2**, 127–130.

Filichkin, S. E., Filichkina, N. E. and Burakovskaia, V. A. (1968). *Zh. Mikrobiol. Epidem. Immunobiol.* **45**, 125–130.

Fisher, M. W., Devlin, H. B. and Gnabasik, F. J. (1969). *J. Bacteriol.* **98**, 835–836.

Fredericq, P. (1963). *Erg. Mikrobiol.* **37**, 114–161.

Fredericq, P., Betz-Bareau, M. and Nicolle, P. (1956). *C. r. Séanc. Soc. Biol.* **150**, 2039–2042.

Freeman, V. J. (1951). *J. Bact.* **61**, 675–688.

Freeman, V. J. and Morse, T. V. (1952). *J. Bact.* **63**, 407–414.

Giammanco, G. and Natoli, D. (1974). IVème Symposium sur "Les bactériophages et les phénomèmes de bactériophagie", Bucarest, 69–70.

Gibson, L. F. and Colman, G. (1973). *J. Hyg.* (Camb.) **71**, 679–689.

Gibson, L. F., Cooper, K., Saragea, A. and Maximescu, P. (1970). *Med. J. Australia* **1**, 412–417.

Gillies, R. R. (1965). *Zbl. Bakt., Abt. I. Orig.* **196**, 370–377.

Gillies, R. R. and Govan, J. R. (1966). *J. Path. Bact.* **91**, 339–345.

Govan, J. R. W. and Gillies, R. R. (1969). *J. med. Microbiol.* **2**, 17–25.

Guinée, P. A. M., Scholtens, R. Th. and Willems, H. M. C. C. (1967). *Antonie van Leeuwenhoek* **33**, 30–40.

Guinée, P. A. M. and Willems, H. M. C. C. (1967a). *Antonie van Leeuwenhoek* **33**, 407–412.

Gullotti, A. and Spano, C. (1960). 4. Colloquium über Fragen der Lysotypie. Wernigerode, 115–119.

Habs, I. (1957). *Z. Hyg. Infekt.-Kr.* **144**, 218–228.

Hallander, H. O. and Laurell, G. (1966). *Postepy Mikrobiol.* **5**, 421–428.

Hamon, Y. (1957). *Ann. Inst. Pasteur* (Paris) **92**, 363–368.

Hamon, Y. (1958). *C. r. Séanc. Acad. Sci.* **247**, 1260–1261.

Hamon, Y. (1960). 4. Colloquium über Fragen der Lysotypie. Wernigerode, 148–160.

Hamon, Y. (1961). *Zbl. Bakt., Abt. I Orig.* **181**, 456–468.

Hamon, Y. and Brault, G. (1958). *C. r. Séanc. Acad. Sci.* **246**, 1779–1780.

Homma, J. Y. (1971). *Jap. J. exp. Med.* **41**, 387–400.

Homma, J. Y., Shionoya, H., Enomoto, M. and Miyao, K. (1972). *Jap. J. exp. Med.* **42**, 171–172.

Hammarström, E. (1949). *Acta med. scand.* **133**, suppl. 223.

Hudemann, H. (1965). 5. Colloquium über Fragen der Lysotypie, Wernigerode, 60–62.

Iosub, C. (1962). *Arch. Roum. Path. exp. Microbiol.* **21**, 283–288.

Iosub, C. (1974). IVème Symposium sur "Les bactériophages et les phénomènes de bactériophagie", Bucarest, 43–44.

Iseki, S. and Sakai, T. (1953). *Proc. Japan. Acad.* **29**, 121.

Iseki, S. and Sakai, T. (1953a). *Proc. Japan. Acad.* **29**, 127.

Istrati, G. (1960). 4. Colloquium über Fragen der Lysotypie, Wernigerode, 53–58.

Istrati, G., Meitert, T., Ciufeco, C., Tunaru, C., Henţiu, V. and Deleanu, L. (1962). *Arch. Roum. Path. exp. Microbiol.* **21**, 288–294.

Junghans, R. (1958). *Dtsch. ges. Wes.* **13**, 246–250.

Junghans, R. (1958a). *Dtsch. ges. Wes.* **13**, 1138–1142.
Junghans, R. (1958b). *Zbl. Bakt., Abt. I. Orig.* **173**, 50–54.
Kallings, L. O. and Laurell, A. B. (1957). *Acta path. microbiol. scand.* **40**, 328–342.
Kallings, L. D., Laurell, A. B. and Zetterberg, B. (1959). *Acta path. microbiol. scand.* **45**, 347–356.
Kameda, M., Harada, K. and Matsuyama, T. (1968). *Jap. J. Bact.* **23**, 343–347.
Kauffmann, F. (1967). *Zbl. Bakt., Abt. I. Orig.* **203**, 458–463.
Kauffmann, F. and Dupont, A. (1950). *Acta path. microbiol. scand.* **27**, 552–564.
Kauffmann, F. and Ørskov, F. (1956). *In* Adam "Säuglings-Enteritis". Stuttgart.
Kende, E. (1964). *Zbl. Bakt., Abt. I. Orig.* **192**, 198–204.
Kilesso, V. A. and Nikityiuk, N. M. (1969). *Zh. Mikrobiol.* (Moscow) **46**, 2, 48–53.
Kiselev, R. N. (1967). *Zh. Mikrobiol.* (Moscow) **44**, 60–64.
Kleinmaier, H. (1957). *Zbl. Bakt., Abt. I. Orig.* **170**, 570–583.
Kleinmaier, H., Schreil, W. and Quincke, G. (1959). *Zbl. Bakt., Abt. I. Orig.* **174**, 229–236.
Knights, H. T., France, D. R. and Harding, S. (1968). *N.Z. med. J.* **67**, 617.
Köhler, W., Ghatak, S. N., Rische, H. and Ziesché, K. (1966). *Zbl. Bakt., Abt. I. Orig.* **201**, 482–488.
Kristensen, M. (1938). *J. Hyg.* (Camb.) **38**, 688–701.
Kristensen, M. and Bojlén, K. (1929). *Zbl. Bakt., Abt. I. Orig.* **114**, 86–108.
Kristensen, M. and Henriksen, H. C. D. (1926). *Acta path. microbiol. scand.* **3**, 551–583.
Krylova, M. D. (1972). *J. Mikrobiol. epidemiol. Immunobiol.* **49**, 27–33.
Krylova, M. D., Reihstat, G. N., Ostrovskaia, Z. S., Tkacenco, A. M., Kuznetova, N. S., Agafonova, L. I. and Pozina, V. S. (1973). *J. Mikrobiol. epidemiol. Immunobiol.* **50**, 93–98.
Kudlaj, D. G., Petrovskaya, V. G. and Kiselev, R. N. (1970). *Zh. Mikrobiol.* (Moscow) **47**, 43–47.
Kunin, M. and Halmagyi, N. E. (1962). *New Eng. J. Med.* **266**, 1297–1301.
Kühn, H., Falta, R. and Rische, H. (1973). Chap. *Salmonella typhimurium* "Lysotypie". VEB G. Fischer-Verlag, Jena, 101–140.
Lalko, J. (1965). *Bull. Inst. Morsk. Med.* (Gdansk) **16**, 147–166.
Lalko, J., Buczowski, Z. and Glosnicka, R. (1967). *Bull. Inst. Morsk. Med.* (Gdansk) **18**, 13–30.
Lányi, B. (1966/67). *Acta microbiol. Acad. Sci. Hung.* **13**, 295–318.
Lányi, B. (1970). *Acta microbiol. Acad. Sci. Hung.* **17**, 35–48.
Laurell, G., Magnuson, J. H., Friselle, E. and Werner, B. (1951). *Acta Ped.* **40**, 302–337.
Lebek, G. (1967). *Path. Microbiol.* **30**, 1015–1036.
Le Minor, L. (1963). *Ann. Inst. Pasteur* (Paris) **105**, 879–896.
Le Minor, L. and Pichinoty, F. (1963). *Ann. Inst. Pasteur* (Paris) **104**, 384–392.
Le Minor, S., Le Minor, L., Nicolle, P. and Buttiaux, R. (1954). *Ann. Inst. Pasteur* (Paris) **86**, 204–226.
Lenk, V. (1955). 1. Colloquium über Fragen der Lysotypie, Wernigerode, 10–12.
Lenk, V. (1956). 2. Colloquium über Fragen der Lysotypie, Wernigerode.
Lilleengen, K. (1948). *Acta path. microbiol. scand.* Suppl. **77**, 11–127.
Levine, M., Rice, P. A., Gangarosa, E. J., Morris, G. K., Snyder, M. J., Formal, S. B., Wells, J. G., Gemski, P. and Hammond, J. (1974). *Am. J. Epidem.* **99**, 30–36.
Marcuse, K. (1934). *Zbl. Bakt., Abt. I. Orig.* **131**, 49–53.

Maresz-Babczyszyn, J., Mrózkurpiela, E., Lachowicz, Z. and Slopek, St. (1967). *Arch. Immunol. Ther. exp.* **15**, 512–516.
Maresz-Babczyszyn, J., Mrózkurpiela, E. and Slopek, St. (1967a). *Arch. Immunol. Ther. exp.* **15**, 517–520.
Matsumoto, H., Tazaki, T. and Kato, T. (1968). *Jap. J. Microbiol.* **17**, 111–119.
Maximescu, P., Saragea, A. and Drăgoi, T. (1972). *Arch. Roum. Path. exp. Microbiol.* **31**, 357–366.
Maximescu, P., Pop, A., Oprişan, A. and Potorac, E. (1974a). *J. Hyg. Epid. Microbiol. Immunol.* (Prague) **18**, 324–428.
Mayr-Harting, A. (1952). *J. gen. Microbiol.* **7**, 382–396.
McGeachie, J. (1965). *Zbl. Bakt., Abt. I. Orig.* **196**, 377–384.
McGeachie, J. and McCormick, W. (1967). *J. clin. Path.* **20**, 887–891.
Meitert, E. (1965). "Lizotipia la *Pseudomonas aeruginosa.*" Doctor's Thesis, Bucharest, Institute of Medicine and Pharmacy.
Meitert, E. (1965a). *Arch. Roum. Path. exp. Microbiol.* **24**, 439–458.
Meitert, E. (1974). IVème Symposium sur "Les bactériophages et les phénomènes de bactériophagie", Bucarest, 65–66.
Meitert, E. and Meitert, T. (1968). *Zbl. Bakt., Abt. I. Orig.* **208**, 515–521.
Meitert, E. and Meitert, T. (1972). *Arch. Roum. Path. exp. Microbiol.* **31**, 443–448.
Meitert, E. and Meitert, T. (1973). Chap. *Pseudomonas aeruginosa.* "Lysotypie", VEB G. Fischer-Verlag, Jena, 398-418.
Meitert, E., Meitert, T., Baron, E., Sulea, I. and Cristea, I. (1969). *Arch. Roum. Path. exp. Microbiol.* **28**, 957–964.
Meitert, T. (1952). Lucrare pentru Examenul de Stat, 1952, Facultatea de Medicină, Bucureşti.
Meitert, T. (1964). *Arch. Roum. Path. exp. Microbiol.* **23**, 679–688.
Meitert, T. and Meitert, E. (1960). *Arch. Roum. Path. exp. Microbiol.* **19**, 623–634.
Meitert, T. and Meitert, E. (1966). *Arch. Roum. Path. exp. Microbiol.* **25**, 427–434.
Meitert, T. and Meitert, E. (1971). *Arch. Roum. Path. exp. Microbiol.* **30**, 37–44.
Meitert, T., Istrati, G., Ciufecu, C., Chiriac, F. and Baron, E. (1968). *Conf. Nat. Epidemiol.* **12–13**, Bucharest, 189–190.
Meitert, T., Istrati, G., Ciufecu, C., Sulea, I. T. and Baron, E. (1969). *Arch. Roum. Path. exp. Microbiol.* **28**, 976–977.
Meitert, T., Pencu, E., Sulea, I. T. and Tempea, C. (1974). IVème Symposium sur "Les bactériophages et les phénomènes de bactériophagie", Bucarest, 60–61.
Meitert, T., Ciufecu, C., Sulea, I., Pencu, E., Dinculescu, E. and Merlaub, I. (1974a). *Arch. Roum. Path. exp. Microbiol.* **34**, 59–66.
Meitert, T., Istrati, G., Sulea, T. I., Pencu, E., Tempea, C. and Gogulescu, L. (1975). 6. Colloquium über Fragen der Lysotypie, Wernigerode, Abstract No. 7.
Meyer, W. (1957). *Zbl. Bakt., Abt. I. Orig.* **168**, 542–552.
Meyer, W. (1966). *Z. med. mikrobiol. u. Immunol.* **152**, 332–341.
Meyer, W., Ziomek, D. and Rische, H. (1973). Chap. *Staphylococcus aureus* in "Lysotypie", VEB G. Fischer-Verlag, Jena, 467–545.
Mihalcu, F. and Vereanu, A. (1974). IVème Symposium sur "Les bactériophages et les phénomènes de bactériophagie", Bucarest, 8–9.
Mihalcu, F., Dumitriu, L. S. and Vereanu, A. (1974). IVème Symposium sur "Les bactériophages et les phénomènes de bactériophagie", Bucarest, 9–10.
Milch, H. (1973). Chap. *Escherichia coli* in "Lysotypie", "VEB G. Fischer-Varlag, Jena, 145–214.

Milch, H. and Deak, S. (1961). *Acta microbiol. Acad. Sci. Hung.* **8**, 411–421.
Milch, H. and Gyenes, M. (1975). 6. Colloquium über Fragen der Lysotypie, Wernigerode 387–394.
Milch, H. and Laszlo, G. V. (1967). *Acta microbiol. Sci. Hung.* **14**, 287–292.
Milch, H., Lásló, V. G. and Biro, G. (1963). *Acta microbiol. Acad. Sci. Hung.* **10**, 41–52.
Milch, H., Gyenes, M. and Hérmán, G. (1974). IVème Symposium sur "Les bactériophages et les phénomènes de bactériophagie", Bucarest, 31.
Mitsumashi, S. (1967). *Jap. J. Microbiol.* **11**, 49–68.
Mukerjee, S. (1963). *Bull. Wld Hlth Org.* **28**, 337–345.
Mukerjee, S. (1973). Chap. *Vibrio comma* in 'Lysotypie", VEB G. Fischer-Verlag, Jena, **2**, 547–572.
Nakagawa, M. (1960). *Jap. J. vet. Res.* **8**, 191–207.
Nestorescu, N., Popovici, M. and Zilişteanu, E. (1953). *Rev. Ig. Microbiol. Epidemiol.* 24–29.
Nestorescu, N., Popovici, M., Novac, S., Cheptea, A. and Alexenco, E. (1956). 2. Colloquium über Fragen der Lysotypie, Wernigerode.
Nestorescu, N., Popovici, M., Palade, C., Novac, S., Alexenco, E., Cheptea, A., Cociaşu, I. and Stoia, A. (1957a). *Arch. Roum. Path. exp. Microbiol.* **16**, 507–515.
Nestorescu, N., Popovici, M. and Palade, C. (1958). Abstracts, VIIth Internat. Congress for Microbiology, Stockholm, 357.
Nicolle, P. (1956). 2. Colloquium über Fragen der Lysotypie, Wernigerode, 64.
Nicolle, P. (1973). Chap. *Yersinia enterocolitica* in "Lysotypie", VEB G. Fischer-Verlag, Jena, 377–388.
Nicolle, P. and Diverneau, G. (1961). *Zbl. Bakt., Abt. I. Orig.* **181**, 385–387.
Nicolle, P. and Hamon, Y. (1951). *C. r. Séanc. Acad. Sci.* **232**, 898–899.
Nicolle, P. and Le Minor, L. (1965). *Ann. Inst. Pasteur* (Paris) **108**, 501–513.
Nicolle, P. and Prunet, J. (1965). 5. Colloquium über Fragen der Lysotypie, Wernigerode, 3–7 Oct., 56–60.
Nicolle, P., Hamon, Y. and Edlinger, E. (1953). *Biol. Méd.* (Paris) **42**, 437–518.
Nicolle, P., Pavlatou, M. and Diverneau, G. (1953a). *C. r. Séanc. Acad. Sci.* **236**, 2453–2455.
Nicolle, P., Pavlatou, M. and Diverneau, G. (1954). *Ann. Inst. Pasteur* (Paris) **87**, 493–509.
Nicolle, P., Van Oye, E., Crocker, C. G. and Brault, I. (1955). *Bull. Soc. Pathol. Exo.* **48**, 492–510.
Nicolle, P., L. Minor, L., Le Minor, S. and Buttiaux, R. (1957). *Zbl. Bakt., Abt. I. Orig.* **168**, 512–528.
Nicolle, P., Le Minor, S., Hamon, Y. and Brault, G. (1960). *Rév. Hyg. Méd. Soc.* **8**, 523–562.
Nicolle, P., Brault, G. and Brault, J. (1963). *C. r. Séanc. Acad. Sci.* **257**, 2194–2197.
Nicolle, P., Mollaret, H. and Brault, J. (1969). *Arch. Roum. Path. exp. Microbiol.* **28**, 1019–1027.
Novgorovskaya, E. M. (1968). Symposium "Aktuelle Fragen der Epidemiologie und Prophylaxie der Ruhr", 4–6.6.1968, Moscow, cited by Sumarokov, A. A., Moscow, 1969, 31.
Ogawa, T., Inagaki, Y., Takamatsu, M., Yoshikane, M. and Yamamoto, T. (1965), *Nagoya Med. J.* **11**, 31–41.
Olitzki, A., Shelubsky, M. and Strauss, W. (1948). *Harefuah*, **34**, 107.
Ortel, S. (1957). 3. Colloquium über Fragen der Lysotypie, Wernigerode, 81–95.

Osman, M. A. M. (1965). *J. clin. Path.* **18**, 200–202.

Papavassiliou, J. and Huet, M. (1962). *Arch. Inst. Pasteur* (Tunis) **39**, 327–340.

Papavassiliou, J. and Samaraki-Lyséropopoulou, V. (1965). *Arch. Inst. Past.* (Hellén.) **11**, 33–43.

Papavassiliou, J., Vandepitte, J., Gatti, F. and Moor, J. (1964). *Ann. Inst. Pasteur* (Paris) **106**, 255–266.

Parker, T. M. (1965). 5. Colloquium über Fragen der Lysotypie, Wernigerode, 144–151.

Parker, M. T. and Jevons, M. P. (1963). In "Infections in Hospitals: Epidemiology and Control" (Williams, R. E. O. and Shooter, R. A., Eds), pp. 55–65. Blackwell Scientific Publications, Oxford.

Pfeiffer, J. and Krüger, W. (1968). *Arch. Immunol. Therp. exp.* **16**, 471–473.

Phillips, I. (1967). *J. Hyg.* (Camb.) **65**, 229–235.

Phillips, I., Lobo, A. Z., Fernandes, R. and Gundara, N. S. (1968). *Lancet* **1**, 11–12.

Popovici, M. (1968). *Arch. de l'Union médicale Balkanique* **6**, 59–67.

Popovici, M., Alexenco, E. and Vianu, I. (1966). *Arch. Roum. Path. exp. Microbiol.* **25**, 957–964.

Popovici, M., Năcescu, N., Filipescu, S., Voina, E., Ghelariu, A., Mucuţă, G. and Vasilescu, G. (1968). *Conf. Nat. Epidemiol.*, Bucureşti, 219–220.

Popovici, M., Greceanu V., and Vianu, I. (1974). IVème Symposium sur "Les bactériophages et les phénomènes de bactériophagie", Bucarest, 36–37.

Pöhn, H. P. (1957a). 3. Colloquium über Fragen der Lysotypie, Wernigerode, 102–103.

Quinh, D. (1968). Cited by Sédlak, J. and Rische, H. in "*Enterobacteriaceae*-Infektionen", VEB G. Thieme, Leipzig, 216–218.

Rische, H. (1955). *Z. ges. Hyg.* **1**, 110.

Rische, H. (1960). 4. Colloquium über Fragen der Lysotypie, Wernigerode, 14–20.

Rische, H. (1968). Chap. VI, Spezielle epidemiologische Laboratoriumsmethoden. "*Enterobacteriaceae*-Infektionen". VEB G. Thieme, Leipzig, 165–250.

Rische, H. (1973). "Lysotypie", VEB, G. Fischer-Verlag, Jena, 23–581.

Rische, H. and Kretzschmar, W. (1962). *Arch. Hyg.* **146**, 530–539.

Rische, H. and Schneider, H. (1956). 2. Colloquium über Fragen der Lyso-typie, Wernigerode.

Rische, H. and Schneider, H. (1960). *J. Hyg. Epid. Microbiol.* **4**, 32–53.

Rische, H. and Ziesché, K. (1973). Chap. *Salmonella typhi* in "Lysotypie", VEB G. Fischer-Verlag, Jena, 23–64.

Rische, H. and Ziesché, K. (1973a). Chap. *Salmonella paratyphi B* in "Lysotypie", VEB G. Fischer-Verlag, Jena, 65–86.

Rurka, G. (1974). *Can. J. Med. Tech.*, **36**, 314–313.

Rusu, V., Baron-Dorbăt, O., Coşman, M. and Lăzăroaie, D. (1974) IVème Symposium sur "Les bactériophages at les phénomènes de bactériophagie" Bucarest, 29–31.

Sandvik, O. (1960). *Acta path. microbiol. scand.* **48**, 56–60

Saragea, A. and Maximescu, P. (1966). *W.H.O. Bull.* **35**, 681–689.

Saragea, A., Maximescu, P. and Meitert, E. (1973). Chap. *Corynebacterium diph-theriae* in "Lysotypie", VEB G. Fischer-Verlag, Jena, 435–466.

Schmidt, A. (1932). *Zbl. Bakt., Abt. I. Orig.* **123**, 207–212.

Schmidt, J. (1962). *Zbl. Bakt., Abt. I. Orig.* **185**, 41–46.

Scholtens, R. Th. (1956). *Antonie van Leeuwenhoek* **22**, 65–88.

Scholtens, R. Th. (1969). *Arch. Roum. Path. exp. Microbiol.* **28**, 984–990.

Sédlak, J. and Rische, H. (1968). *"Enterobacteriaceae*-Infektionen", VEB G. Fischer-Verlag, Jena, 204–205.

Sedlak, J., Mulczyk, M., Slopek, St. and Slajsova, M. (1967). *Zbl. Bakt.*, *Abt. I. Orig.* 202, 448–462.

Seidel, G. and Eilsberger, G. (1962). *Zbl. Bakt.*, *Abt. I. Orig.* 185, 175–181.

Shannon, R. (1957). *J. med. Lab. Technol.* 14, 199–214.

Shooter, R. A., Walker, K. A., Williams, V. R., Horgan, G. M., Parker, M. T., Asheshov, E. H. and Bullimore, J. F. (1966). *Lancet* II, 1331–1334.

Sjöberg, L. and Lindberg, A. A. (1968). *Acta path. microbiol. scand.* 74, 61–68.

Sjöberg, L. and Nord, C. E. (1975). 6. Colloquium über Fragen der Lysotypie, Wernigerode, 520–525.

Slopek, St. and Maresz-Babczyszyn, J. (1967). *Arch. Immunol. Ther. exp.* 15, 525–529.

Sonnenschein, C. (1925). *München. med. Wschr.* 72, 1443–1444.

Sonnenschein, C. (1928). *Dtsch. med. Wschr.* 54, 1034–1036.

Sonnenschein, C. (1929). *München. med. Wschr.* 76, 355–356.

Stamatin, N. (1969). *Arch. Roum. Path. exp. Microbiol.* 28, 879–884.

Stamatin, N. and Li Van Sob (1959). *Arch. Roum. Path. exp. Microbiol.* 18, 31–32.

Stepankovskaja, L. D. and Brutman, E. J. (1969). *Zh. Mikrobiol* (Moscow) 46, 2, 31–34.

Stepankovskaja, L. D., Brutman, E. J., Germanyuk, J. V. and Korsun, E. A. (1968). *Zh. Mikrobiol.* (Moscow) 45, 12, 43–45.

Szégli, L., Popovici, M., Soare, L., Neguţ, M., Călin, C. and Florescu, E. (1974). IVème Symposium sur "Les bactériophages et les phénomènes de bactériophagie", Bucarest, 44–45.

Szturm-Rubinsten, S. (1964). *Ann. Inst. Pasteur* (Paris) 106, 114–122.

Szturm-Rubinsten, S. (1970). *Ann. Inst. Pasteur* (Paris) 118, 34–40.

Tagg, J. R. and Mushin, R. (1973). *J. med. Microbiol.* 6, 559–563.

Tinne, J. E., Gordon, A. M., Bain, W. H. and Mackey, W. A. (1967). *Brit. med. J.* 4, 313–315.

Tomasic, P. (1960). 4. Colloquium über Fragen der Lysotypie, Wernigerode, 144–148.

Toucas, M. (1974). IVème Symposium sur "Les bactériophages et les phénomènes de bactériophagie", Bucarest, 28–29.

Tschäpe, H. and Rische, H. (1970). *Zbl. Bakt.*, *Abt. I. Orig.* 314, 91–100.

Tschäpe, H. and Rische, H. (1970a). *Zschr. ges. Hyg.* 16, 662–664.

Tschäpe, H. and Rische, H. (1972). *Zschr. allg. Mikrobiol.* 12, 59–68.

Twort, T. W. (1915). *Lancet* 2, 1241–1243.

Verder, E. and Evans, J. (1961). *J. infect. Dis.* 109, 183–193.

Véron, M. (1961). *Ann. Inst. Pasteur* (Paris) 101, 456–460.

Vieu, J. F. (1969). *Bull. Inst. Pasteur* 67, 1231–1249.

Vieu, J. F. and Ducrest, P. (1960). 4. Colloquium über Fragen der Lysotypie, Wernigerode, 161–168.

Wahba, A. H. (1965). *Br. med. J.* 1, 86–89.

Wahba, A. H. (1965a). *Zbl. Bakt.*, *Abt. I. Orig.* 196, 389–394.

Wahl, R. and Blum-Emmerique, L. (1952). *Ann. Inst. Pasteur* (Paris) 82, 29–43.

Wahl, R. and Blum-Emmerique, L. (1952a). *Ann. Inst. Pasteur* (Paris) 82, 44–49.

Wahl, R. and Fouace, J. (1958). *Zbl. Bakt.*, *Abt. I. Orig.* 171, 573–583.

Watanabe, T. (1968). *Proc. XII. Congr. Genetics* 2, 237.

Wiedemann, B. and Knothe, H. (1968). *Zbl. Bakt.*, *Abt. I. Orig.* 208, 177–185.

Williams, R. E. O. and Jevons, M. P. (1960). 4. Colloquium über Fragen der Lysotypie, Wernigerode, 90–98.

Williams, R. E. O., Rippon, J. and Dowsett, L. M. (1953). *Lancet* 1, 510–514.

Witte, W. (1975). 6. Colloquium über Fragen der Lysotypie, Wernigerode, 207–212.

Wokatsch, R. (1964). *Zbl. Bakt., Abt. I. Orig.* 192, 468–476.

Zabransky, R. J. and Day, F. E. (1967). *Bact. Proc.*, 97.

Zamiri, I. and McEnegart, ? (1973). *J. med. Microbiol.* 6, Pxxi.

Zarikova, M. S. (1965). *Zh. Mikrobiol.* (Moscow) 42, 141–142.

Zaritski, A. M. (1968). *J. Mikrobiol.* (Moscow) 45, 46–50.

Ziesché, K. (1974). IVème Symposium sur "Les bactériophages et les phénomènes de bactériophagie", Bucarest, 42–43.

Ziesché, K. and Rische, H. (1973). Chap. *Shigella sonnei*, pp. 245–342, in Lysotypie (Rische, H., Ed.), VEB G. Fischer-Verlag, Jena, 245–342.

CHAPTER II

The Application of Typing Methods to Nosocomial Infections

G. A. J. AYLIFFE

Hospital Infection Research Laboratory, Summerfield Hospital, Birmingham, England

I. INTRODUCTION

In this Chapter typing methods are considered within the general context of investigation of outbreaks of nosocomial, i.e. hospital-acquired infection. The collection of epidemiological information is necessary to interpret the results of typing and will be discussed in most of the investigations described. The examples of outbreaks or epidemiological investigations were whenever possible selected from situations in which the author was involved or personally acquainted. Outbreaks of recognized communicable diseases (e.g. salmonellosis, shigellosis, respiratory virus infections and childhood fevers) often occur in hospital, but will not be dealt with in this Chapter. The organisms to be considered are shown in Table I and are present in the normal flora of patients, staff and visitors and in the inanimate environment of the hospital.

A. Incidence of infection

The incidence of hospital-acquired infection is often uncertain, but from available reports and from our own data, it would seem to be about 3–5% in general hospitals. Urinary tract, surgical wound and respiratory tract infections are the most frequent. The common organisms causing hospital-acquired urinary tract and surgical wound infections are shown in Table I.

TABLE I

Organisms isolated from operation wounds and acquired urinary tract infection in a general hospital (1972)

	% of isolations from	
Organism	Wounds	Urines
Staphylococcus aureus	33	2
Escherichia coli	25	39
Klebsiella sp.	6	18
Proteus sp.	11	20
Pseudomonas aeruginosa	3	5
Others, e.g. *Streptococcus faecalis, Candida* sp., other Gram-negative bacilli, etc.	22	16
Number of infections	760	1110

B. General properties of organisms

Any investigation of an outbreak of infection requires some knowledge of the properties of the organisms involved. For practical purposes in hospital, these are mainly staphylococci and Gram-negative bacilli. *Staphylococcus aureus* is found in the nose of 20–30% of normal people, and much less frequently in the perineal region (Williams *et al.*, 1966). Transmission in hospital is often from a patient or a member of staff with an infected lesion. Staphylococci are commonly spread on skin scales, especially by patients shedding large numbers of organisms into the environment. Staphylococci survive drying much better than Gram-negative bacilli but do not grow in the inanimate environment. People are the sources, but the isolation of strains from certain environmental sites may help to establish routes of transmission.

All of the Gram-negative bacilli described may be found in the faeces of normal people, but some are also commonly found in the moist environment of the hospital. *Pseudomonas aeruginosa, Klebsiella* sp. and *Serratia marcescens* are able to grow at room temperature in a moist environment with minimal nutrients. In contrast to *S. aureus*, the environment may be a true source of an outbreak of infection caused by these organisms, although person to person spread also occurs.

C. General applications of typing methods

The typing methods already described, e.g. phage, bacteriocin and serological, are all used in the investigation of hospital infection, but biochemical profiles and antibiotic or chemical resistance patterns may also be useful. Apart from phage-typing of *S. aureus* and possibly pyocin typing, methods for typing other organisms are less well established in routine hospital epidemiology.

Infections may arise from a common source, or may occur sporadically, or in endemic or hyperendemic conditions (Parker, 1971). A single source in an operating theatre could be a nurse with an infected finger, or a contaminated solution used for skin disinfection. In addition to the original single source, secondary person to person spread may take place, e.g. a staphylococcal infection acquired from a member of the operating room staff may subsequently spread from patient to patient in a ward. Often when the outbreak is investigated, the original source is no longer apparent.

A number of unrelated infections may occur in a unit or hospital at the same time, possibly due to a general failure in aseptic techniques. These will usually be endogenous infections and by means of a typing method, the sources in each individual infection may be identified as the patient's own flora. Staphylococcal wound infections may arise from the patient's own nasal flora, and urinary tract infection caused by Gram-negative bacilli may originate from organisms in the faeces. Sporadic infections of endogenous origin may be distributed throughout the hospital and typing will show a number of different patterns (e.g. Darrell and Wahba, 1964). An endemic or hyperendemic situation may often be found in special units, e.g. intensive-care or burns. Similar strains are isolated from more than one patient at one time and will be consistently isolated in the unit, although the endemic strain will probably be different from time to time. Typing methods will enable gradual changes to be followed over months and years. A sudden increase in cross-infection caused by a single strain of an organism in a unit where cross-infection was usually absent or uncommon, or an increase above the level usually found in the unit may indicate an epidemic or a potential epidemic situation.

Typing methods may also indicate the possible presence of an especially virulent strain, or a strain of a certain type associated with a particular infection, e.g. *S. aureus* phage type 71 is often a cause of impetigo in children. However, epidemic type and virulence are independant characteristics and in these instances a typing method is only an indication of possible virulence. Thus, strains of *S. aureus* of phage type 71 may be isolated both from people without infectious disease and from persons who have never transmitted infection to others. Other uses of typing in hospital include the recognition of the emergence of resistance in previously sensitive strains in patients treated with a certain antibiotic. Typing may also aid the differentiation between human and animal, or human and environmental strains.

II. INVESTIGATION OF STAPHYLOCOCCAL INFECTIONS

Coagulase-positive strains are still the most important of the Gram-positive cocci causing acute hosital infection, but coagulase-negative strains have become increasingly responsible for infections in particularly suscept-ible patients, e.g. following implant surgery. The biochemical subdivision of staphylococci and micrococci (Baird-Parker, 1965) and antibiotic resistance patterns may be of clinical value in identifying a predominant strain in certain infections. In primary urinary tract infections, the com-monest type of *Staphylococcus* is Baird-Parker's biotype M.3 (Mitchell, 1968) which is novobiocin-resistant, and uncommon on normal skin (see also Noble and Somerville, 1974). Phage typing of coagulase-negative strains is not yet as well established a method as for *S. aureus*. Identical phage patterns have been isolated from Spitz–Holter valves, blood cultures and sometimes from the skin of patients (Verhoef *et al.*, 1972), suggesting endogenous infections. However, a wide range of coagulase-negative cocci is normally found on the skin and in the hospital environment. Epidemio-logical studies accordingly involve much more laboratory work than in the investigation of coagulase-positive strains.

A. Infections caused by *S. aureus*

Outbreaks have been frequently described and most have been elucidated by means of antibiotic sensitivity patterns and phage-typing (Blair and Williams, 1961). Examples of outbreaks in surgical, neonatal and derma-tological wards are described in the following Sections.

1. *Surgical wards*

Infection may arise in the operating theatre or in the ward. The possible sources are shown in Fig. 1. An epidemiological investigation is necessary when two or more infections are recognized either in one ward, or in patients operated on in one operating theatre. This information should be obtained from routine infection surveillance methods in the hospital. The laboratory reports will indicate that *S. aureus* is involved and also provide the antibiotic sensitivity pattern. A similar antibiotic sensitivity pattern in strains from several patients, particularly if the organism is resistant to four or five antibiotics may be initially helpful, but often phage typing is necessary to show that a particular strain of *Staphylococcus* is involved.

The most important part of the investigation is the collection of epidemiological data, e.g. types and dates of operations, wound drainage, presence of haematoma, when the wounds were first dressed, date of admission of infected patients, other simultaneous infections in the ward, name of surgeon and members of surgical team and operating theatre. At this stage it should be known whether there is a definite outbreak of infection, the possible area of origin, and whether a detailed investigation is required.

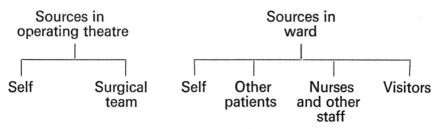

FIG. 1. Staphyloccal infections in surgery

The site of origin of the infection can often be obtained from the epidemiological data, e.g. deep infections in clean, undrained wounds are usually of theatre origin; infection appearing before the first dressing in the ward is another indication of a possible theatre source of infection. Antibiotic sensitivity patterns and phage typing may indicate whether a common "ward" strain is involved. The following describes a study of an outbreak of theatre-acquired infections. A series of wound infections in several wards from which were isolated strains of *S. aureus* with an unusual antibiotic sensitivity pattern and of the same phage pattern was recognized. From clinical criteria, it seemed that some of these infections probably originated in the operating theatre. Table II shows that Theatre C was a likely source of the outbreak and that the surgeon was not responsible.

Nasal swabs were taken from all the staff, slit-sampling studies were made, and settle-plates were exposed during operations in Theatre C. A theatre porter was found to be carrying the epidemic strain in his nose, and a similar strain was isolated from the air-sampling plates. The porter was later found to be suffering from a desquamating skin lesion (Ayliffe and Collins, 1967). He was asked to perform standard exercises in the laboratory and slit-sampling studies showed him to be a heavy disperser of the epidemic strain. It is often possible to detect the probable source quickly without any preliminary screening if a member of the operating staff is found with a septic lesion. Outbreaks of theatre-acquired infection are

TABLE II

Wound infections due to a strain of *Staphylococcus*
aureus **resistant to Tetracycline, Novobiocin and**
Neomycin (phage pattern 80/81)

Operation	Ward	Surgeon	Operating theatre
Varicose veins	1	A	C
Cholecystectomy	1	A	C
Mastectomy	2	C	C
Herniorrhaphy	3	C	C
Nephrectomy	3	C	C
Amputation of leg	2	B	C

commonly due to a septic lesion on the hands or fore-arms of a member of the operating team (e.g. McDonald and Timbury, 1957).

Air sampling may detect the presence of a disperser, who is not a nasal carrier and has no infected lesion. Male perineal carriers are often heavy dispersers, whilst normal females are rarely dispersers (Blowers *et al.*, 1973). Sampling of fingers, face and hair may show heavy growth of the epidemic strain and indicate a possible disperser or source (Ayliffe *et al.*, 1973). Epidemic strains of *S. aureus* of theatre origin are often sensitive to all antibiotics, apart from Penicillin, and 20–30% of operating staff may be nasal carriers of sensitive strains. Phage-typing, dispersal tests, and tests for skin and finger carriage may help to define the source.

Outbreaks of staphylococcal infection of ward origin may be more difficult since a number of infections often occur simultaneously without any single source being apparent. These infections may occur at intervals over a long period of time and unless strains are typed, any connection between them may not be recognized. The ward epidemic strains are usually resistant to several antibiotics and the antibiogram may be helpful for identifying the epidemic or endemic strain. A strain resistant to Penicillin, Tetracycline, Erythromycin, Kanamycin and Methicillin is probably sufficiently characteristic to make phage-typing unnecessary, whereas phage-typing would be important in the identification of a strain resistant to Penicillin and Tetracycline only. The epidemiological data will be helpful, since most of the ward-acquired infected wounds will have been dressed in the ward and will often be moist or have drains. All wounds and lesions in the ward should be sampled and careful enquiry made as to the presence of staff with infections, or of bed-sores in patients. Figure 2 shows the spread of *S. aureus*, phage-type 53/75 in a surgical ward. There appeared initially to be a period between patients B and D when there were none with colonized noses and none with infections in the ward. The strain was found on a bed-pan and later it was determined that patient C had been in the ward throughout this period and had a colonized bed-sore. This was not recognized until much later (Gillespie *et al.*, 1961). To control an outbreak it is necessary to isolate heavy dispersers of the epidemic strain in single-wards or in a special isolation unit. Dispersers in the ward may be identified by the presence of a large number of colonies on air-sampling plates in their vicinity, or on contact plates taken from the floor near the bed, or on sweep-plates from bedding.

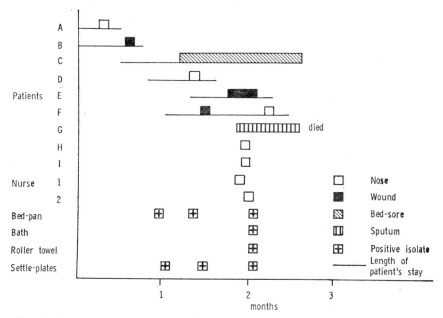

FIG. 2. Spread of *Staphylococcus aureus* phage pattern 53/75 in a surgical ward.

When the type identity of the epidemic strain is established, a routine screening method may be used. Strains may be screened for resistance to one antibiotic, e.g. Tetracycline or Methicillin, or if more useful, a single phage or group of phages, e.g. 80/81, without using the complete set of phages. If additional bacteriological sampling is not possible, patients with heavily discharging wounds or lesions which cannot be adequately en-closed, e.g. eczema, pneumonia, should be treated as dispersers. If eradi-cation of the strain from a unit is necessary, nasal carriers will also require treatment. This should include staff, although these are usually victims rather than the cause of the outbreak (see Fig. 2). However, a member of staff with an infected lesion, particularly on the hands or fore-arm may infect a number or patients in the ward as well as in the operating theatre.

When treating a member of staff with an infected lesion, or with recurrent sepsis, it is useful to know if the same strain is present in a carriage site such as the nose or perineum. Since these strains are often resistant to Penicillin only, phage typing may be particularly useful.

Visitors are rarely sources of staphylococcal infection in hospital and investigation for carriage is usually unnecessary.

2. *Neonatal wards*

The investigation of an outbreak in neonatal wards is similar to that in surgical wards, except that the umbilicus as well as the nose and other lesions are also sampled. Sampling of the environment, e.g. babies' baths, scales, napkin changing table, may be of some value in tracing the possible mode of transmission.

The babies themselves are the main sources of infection; the nose, umbilicus and groins are often colonized. A member of the staff may sometimes be the major source, especially if she has an infected lesion (Gillespie and Alder, 1957). More often the carrier on the staff infects one baby, who in turn becomes a disperser and infects other babies. An investigation in a nursery becomes necessary when septic spots or other staphylococcal

TABLE III

Survey for *Staphylococcus aureus* in a neonatal ward
(15 babies)

Site	Antibiotic resistance pattern	Phage pattern (R.T.D.)†
Babies' noses or	P	29/52/80
umbilical cords	P	29/52
	PT	85/80/47/53/ 54/75/88
	P	NT (3A/29 at 100 × RTD)
	PT	47/53/75/83A
	PTE	NT
	P	29/52/52A/80
	P	29/80
Septic spots	P	71
	P	71
Nose of member of staff	P	71

P = resistant to Penicillin; T = Tetracycline; E = Erythromycin.
† R.T.D. = routine test dilution.

lesions appear in more than one baby. The epidemic strains are usually resistant to Penicillin only, and phage typing may distinguish the epidemic strain from others which are not causing lesions. An example of a ward survey is shown in Table III. Infections were caused by phage-type 71, but the strain was not widely distributed. The strains isolated were mainly phage Group 1. It seemed likely that these babies were infected by the member of staff who was a nasal carrier. The outbreak was terminated after isolation of the two babies with septic spots and treatment of the single member of the staff carrying the strain. Although *S. aureus* was found in the environment, none was phage-type 71.

Sometimes a potentially virulent strain is not recognised in the nursery, but infections of hospital origin may be isolated from babies after discharge (Ayliffe *et al.*, 1972) or from breast abscesses (in the mothers) (Corner *et al.*, 1960). Phage-typing of strains will help to detect these strains in the nursery of origin.

3. Dermatological wards

Cross-infection is common in these wards and difficult to prevent. The antibiograms and phage patterns of strains are often characteristic. Although of limited use within a unit, typing assists in recognizing the "dermatological" origin of strains causing outbreaks in other areas especially in surgical wards. A problem with dermatological patients is the variety of strains occurring not only in the unit, but in individual patients as well (Ayliffe, 1970). Table IV shows a variety of antibiotic sensitivities and phage patterns, which often appear to be related. Conventionally an antibiotic sensitive strain is considered to be different from a strain of similar phage type, but resistant to several antibiotics. This is obviously much less certain in dermatological units where staphylococcal populations on patients and in the environment are large and varied.

III. INFECTIONS CAUSED BY
LANCEFIELD GROUP A β-HAEMOLYTIC STREPTOCOCCI

These are now rarely found in hospital outbreaks in Europe or North America, but used to be common in burns, obstetric units, and in surgical wards. The organism is commonly found in the throat and less often in the nose or on the skin of patients with impetigo or eczema. If post-puerperal sepsis occurs, nose and throat swabs should be taken from the patient and all likely staff. Serological typing confirms the probable source, although the staff members from whom a strain is isolated could equally well be victims rather than primary sources. As with *S. aureus* people are the

TABLE IV

Strains of *Staphyloccus aureus* isolated from patients in dermatology wards

Antibiotic resistance pattern	Phage pattern (R.T.D.)
Sensitive	84
Sensitive	84/85/47/53/54/75/77/88
PT	84/29/79/80/88/88
PTE	84/77/81
PTF	85
PTN	84/85
PTEN	84/85/77
PTEL	84/85/52/80
PTENF	84
PTENFL	84/85
PTENFL	84/77

P = resistant to Penicillin; T = Tetracycline; E = Erythromycin; F = Fusidic acid; N = Neomycin/Kanamycin; L = Lincomycin.
Sensitive—to all antibiotics tested.

important sources, but environmental strains may indicate routes of transfer (Williams *et al.*, 1966).

IV. INVESTIGATION OF GRAM-NEGATIVE INFECTIONS

A. *Escherichia coli*

This organism is the most common cause of hospital-acquired infection, although most infections are endogenous in origin. Outbreaks, apart from gastroenteritis in infants, are rarely reported. This may be partly due to the circumstance that suitable typing methods are rarely used for *E. coli*; serological typing is commonly used for tracing the spread of entero-pathogenic strains, but has only recently been used for other strains. Strains of *E. coli* are usually similar in colonial appearance and many colonies have to be tested before it is possible to determine whether a certain serotype is either present, predominant or absent in a sample of faeces. This is a difficulty which involves all investigations on the normal flora and has already been discussed in relation to coagulase-negative cocci on the skin.

Serological typing may be of value in recognizing that the source of an infection is endogenous, e.g. a urinary tract infection caused by an organism present in the patient's own faeces (Gruneberg *et al.*, 1968). Bacteriocin typing has also been used successfully for this purpose (Linton, 1960).

Predominant strains in faeces may be recognized and possible animal or food origins determined (Bettelheim *et al.*, 1974a, b).

Serological typing is most widely used for investigating outbreaks of infantile gastroenteritis in paediatric or neonatal wards (Rogers, 1963). A single infection in a neonatal ward usually does not require an extensive investigation, but the same serotype may be found in the mother. If an outbreak occurs, spread is usually from baby to baby. The ward is closed to further admissions (under 18 months in paediatric wards) and all patients are screened for the presence of the epidemic strain. It is not usually necessary to examine the faeces of staff, although if looking after infected babies and contacts, members of staff should not nurse other babies or prepare feeds.

Routine screening of admissions for any enteropathogenic strain is not usually necessary, but it may be worthwhile for a limited period to screen for a specific strain known to be present in the surrounding community. Babies are often admitted carrying an apparently enteropathogenic strain, which may spread in a unit without causing any clinical symptoms (Noy *et al.*, 1974). Occasionally an outbreak may occur and no strain of a recognized enteropathogenic serotype is isolated. It may be worthwhile to collect strains from babies with clinical symptoms of diarrhoea and send to a reference laboratory for further investigation and possible preparation of new antisera.

B. *Proteus mirabilis*

P. mirabilis is a common cause of urinary tract infection in hospital. Infection is usually endogenous and of faecal origin. Outbreaks are rare and cross-infection occurs mainly in urological wards. Strains may be isolated from the environment, but it is not usually an important source. Examination of relevant areas of the environment (e.g. urine, bottles and bedpans) may help to determine the mode of spread. Most strains of *P. mirabilis* show similar biochemical profiles and antibiotic resistance patterns. An additional typing method is required and in routine laboratories the Diene's test is usually adequate. In this test, a line of inhibition is seen between the spreading haloes of different strains of *P. mirabilis* growing on a plate. No zone of inhibition is seen when the spreading haloes are from the same strain (Skirrow, 1969). In some circumstances, serological, proticin, phage or resistogram methods are of value. Interpretation, however, is sometimes difficult and methods do not always agree. Table V shows a comparison of typing results of five strains of *P. mirabilis* of serological type O3 H2. Strains 1 and 2 were similar in Diene's, phage and proticin types. Strains 3, 4 and 5 were different, but similar in Diene's and proticin types. Phage typing alone was of limited value. Table VI shows

3

TAPLE V

**Typing results of five strains of *Proteus mirabilis*
serotype O3 H2**

Strain	Diene's type	Phage-type	Proticin type
1	D1	19/28	1
2	D1	19/28+	1
3	D2	19/28	3
4	D2	8/19/20/28/31	3
5	D2	8/19/20/28/31	3

the variation in other typing methods with strains showing phage pattern 8/19/20/28/31.

A probable common source of an outbreak was described by Burke *et al.* (1971). Eleven serious infections caused by a strain of similar Diene's and phage type occurred in a nursery over a four year period. The same strain was found on the hands and in the vagina and rectum of a nurse. It was also found in 7/12 neonates which she admitted. No environmental source was found. The phage type was a common one (8/19/20/28) and the Diene's test appeared to be of greater value than either phage or proticin typing. The source in a nursery may be much less certain and examination of faecal strains of staff may show no common source. In a Birmingham maternity unit, three babies died of meningitis caused by *P. mirabilis* within a few days of each other. Proteus meningitis is uncommon and three cases occurring together suggested cross-infection. The strains isolated from two of the cases and the umbilicus of other babies in the unit were

TABLE VI

**Comparison of six strains of *Proteus mirabilis*
phage-type 8/19/20/28/31**

Strain	Serotype O	Serotype H	Diene's type	Proticin type
1	NT	2	D26	4
2	3	2	D 3	3
3	6	2	D 6	3
4	10	3	D 8	NT
5	24	3	D17	1
6	10	4	D 9	8

similar as shown by the Diene's test and serological typing. The organism was not found in the faeces of staff or in the environment, and no further cases occurred. The Diene's test was sufficient to identify a single epidemic strain in the unit, and this was confirmed by serological typing (Skirrow, 1969).

In a urological unit, cross-infection may be due to poor aseptic techniques or inadequate disinfection of relevant equipment. The presence of an outbreak rather than simultaneously occurring infections caused by different strains can be confirmed by a typing method. The faeces and urines of patients should be examined, also the urethral meatus in patients with indwelling catheters. Hands of staff, hand-washing preparations, nail-brushes, hand-creams, antiseptic solutions used for catheter care, catheter lubricating ointments, urine bottles, bed-pans and other relevant sites should be examined. In an outbreak involving patients in a urological ward, examination of faeces of staff is rarely of value; spread is usually by transfer between patients and not directly to individuals from one major source.

Typing may also be of value in determining the endogenous origin of infection or the presence of a single strain on a number of sites in one patient. Strains from faeces and urines have often been found to be similar as evidenced by a variety of methods, e.g. strains from the nose, fingers, sheets, pillows and sputum of one patient were similar in serological type, phage, proticin, resistogram patterns and Diene's phenomenon. However, as already described, agreement between methods is not always apparent (Kashbur *et al.*, 1974).

C. *Klebsiella* sp.

Klebsiella sp. have become increasingly important as a cause of hospital infection in recent years. Chronic urinary tract infections are the most common, but *Klebsiella* sp. may cause wound, respiratory infection and bacteraemia. As with *P. mirabilis*, *Klebsiella* sp. can be isolated from the faeces of most normal people. They are able to grow in moist areas of the environment, especially in fluids, such as weak solutions of disinfectants. Biochemical profiles and antibiotic sensitivity patterns are more useful for identifying strains than they are for *P. mirabilis* or *E. coli*. Typing methods include phage and bacteriocin, but serological typing based on capsular antigens is probably the most reliable. Phage and bacteriocin typing methods are insufficiently discriminating for routine use, but may be useful in occasional outbreaks.

Common source outbreaks have been reported. In one instance contamination of infant feeds with *Klebsiella* was associated with the same strain in all babies in a nursery (Ayliffe *et al.*, 1970). There was no instance of clinical infectious disease but all strains isolated were identified by bacteriocin typing (Hall, 1971). In another outbreak, six infections of intravenous injection sites were caused by a *Klebsiella* (serological type 18) isolated from a lanolin handcream used by the staff (Morse *et al.*, 1967). Investigation of outbreaks of urinary tract infection is similar to that described for *P. mirabilis*, and investigations for respiratory tract infections are similar to those described for *Pseudomonas aeruginosa* (*vide infra*). In most outbreaks, patient to patient transfer occurs, possibly on the hands of the staff *Klebsiella* sp. isolated from faeces of newborn babies in different wards are shown in Table VII.

TABLE VII
Klebsiella strains isolated from babies' faeces

Ward	Number of isolates	Capsular type	Bacteriocin type
1	2	11	27/30
	2	11	27/9137
	3	11	27
	2	11	NT
	3	9	4/7/24/77
2	1	47	3/4/5/7/24/77
		63	27
3	2	11	4/7/24/27
	1	43	4/7/24/27
4	1	77	7/24/27

Capsular typing suggested cross-infection with two strains in ward 1, which was a special care unit. These differed from those in other wards except for two strains in ward 3. Bacteriocin typing alone was sufficiently discriminating and could have indicated a different epidemiological situation. The epidemic strains in ward 1 were not found in infant feeds, soap solutions, baby baths, humidifiers, antiseptic hand preparations, hand and baby creams or in any other moist site on the ward. The faeces of staff were not examined, but it seemed likely that transfer of infection was from baby to baby. The strains differed in serotype from those isolated from babies in a special care unit in another hospital. These were resistant to Ampicillin, Tetracycline and Chloramphenicol, capsular type 30, and showed a bacteriocin pattern of 4/7/24/27. None of these babies was clinically infected with the endemic *Klebsiella* strain. However, in an outbreak in a baby unit in the U.S.A., eight premature babies and two full-term babies developed septicaemia with a strain of *Klebsiella pneumoniae* (serologically type 33). The strain was found in 12/17 rectal swabs from babies, but only in 2/35 samples of faeces from staff. Few strains were isolated from the environment and it was again concluded that spread was from baby to baby probably on hands of staff. The strain was isolated from the fingers of four nurses (Hable *et al.*, 1972).

Klebsiella sp. are often isolated from plants and natural waters outside of the hospital environment. Serotyping of hospital strains and strains from water supplies showed little difference in the range of biotypes (Matsen *et al.*, 1974). Typing methods have generally failed to distinguish between hospital and other strains.

D. *Pseudomonas aeruginosa*

Ps. aeruginosa is an "opportunist" organism of low pathogenicity and is mainly responsible for infections in patients with low immunity (e.g. leukaemic or immunosuppressed) or in sites with a poor immunological defence mechanism (e.g. the anterior chamber of the eye). *Ps. aeruginosa* may be isolated in chronic urinary tract infections, particularly in patients treated with repeated courses of antibiotics, also it is an important cause of septicaemia and graft failure in patients with severe burns. *Pseudomonas* infections are also associated with medical procedures such as respiratory ventilation and indwelling urinary catheters.

The organism is widely distributed in the moist environment of the hospital and will grow in fluids with minimal nutrients (Favero *et al.*, 1971). It is also a normal inhabitant of the large intestine and has been isolated from 38% of hospital patients (Shooter *et al.*, 1966). Sporadic infections are often endogenous. Table VIII shows some sites from which *Ps. aeruginosa* can often be isolated. Many of these are unlikely sources of infection and a typing method is obviously required to eliminate them from further consideration as a major source. Other species of *Pseudomonas* as well as other Gram-negative bacilli may be isolated from these sites, but these are much less often responsible for infection. An outbreak due to another species of *Pseudomonas*, such as *Ps. cepacia*, can often be identified by its distinctive biochemical characteristics. Table VIII also indicates the more important sources (major) and other sites such as sinks and drains which can usually be ignored as sources in an investigation (minor sources).

Most sites may be sampled with cotton wool swabs, which should not be allowed to dry before culturing. Whenever possible, fluid should be collected with a sterile pipette. Many of the environmental sites contain a variety of Gram-negative bacilli and selective media are required for the isolation of *Ps. aeruginosa*. A modified King's medium containing cetrimide

TABLE VIII

Sources and routes of spread of *Pseudomonas aeruginosa*

Major sources and routes
Other infected patients (lesions or colonized sites)
Faeces of patient with infection
Hands of staff

Humidifiers (nebulizers)
Ventilators and suction equipment

Food
Food mixers and dispensing equipment, especially infant feeds

Contaminated solutions used for aseptic techniques (e.g. saline, antiseptics and other medicaments)
Hand-creams
Washing bowls, baths, face-flannels
Shaving and nail-brushes

Minor or uncommon sources
Sinks, drains, flower-water, aquaria
Floor-mops and cleaning equipment†
Faecal carriers (staff)

† If aerosols are produced, cleaning equipment could be a major hazard.

(Brown and Lowbury, 1965) with or without nitrofurantoin or nalidixic acid is satisfactory.

The typing methods have been reviewed in Chapters 3 and 5. In our studies a combination of pyocin, serological and phage typing have been used. Routine typing of all isolates from patients is rarely required, except possibly in special units, e.g. burns and intensive care. More than one type may be present in one site and it may be necessary to type a selection of colonies, particularly if there are colonial differences. Most strains of *Ps. aeruginosa* are resistant to commonly used antibiotics and antibiograms are not usually of much value in identifying different types unless the endemic strain has an unusual resistance pattern, e.g. Gentamicin or Carbenicillin resistance.

When an outbreak occurs, collection of epidemiological data is of major importance as in staphylococcal outbreaks, to determine the probable site of origin, i.e. operating theatre or ward. The possible common use of equipment or solutions by the affected patients, e.g. cystoscopes, respiratory ventilators, suction equipment, eye-drops, is investigated. It is also important to find out whether equipment is adequately disinfected or sterilized between use by different patients. Often the probable source becomes apparent from the collection of data and typing of the strains will confirm the origin. Urinary tract infection developing within a day or two after cystoscopy in one instance suggested that an inadequately disinfected resectoscope was the probable source (Moore and Forman, 1966). Serological typing of the strains was of little extra value since the source was already obvious from the isolation of *Pseudomonas*. In a neonatal unit, ten babies were infected with a single strain as shown by pyocin and phage typing. The infections were mainly respiratory and six of the babies had received oxygen in the labour ward. The epidemic strain was isolated from a delivery room resuscitator (Fierer *et al.*, 1967). A rather similar outbreak in which aspirators were thought to be the main source of infection was

TABLE IX

Phage patterns of *Pseudomonas aeruginosa* in an eye hospital

Site of isolation	Phage-pattern
Bath and sink	7/31/73
Sluice room cloth and sink ⎱ Urine bottles ⎰	7/31/73/109/119X
Mop and bucket	7/31/73
Mop	109/119X
Mop and bucket	7/31/73 109/119X
Saline solution	7/24/68/1214
Infected eyes	7/24/68/1214

reported by Bassett *et al.*, (1965). Post-operative infections of the eye occurring soon after operation are likely to be due to contaminated solutions or instruments used at the time of operation. An outbreak of post-operative infection in which six patients lost an eye, was traced to contaminated saline solution applied to the eye at operation (Ayliffe *et al.*, 1966). Although the isolation of *Pseudomonas* from the solution was in itself sufficient evidence to indicate it was the probable source, this was confirmed by typing the strains. Other possible environmental sources were sampled and Table IX shows that the strain was not present elsewhere in the environment. A single method of typing is not always adequate, and Table X shows that either serological or pyocin typing alone might have indicated several possible environmental sources in an outbreak in a neurosurgical unit. A combination of both methods of typing reduced the number of possible sources, but a characteristic phage pattern (E) provided the final evidence of the primary source.

A more discriminate single pyocin typing method (e.g. Govan and Gillies, 1969; Rampling *et al.*, 1975), or the finger-printing method of Farmer and Herman (1969) may have also revealed the difference between these strains.

In some outbreaks the common source is not apparent, especially if cross-infection has also occurred between the infected patients. In the outbreak described in Table X, there were wound and urinary tract infections, and it seemed possible that cross-infection was occurring in the

TABLE X

Isolations of *Pseudomonas aeruginosa* from environment and infected patients

Sites	Types		
	Serological	Pyocine	Phage
Sinks, floors, hand-cream	11	D	
Urine bottles	9	NT	
Soap tray	10	NT	
sink-cloth	4	F	
Cap of	1	NT	
disinfectant	11	A	
bottle	7	B	
	6	A	
	6	D	
	10	B	
Shaving-brush	6	D	†E
Infected patients	6	D	†E

† E = epidemic strain.

ward. On a preliminary study of the environment, the typing methods showed that none of the environmental sites was the source. The eventual isolation of the epidemic strain from the skin of the scalp before operation suggested the possibility that a shaving-brush was the source and the characteristic strain (phage type E) was isolated from it (Ayliffe *et al.*, 1965). The shaving-brush was used unofficially by one of the staff for pre-operative shaving which the preliminary investigation had failed to disclose. Presumably some patient to patient transmission had also occurred which obscured the presence of a common source of the post-operative severe infections. This demonstrates the importance of collecting all available information and studying the relevant clinical techniques in

detail, or an important clue may be missed. Often the use of a less discrimi-
natory method, e.g. serological typing method, alone will suggest a different
epidemiological pattern. In a study of *Ps. aeruginosa* in faeces, Shooter *et al.*
(1966) found three distinct pyocine patterns and eight different phage
patterns associated with serogroup O:6. Subdivision into too many types
may obscure the epidemiological pattern and also has to be avoided.

A number of other single common sources have been reported and include disinfectants and food. Others seem much less likely, for instance
Ps. aeruginosa from sinks seem to be rarely responsible for outbreaks, and
this has been confirmed by typing.

Endemic infections in burns units or intensive care units are more
difficult to investigate. As with staphylococcal and other Gram-negative
infections in wards, patient to patient transfer on the hands of staff is the
probable common mode of spread. A useful study in a major injuries unit
showed that over a period of 18 months, infections were caused by a
variety of strains (Lowbury *et al.*, 1970).

Strains were typed serologically and with phages; distinct strains as
determined by both typing methods are shown in Table XI by capital letters.
Sixteen periods were studied and nine are shown in the table. Sources of
strains were varied, some were probably transferred from other patients or
wards. Less frequently infections were of endogenous origin and rarely
they were acquired from wash hand basins or sinks. Strains were usually
isolated from sinks only when a patient was already infected with the
strain, and tended to disappear when the infection disappeared. Strain A

TABLE XI

Types of *Pseudomonas aeruginosa* in a major injuries unit

Length of period	Infections in tracheostomies	Isolates from wash hand basins and other sinks	Isolates from hands of staff
1 (37 days)	A (7), B (2)	A, NT	A, B, C, NT
2 (16 days)	None	A, C	C, H
3 (45 days)	B (1)	A, C, X, NT	B, C, NT
4 (74 days)	None	A, B, C, NT	C
5 (55 days)	E (1)	A, C, NT	C, E
6 (43 days)	None	A, J	A
7 (84 days)	A (1), F (5), L (1), NT (2)	A, F	A, F
8 (23 days)	None	A	NT
9 (30 days)	A (2), G (1), F (1), L (1)	A, F	A, D, F, G

( ) Number of infections.   Lowbury *et al.*, 1970.

seemed to be a "sink" strain. Numerous strains of *Ps. aeruginosa* were found in the environment, but there was little indication that many infections occurred from any of these possible sources. It seemed more likely that cross-infection occurred from infected patients on the hands of staff.

Patient to patient spread is probably the most important mode of spread of *Ps. aeruginosa* in burns units, although other sources have also been implicated. Over a period of four months in a burns unit, all strains of *Ps. aeruginosa* were typed by serological and phage techniques. Of 59 strains acquired by the patients, 46 were of the same type as strains previously isolated from other patients (Davis *et al.*, 1968). Environmental sources are less likely to cause endemic infection in a burns unit, although similar pyocin types have been isolated from food (e.g. salad) and on burns.

The possibility of transferable antibiotic resistance in *Ps. aeruginosa* was indicated in a burns unit after strains were serotyped. Three serogroups O:3, 5c and 10 showed the rapid emergence of Carbenicillin resistance within a few days of treating a patient with Carbenicillin. All three serotypes were previously Carbenicillin-sensitive (Lowbury *et al.*, 1969). Later studies confirmed that the three strains as well as coliforms in the unit contained a similar transferable plasmid.

E. *Serratia marcescens*

Serratia marcescens is another opportunist organism which has caused occasional outbreaks in intensive care units, mainly in the U.S.A. The organism may occasionally be found in faeces, but more often in the moist environment of the hospital. Infection is particularly likely to occur in debilitated patients in intensive care units, or following instrumentation of the respiratory or urinary tract, and is associated with antibiotic therapy. The organism may often be characterized by pigment production, biochemical profile and antibiogram, but sometimes serological or bacteriocin typing is helpful. The investigation of an outbreak is rather similar to that of *Ps. aeruginosa*, but recognition may be more difficult as many strains are non-pigmented. A common source outbreak was described in a Birmingham intensive care unit (Whitby *et al.*, 1972). Thirteen patients (12 of whom were males) were infected with the strain. Most of these patients had a tracheostomy and the organism, a non-chromogenic strain, was mainly found in tracheal aspirates or sputum. It was not found in the environment, apart from a shaving-brush which was assumed to be the source.

In another study, two strains spread within an intensive care unit as evidenced by means of bacteriocin typing (Traub, 1972). It was considered that spread in these special units occurred as usual from person to person via the hands of the staff.

During one month, strains of *Serratia* were isolated from 7 of 20 patients in a paediatric intensive care unit (Cardos *et al.*, 1974); five of these children died. Serological typing, antibiotic sensitivity patterns and sensitivity to normal serum indicated that five of these strains were different. Since this was not an epidemic situation, the unit was not closed. Additional markers are obviously useful in investigating outbreaks of infection with this organism.

ACKNOWLEDGEMENTS

I wish to thank Dr M. T. Parker and the Central Public Health Laboratory, Colindale, for typing the strains of *Ps. aeruginosa*, and for supplying the staphylococcal phages; Mr I. Kashbur, Dept. of Microbiology, University of Benghazi, for the results of *Proteus* typing methods, and Dr I. Orskov, State Serum Institute, Copenhagen, for serotyping the *Klebsiella* strains.

REFERENCES

Ayliffe, G. A. J. (1970). *J. clin. Path.*, **23**, 19–23.
Ayliffe, G. A. J., Babb, J. R., and Collins, B. J. (1973). *In* "Airborne transmission and Airborne Infection" (Ed. J. F. Ph Hers and H. C. Winkler), pp. 435–437. Oosthoek Publishing, Utrecht.
Ayliffe, G. A. J., Barry, D. R., Lowbury, E. J. L., Roper-Hall, M. J., and Martin-Walker, W. (1966). *Lancet* **1**, 1113–1117.
Ayliffe, G. A. J., Brightwell, K., Ball, P., and Derrington, M. (1972). *Lancet* **2**, 479–80.
Ayliffe, G. A. J., and Collins, B. J. (1967). *J. clin. Path.*, **20**, 195–198.
Ayliffe, G. A. J., Collins, B. J., and Pettit, F. (1970). *Lancet*, **1**, 559–560.
Ayliffe, G. A. J., Lowbury, E. J. L., Hamilton, J. G., Small, J. M., Asheshov, E. A., and Parker, M. T. (1965). *Lancet*, **2**, 365–369.
Baird-Parker, A. C. (1965). *J. gen. Microbiol.*, **38**, 365–387.
Bassett, D. C. J., Thompson, S. A. S., and Page, B. (1965). *Lancet*, **1**, 781–784.
Bettelheim, K. A., Breadon, A., Favers, M. C., O'Farrell, S. M., and Shooter, R. A. (1974a). *J. Hyg. (Camb.)*, **72**, 67–70.
Bettelheim, K. A., Bushrod, F. M., Chandler, M. E., Cooke, E. Mary, O'Farrell, S. M., and Shooter, R. A. (1974b). *J. Hyg. (Camb.)*, **73**, 467–471.
Blair, J. E., and Williams, R. E. O. (1961). *Bull. Wld Hlth Org.*, **24**, 771–784.
Blowers, R., Hill, J., and Howell, A. (1973). *In* "Airborne Transmission and Airborne Infection" (Ed. J. F. Ph Hers and H. C. Winkler), pp. 432–434. Oosthoek Publishing, Utrecht.
Brown, V. I., and Lowbury, E. J. L. (1965). *J. clin. Path.*, **18**, 752–756.
Burke, J. P., Ingall, D., Klein, J. O., Gezon, H. M., and Finland, M. (1971). *New Engl. J. Med.*, **284**, 115–121.
Cardos, S. F., Florman, A. L., Simberkoff, M. S., and Lanier, L. (1974). *Am. J. med. Sci.*, **266**, 447–452.
Corner, Beryl D., Crowther, S. T., and Eades, S. M. (1960). *Br. med. J.*, **1**, 1927–1929.
Darrell, J. H., and Wahba, A. H. (1964). *J. clin. Path.*, **17**, 236–242.
Davis, B., Lilly, H. A., and Lowbury, E. J. L. (1969). *J. clin. Path.*, **22**, 634–641.
Farmer, J. J. III, and Herman, L. G. (1969). *Appl. Microbiol.*, **18**, 760–765.

60   G. A. J. AYLIFFE

Favero, M. S., Carson, L. A., Bond, W. W., and Peterson, N. J. (1971). *Science*, **173**, 836–838.
Fierer, J., Taylor, P. M., and Gezon, H. M. (1967). *New Engl. J. Med.*, **276**, 991–996.
Gillespie, W. A., and Alder, V. G. (1957). *Lancet*, **1**, 632–634.
Gillespie, W. A., Alder, V. G., Ayliffe, G. A. J., Powell, D. E. B., and Wypkema, W. (1961). *Lancet*, **1**, 1299–1303.
Govan, J. R. W., and Gillies, R. R. (1969). *J. med. Microbiol.*, **2**, 17–25.
Gruneberg, R. N., Leigh, D. A., and Brumfitt, W. (1968). *In* "Urinary Tract Infection" (Ed. F. W. O'Grady and W. Brumfitt), pp. 68–80. Oxford University Press, London.
Hable, K. A., Matsen, J. M., Wheeler, P. J., Hunt, Carl E., and Quie, P. G. (1972). *J. Pediat.*, **80**, 920–924.
Hall, F. (1971). *J. clin. Path.*, **24**, 712–716.
Kashbur, I. M., Gearge, R. H., and Ayliffe, G. A. J. (1974). *J. clin. Path.*, **27**, 572–577.
Linton, K. B. (1960). *J. clin. Path.*, **13**, 168–172.
Lowbury, E. J. L., Kidson, A., Lilly, H. A., Ayliffe, G. A. J., and Jones, R. J. (1969). *Lancet*, **2**, 448–452.
Lowbury, E. J. L., Thom, B. T., Lilly, H. A., Babb, J. R., and Whittall, K. (1970). *J. med. Microbiol.*, **3**, 39–56.
Matsen, J. H., Spindler, J. A., and Blosser, R. O. (1974). *Appl. Microbiol.*, **28**, 672–678.
McDonald, S., and Timbury, M. G. (1957). *Lancet*, **2**, 863–864.
Mitchell, R. G. (1968). *J. clin. Path.*, **21**, 93–96.
Moore, B., and Forman, A. (1966). *Lancet*, **2**, 929–931
Morse, L. J., Williams, H. L., Grenn, F. P., Eldridge, E. E. and Rotta, J. R. (1967). *New Engl. J. Med.*, **277**, 472–473.
Noble, W. C., and Somerville, D. A. (1974). *In* "Microbiology of Human Skin", pp. 152–154. W. B. Saunders Co. Ltd., London, Philadelphia and Toronto.
Noy, J. H., Ayliffe, G. A. J., and Linton, K. B. (1974). *J. med. Microbiol.*, **7**, 509–520.
Parker, M. T. (1971). *Proc. R. Soc. Med.*, **64**, 979–980.
Rampling, A., Whitby, J. L., and Wildy, P. (1975). *J. med. Microbiol.*, **8**, 531–541.
Rogers, K. B. (1963). *In* "Infection in Hospitals: Epidemiology and Control" (Ed. R. E. O. Williams and R. A. Shooter), pp. 131–144. Blackwell, Oxford.
Shooter, R. A., Walker, K. A., Williams, V. R., Horgan, G. M., Parker, M. T., Asheshov, E. H., and Bullimore, J. F. (1966). *Lancet*, **2**, 1331–1334.
Skirrow, M. B. (1969). *J. med. Microbiol.*, **2**, 471–477.
Traub, W. A. (1972). *Appl. Microbiol.*, **23**, 982–985.
Vierhoef, J., Van Boven, C. P. A., and Winkler, K. C. (1972). *J. med. Microbiol.*, **5**, 9–19.
Whitby, J. L., Blair, J. N. and Rampling, A. (1972). *Lancet*, **2**, 127–128.
Williams, R. E. O., Blowers, R., Garrod, L. P., and Shooter, R. A. (1966). *In* "Hospital Infection, Causes and Prevention". Lloyd Luke, London.

CHAPTER III

Pyocin Typing of *Pseudomonas aeruginosa*

J. R. W. GOVAN

*Department of Bacteriology, Medical School, University of Edinburgh,
Edinburgh, Scotland*

I. INTRODUCTION

The emergence of *Pseudomonas aeruginosa* in the last two decades as an important opportunist pathogen in nosocomial infections can be attributed to factors relating to both the organism and the human host. First, *Ps. aeruginosa* has a widespread distribution in nature, physiological adaptability and innate resistance to many antimicrobial agents. Second, there is an increasing number of patients who are susceptible to infection with such an organism because of age, debilitation, or predisposing therapy, such as treatment with antibiotics, immunosuppressive agents or antimetabolites. The range of *Pseudomonas* infections is extensive and virtually no part of the human body is sacrosanct. No less extensive is the variety of sources in the hospital from which *Ps. aeruginosa* can be isolated. These factors and the difficulty encountered in successfully treating established infections make it essential constantly to monitor the different strains of *Ps. aeruginosa* present in the hospital environment in order to determine the mode of spread of a particular strain in an outbreak.

Three methods have been used to type *Ps. aeruginosa*, serotyping, phage typing and pyocin typing. The aim of this Chapter is to describe the techniques of pyocin typing and to comment on the value of this method for epidemiological studies.

II. PYOCIN TYPING

A. Pyocins (aeruginocins)

Pyocins are the bacteriocins of *Ps. aeruginosa*, i.e. antibiotic substances produced by strains of the species which have the characteristic property of being lethal only for other strains of *Ps. aeruginosa* or closely related species.

Pyocinogeny (the ability to produce pyocin) was first described by Jacob (1954) and is a stable characteristic which is normally repressed in most bacterial cells since synthesis and release of pyocin is lethal. The number of cells in which synthesis is initiated, can be increased by induction with ultra-violet light or Mitomycin C.

Several distinct categories of pyocin are now recognized (Holloway and Krishnapillai, 1974). R-type pyocins resemble the tail of contractile phage (Ishii *et al.*, 1965; Higerd *et al.*, 1967; Govan, 1968, 1974a, b) whilst morphologically distinct rod-shaped, flexuous or F-type pyocins resemble the tail of non-contractile *Pseudomonas* phage (Takeya *et al.*, 1969; Govan, 1974b). R-type pyocins may show immunological cross-reactivity with contractile phages (Ito and Kageyama, 1970) and synthesis of pyocin R is directed from a chromosomal locus (Kageyama, 1970a, b). Low molecular weight pyocins have also been described, pyocin A2 (Homma and Suzuki, 1966) associated with endotoxin from the bacterial cell wall and A3 derived from protoplasm. S-type pyocins, also of low molecular weight (approximately 10^5 Daltons), have been isolated by Ito *et al.* (1970).

Strains of *Ps. aeruginosa* are immune to their own pyocin, but sensitive cells are killed following attachment of pyocin to specific receptors on the cell surface. In the case of R-type pyocins, the receptors are lipopolysaccharide (Ikeda and Egami, 1969); contraction occurs following adsorption to the cell surface and is also observed following attachment of the pyocins to purified lipopolysaccharide from sensitive cells (Govan, 1974a). The nature of the receptor for F-type and low molecular weight pyocins remains unknown. Kaziro and Tanaka (1965a, b) have shown that in the case of pyocin R, cells are most sensitive in the logarithmic growth phase, synthesis of RNA, DNA and protein is interrupted at the ribosomal level without direct contact with ribosomes. The activity of F-type and S-type pyocins has not received much attention. When produced on solid medium,

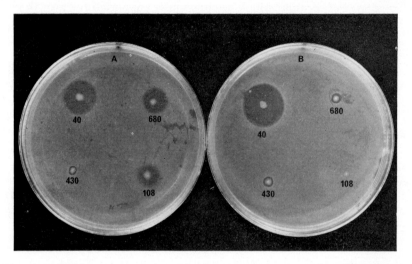

FIG. 1. Inhibition zones produced by four pyocinogenic strains of *Pseudomonas aeruginosa* against indicator strain 5. Plate A. Medium is Tryptone Soya Agar. Strains 40, 680 and 108 produce S-type pyocin activity; R-type pyocin activity is produced by strain 430. Plate B. Medium is Tryptone Soya Agar containing 0·05% trypsin. Strain 40 produces trypsin-resistant S-type activity; strain 680 now shows R-type activity—previously masked by S-type pyocin; strain 430 demonstrates the trypsin-resistance of R-type pyocin whilst the S-type pyocin of strain 108 is trypsin sensitive.

R- and F-type pyocins do not diffuse readily and their inhibitory action is restricted to an area beneath or closely surrounding the producer strain growth; in contrast S-type pyocins produce a wide zone of inhibition on solid media. S-type pyocins are generally trypsin sensitive but a trypsin resistant category has been observed (Govan, unpublished). These distinct types of pyocin can be produced alone or in combination (Ito *et al.*, 1970; Govan, 1974b; Figs. 1, 3 and 5) and, on the basis of biochemical studies, spectrum of activity and lack of serological cross-reactivity, represent distinct bacteriocins and not integrated forms or precursors.

B. Development of the method

Holloway (1960) reported that pyocinogeny was common in strains of *Ps. aeruginosa* and suggested that pyocin production might prove a useful epidemiological marker of this species. Darrell and Wahba (1964) described a cross-streaking technique based on the earlier colicin typing method for *Escherichia coli* of Abbott and Shannon (1958). The cross-streaking technique depends on the ability of a set of indicator strains of *Ps. aeruginosa* to provide patterns of inhibition when inoculated by "cross-streaking" over an area of medium which has previously supported the growth of the test or producer strain. According to the particular pattern of inhibition produced, the test strain is given a type designation. Strains producing no inhibition on any indicator strain are designated untypable (UT).

Darrell and Wahba used a set of 12 indicator strains and identified 11 types, labelled A-P, in 494 strains from 219 patients. Of these strains 91% were typable by this method and its reliability was supported by evidence of type stability in replicate isolates from the same patient. Wahba (1963) had attributed occasional heavy resistant growth in the area of inhibition to the production of extracellular enzymes which destroyed pyocin activity. Darrell and Wahba employed Oxoid Tryptone Soya Agar supplemented with iodoacetic acid, sodium citrate and dipotassium hydrogen phosphate to suppress the action of the pyocin-inactivating substances. Growth of the producer strain during the primary period of incubation was for 24 h at 37°C.

In 1966, Gillies and Govan described a cross-streaking technique which had been developed over several years, during which time the optimum conditions for production and detection of pyocins had been investigated and a set of indicator strains selected. Using eight indicator strains and growing the producer strain for 14–18 h at 32°C on Oxoid Tryptone Soya Agar incorporating 5% defibrinated blood, 88% of 5690 strains were typable and allocated to 37 pyocin types. The reliability of the technique for epidemiological purposes was satisfactorily validated in an extensive study (Gillies and Govan, 1966; Govan, 1968).

C. Method for pyocin typing (Gillies and Govan, 1966)

The strain to be typed is streaked diametrically across the surface of Oxoid Tryptone Soya Agar supplemented with 5% defibrinated horse blood to give an inoculum width of approximately 1 cm. After incubation for 14–18 h at 32°C the growth is removed with a microscope slide which has been dipped in chloroform and the remaining viable growth is killed by pouring approximately 3 ml chloroform into the lid of the Petri dish and replacing the medium-containing portion for 15 min. The plate is then opened and traces of chloroform vapour eliminated by exposing the medium

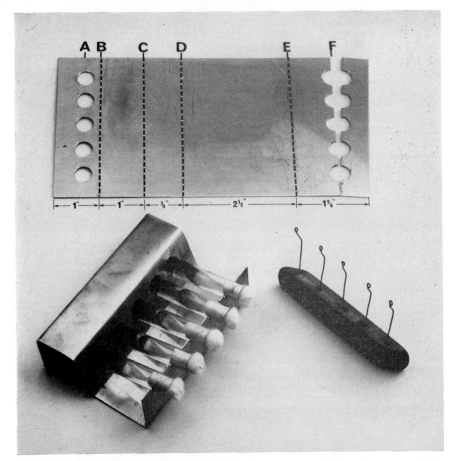

Fig. 2. Simple apparatus for application of indicator strains (Brown, 1973a). Reproduced by kind permission of *Medical Laboratory Technology*.

to the air for a few minutes. Plastic Petri dishes are not recommended but can be used provided that liquid chloroform is not allowed to come into direct contact with the plastic. The medium-containing portion of the dish can however be inverted over a small filter paper that has previously been saturated with chloroform.

Cultures of the indicator strains, grown under static conditions in Oxoid Nutrient Broth No. 2 for 4 h at 37°C, are streaked on to the medium by means of a multiple loop inoculator (Fig. 2) at right angles to the line of the original inoculum, starting from the original test strain growth area; indicator strains no. 1–5 are applied on the left side of the plate and no. 6–8 on the right side. When further indicator strains, A–E, are used, these

Fig. 3. Pyocin typing plate of a strain of *Pseudomonas aeruginosa* belonging to type 1, i.e. only indicator strain 6 (top right) remains uninhibited. Note extended inhibition zone against indicator strains 3 and 7.

Fig. 4. Pyocin typing plate of a strain of *Pseudomonas aeruginosa* belonging to type 16. The zones of inhibition against indicator strains 1, 3, 4, 7 and 8 are uniform in size.

are streaked across a second plate from left to right. The plate is then reincubated at 37°C for 18 h.

Any pyocins produced by the original inoculum diffuse into the medium during the first period of incubation and then exert their inhibitory action on the indicator strains during the subsequent incubation (Figs. 3–4). The pyocin types of the strains under examination are recognized from the patterns of inhibition which they produce on the eight indicator strains, no. 1–8 (Table I) and the five additional indicator strains, A–E (Table II).

TABLE I

Inhibition patterns of pyocin types of *Pseudomonas aeruginosa* using the Gillies and Govan method

Pyocin type	Inhibition of indicator strain no.							
	1	2	3	4	5	6	7	8
1	+	+	+	+	+	−	+	+
2	−	+	−	−	−	−	−	−
3	+	+	+	−	+	−	+	−
4	+	+	+	+	+	−	−	+
5	−	−	−	−	+	−	−	−
6	+	+	+	+	+	−	+	−
7	+	+	+	−	−	−	+	+
8	−	+	+	+	−	−	+	−
9	−	−	−	−	+	−	+	−
10	+	+	+	+	+	+	+	+
11	+	+	+	−	−	−	+	−
12	+	+	−	+	+	−	−	+
13	−	−	−	+	−	−	−	+
14	−	−	+	−	+	−	+	−
15	−	+	−	−	+	−	+	−
16	+	−	+	+	−	−	+	+
17	−	−	+	−	−	−	+	−
18	+	−	+	+	+	−	+	+
19	−	−	+	+	−	−	+	−
20	−	−	−	−	+	+	−	−
21	−	+	−	+	+	−	−	−
22	+	+	+	−	+	+	+	−
23	+	−	−	−	+	−	+	−
24	−	−	+	+	+	−	+	+
25	+	−	+	−	−	−	+	−
26	+	−	−	−	−	−	+	−
27	+	−	+	−	+	−	+	−
28	−	−	−	+	−	−	+	−
29	−	+	−	−	+	−	−	−
30	−	+	+	−	−	−	−	−
31	−	−	−	−	−	−	+	−

J. R. W. GOVAN

TABLE I (*continued*)

Pyocin type	Inhibition of indicator strain no.							
	1	2	3	4	5	6	7	8
32	−	−	−	+	+	−	−	+
33	+	+	+	+	+	+	+	−
34	−	−	−	−	−	−	−	+
35	+	+	−	−	+	−	+	−
36	−	+	−	+	−	−	−	+
37	−	+	+	+	+	−	+	−
38	−	+	+	−	−	−	+	−
39	−	+	+	+	−	−	+	+
40	+	+	−	−	+	−	−	−
41	−	+	+	−	+	−	+	−
42	−	−	+	−	−	−	+	+
43	−	+	+	+	+	−	+	+
44	+	+	+	−	+	−	−	−
45	+	+	+	−	+	−	+	+
46	+	+	+	+	−	−	+	−
47	−	−	+	−	−	+	+	−
48	+	+	−	−	+	+	+	−
49	−	−	+	−	+	−	−	−
50	−	−	+	−	−	−	−	−
51	+	+	+	+	−	−	−	+
52	+	+	−	−	+	+	−	−
53	−	+	−	+	+	−	−	+
54	−	+	+	+	−	−	−	−
55	+	−	−	−	−	−	−	−
56	+	−	−	−	+	−	−	−
57	−	+	+	+	−	−	−	+
58	+	+	+	−	−	−	−	−
59	+	−	+	−	−	−	−	−
60	+	+	−	−	−	−	+	−
61	+	−	−	+	−	−	−	+
62	+	+	+	−	−	+	+	−
63	+	−	+	+	+	−	+	−
64	−	−	+	−	−	−	−	+
65	−	−	+	+	−	−	−	+
66	−	+	+	−	+	−	−	−
67	−	−	−	−	−	+	+	−
68	−	−	−	+	−	−	−	−
69	−	+	+	−	−	+	+	−
70	−	+	−	+	−	−	−	−
71	−	+	−	+	−	−	+	−
72	−	+	−	−	+	+	−	−
73	−	+	−	−	−	+	−	−
74	−	+	+	−	−	−	+	+

TABLE I (*continued*)

Pyocin type	Inhibition of indicator strain no.							
	1	2	3	4	5	6	7	8
75	+	−	+	+	−	+	+	−
76	+	+	−	+	+	+	+	−
77	−	+	+	−	−	−	−	+
78	−	+	−	+	−	+	+	+
79	−	−	−	+	+	+	+	+
80	−	+	−	+	−	−	+	+
81	−	+	−	−	+	−	−	+
82	−	+	−	−	+	−	+	+
83	−	−	−	+	+	−	+	+
84	−	+	−	−	−	−	+	−
85	−	+	−	−	−	−	+	+
86	−	+	+	−	−	+	−	−
87	−	+	+	+	−	+	−	+
88	+	−	−	−	+	−	−	+
89	−	+	+	+	−	+	−	−
90	−	−	+	+	−	−	−	−
91	−	−	+	+	−	+	−	−
92	−	−	+	+	+	−	+	−
93	+	−	−	+	−	−	−	−
94	+	−	−	+	+	−	−	+
95	+	−	+	−	−	+	+	−
96	+	−	+	+	−	−	−	−
97	+	−	+	+	+	−	−	+
98	+	−	+	+	−	−	+	−
99	+	−	+	+	+	+	+	+
100	+	+	−	−	−	+	+	−
101	+	+	−	−	+	−	−	+
102	−	−	−	+	−	+	+	−
103	−	−	−	+	+	+	−	+
104	−	−	−	+	−	−	+	+
105	+	+	+	+	−	−	+	+

+ = Inhibition; − = no inhibition.

D. Additional notes on the use of the pyocin typing technique

1. *Test strain*

The technique described does not stipulate the nature of the test strain inoculum. Experience, however, has shown that the best results are obtained from single colonies taken from non-inhibitory medium, e.g. nutrient agar. If desired, the test strain inoculum may be applied to the agar surface by means of a sterile swab rather than with a bacteriological loop.

Edmonds *et al.* (1972) used a modified pyocin typing technique whereby the test strains were grown in Oxoid Tryptone Soya Broth at 32°C for 2–4 h before inoculation on to the typing medium. The reason for this additional step is not stated.

2. *Growth conditions during pyocin production*

In the course of developing the standardized pyocin typing technique,

TABLE II

Inhibition patterns of subtypes of common pyocin types using the Govan and Gillies method

Pyocin subtype†	Inhibition of indicator strain				
	A	B	C	D	E
a	+	+	+	+	+
b	−	+	+	+	+
c	−	−	+	+	+
d	+	−	+	+	+
e	−	+	+	−	+
f	−	−	−	−	−
g	−	−	+	−	+
h	−	+	−	+	+
j	+	−	−	−	+
k	−	−	−	−	+
l	−	+	+	−	−
m	+	+	+	−	−
n	+	+	+	−	+
o	−	+	−	−	−
p	+	−	+	+	−
q	+	−	+	−	+
r	+	−	−	+	−
s	−	−	+	+	−
t	+	−	+	−	−
u	−	+	−	+	−
v	−	−	−	+	−
w	+	+	+	+	−
x	−	−	−	+	+
y	−	−	+	−	−
z	+	−	−	−	−

+ = inhibition; − = no inhibition.

† Strains in these subtypes are designated as type 1/a, 5/f, UT/k, etc.

the clarity of inhibition was found to be greatly influenced by the duration and temperature of incubation of the test strain and the culture medium used (Gillies and Govan, 1966; Govan, 1968). There was considerable improvement in the clarity of inhibition when primary incubation was reduced from 48 h to 24 h and finally to 14 h (Fig. 5). In practice, incubation for 14–18 h is satisfactory. Even more important than the duration of incubation was the temperature employed during this phase; regardless of the duration of incubation employed, many strains, particularly those belonging to pyocin types 5 and 16, produced clear-cut inhibition at 32°C but gave inferior results at 35·5°C and failed to show any pyocin activity whatsoever after primary incubation at 37°C. Some strains, however, produced identical inhibition patterns at all three temperatures, though once again, inhibition is more clear-cut at the lower temperatures. Oxoid Tryptone Soya Agar supplemented with 5% defibrinated horse blood was found to be the most satisfactory culture medium for pyocin typing; equally good results have been obtained by the author with BBL Trypticase Soy Agar. Addition of blood is not essential, but provides a good contrast background for the reading of inhibition. No appreciable difference has been found using horse, sheep or human blood. Incorporation of iodoacetic acid, sodium citrate and dipotassium hydrogen phosphate (Wahba, 1963; Darrell and Wahba, 1964) does not improve the clarity of inhibition in the author's experience.

These optimum conditions (32°C for 14–18 h) for spontaneous pyocin production have been confirmed by Tagg and Mushin (1971) and Bergan (1973a). Tripathy and Chadwick (1971) reduced the number of untypable strains encountered by inducing pyocin production with Mitomycin C (0·5 μg/ml) in Difco Tryptose Agar and employing a 6 h incubation period at 32°C. Kohn (1966) reported that removal of the primary growth from the culture medium could be facilitated by inoculating the test strain directly on to Oxoid cellulose acetate strips. Not all pyocins are capable of passing through cellulose acetate spontaneously (Wahba, 1963; Govan, 1968, 1974b; Macpherson and Gillies, 1969) and the use of such membranes is not recommended for routine typing purposes.

3. Indicator strains

(a) *Maintenance.* Stock indicator strains can be maintained as freeze-dried cultures or as cultures grown on nutrient agar slopes contained in screw-capped $\frac{1}{4}$ oz bottles and held at 4 or 37°C. Routinely, cultures are maintained on nutrient agar, held at 4°C, and subcultures prepared after 14 days.

The stability of the indicator strains and the maintenance of suitable typing standards should be monitored by including several standard pyocin producer strains of known pyocin type in each group of tests.

FIG. 5. Pyocin typing plates of a strain of *Pseudomonas aeruginosa* belonging to type 1. Following inoculation with the pyocinogenic strain both plates were incubated at 32°C for either 14 h (left) or 24 h (right). The eight indicator strains were then applied and both plates reincubated for 18 h at 37°C. Note the increased resistant growth against indicator strains 1, 2, 3, 4, 7 and 8 when primary incubation was for 24 h; a wide zone of inhibition is evident in both instances against indicator strain 5 and remains unaffected by the duration of incubation of the pyocinogenic strain.

(b) *Preparation*. A single colony is used to inoculate 2 ml of prewarmed Oxoid Nutrient Broth No. 2 contained in test-tubes measuring $3 \times \frac{3}{8}$ in. and incubated without agitation for 3–4 h at 37°C to yield a log phase culture containing approximately 1×10^8 cells/ml. Pellicle formation is usually minimal in such cultures, nevertheless before use each tube is agitated to ensure uniform turbidity. No significant improvement in the clarity of typing results was observed by the author when 18 h broth cultures were employed as indicators at various dilutions. Indeed, the best results using such diluted cultures were found using a dilution which matched turbidimetrically a standard undiluted 3–4 h broth culture. Bergan (1973a) observed that a 1/100 or 1/150 dilution of an indicator culture gave better results than undiluted cultures. It is difficult to assess the value of this modification since the parent 3 h broth culture had been prepared under vigorous agitation and therefore initially would contain a larger bacterial population than those employed in the standardized typing technique, i.e. after growth in test-tubes without agitation.

4. *Application of the indicator strains*

When pyocin typing is carried out on a large number of strains, the application of indicator strains individually by hand is tedious and time-consuming. Several types of applicator apparatus have been described (Wahba and Lidwell, 1963; Merrikin and Terry, 1969; Tagg and Mushin, 1971). Since 1967 we have routinely used a simple, yet effective, instrument (Brown, 1973a) which allows the processing of approximately 200 typing plates/h. The apparatus is inexpensive to manufacture, easy to sterilize and possesses a simplicity in keeping with the typing technique itself.

The apparatus (Fig. 2) consists of an aluminium stand to hold $3 \times \frac{3}{8}$ in. tubes of indicator strains and a rubber block containing bacteriological wire loops to spread these indicators. The tube holder is made from 32 S.W.G. sheet aluminium measuring $6\frac{7}{8} \times 3\frac{3}{4}$ in.; five holes each of diameter $\frac{7}{16}$ and $\frac{5}{8}$ in. between centres, are drilled out along the lines A and F and the end of the sheet cut off along line F to leave semi-circular notches. The sheet is then shaped to form the holder, with the area between lines D and E acting as the base.

The loop holder is a rubber eraser measuring $3\frac{1}{2} \times \frac{5}{8} \times \frac{3}{8}$ in. and the loops are made from 24 S.W.G. Ni-chrome wire. Each wire is fashioned from a $2\frac{3}{4}$ in. length. The end to be inserted in the rubber is turned back on itself for $\frac{1}{8}$ in. for better grip. A loop of $\frac{1}{12}$ in. diameter is made at the other end and the five wires are inserted into the rubber block at $\frac{5}{8}$ in. intervals to a depth of $\frac{1}{2}$ in. The free distal $\frac{1}{2}$ in. of the loops is curved to an angle of approximately 30° to allow easier inoculation of the culture plate and yet still permit the loops' insertion into the tubes of indicator broth culture.

The loops are sterilized to red heat in a bunsen flame and the charged loops are applied to the culture plate and drawn across it from the centre of the producer strain growth area to the edge of the plate. The loops are recharged after each inoculation without being resterilized. This model was designed for the application of five indicators to one side and another loopholder consisting of three loops is used to apply indicator strains to the other side. A composite model consisting of eight loops has also been employed.

5. *Incubation conditions following application of the indicator strains*

It was recommended (Gillies and Govan, 1966) that incubation of the test strain should be at 32°C for 14–18 h to ensure maximum spontaneous pyocin production, but incubation for a similar period at 37°C should be employed following addition of the indicator strains. Edmonds *et al.* (1972) and Shriniwas (1974) employed 32°C and a 14–18 h incubation period for pyocin production and during the subsequent incubation period. No reason is given for the use of 32°C during this second incubation period. The use of various periods and temperatures of incubation following the indicator strain application have been studied (Govan, 1968) and 14–18 h at 37°C found to give optimum results.

6. *Reading of results*

The style adopted for assignment of a strain of *Ps. aeruginosa* to a particular pyocin type is to decide qualitatively whether inhibition of an indicator strain has taken place (+) or whether no inhibition is present (−) and then allot a pyocin type by consulting the pattern charts.

The inhibition reactions encountered in pyocin typing are, (a) complete inhibition corresponding to the growth area of the test strain and with little or no resistant growth, (b) inhibition with many resistant colonies, (c) inhibition zones containing areas of confluent resistant growth.

The high molecular weight R and F pyocins do not diffuse readily through agar and give rise to zones of inhibition corresponding closely to the original growth area of the producer strain. The low molecular weight pyocins, however, give rise to areas of inhibition extending beyond the original growth area. Compare the extent of inhibition of indicator strains 3 and 7 (Fig. 3) and indicator strain 5 (Fig. 5) with that against the other indicator strains.

Typing results can be more fully recorded by noting both (a) the presence of inhibition over the producer growth area only (+) or inhibition extending beyond this area (+ + +), and (b) the presence of confluent resistant growth (RG) or significant numbers of resistant colonies (RC).

Although details of zone size and resistant growth do not alter the particular pyocin type allotted to a strain of *Ps. aeruginosa*, such information is often of considerable value in confirming the relationship of strains in epidemic situations. It should be noted that the amount of resistant growth can vary when a strain is typed on separate occasions. It is advisable, therefore, to compare the nature of inhibition obtained with two or more isolates, only when these are tested on the same occasion.

III. VALIDITY OF THE TECHNIQUE

Ideally, a typing technique should give reproducible results which are epidemiologically valid. It should also be applicable on an international level and allow the characterization of the maximum number of strains tested into a reasonable number of distinct types.

A. Epidemiological validity

The indices of reliability used in determining the validity of this method of characterizing strains of *Ps. aeruginosa* for epidemiological purposes were:

> *In vitro*. Constancy of pyocin production after prolonged storage and/or subculture.
>
> *In vivo*. (a) Constancy of pyocin type in replicate isolates from the same site in a given patient. (b) Uniformity of pyocin type in strains from an epidemic outbreak.

Considerable evidence that the technique described fulfils these criteria was obtained in studies of many clinical isolates over a three year period (Govan, 1968). Eight strains of *Ps. aeruginosa*, one each from pyocin types 1, 3, 5, 9, 10, 11, 16 and 31 were subcultured on nutrient agar once every 14 days and typed once a week for over two years without any alteration in the type pattern or quality of inhibition produced. In a much larger series of 260 strains, however, representing 22 pyocin types and stored for periods ranging from three months to three years, at room temperature, variations were noted. On retyping, 15 strains (5·7%) produced patterns of inhibition which differed from the original. All but two of these strains, however, had been stored for more than six months and in the two exceptions loss of activity towards only one indicator strain was observed.

Replicate isolates from the same site in 530 patients (2523 strains) treated in hospital were of the same pyocin type as the original isolate but in 68 instances (268 strains) different pyocin type patterns were encountered on different days of testing. In some instances this variation in type involved only one isolate differing from the majority. The interval between isolations varied from one day to six months and the number of replicates

1 to 55. In the case of patients treated at home the stability of pyocin production is even more impressive. Twenty-seven patients (59 strains) showed no variation in the pyocin type of replicate isolates from the same site and in only one instance was variation observed.

An examination of replicate isolates made on different days from different sites in the same patient also suggested considerable stability of pyocin production *in vivo*. Such replicate isolates from 168 hospitalized patients (519 strains) were of the same type in 133 patients and of different types in 35 patients (129 strains). One patient over a six month period produced 137 isolates of *Ps. aeruginosa* from nine types of specimen and a further 89 isolates from culture plates exposed at his bedside and all belonged to pyocin type 35.

The reason that not all isolates from the same site in a patient are of the same pyocin type could be due to simultaneous infection with more than one strain, instability of pyocin production or instability of sensitivity or resistance to pyocins in the indicator strains. When an average of six colonies were typed from each diagnostic plate, it was found that more than one pyocin type was found more frequently in hospital patients (10·2%) than in patients treated at home (3·8%). Deighton *et al.* (1971) found more than one pyocin type of *Ps. aeruginosa* from the same site in 15% of hospital patients and Heckman *et al.* (1972) in 13% of similar patients; no home-treated patients were present in these series. In view of the considerable stability of pyocin production both *in vitro* and *in vivo* and the difference in results obtained from hospital patients and those treated at home it is suggested (Govan, 1968; Govan and Gillies, 1969) that, in the majority of cases, the presence of more than one type in a specimen is due to multiple infection and reflects the high incidence of different strains of *Ps. aeruginosa* in the hospital environment.

It would be unreasonable to assume that loss of pyocin producing ability never occurs *in vivo*. Instability of pyocin production after storage has been reported by Hamon *et al.* (1961). A change in pyocin type after storage, noted in a minority of strains, usually entails loss of inhibition of one or more indicator strains rather than a complete loss of pyocin production (Govan, 1968; Zabransky and Day, 1969; Merrikin and Terry, 1972). Since approximately 50% of strains produce more than one form of pyocin simultaneously (Govan, unpublished), loss of inhibition against certain indicator strains could be due to the loss of the genetic determinant for one pyocin only.

B. Validation of the typing technique with respect to percentage of strains typed, type distribution and international application

The data presented in Table III summarizes the application of this

Pyocin typing of 10,708 strains of *Pseudomonas aeruginosa* in 11 countries using the method of Gillies and Govan

Country	No. of strains examined	Percentage distribution of most frequent pyocin types				No. of pyocin types encountered	Percentage of untypable strains	Percentage of strains allocated to one or other of the 37 types	Reference
		1	3	5	10				
Australia									
Victoria	1114†	30	21	4	11	25	9	82 }	Tagg and Mushin (1971)
New South Wales	219†	37	16	2	23		6	89 }	
Singapore	99†	47	10	0	17		10	85	
Canada									
Toronto	1820†	46	8	3	10	NS	10	NS	Duncan and Booth (1975)
Kingston	336†	43	10	4	9	21	11	87	Tripathy and Chadwick (1971)
Scotland	2396†	34	25	8	3	35	8	87	Govan and Gillies (1969)
Hungary	1043†	29	20	6	15	32	9	83	Csiszar and Lanyi (1970)
England	156†	42	11	5	11	15	4	84	Al-Dujaili and Harris (1974)
Holland									
Amsterdam	593	33	11	3	4	18	7	87 }	Siem (1972)
Arnhem	299	33	23	7	8	16	7	85 }	
Germany	210	18	16	9	7	NS	NS	NS	Neussel (1971)
Israel	199	40	8	5	11	18	5	87	Mushin and Ziv (1973)
Norway	486	32	20	14	6	NS	3	NS	Bergan (1973a)
U.S.A.									
Albany	238	31	10	14	8	20	10	76	Baltch and Griffin (1972)
Milwaukee	1500	52	7	3	11	NS	12	85	Heckman et. al. (1972)

† Only one strain from each patient included.
NS = not stated.

pyocin typing technique in the examination of 10,708 strains of *Ps. aeruginosa* in 15 centres located in 11 countries. In assessing the validity of the
technique in epidemiological studies, two items are worthy of comment and
further consideration; (a) The set of indicator strains isolated in Scotland,
labelled no. 1–8, have proved suitable for use on a world-wide basis and
allow a high proportion of strains to be allocated to one or other of the 37
types. (b) Strains belonging to pyocin types 1, 3, 5, 10 and those designated
untypable (UT) are those most commonly encountered, regardless of the
geographical location.

1. *Pyocin type inhibition patterns 38–105.*

Originally, Gillies and Govan (1966) described 36 inhibition patterns
encountered with the eight indicator strains and later introduced a 37th
(Govan and Gillies, 1969). Each type had been confirmed on the basis of
maintenance of the typing pattern (a) after strains had been subcultured
and retested (b) in replicate isolates made from the same site in a patient.

Since 1964 over 15,000 strains of *Ps. aeruginosa* have been examined in
this laboratory and many inhibition patterns have been encountered other
than the 37 previously described. Because, with few exceptions, they are
only seldom encountered, these potential new pyocin type patterns have
not been published. However, because several of these patterns have also
been encountered by other workers an extended list of 105 inhibition
patterns is included on this occasion. This also contains patterns of inhibition encountered only by other workers.

It should be emphasized that the validity of these new pyocin types is
based only on the stability of the inhibition pattern on repeated testing. In
the absence of epidemiological data, the number of isolations of these new
types have been included to allow estimation of their relative importance.

Bergan (1975) introduced the new pyocin type patterns 38–51 on the
basis of at least four isolations. We have also encountered most of these new
types on more than four occasions the only exception being type 49 which
we have never encountered. In Australia, Tagg and Mushin (1971) isolated
more than four strains belonging to types 46, 47 and 48, and type 47 has
also been encountered on four occasions in Holland (Siem, 1972).

In addition, the following new pyocin types are suggested. Types 52–61
isolated by us on more than four occasions with type 52 also encountered
by Siem (1972) and type 60 by Tagg and Mushin (1971). Types 61–69
were isolated on three occasions and include types 62, 68 and 69 isolated by
Tagg and Mushin (1971); type 69 has also been observed by Siem (1972).
Types 70–78 were isolated on two occasions and types 79–104 on one
occasion only. Siem (1972) reported seven isolates of type 80 and more

than three isolations of type 88. Strains belonging to type 105 have been observed by Tagg and Mushin (1971) on more than four occasions.

2. *Subdivision of common pyocin types*

Universally, the most common pyocin inhibition pattern encountered is that of pyocin type I (Table III) and such strains together with those belonging to types 3, 5, 10 and UT account for 58% (Siem, 1972) to 85% (Heckman *et al.*, 1972) of all isolates. Clustering of so many isolates into relatively few types reduces the value of this pyocin typing method for epidemiological purposes and further subdivisions of these types would be beneficial.

In studies of pyocinogeny and the nature of the various pyocins produced by strains belonging to the common pyocin types, it became apparent that these common types were not homogeneous groups, but could be subdivided, e.g. compare the size of inhibition zones obtained with two strains of pyocin type 1 in Figs. 3 and 5.

The use of five additional indicator strains, labelled A–E, allowed subdivision of 795 strains belonging to type 1 into eight subtypes (Govan and Gillies, 1969). The technique was validated using the same criteria as were employed for the primary typing method and has proved a valuable additional aid for further characterization (Phillips *et al.*, 1968; Smith and Tuffnell, 1970; Rose *et al.*, 1971; Mushin and Ziv, 1973; Duncan and Booth, 1975).

To investigate the possibility of subdividing the other common pyocin types 2400 consecutive isolates of *Ps. aeruginosa* were examined for pyocin production against the eight primary indicator strains, the five indicators A–E and four additional strains, two of which had been used in a successful subdivision of strains belonging to pyocin type 5 (Brown, 1973b).

The subtyping indicators A–E, used in conjunction with the primary set, were sufficient to subdivide strains belonging to types 3, 5 and 10. In addition it allowed detection of pyocin activity, and therefore subdivision, in certain strains previously designated UT (untypable). The patterns of inhibition observed with indicators A–E have therefore been extended (Table II) and currently consist of 25 patterns labelled a–z. These include all the inhibition patterns obtained with the types 1, 3, 5, 10 and UT against this subtyping set. It should be noted that an inhibition pattern obtained with this set may be shared by two strains which have already been distinguished by their inhibition pattern against indicator strains no. 1–8. No confusion arises since type designation follows the convention type 1/a, type 3/e, type UT/k, etc.

Five hundred and sixteen strains belonging to pyocin type 1 could be allocated to one or other of the eight subtypes (1/a–1/h) already described

(Govan and Gillies, 1969) but a further 47 strains were distributed between a further 13 subtypes. Eleven of these 47 strains produced the inhibition pattern representing type 1/v and similar strains have been described by Rose *et al.* (1971) and Mushin and Ziv (1973). Strains belonging to types now designated 1/u and 1/y have also been isolated (Mushin and Ziv, 1973).

One hundred and forty-two of 289 strains belonging to pyocin type 3 could be allocated to type 3/e but types 3/a, 3/b, 3/l and 3/n are also represented.

Although they inhibit only one indicator strain of the primary set and might be considered to form a homogeneous group, strains of type 5 could be allocated to three subtypes, namely, 5/f, 5/j and 5/k.

One hundred and fifty-five strains belonging to pyocin type 10 could be allocated to eight subtypes predominantly 10/a, 10/b and 10/c.

Of particular value was the observation that of 170 strains previously designated UT, i.e. which had shown no pyocin activity against the eight primary indicators, 46 produced inhibition against one or more of the indicators A–E and could be allocated to at least four groups, namely UT/k, UT/l, UT/y and UT/z. The possibility of finding further indicators to detect activity in the remaining untypable strains was diminished by the evidence that these strains did not produce pyocin activity against any of the additional four indicator strains used in the investigation.

Ziv *et al.* (1971) have already used two of their own isolates as indicator strains and subdivided types 1, 3 and 10 each into two subgroups. The author, however, recommends the general use of indicator strains A–E for subtyping purposes. These strains have been shown capable of subdividing each of the common types into a reasonable number of subgroups and have already been distributed widely because of their present value in the subdivision of strains of pyocin type 1.

IV. TYPING OF MUCOID STRAINS OF *PSEUDOMONAS AERUGINOSA* BY PYOCIN PRODUCTION

A modified version of the standardized pyocin typing technique is used for one purpose only, namely to characterize the very mucoid strains of *Ps. aeruginosa* often isolated from patients suffering from cystic fibrosis (Fig. 6). In view of the failure, on many occasions, to detect any inhibition pattern against the indicator strains Schwarzman and Boring (1971) assumed that such strains were apyocinogenic. The present author considers it more likely, however, that such strains did produce pyocins but that these were prevented from diffusing into the medium by the mucus surrounding the bacterial surface.

The following modified technique (Williams and Govan, 1973) was found

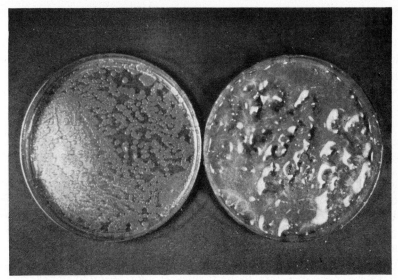

Fig. 6. Non-mucoid (left) and mucoid (right) strains of *Pseudomonas aeruginosa* grown on Oxoid Tryptone Soya Agar for 18 h at 32°C.

useful in typing mucoid strains. It consists of growing the mucoid strain in liquid culture and then assaying the cell-free supernate for pyocin activity against the standard indicator strains. The method is as follows.

A. Production of pyocins in liquid culture

A 100 ml volume of Oxoid Tryptone Soya Broth contained in a 2 litre flask is inoculated with 2 ml of an overnight broth culture of the mucoid strain and incubated at 32°C with vigorous agitation for 4 h. Pyocin production can be increased by addition of the inducing agent Mitomycin C (1·5 μg/ml final concentration) and further incubation for 2 h. The culture is centrifuged to remove cells and the supernate, containing pyocins, sterilized with 5% (v/v) chloroform for 15 min and decanted.

B. Detection of pyocin activity

Four-hour broth cultures of the indicator strains are used to prepare lawns on 9 ml nutrient agar contained in plastic Petri dishes (diameter 9 cm). Drops (0·02 ml) of serial two-fold dilutions of supernatants in sterile physiological saline are spotted on to well-dried indicator lawns. The drops are allowed to dry and the plates incubated for 18 h at 37°C. Pyocin activity is indicated by zones of inhibition on the indicator lawns.

The application of a range of dilutions to the indicator lawns allows

4

simultaneous recognition of phage activity which can be a useful additional epidemiological marker.

This technique is recommended for use only with mucoid *Ps. aeruginosa*; it is more time-consuming and requires more basic materials than the standardized pyocin typing technique. Provided that suitable agitation is used, the volume of primary culture could probably be reduced. Identical inhibition patterns, corresponding to recognized pyocin types, were obtained using induced and uninduced cultures.

V. CORRELATION BETWEEN TYPING METHODS

Regardless of the phage or pyocin typing scheme employed there appears to be little correlation between results of phage or pyocin typing (Sjoberg and Lindberg, 1967, 1968; Govan, 1968; Farmer and Herman, 1969; Bergan, 1973b). Considerable correlation does exist between certain pyocin types and serotypes.

Wahba (1965) noted that strains belonging to his pyocin types G, K, L, O and P belonged in general to the Wahba serotype 14 and to Habs serotypes 1, 3, 9 and 6 respectively. Further confirmation of correlation has been obtained using the pyocin typing technique introduced by the author and the serotyping schemes of Habs (1957) and Lanyi (1966). To avoid confusion in the following discussion, the serotype nomenclature of Lanyi has been converted to the corresponding Habs serotype designations. A significant correlation has been found between strains belonging to pyocin type 3 and serotype 6 (Govan, 1968; Csiszar and Lanyi, 1970; Siem, 1972; Bergan, 1973a). The ability of pyocin typing to subdivide particular serotypes and the relationship between specific pyocin types and a serotype is also evident from the following. Siem (1972) noted that of 149 strains of the unusual pyocin type 2, 131 belonged to serotype 6 and Govan (1968) found that all nine pyocin type 17 strains examined and all three pyocin type 19 strains also belonged to serotype 6. Csiszar and Lanyi (1970) observed that 12 of 13 pyocin type 29 strains and 14 of 25 pyocin type 5 strains belonged to serotype 3. Bergan (1973a) confirmed the latter correlation observing that 48 of 66 pyocin type 5 strains belonged to serotype 3. Pyocin typing carried out by Siem (1972) further confirmed this correlation and simultaneously showed a considerable subdivision of serotype 3 into five pyocin types; 17 of 36 pyocin type 5 strains, 10 of 11 pyocin type 9 strains, all five pyocin type 15 strains, 8 of 12 pyocin type 29 strains and 12 of 14 pyocin type 35 strains all belonged to serotype 3. Siem also confirmed that 10 of 11 strains of pyocin type 11 belonged to serotype 1. Initially there appeared to be little correlation between strains of pyocin type 1 and any particular serotype. However, when such strains are allocated to subtypes on the basis of their activity against indicator strains A–E, certain correlations emerge. Csiszar and Lanyi (1970) observed that pyocin types 1/c and 1/d accounted for 80% of all strains of serotype 2; 15 of 17 strains belonging to pyocin type 1/f were of serotype 9 and 15 of 34 strains belonging to pyocin type 1/b were of serotype 11. Al-Dujaili and Harris (1974) noted that 11 of 15 strains belonging to pyocin type 1/h were of serotype 11.

Since it has already been shown that strains of pyocin types 3 and 5 may be subdivided using indicator strains A–E, it is not unexpected that the correlation between these primary types and serotypes 6 and 3 respectively is less than absolute. It would be interesting to observe the correlation results when subdivision of these pyocin types is investigated in conjunction with serotyping.

Pyocin typing as described here examines the ability of strains to produce a substance whereas serotyping is determined by the presence of antigens on the cell surface. The fact that the two techniques are based on different biological systems and yet demonstrate a degree of correlation does not present a conflict in regard to their value for epidemiological studies. If all the causal strains in an epidemic have a single ancestral origin and the two methods of typing used are considered reliable, then correlation should be absolute. The lack of complete correlation between a serotype and a pyocin type suggests the ability of one technique to subdivide the other, but could also result from occasional instability in the biological determinants of one or other technique.

VI. ALTERNATIVE METHODS OF PYOCIN TYPING

A different approach to pyocin typing has been to characterize strains of *Ps. aeruginosa* on the basis of their sensitivity to pyocins.

Lewis (1967) grew seven pyocin producer strains in agar for 18 h at 30°C, then examined the sensitivity of the test strain to the pyocins produced, by incorporating it in an agar overlay. Growth inhibition in the top layer appeared over primary growths and for 169 strains examined 17 types were distinguished.

The use of stock preparations of pyocins, resulting in a technique resembling phage typing, has received more attention. Osman (1965) used pyocin preparations obtained from four producer strains and differentiated 101 isolates into ten pyocin sensitivity patterns. A more elaborate two-stage technique was described by Farmer and Herman (1969). Firstly, pyocin and phage production was induced in a log phase culture of the test strain using Mitomycin C and the lysate tested for inhibitory activity against a set of 27 indicator strains. Secondly, 24 standard pyocin-phage lysates were employed to test the sensitivity of the test strain which had been prepared under carefully standardized conditions. In this way an "epidemiological fingerprint" consisting of 51 operational characteristics could be established for each isolate. Each of the 157 strains examined was typable by this method and the "fingerprinting" technique was considered a sensitive tool for epidemiological studies.

Later in conjunction with other workers, Farmer considered that pyocin sensitivity was too unstable a property for use in epidemiological typing (Bobo *et al.*, 1973) and a simplified version of the "fingerprinting" technique based on pyocin production only was described (Jones *et al.*, 1974). In this method, pyocins are produced from test strains grown for 18 h at 32°C in Trypticase Soy Broth (without glucose) incorporating 1% potassium nitrate. These authors considered that the ability of most strains of *Ps. aeruginosa* to use nitrate as a terminal electron acceptor and thus grow uniformly throughout the broth eliminated the need for mechanical shaking during pyocin production and also induction with Mitomycin C. A set of 18 indicator strains was chosen from 250 strains, including 60 strains already used in other pyocin typing systems; the final set included 11 of the latter. The simplified technique gave the identical epidemiological results when used to type 23 isolates of *Ps. aeruginosa* from a nursery outbreak, previously investigated using the more elaborate "fingerprinting" method.

Rampling *et al.* (1975) described a technique based on pyocin sensitivity in which pyocin-phage lysates were rendered "phage-free" by ultraviolet irradiation; 27 such lysates were used to divide 105 isolates into 40 sensitivity patterns. When the reproducibility of the pyocin sensitivity patterns was examined by testing six control strains eight times in one experiment, only two strains gave consistent results.

VII. APPLICATIONS OF THE GILLIES AND GOVAN PYOCIN TYPING TECHNIQUE

Pyocin typing (Gillies and Govan, 1966; Govan and Gillies, 1969) has proved to be a valuable aid in epidemiological studies of *Ps. aeruginosa*. The technique has been used to determine the incidence of exogenously and endogenously acquired infections and to elucidate the sources, reservoirs and mode of spread of the organism in the hospital environment.

In an early application of the technique (Govan, 1968) two long-term episodes of cross-infection in two adjacent wards were detected retrospectively. During a 16-month period, strains of the relatively uncommon pyocin type 35 accounted for 26 (72%) of the 36 cases of infection with *Ps. aeruginosa* in unit A. Concurrently in unit B, strains of the equally rare pyocin type 29 were isolated from 23 (70%) of the 33 similar cases of infection.

Outbreaks involving many patients in a short period of time are easily recognized. Insidious outbreaks of cross-infection, such as those just described, in which only a few cases are present simultaneously, are more difficult to detect and demonstrate the value of constant monitoring of infections with pyocin typing.

The use of pyocin typing has implicated faulty sterilization techniques and many inanimate vehicles in the spread of infections due to *Ps. aeruginosa*. Improper sanitization of urine bottles and milk feed stoppers was the cause of two large outbreaks (Govan, 1968). Duncan and Booth (1965) encountered an outbreak of infection due to an uncommon subtype of type 1. The causal organisms were isolated from rubber urine collection bags and the surrounds of the physiotherapy treatment pool. All three outbreaks ceased following improved sanitization procedures.

With hospital equipment, e.g. respirators, sterilization may be more apparent than real. Tinne *et al.* (1967) described an outbreak of respiratory tract infection in a cardiac surgery unit which affected seven cases with three deaths. All cases were due to pyocin type 10 strains and post-operative mechanical ventilation implicated. It was significant that the last three cases of infection occurred after "sterilization" of the respirator by disinfection and exposure to ethylene oxide. The unit was closed, sanitized and intricate equipment dismantled before exposure to ethylene oxide. On reopening the unit another case of respiratory tract infection with a type 10 strain was encountered raising doubts whether these measures had been effective. It was found, however, that this patient had been present in the unit during the outbreak. The organism was eradicated from this patient's sputum by chemotherapy but not before cross-infection had occurred to the patient in the adjoining bed.

The role of the infected patient and human carrier following successful sterilization of implicated apparatus was further emphasized by Fierer *et al.* (1967) in the first reported use of pyocin typing in the U.S.A. The original cause of an epidemic which involved 22 new-born infants and resulted in two deaths, was found to be delivery room resuscitation equipment that had been contaminated with *Ps. aeruginosa* via a wash-sink aerator. After disinfection the causal strain was never again isolated in the nursery except from infected babies. Cross-infection through the contaminated hands of personnel was considered the most likely means of transmission to infants not resuscitated at birth and for the 12 new cases encountered after eradication of the causal organism from the equipment. Deighton *et al.* (1971) used pyocin typing to show that infected hands of personnel contributed to the spread of infection during bathing of infants. Repeated outbreaks of cross-infection were encountered and it was shown that objects and persons in contact with infected patients became contaminated with the causal strain. In contrast, Baltch and Griffin (1972) found no evidence of cross-infection with *Ps. aeruginosa* in a comprehensive study lasting 12 months; they were unable to detect the same pyocin type in several patients on one ward or room at a given time.

Although there was clear evidence for cross-infection in extended-care and urology wards, Duncan and Booth (1975) were tempted to conclude from pyocin typing results, obtained in a three year investigation, that endogenous rather than exogenous spread was the most common method of spread in *Ps. aeruginosa* infections. Patients acquire an increased faecal carriage of *Ps. aeruginosa* following admission to hospital (Shooter *et al.*, 1966) and pyocin typing has demonstrated that faecal carriage may lead to endogenous infection (Govan, 1968; Deighton *et al.*, 1971). The manner in which colonization of the gut occurs is not clearly understood but may originate in contaminated foods.

More unusual evidence for endogenously acquired infection derives from a microbiological study of submarine crews during long patrols. Morris and Fallon (1973) encountered an outbreak of otitis externa which was shown by pyocin typing to be due to the same strain of *Ps. aeruginosa* as that isolated a few days previously from apparently healthy throats.

Heckman *et al.* (1972) made valuable use of pyocin typing to determine the sites of colonization of patients with the same pyocin type. In addition to a study of sites and patterns of colonization, results from 17 patients demonstrated correlation between clinical diagnosis and the pyocin types of organisms isolated from one or more ante-mortem sites and post-mortem material.

Williams and Govan (1973) used both the standard technique and the modified method, described in this Chapter, to investigate the relationship between mucoid and non-mucoid strains of *Ps. aeruginosa* isolated from the sputa of children with cystic fibrosis. Mucoid strains are frequently observed in the sputa from such children (Doggett, 1969). Mucoid and non-mucoid strains of *Ps. aeruginosa* are often isolated from the same specimen, and as the infection progresses the mucoid strain predominates with a concomitant deterioration in the condition of the patient (Doggett *et al.*, 1966). Mucoid and non-mucoid strains isolated from the same specimen belonged to the same pyocin type suggesting that the mucoid variant was derived from the non-mucoid strain.

Pyocin typing has been used in studies of chemotherapeutic agents and in the therapeutic use of pyocins themselves, to determine relapse or reinfection (Brumfitt *et al.*, 1967; Phillips *et al.*, 1968; Govan, 1968; Williams, 1974). Shulman *et al.* (1971) used pyocin typing to demonstrate the emergence and spread, in a burns unit, of a Gentamycin-resistant strain of *Ps. aeruginosa* belonging to pyocin type 5. The Gentamycin-resistant strain did not spread to areas of the hospital which did not use Gentamycin and the outbreak was dramatically reduced following discontinuation of the routine use of the antibiotic.

Pyocin typing has been shown to be applicable in the study of *Ps. aeruginosa* from non-human sources such as turkeys and horses (Govan, unpublished) and in cattle and many other animals (Mushin and Ziv, 1973).

The use of pyocin typing in many studies of the epidemiology of *Ps. aeruginosa* infections reveals numerous routes, sources and vectors. Several common factors emerge, however, which are important if such infections are to be prevented or controlled.

1. The hospital environment usually harbours many different pyocin types of *Ps. aeruginosa* and, without a suitable method of characterizing the organism, it is impossible to monitor infections or investigate and control outbreaks.

2. Except in episodes of cross-infection, the distribution of pyocin types encountered in infections in a unit, over a period of time, follows no regular pattern. The epidemiology of nosocomial infections due to *Ps. aeruginosa* is therefore different from similar staphylococcal infections where a large proportion of infections are caused by a few resident "hospital" staphylococci.

VIII. BIOLOGICAL PROPERTIES AND PYOCIN TYPES

No statistically valid evidence has been reported to correlate particular pyocin types of *Ps. aeruginosa* with pigment production and colonial morphology (Csiszar and Lanyi, 1970), preference for a particular site or type of infection (Heckman *et al.*, 1972; Duncan and Booth, 1975) or virulence (Baltch and Griffin, 1972; Al Dujaili and Harris, 1975).

IX. THE FUTURE

A. International standardization of pyocin typing

Formal pleas have been made for international standardization of a single technique of pyocin typing and for a mnemonic system of type nomenclature (Herman and Farmer, 1970; Farmer, 1970).

Table III illustrates the widespread use of the Gillies and Govan technique and suggests that *de facto* standardization already exists. To the author's knowledge the indicator strains have already been distributed from this laboratory to more than 200 centres.

B. Choice of a particular typing method

No single typing technique for *Ps. aeruginosa*, phage typing, pyocin typing or serotyping has proved completely satisfactory and in many epidemiological studies strains have been examined using more than one typing method.

Phage typing requires preparation, maintenance and standardization of phage stocks and of the three methods, is probably the most laborious to undertake. The method is less reproducible than pyocin typing and serotyping and sensitivity to phage is altered by changes in colonial morphology due to dissociation (Shionoya and Homma, 1968). An advantage of phage typing is that it divides strains into a large number of phage types. Bobo *et al.* (1973) investigated an outbreak of *Ps. aeruginosa* infection in a nursery using five typing methods including phage typing. Pyocin production and serotyping proved to be the most useful and stable markers.

Serotyping shows good reproducibility, but the preparation or purchase of antisera is relatively expensive. The main disadvantages of this technique are that it does not provide as large a number of distinct types as the other methods and, in addition, the majority of strains can be allocated to only a few common types.

Similarly, one of the main criticisms of the Gillies and Govan pyocin typing scheme was that the majority of isolates examined belonged to a relatively few common pyocin types. Subdivision of the most common type, pyocin type 1 (Govan and Gillies, 1969), has greatly improved the sensitivity of the technique. Even better differentiation is now possible following the introduction of a scheme for subdividing the other common pyocin types using the existing indicator strains A–E. A disadvantage of this method of typing is that the technique requires three days to complete.

Following the improvements outlined in this Chapter, pyocin typing now has the necessary properties to recommend it as the sole typing system for *Ps. aeruginosa* in all laboratories. It is suggested, however, that reference centres use both pyocin typing and one other technique. Phage typing has much to offer but, if serotyping was chosen, this would allow further analysis of the obvious correlation between certain serotypes and pyocin types.

C. Future developments

Pyocin typing benefits considerably from basic knowledge of pyocins and pyocinogeny and will continue to do so in future. Already the nature of the individual pyocins produced alone or in combination by strains belonging to several pyocin types has been determined (Govan, 1973b and unpublished; Brown, 1973b). Electron microscopy, pyocin-resistant mutants, diffusibility and trypsin sensitivity can be used to determine heterogeneity of pyocin production.

Subdivision of the more common pyocin types, using indicator strains A–E, increases the sensitivity of the technique and further subdivision of these and other pyocin types is probable. The number of untypable strains may be further reduced by selection of further indicator strains but a lack of detectable pyocin activity *per se* is a useful epidemiological marker. The introduction of certain R factors into a pyocinogenic strain of *Ps. aeruginosa* can lead to the apparent loss of pyocin production (Jacoby, 1974; Govan, unpublished), and further investigation of this phenomenon could be relevant to pyocin typing in epidemiological investigations.

Although the optimum condition may have been found for pyocin production it seems reasonable that future use of pyocin typing techniques will encounter typing patterns not yet published.

D. Pyocin(e) or aeruginocin(e) typing

The name "pyocine" was first introduced by Jacob (1954) in a paper, written in French, to describe a bacteriocin of the species *Pseudomonas pyocyanea* (the alternative species epithet for *Pseudomonas aeruginosa*). At present, the term "pyocin" or the French form "pyocine" is used by many workers. In 1970 the Judicial Commission of the International Committee on the Nomenclature of Bacteria accepted the name *Pseudomonas aeruginosa* in place of *Pseudomonas pyocyanea*. To avoid confusion the term "pyocin typing" has been retained throughout this Chapter but it seems logical that in future the more correct term would be "aeruginocin typing".

REFERENCES

Abbot, J. D., and Shannon, R. (1958). *J. clin. Path.*, **11**, 71–77.
Al-Dujaili, A. H., and Harris, D. M. (1974). *J. clin. Path.*, **27**, 569–571.
Al-Dujaili, A. H., and Harris, D. M. (1975). *J. Hyg. (Camb.)* **75**, 195–201.
Baltch, A. L., and Griffin, P. E. (1972). *Am. J. med. Sci.*, **264**, 233–246.
Bergan, T. (1973a). *Acta path. microbiol. scand.*, **81B**, 70–80.
Bergan, T. (1973b). *Acta path. microbiol. scand.*, **81B**, 81–90.
Bergan, T. (1975) Epidemiological typing of *Pseudomonas aeruginosa. In* "Resistance of *Pseudomonas aeruginosa*" (Ed. M. R. W. Brown). John Wiley, London.
Bobo, R. A., Newton, E. J., Jones, L. F., Farmer, L. H., and Farmer, J. J. (1973). *Appl. Microbiol.*, **25**, 414–420.
Brown, D. O. (1973a). *Med. Lab. Technol.*, **30**, 351–353.
Brown, D. O. (1973b). Filamentous pyocines of *Pseudomonas aeruginosa*. Department of Bacteriology, University of Edinburgh. Thesis presented for Fellowship of the Institute of Medical Laboratory Sciences.
Brumfitt, W., Percival, A., and Leigh, D. A. (1967). *Lancet*, **2**, 1289–1293.
Csiszár, K., and Lányi, B. (1970). *Acta microbiol. Acad. sci. hung.*, **17**, 361–370.

Darrell, J. H., and Wahba, A. H. (1964). *J. clin. Path.*, **17**, 236–242.

Deighton, M. A., Tagg, J. R., and Mushin, R. (1971). *Med. J. Aust.*, **1**, 892–896.

Doggett, R. G. (1969). *Appl. Microbiol.*, **18**, 936–937.

Doggett, R. G., Harrison, G. M., Stillwell, R. N., and Wallis, E. S. (1966). *J. Pediat.*, **68**, 215–221.

Duncan, I. B. R. and Booth, V. (1975). *Can. med. Ass. J.*, **112**, 837–843.

Edmonds, P., Suskind, R. R., MacMillan, B. G., and Holder, I. A. (1972). *Appl. Microbiol.*, **24**, 213–218.

Farmer, J. J. (1970). *Lancet*, **2**, p. 96.

Farmer, J. J., and Herman, L. G. (1969). *Appl. Microbiol.*, **18**, 760–765.

Fierer, J., Taylor, P. M., and Gezon, H. M. (1967). *New Engl. J. Med.*, **276**, 991–996.

Gillies, R. R., and Govan, J. R. W. (1966). *J. Path. Bact.*, **91**, 339–345.

Govan, J. R. W. (1968). The pyocines of *Pseudomonas pyocyanea*. Department of Bacteriology, University of Edinburgh. Thesis presented for the Degree of Doctor of Philosophy, Edinburgh.

Govan, J. R. W. (1974a). *J. gen. Microbiol.*, **80**, 1–15.

Govan, J. R. W. (1974b). *J. gen. Microbiol.*, **80**, 17–30.

Govan, J. R. W., and Gillies, R. R. (1969). *J. med. Microbiol.*, **2**, 17–25.

Habs, I. (1957). *Z. Hyg. InfecktKrankh.*, **144**, 218–228.

Hamon, Y., Véron, M., and Peron, Y. (1961). *Annls. Inst. Pasteur*, **101**, 738–753.

Heckman, M. G., Babcock, J. B., and Rose, H. D. (1972). *Am. J. clin. Path.*, **57**, 35–42.

Herman, L. G., and Farmer, J. J. (1970). Abstracts. *Tenth International Congress for Microbiology*, **8**, p. 98.

Higerd, T. B., Baechler, C. A., and Berk, R. S. (1967). *J. Bact.*, **93**, 1976–1986.

Holloway, B. W. (1960). *J. Path. Bact.*, **80**, 448–450.

Holloway, B. W., and Krishnapillai, V. (1974). Bacteriophages and bacteriocines. *In* "Genetics and Biochemistry of Pseudomonas" (Ed. P. H. Clarke and M. H. Richmond). John Wiley, London.

Homma, J. Y., and Suzuki, N. (1966). *Jap. J. exp. Med.*, **31**, 209–213.

Ikedi, K., and Egami, F. (1969). *J. Biochem. (Tokyo)*, **65**, 603–609.

International Committee of Nomenclature of Bacteria, Judicial Commission (1970). *Inst. J. syst. Bact.*, **20**, 15–16.

Ishii, Y., Nishi, Y., and Egami, F. (1965). *J. molec. Biol.*, **13**, 428–431.

Ito, S., and Kageyama, M. (1970). *J. gen. appl. Microbiol. (Tokyo)*, **16**, 231–240.

Ito, S., Kageyama, M., and Egami, F. (1970). *J. gen. appl. Microbiol.*, **16**, 205–214.

Jacob, F. (1954). *Annls. Inst. Pasteur*, **86**, 149–160.

Jacoby, G. A. (1974). *Antimicrob. Ag. Chemother.*, **6**, 329–352.

Jones, L. F., Zakanycz, J. P., Thomas, E. T., and Farmer, J. J. (1974). *Appl. Microbiol.*, **27**, 400–406.

Kageyama, M. (1970a). *J. gen. appl. Microbiol. (Tokyo)*, **16**, 523–530.

Kageyama, M. (1970b). *J. gen. appl. Microbiol. (Tokyo)*, **16**, 531–535.

Kaziro, Y., and Tanaka, M. (1965a). *J. Biochem. (Tokyo)*, **57**, 689–695.

Kaziro, Y., and Tanaka, M. (1965b). *J. Biochem. (Tokyo)*, **58**, 357–363.

Kohn, J. (1966). *J. clin. Path.*, **19**, p. 403.

Lanyi, B. (1966/67). *Acta path. microbiol. Acad. sci. hung.*, **13**, 295–318.

Lewis, M. S. (1967). *J. clin. Path.*, **20**, p. 103.

Macpherson, J. N., and Gillies, R. R. (1969). *J. med. Microbiol.*, **2**, 161–165.

Merrikin, D. J., and Terry, C. S. (1969). *J. appl. Bact.*, **32**, 301–303.

Merrikin, D. J., and Terry, C. S. (1972). *J. appl. Bact.*, **35**, 667–672.
Morris, J. E. W., and Fallon, R. J. (1973). *J. Hyg. (Camb.)*, **71**, 761–770.
Mushin, R., and Ziv, G. (1973). *Israel J. med. Sci.*, **9**, 155–161.
Neussel, H. (1971). *Arzneimittel-Forsch.*, **21**, 333–335.
Osman, M. A. M. (1965). *J. clin. Path.*, **18**, 200–202.
Phillips, I., Fernandes, R., and Gundara, N. S. (1968). *Lancet*, **1**, 11–12.
Rampling, A., Whitby, J. L., and Wildy, P. (1975). *J. med. Microbiol.*, **8**, 531–541.
Rose, H. D., Babcock, J. B., and Heckman, M. G. (1971). *Appl. Microbiol.*, **22**, p. 475.
Schwarzmann, S., and Boring, J. R. (1971). *Infect. Immun.*, **3**, 762–767.
Shionoya, H., and Homma, J. Y. (1968). *Jap J. exp. Med.*, **38**, 81–94.
Shooter, R. A., Walker, K. A., Williams, V. R., Horgan, G. M., Parker, M. T., Asheshov, E. H., and Bullimore, J. F. (1966). *Lancet*, **2**, 1331–1334.
Shriniwas (1974). *J. clin. Path.*, **27**, 92–96.
Shulman, J. A., Terry, P. M., and Hough, C. E. (1971). *J. Infect. Dis.*, **124**, (Suppl.), 518–523.
Siem, T. H. (1972). Het typeren van *Pseudomonas aeruginosa* met behulp van een gecombineerde sero-pyocine typeringsmethode. Doctorate thesis presented in the University of Amsterdam.
Sjoberg, L., and Lindberg, A. A. (1967). *Acta path. microbiol. scand.*, **70**, 639–640.
Sjoberg, L., and Lindberg, A. A. (1968). *Acta path. microbiol. scand.*, **74**, 61–68.
Smith, H. B. H., and Tuffnell, P. G. (1970). *Can Anaesth. Soc. J.*, **17**, 516–521.
Tagg, J. R., and Mushin, R. (1971). *Med. J. Aust.*, **1**, 847–852.
Takeya, K., Minamishima, Y., Ohnishi, Y., and Amako, K. (1969). *J. gen. Virol.*, **4**, 145–149.
Tinne, J. E., Gordon, A. M., Bain, W. H., and Mackay, W. A. (1967). *Br. med. J.*, **4**, 313–315.
Tripathy, G. S., and Chadwick, P. (1971). *Can. J. Microbiol.*, **17**, 829–835.
Wahba, A. H. (1963). *J. Hyg. (Camb.)*, **61**, 431–441.
Wahba, A. H. (1965). *Zentbl. Bakt. I. Orig.*, **196**, 389–394.
Wahba, A. H., and Lidwell, O. M. (1963). *J. appl. Bact.*, **26**, 246–248.
Williams, R. J. (1974). Pyocines and the treatment of *Pseudomonas aeruginosa* infections. Department of Bacteriology, University of Edinburgh. Thesis presented for the degree of Doctor of Philosophy, Edinburgh.
Williams, R. J., and Govan, J. R. W. (1973). *J. med. Microbiol.*, **6**, 409–412.
Zabransky, R. J., and Day, F. E. (1969). *Appl. Microbiol.*, **17**, 293–296.
Ziv, G., Mushin, R., and Tagg, J. R. (1971). *J. Hyg. (Camb.)*, **69**, 171–177.

CHAPTER IV

Serological Characterization of *Pseudomonas aeruginosa*

B. Lányi and T. Bergan

National Institute of Hygiene, Budapest, Hungary
Department of Microbiology, Institute of Pharmacy,
and Department of Microbiology, Aker Hospital, University of Oslo, Oslo, Norway

I. INTRODUCTION

The rise in infections due to *Pseudomonas aeruginosa* has been commented upon frequently during the past decades (Bergan, 1967, 1968; Finland, 1971; Shooter, 1971, 1973). In Finland's experience, during the period 1935–1965 the frequency of pseudomonas rose from 3–4 to 9% of all isolates from blood cultures.

Pseudomonas infections are mainly a consequence of modern hospitalization. The mechanisms responsible for this change are discussed elsewhere (Lowbury, 1974).

Clinical aspects of pseudomonas† infections have been detailed by Forkner (1960), Caselitz (1966) and Young and Armstrong (1972). Most common are infections of the urinary tract, respiratory tract—particularly in the aged, in premature babies, and in tracheostomized patients—and burn wounds (Bergan, 1968). Patients with infections to a considerable extent maintain the nosocomial situation since they constitute reservoirs from which spread may occur to the environment. It is also important that there are healthy carriers of pseudomonas (Shooter *et al.*, 1966). Spreading occurs easily.

Because of extensive resistance to antibiotics, pseudomonas infections may be difficult to eradicate and have particularly serious consequences.

In this situation, it is desirable to identify the sources and follow the routes of transmission. As tools to this end epidemiological typing methods have been developed: pyocine typing, bacteriophage typing and serological typing.

Serological characterization is a requirement for attempts of active or passive immunization against pseudomonas in animals and man (editorial *Lancet*, 1975; Feller and Pierron, 1968; Jones and Roe, 1975; Pennington *et al.*, 1975; Young and Armstrong, 1972). Serological know-how is also necessary for identification of specific antibodies in patient sera. Kumari *et al.* (1973) have found higher titres against pseudomonas in patients suffering from pseudomonas infections than in normal controls, and patients with deep-seated lesions had higher titres than those with superficial lesions. Similarly, Høiby and Wiik (1975) with crossed immunoelectrophoresis found that patients with cystic fibrosis had responded to several pseudomonas antigens, whereas no controls exhibited corresponding antibody. Prevalence of antibodies against *P. aeruginosa* in normal subjects increases with age (Høiby, 1975c).

It is the purpose here to review methodology and application of serology

† In the following the term "pseudomonas" is used synonymously with *P. aeruginosa*.

and show how the serotyping system of Habs can be constructed to recognize the cross-reactions among serogroups.

II. IDENTIFICATION OF *P. AERUGINOSA*

In order to ensure correct diagnosis of an isolate, it is important to define *P. aeruginosa*. It is important that isolates considered for typing by an epidemiological typing method meet certain standards such that aberrant results or lack of typability are not due to simple error in classification.

Pseudomonas aeruginosa belongs to the family *Pseudomonadaceae*, genus *Pseudomonas*. It is strictly aerobic, exhibits straight, Gram-negative rods, generally 0·5–0·8 by 1·5–3·0 nm. Cells are motile by polar, monotrichous flagella. Characteristically, pyocyanin, a water and chloroform soluble phenazine pigment, is produced by the majority of strains. This is blue-green at a neutral or alkaline reaction and red in acid media. Some strains produce a dark, reddish brown pigment, pyorubin. All produce a diffusible green fluorescent fluorescin, pyofluorescin. The oxidase reaction is positive, the organism always has an oxidative, respiratory metabolism. *P. aeruginosa* grows at 42 but not at 4°C. The mole $\%(G+C)$ of deoxyribonucleic acid is around 67.

Cultures of *P. aeruginosa* usually have a rough appearance with an uneven margin, although occasionally mucoid strains with a glistening, shiny surface and large, 1–3 mm diameter colonies are seen. A smell of spoiled fish is typically noticed, and almost diagnostic. Differentiation from other fluorescent pseudomonads is achieved by further observation of the following characteristics:

Growth at 42°C
Reduction of nitrate to nitrogen gas
Liquefaction of gelatin (in broth with 15% gelatin)
Acid production from glucose and mannitol
Lack of acid production from:

Adonitol
Dulcitol
Inositol
Saccharose
Sorbitol.

The biochemical-cultural characteristics are determined after cultivation at 37°C for 4 days and cultures processed according to Jessen (1965).

Minor deviations from the above reactions are sometimes seen. Jessen (1965) considers absence of growth at +5°C and/or failure to produce an egg-yolk reaction as being of particular diagnostic importance.

III. SEROLOGICAL TYPING

A. Serological approaches

Serological examinations of *P. aeruginosa* have been carried out since the beginning of this century (Jacobsthal, 1912; Plehn and Trommsdorff, 1916; St. John-Brooks *et al.*, 1925). Trommsdorff (1916) separated 24 isolates into 5 serogroups. The number of distinct groups seems high considering the few strains examined. Other pioneers were Aoki (1926) and Kanzaki (1934). There is no agglutinogen common to all *P. aeruginosa* strains, but there are many cross-reactions among minor antigens.

The evolution of *P. aeruginosa* serology has been discussed by Caselitz (1966), Köhler (1957, 1958), and by Govan (1968).

Instead of starting from previous results, the tendency has often been to build up independent serogrouping systems from scratch. This has hampered comparison of results and is a situation which might now change. Several independent serogrouping systems have been established (Chia-Ying, 1963; Christie, 1948; van den Ende, 1952; Fisher *et al.*, 1969; Habs, 1957; Homma, 1974; Lányi, 1966/67, 1970; Mayr-Harting, 1948; Meitert and Meitert, 1966; Sandvik, 1960b; Verder and Evans, 1961; Wokatsch, 1964) (see Table I). Of these, the systems of Lányi (1966/67, 1970) and Verder and Evans (1961) are the most detailed and take account of cross-reactions and both heat stable and heat labile antigens.

Under the auspices of the Subcommittee of *Pseudomonadaceae* and Related Organisms of the International Association of Microbiological Societies, Professor P. V. Liu, Louisville, Ky., is heading an International Collaborative Study on *Pseudomonas aeruginosa* Serology (ICSPS) attempting to establish an International Antigenic Typing Scheme (IATS).

This has been based on the first 12 O-groups of the Habs scheme (Habs, 1957) which is the first system to have gained more widespread recognition. This has been supplemented by the O: II of Sandvik (1960a, b) which was designated as O: 13 previously by Wahba (1965a, b) and subsequently used as O: 13 by, for example, Bergan (1972a, 1973a) and Mikkelsen (1970). Further serogroup antigens have also been derived from other typing sets and given continuous numbers in the collaborative study according to the priority of their inclusion in the scrutiny. Accordingly, number 14 in the continuous numbering system is the O: V, represented by type strain 1M-1, in the system of Verder and Evans (1961). It may be mentioned that Wahba (1965a), Bergan (1973a) and Mikkelsen (1970) have, although using the system of IATS up to O: 13, referred to different antigens as O: 14. The continuous number 15 is the O: 12, represented by type strain 170022, of Lányi (1966/67). The continuous number 16 is an O-antigen present in Homma's O:13 type strain YS–74,

TABLE I
Independent serogrouping schemes for *Pseudomonas aeruginosa* published after 1955

Serogrouping system	No. of O-antigens	Typing results with individual sets		
		Publication	% Typed	Self-agglutinable
Habs (1957)	12	Kleinmaier and Quincke (1959)	84	5
		Wokatsch (1964)	62	0
		Borst and deJong (1970)	86	?
		Wahba (1965b)†	99·7	0
		Mikkelsen (1970)	87	12
		Bergan (1972a)	71	14
		Bergan (1973a)	86	7
	16	Agarwal *et al.* (1972)	84	0
Fisher *et al.* (1969)	7	Fisher *et al.* (1969)	94	?
		Adler and Finland (1971)	88	0
		Moody *et al.* (1972)	99	0
Chia-Ying (1963)	5	Chia-Ying (1963)	96	?
		Homma *et al.* (1970)	72*	1
Homma (1974)	16	Maruyama *et al.* (1971)	73	0
		Yoshioka *et al.* (1970)	81	0
Lányi (1966/67)	27 (supplemented by 7 H-antigens, 1970)	Lányi (1966/67)	88‡	1
		Zellner *et al.* (1975)	100	0
Meitert (1964)	10	Meitert and Meitert (1966)	85	?
Sandvik (1960a and pers. comm., 1971)	8	Sandvik (1960a, b)	98	2
Verder and Evans (1961)	13 (supplemented by 10 H-antigens)	Verder and Evans (1961)	100	0
Wokatsch (1964)§	25	Wokatsch (1964)	100	0

* Polyagglutinable, 15%; non-groupable, 12%.
† With 2 additional O-antigens such that a total of 14 O-groups was included.
‡ One per cent self-agglutinable and 11% polyagglutinable.
§ Used Habs's 12 serogroups extended with 13 O-sera to type animal strains. The latter 13 sera were probably not factor sera since many bacteria reacted within 2–4 of them.

which appears to cross-react with strain 170003 of Lányi (1966/67). The continuous number 17 is a unique antigen found in O:X (Meitert, 1964). Typing by thermolabile antigens (Kleinmaier et al., 1958; Lányi, 1970; Verder and Evans, 1961) has not gained wide recognition. The thermolabile antigens may be flagellar, fimbrial or other surface antigens (Bradley and Pitt, 1975; Lányi, 1970; Pitt and Bradley, 1975). Lányi (1970) recognized two distinct thermolabile antigens, each subdivided into minor components leading to a total of 8 determinants (Lányi, 1970). By combining O- and H-antigen determination, Lányi distinguished 58 types and Verder and Evans (1961) 29 serotypes.

Other serological procedures than the widely used agglutination procedures have been explored experimentally, such as the fluorescent antibody technique (Nishimura et al., 1973), passive haemagglutination, precipitation with O-antigen extracts, slime layer substance, mucoid material, double gel immunodiffusion, immunoelectrophoresis—both one-dimensional and crossed immunoelectrophoresis. These techniques will be described below.

IV. ANTIGENIC STRUCTURE OF P. AERUGINOSA

A. History

The first studies on the antigenic structure of P. aeruginosa were centred around heat-stable and heat-labile factors. Since basic features of the chemical or cellulotopographic composition was largely unknown, several of the earlier studies used techniques which—in retrospect—were insufficient for the separation of reactions due to antigens with different physico-chemical properties. More recent studies, utilizing experience from the serology of Enterobacteriaceae and new techniques have made great progress in the elucidation of the antigenic constitution of P. aeruginosa antigens. In many respects, antigens in Enterobacteriaceae and in pseudomonads are basically different, especially as regards the optimal conditions for their determination.

B. Characteristics of O-antigens

1. Immunogenicity

The production of O-antibodies may be elicited by living or heated cell suspensions or bacteria treated with ethanol, hydrochloric acid, or formaldehyde (Lányi, 1966/67), see Table II. Since serogrouping in practice is preferably carried out with O-sera without antibodies against heat labile antigens, heated suspensions are, as a rule, used for immunization. To obtain highly titred O-sera, relatively large doses of the bacteria should be

TABLE II

Characteristics of the O-antigens of *P. aeruginosa*

Antigen	Agglutin-ability	Immuno-genicity	Agglutinin-binding capacity
Living	+ + + +	+ + + +	+ + + +
50–75°C 1 h, 80°C ½ h	−	+ + + +	+ + + +
80°C 1 h	±	+ + + +	+ + + +
100°C 1 h	+	+ + + +	+ + + +
100°C 2½ h	+ +	+ + + +	+ + + +
120°C 2½ h	+ + +	+ +	+ + + +
100°C 2½ h + 130°C 1 h	+ + +	+ +	+ + + +
Saturated NaCl	−	+ + + +	+ + + +
Ethanol, 50%	−	+ + + +	+ + + +
HCl, 0·001 N	−	+ + + +	+ + + +
HCl, N	+ + +	+ + + +	+ + + +
Formaldehyde, 0·5%	−	+ + + +	+ + + +

injected intravenously and the immunization course should be of short duration (Homma *et al.*, 1971; Lányi, 1966/67; Mikkelsen, 1968; Verder and Evans, 1961). Usually maximum O-antibody titre is reached within 2 weeks (Pitt and Bradley, 1975).

2. *Antibody-binding capacity*

Similarly to immunogenicity, antibody-binding by *P. aeruginosa* O-antigens is uninfluenced by heating or by treatment with the usual chemical substances (Lányi, 1966/67), see Table II. In practice, absorption of O-antibodies is carried out with cultures heated at 100°C for 1 to 2½ h.

3. *Agglutinability*

Mayr-Harting (1948) was the first to conclude correctly that the agglutination of living *P. aeruginosa* was due to O-antibodies. In homologous OH-serum, the flagellar reaction was suppressed by a marked, high-titred somatic reaction. She showed that cells lost their H-agglutinability after heating or alcohol treatment. Since Mayr-Harting's report appeared, several authors have studied the effect of chemical substances and heat on O-agglutination of *P. aeruginosa*. An inhibitory effect of alcohol has been confirmed by Munoz *et al.* (1949), van den Ende (1952), and Lányi (1966/67). The behaviour of living *P. aeruginosa* in antiserum has been investigated (Hobbs *et al.*, 1964; Lányi, 1966/67; Meitert and Meitert, 1960). The effects of acid have been studied by Lányi (1966/67) and by Müller *et al.* (1973). The first systematic study on the effect of heat on O-agglutinability of *P. aeruginosa* was reported by Habs (1957), the observations of whom were confirmed and extended by Homma *et al.* (1970), Lányi (1966/67), Müller *et al.* (1973) and Verder and Evans (1961). The results may be summarized as in Table II.

Living cells of *P. aeruginosa* show high titred tube-agglutination in homologous O-antiserum after incubation at 37°C for 2 h. Alternatively, an immediate slide reaction in diluted O-serum is observed. The agglutination is characterized by a coarse, granular bacterial clumping which morphologically resembles the O-agglutination of *Enterobacteriaceae*. After further incubation at 37°C, however, living cells of *P. aeruginosa* undergo lysis resulting in bacterial debris adhering to the test-tube walls.

After exposure of living *P. aeruginosa* to 55–75°C for 30–60 min, the suspension becomes slimy and the cells loose their agglutinability entirely. Cultures incubated at 80°C for 30 min still fail to agglutinate, but after 60 min a slight agglutinability appears. The reaction gradually becomes stronger during the next 4–5 h. Heating at 100°C for 60 min, renders the cells agglutinable at low titres. After boiling for $2\frac{1}{2}$ h, the reactivity is further markedly increased and the viscosity of the suspension disappears.

The highest O-titres are obtained with cells which have been autoclaved at 120°C for 2–$2\frac{1}{2}$ h, exposed to 100°C for $2\frac{1}{2}$ h in saline, or kept at 130°C for 1 h as a glycerol suspension.

Treatment of cells with formalin or ethanol reduces O-agglutinability. The same effect is seen with suspensions in saturated sodium chloride. In contrast, cells treated with 1N hydrochloric acid or glacial acetic acid are O-agglutinable and retain their reactivity even after exposure to 75°C. Treatment with lower concentrations of hydrochloric acid (pH 3–4), resembles mild heat in causing inagglutinability. Agglutinates of *P. aeruginosa* heated at 100–130°C or treated with acid are finely granular. The clumps are smaller than those resulting with living cells.

If tube agglutination proceeds at 50°C (water bath), the titres become raised, usually by one dilution step compared to incubation at 37°C.

Since living cells agglutinate readily, whereas suspensions exposed to moderate heat may fail to react or show lower titres, the question arose as to whether *P. aeruginosa* has a somatic factor similar to the "envelope" (B or L) antigens of *Escherichia coli*, which inhibit O-agglutination of living cells (Habs, 1957; Tchernomordik, 1956; Verder and Evans, 1961). In an earlier study, van den Ende (1952) concluded that the masking effect of alcohol on O-agglutination of *P. aeruginosa* was due to a nucleoprotein precipitate on the surface of the cells. This formation appeared to be relatively inert. As living cultures and suspensions heated to 100°C or more give identical cross-agglutination patterns (Kleinmaier, 1957/58; Lányi, 1966/67; and Wahba, 1965a, b), the presence of B- or C-type antigens can be excluded. It would appear that mild heat, alcohol, formalin, saturated sodium chloride, or low concentrations of acid cause a swelling of or chemical damage to a presently undefined substance on the surface of the cells and in this manner interfere with their agglutinability. Heating at high temperature or exposure to more concentrated acid leads to agglutinable cells, presumably by destroying a hypothetical surface substance.

4. *Precipitation*

Previous failures to classify *P. aeruginosa* adequately by agglutination, inspired studies of antigen precipitation. Homma *et al.* (1951) and Hosoya *et al.* (1949) isolated strain-specific factors which were resistant to pepsin and trypsin. Van den Ende (1952) using trichloroacetic acid extracts, classified *P. aeruginosa* strains into 6 groups. Köhler (1957/58) made extensive studies on the group-specific antigen of organisms extracted with hydrochloric acid or with Fuller's formamide method.

Kleinmaier and Müller (1958) demonstrated that tube precipitation with *P. aeruginosa* extracts reflected the same antigenic pattern as that obtained by tube agglutination. With Ouchterlony's double agar gel immunodiffusion technique, Müller and Kleinmaier (1958) showed that in *P. aeruginosa* antigen-antibody systems, varying with the antigens used, 1 to 4 precipitation lines developed. Hobbs *et al.* (1964) with the same technique demonstrated several antigens in pseudomonads. At least one of the components was shared by all isolates. Van Eeden (1967) classified *P. aeruginosa* according to agar gel precipitation with trichloroacetic acid extracts. Ádám *et al.* (1971) have demonstrated group-specific reactions with lipopolysaccharides from Lányi's type strains by capillary precipitation and haemagglutination tests. Chester *et al.* (1973) have also demonstrated that lipopolysaccharides prepared from Habs's strains give specific reactions with capillary, ring and double diffusion technique. Lányi and Ádám (1973) have confirmed the agglutination pattern in double agar gel precipitation with various kinds of extracts which give, as a rule, identical and specific cross-reaction patterns for *P. aeruginosa* O-antigens.

These studies have indicated that lipopolysaccharides are responsible for the O-antigen specificity of *P. aeruginosa*.

5. *Classification by O-antigens*

Sandvik (1960) was the first to compare independently elaborated anti-

genic schemes (The Habs and Sandvik systems). Subsequently the follow
ing systems were compared: Habs *vs.* Verder and Evans (Muraschi *et al.*,
1966a, b); Verder and Evans *vs.* Lányi (Matsumoto and Tazaki, 1969);
Habs *vs.* Verder and Evans *vs.* Lányi (Thom, 1968, pers. comm.); Habs *vs.*
Homma *vs.* Lányi *vs.* Sandvik (Bergan, 1973a); Habs *vs.* Fisher *vs.* Lányi
(Lányi and Ádám 1973); Habs *vs.* Verder and Evans *vs.* Meitert *vs.* Lányi
vs. Fisher *vs.* Homma (Homma, 1973, pers. comm.); Habs *vs.* Meitert *vs.*
Lányi *vs.* Homma (Meitert, 1974, pers. comm.).

These findings have been summarized in Table III, showing the
correspondence of O-antigen-symbols within different serogrouping systems. The first column presents symbols for a scheme proposed by the
authors of this Chapter (Table IV, *vide infra*). Up to O: 12, this is based
on the group antigen designations of Habs (1957) which have priority by
date of publication over the other antigenic schemes. Subsequently identified new O-antigens and cross-reactivity with Habs group antigens as well
as cross-reactions of major antigens within the Habs scheme have been
duly acknowledged according to modern rules of serological classification
as expressed, for example, in the serotyping schemes of *Salmonella*, *Shigella*,
and other enterobacteriae. The recognition of cross-reactions must have
consequences for the constitution of a typing scheme, and its use is imperative as the most practical way of encompassing the complexity of the
antigenic mosaic of the species *Pseudomonas aeruginosa*.

The numbers in the second column in Table III, which is designated
"continuous numbering system" and is repeated in the column to the far
right in Table IV, correspond to the acquisition numbers and labels under
which the O-antigens have been compared/studied by the international
collaborative study on serogrouping.

In the proposed system, the O-antigen groups O: 2 and O: 5 of Habs
have been joined into one group, O: 2, by virtue of the fact that they share
a well-defined common antigen, O: 2a. The factor O: 2a is the common
specificity of group O: 2. This is also shared by the type strain YS-74 of
Homma (O: 13 in the scheme of Homma, 1974) which in antigenic constitution is identical to strain 170003 of Lányi (1966/67) (representing
O: 3a, 3b in the original grouping scheme of Lányi). The strains 170003 and
YS-74 also have a specific antigen, O: 2b, which is unique compared to
other group O: 2 type strains. In the international collaborative study, the
strain YS-74 has received the continuous number designation 16. In addition, strains 170006 and 170007 of Lányi (1966/67) have other partial
antigens, O: 2d, 2e, 2f. The cross-reactions between O: 2 and O: 5 were
recognized by Habs (1957) from the beginning. As these were one of the
more frequent in clinical strains. Véron (1961) studied the cross-reactions
between the Habs type strains and other isolates. He considered these to

Arabic–Latin system†	Continuous numbering system‡	Habs 1957	Sandvik 1960	Verder and Evans, 1961	Meitert, 1964; Meitert and Meitert, 1966	Lányi 1966/67	Fisher et al., 1969	Homma, 1974	Homma, 1976
1	1	1	VII	IV	–	6	4	10	I
2 (five subgroups)	2, 5, 16	2, 5, –	–	I (three subgroups), X	–, II, VI	3 (five subgroups)	3, 7, –	2, 7, 13, 16	B
3	3	3	III	VI	V	1	–	1	A
4 (two subgroups)	4	4	IV	–	VIII	11	–	6	F
6 (four subgroups)	6	6	I	II	I, IV	4 (four subgroups)	1	8	G
7 (three subgroups)	7, 8	7, 8	–, VIII	–, VIII	–, III	5 (three subgroups)	6	–, 3	C
9 (two subgroups)	9	9	V	IX	–	10 (two subgroups)	–	4	D
10 (two subgroups)	10	10	–	–	–	2	5	9	H
11 (two subgroups)	11	11	VI	III	–	7 (two subgroups)	2	5	E
12	12	12	–	VII (two subgroups)	VII	13	–	–, 14	L
13 (two subgroups)	13, 14	–	II, –	–, V	–	–	–	12, –	K
14	17	–	–	–	X	–	–	–	
15	15	–	–	–	–	12	–	11	J

† Proposed at present by Lányi and Bergan; O-antigenic groups are designated with Arabic numerals, partial antigens characterizing the subgroups within the groups are designated with additional Latin letters. The system scheme has been presented at a meeting of the International Collaborative Study Group on *Pseudomonas aeruginosa* Serology (ICS PS), September 2, 1976, at Dundee, Scotland, UK.

‡ Proposed by Liu (pers. comm., 1974); O-antigens are designated with continuous numbering; several partial antigens described in the literature are not included.

§ Proposed by Homma (pers. comm., 1976; O-antigenic groups are designated with capital Latin letters.

be related and recognized 4 subgroup antigens, a, b, c and d. These were represented by the type strains for the respective groups O: 2c, O: 2b, O: 5c and O: 5d. The first of these was identical with the Habs O: 2 and the O: 5c to the Habs O: 5. At Colindale, a subgrouping system is employed for the O: 2 complex as suggested and conceived in this

TABLE IV

O-antigens of *Pseudomonas aeruginosa*

Group	O-antigen	Type strain	Continuous numbering system
1	1	Habs 1	1
2	2a, 2b	170003	16
	(2a), 2c	Habs 2	2
	2a, 2d	Habs 5	
	2a, 2d, 2e	170006	
	(2a), 2d, 2f	170007	
3	3	Habs 3	3
4	4a, 4b	Habs 4	4
	4a, 4c	170040	
6	6a	Habs 6	6
	6a, 6b	170008†	
	6a, 6c	170009	
	6a, 6d	170010	
7	7a, 7b, 7c	170011	7
	7a, 7b, 7d	Habs 8	8
	7a, 7d	170013	
9	9a	170019	9
	9a, 9b	170020	
10	10a, 10b	Habs 10	10
	10a, 10c	170002	
11	11a, 11b	Habs 11	11
	11a, 11c	170016	
12	12	Habs 12	12
13	13a, 13b	Sandvik II	13
	13a, 13c	Verder & Evans V, strain 1M-1	14
14	8	Meitert X	17
15	5	170022	15

† Antigen 6b less prominent O: 6a, 6b→6a variation frequently encountered. (Figures in brackets indicate antigens that are frequently weakly developed.)

Pseudomonas aeruginosa O-antigen type strains

Arabic–Latin system	Continuous system	Type strain proposed	Remarks
1	1	Habs 1 (1 : 2a, 2b)	O-antigen identical with 170014 (1 : 2a, 2b)
2a, 2b	16	170003 (2a, 2b: 1)	O-antigen identical with YS-74† (2a, 2b?)
(2a), 2c	2	Habs 2 (2a, 2c: 1)	O-antigen identical with 170004 (2a, 2c: 1)
2a, 2d	5	Habs 5 (2a, 2d: ?)	O-antigen identical with 170005† (2a, 2d: 1)
2a, 2d, 2e	—	170006 (2a, 2d, 2e: 1)	
(2a), 2d, 2f	—	170007 (2a, 2d, 2f: 1)	
3	3	Habs 3 (3 : 1)	O-antigen identical with 170001 (3: 1)
4a, 4b	4	Habs 4 (4a, 4b: 1)	O-antigen identical with 170021 (4a, 4b: 2a, 2c, 2f)
4a, 4c	—	170040 (4a, 4c: 2a, 2c)	
6a	6	Habs 6 (6a: 2a, . . .)	
6b, 6b	—	170008 (6a, 6b: 2a, 2b)	
6a, 6c	—	170009 (6a, 6c: —)	
6a, 6d	7	170010 (6a, 6d: 2a, 2b, 2f)	O-antigen identical with Wahba 14† (6a, 6d: ?)
7a, 7b, 7c	7	170011 (7a, 7b, 7c: 1)	O-antigen closely related to Habs7† (7a: ?)
7a, 7b, 7d	8	Habs 8 (7a, 7b, 7d: ?)	O-antigen closely related to 170012 (7a, 7b, 7d; 2a, 2d)
7a, 7d	—	170013 (7a, 7d: 1)	
9a	9	170019 (9a: 1)	O-antigen closely related to Habs 9; O-group 10 strains cross-react with Habs 9 but not with 170019
9a, 9b	—	170020 (9a, 9b: 2a, 2c)	
10a, 10b	10	Habs 10 (10a, 10b: 1)	
10a, 10c	—	170002 (10a, 10c: 2a, 2b)	Cross-reacts with O-group 9
11a, 11b	11	Habs 11 (11a, 11b: 1)	
11a, 11c	—	170016 (11a, 11c: 2a, 2c)	O-antigen identical with 170015 (11a, 11b: 2a, 2c)
12	12	Habs 12 (12: 1)	O-antigen identical with 170023 (12: 1)
13a, 13b	13	Sandvik II (13a, 13b: 2a, . . .)	
13a, 13c	14	V.-E. 1M-1 (13a, 13c: 2a, . . .)	
14	17	Meitert X (14: 2a, 2d)	
15	15	170022 (15:1)	

† Not tested for production of absorbed serum.

Chapter, cf. Table V and Parker (1976). During the past 20 years, the Habs groups O: 1, O: 3 and O: 12 have remained without subdivisions.

The O: 4-group has recently been split into subgroup antigens. It now consists of O: 4a, 4b represented by Habs type strains for O: 4, and the O: 4a, 4c recently defined by Lányi and Lantos (1976) and represented by their type strain 170040 (Ar122). This strain was recently isolated from an infant and was thought probably to have developed in the patient from an isolate of O: 4a, 4b. Actually, this event clearly illustrates the superior flexibility and usefulness of the O-group–O-subgroup arrangement and the rearranged Habs system presented for the first time in this review (Table

TABLE V

Subgrouping pattern of the serogroup O: 2 complex used at the Cross-Infection Reference Laboratory, Colindale, London (Parker, 1976)

Subgroup antigen	Frequency†
2A	1
2A/2B	2
2A/5C	5
2B/5C	0·8
5C	2
5D	1
PS11 (=170003 of Lányi, 1966/67)	2
Other	0·6
Balance	0·6
Total reactive with sera against Habs O: 2 and O: 5	15

† Based on 1260 hospital isolates from 1974.

IV). It is far better suited to acknowledge later discoveries of partial O-antigen relationships than the systems of Habs or that hitherto employed by the international collaborative study—in the way the antigens have been arranged, i.e. without recognizing well established and major cross-reactions explicitly.

A very common O-group is that of Habs O: 6. Within this group, a number of strains with special partial antigens have been discovered. The type strain of Habs has only the O-factor O: 6a. Other subgroup antigens within the group are O: 6b, O: 6c and O: 6d represented by the type strains 170008, 170009 and 170010 of Lányi (1966/67). The Cross-Infection Reference Laboratory at Colindale, London, operates with another local set of subgroup antigens (Parker, 1976) (Table VI). This

TABLE VI

Subgrouping pattern of the O: 6 complex used at the Cross-Infection Reference Laboratory, Colindale, London (Parker, 1976)

Subgroup antigen	Frequency†
6	8
6, 6A	0·4
6, 6C	8
6, W14‡	0·4
6, 6A, 6C	2
6, 6A, W14	1
6, 6C, W14	2
6, 6A, 6C, W14	0·2
Balance	1
Total reactive with sera against Habs O: 6	23

† Based on 1260 hospital isolates from 1974.
‡ W14 corresponds to Wahba (1965a, b) group O: 14.

includes the O: 14 of Wahba (1965a, b) which cross-reacted with Habs O: 6 and was also recognized as a separate group by Bergan (1972a, 1973a). The elucidation of antigenic relationship within the group is the subject of ongoing studies.

The well known cross-reactions between Habs types O: 7 and O: 8 (Bergan, 1973a; Habs, 1957; Mikkelsen, 1970; Wahba, 1965a, b) have as a natural consequence that the two have been united into the group complex, O: 7, of the new scheme. Habs O: 9 and O: 10 each have been placed in separate groups, O: 9 and O: 10 of the new scheme. Cross-reactions between them have been reported several times (Bergan, 1973a; Wahba, 1965a, b), but have been minor. Each of the two new groups have been subdivided into partial antigens, O: 9a and O: 9b, and O: 10a, O: 10b and O: 10c. Lányi's 170019 has only O: 9a and is, therefore, suitable in lieu of Habs type strain O:9. The antigen O:9b is found in strain 170020 of Lányi (1966/67). Habs type strain O:10 has both partial antigens O:10a and O:10b. The O:10c is found in strain 170002 of Lányi (1966/67).

The Habs type strain O: 11 has been found to cross-react with 170016 (Lányi, 1966/67) by virtue of the factor O: 11a. Each have their own additional partial antigen, 11b and 11c respectively, and have been combined to form group O: 11 of the new system. O-group 13 of the new typing cheme by priority consists of the O: II of Sandvik (1960a, b) which has the partial antigens 13a and 13b. In addition, group 13 contains O: V, represented by the type strain 1M-1 of Verder and Evans (1961), which cross-reacts by virtue of the factor 13a and also has the partial antigen O: 13c. The Verder and Evans antigen has been referred to as O: 14 in the continuous numbering system of the international collaborative study.

In the new typing scheme, the group designations O: 5 and O: 8 are left vacant to avoid confusion with the corresponding Habs O-groups after their transfer to other group complexes. Since the continuous numbering system of the collaborative study has not appeared in print, the two remaining distinct O-antigens represented by strain 170022 (O: 12 of Lányi, 1966/67) and the type strain of Meitert (1964) O: X, each by priority according to date of publication, are referred to groups O: 14 and O: 14 in the new scheme (Tables IV and IVb).

It should be noted that strains representing the different serogrouping systems may vary in minor cross-reactions and, accordingly, the balance table between individual systems is to be interpreted as involving reactions of major factors only. Certain antigens described as O-factors (e.g. Lányi's O: 8 and O: 9 and Meitert's related antigen O: IX) have been omitted from Table IV, since these antigens have been shown to be R-like (e.g. Lányi and Lantos, 1976) and are deficient in O-antigens.

In a presentation like Table III where corresponding O-groups of different, independent typing schemes are compared, it is inevitable that other workers might conceive a few reactions somewhat differently. This depends upon the particular rabbit response to minor antigens, and, perhaps, to secondary changes of partial antigens in the local substrain of each type strain. Thus, in a balance scheme which appeared in 1974, Homma had several deviations from Table III which have been brought more in conformity with our balance table in a privately circulated scheme from Homma (Sept. 11, 1976). Similar schemes for private circulation received August 1976 from Liu, and September/October 1976 from Pitt, were essentially identical to our Table III but for a couple of places. Accordingly, we present this Table mainly for orientation purposes. It is to be interpreted with some care, as it is to be conceived as indicative primarily of major antigens. Comparisons between independent schemes will, however, be easier with a subgrouping scheme like the one presented in Table IV. Part of the reason for the difficulties in constructing a balance table like Table III is that only the Lányi (1966/67) and Verder–Evans schemes recognize subgroup antigens within the very framework of their schematic constructions.

In a proposal for renaming and grouping of strains circulated privately by Homma (personal communication, September 11, 1976), the Arabic numbering system used hitherto by Habs and the derived scheme of the international collaborative study has been rearranged. The rearrangement is made with the Homma (1974) scheme type strains (in which actual strains have varied from time to time) and starts using a capital Latin lettering system instead. The letter system (Table III) groups together cross-reacting entities in the same way as is done in Table IV. Reference to O-groups by letters resembles the convention within the genus *Salmonella* where letters designate groups and continuous Arabic numbers are employed to label each antigen. It is, however, incomplete in that it fails to designate or identify the pseudomonas antigens which are responsible for the very cross-reactions that are the reason for lumping in serogroups such as is the hallmark of the *Salmonella* system.

The rationale for converting to a letter system was to avoid confusion and to postpone final numbering until reachable by international agreement. The trouble is, however, that there seems to be an international agreement already of basing a serogrouping system on the scheme of Habs and of employing a numbering system. This is a convention which has the support of the Subcommittee on *Pseudomonas* and Related Organisms and most workers participating in the international collaborative study. We have wanted to retain the designations derived from the Habs antigen scheme since these are already the best known to most centres. It is interesting to note, though, that although not quite as detailed in defining subgroups, the major Homma groups coincide with the O-antigen complexes employed in Table IV. The new Homma scheme contains a group M which corresponds to Lányi's group antigen O: 9 and is excluded from the presently proposed scheme because it is an R-like antigen in a strain deficient in O-antigen. Other analogous antigens, such as Lányi O: 8 and Meitert and Meitert O: IX, have not been adopted by Homma. The new Meitert and Meitert group antigens O: XII and O: XVII appear not to have any counterparts in other grouping schemes.

Since the only other typing scheme that has formally taken into account the existence of subgroups is the Verder–Evans scheme (1961), it is of interest to compare it with the presently proposed rearranged Habs-derived scheme. These schemes, also, are the only two recognizing H-antigens. Table VII shows the number of corresponding O-subgroups within each entity. In most places the new scheme has more subgroup antigens than the Verder–Evans scheme, 17 in all. This is the result of 20 years of maturation and indirectly has benefited from the catalytic effect of the work of many interested workers over the years. Within the Verder–Evans subgroup O: VII, though, a finer subdivision is noted.

6. *Immunoelectrophoretic grouping*

Van Eeden (1967) showed three kinds of immunoelectrophoretic pat-

TABLE VII

Balance of number of O-subgroup antigens in the new antigenic scheme
and the scheme of Verder and Evans (1961)

Arabic–Latin system		Verder and Evans		No. of serogroup antigens more in new scheme
O-group	No. of subgroup antigens	O-group	No. of subgroup antigens	
1	1	IV	1	
2	6	I+X	6	
3	1	VI	1	
4	3			3
6	4	II	1	3
7	4	VIII	1	3
9	2	IX	1	1
10	3			3
11	3	III	2	1
12	1	VII	3	−2
13	3	V	1	2
14	1		1	1
15	1			1
Total no. O-subgroups more in new scheme than in Verder and Evans scheme				16

terns with trichloroacetic acid extracts of *P. aeruginosa*. Using heated saline extracts, supernatants of phenol and water extracts (L_1 fractions), purified lipopolysaccharide, trichloroacetic acid, and sodium hydroxide extracts, Lányi et al. (1975) classified *P. aeruginosa* O-antigens into various immunoelectrophoretic groups and subgroups (Table XVI). They showed that serologically established O-antigens corresponded closely with the immunoelectrophoretic pattern; groups of strains with identical O-antigens or which share major somatic components with one exception, belonged to the same immunoelectrophoretic group (Figs 1–7).

7. *Immunochemistry of O-antigens*

Similarly to other Gram-negative bacteria, cell wall lipopolysaccharide of *P. aeruginosa* is composed of phospholipids and proteins (Ádám et al., 1971; Boivin and Mesrobeanu, 1937; Mlynarcik and Muszyński, 1974). Phenol extracted lipopolysaccharide (LPS) corresponds to the O-antigens (Lányi and Ádám, 1973). The lipopolysaccharides correspond to those of the *Enterobacteriaceae* in that they have side-chain polysaccharides attached

TABLE VIII

Correlation between amino-sugar composition of lipopolysaccharide and serogroup specificity of *Pseudomonas aeruginosa* (Koval and Meadow, 1975)†

Habs serogroup	2-Amino-2-deoxy-galacturonic acid	Quino-vosamine	Fucosamine	Others
1	−	+	+	U5, U6, U7
2	−	−	tr	Y
3	+	−	tr	Y
4	−	+	+	.
5	+/−	−	+	U8/.
6	+	tr	tr	U1, U5, U6, U7, X/.
7	−	−	+	.
8	−	−	+	.
9	−	+	+	.
10	+	+	tr	.
11	−	−	+	.
12	−	+	tr	.
13	tr	+	tr	U5, U6, U7

† − = Not detectable; + = present; tr = trace.
U1, U5, U6, U7, U8, X and Y are unidentified amino compounds.

to a common core polysaccharide (Chester *et al.*, 1972; Drewry *et al.*, 1971, 1972a, b; Fensom and Gray, 1969; Fensom and Meadow, 1970). In 1973, Chester *et al.* reported on the classification of *P. aeruginosa* O-antigens into chemotypes. They found that the lipopolysaccharides of each Habs type strain contained glucose, heptose, rhamnose, 2-keto-3-deoxyoctonic acid and alanine, usually in equivalent amounts. Many strains contained additional sugars and amino-compounds, such as amino-sugars. Koval and Meadow (1975) were able to show that some amino-sugars were, in fact,

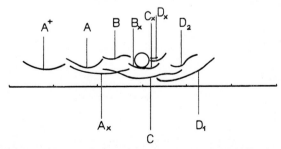

Fig. 1. Schematic diagram of precipitation arcs obtained with *P. aeruginosa* antigens. Anode on left; each division on the scale = 10 mm.

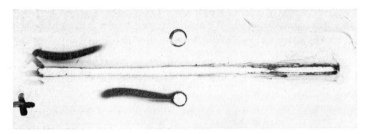

FIG. 2. *P. aeruginosa* precipitation arc A$^+$ (above trench) and fused arcs A and B (below trench).

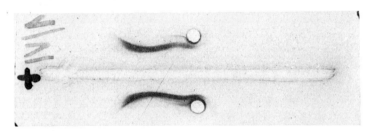

FIG. 3. *P. aeruginosa* precipitation arcs A, B and B$_x$.

FIG. 4. *P. aeruginosa* precipitation arc A$_x$.

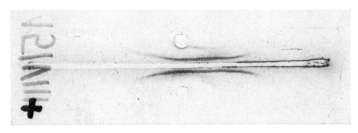

FIG. 5. *P. aeruginosa* precipitation arcs C and D$_x$.

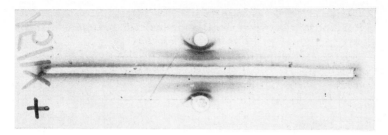

FIG. 6. *P. aeruginosa* precipitation arcs C and C_x (double line).

FIG. 7. *P. aeruginosa* precipitation arcs D_x, D_1 and D_2.

specific for certain antigens (Table VIII). In contrast to *Enterobacteriaceae* O-antigens, characterized by several neutral sugars in their side chains, in the high molecular weight side chain fraction of *P. aeruginosa* only two sugars (mannose and xylose) were present in significant amounts. In addition to these, substances characteristic of *P. aeruginosa* side chains were unidentified amino-compounds, the presence or absence of which yielded a basis for the classification of O-antigens into chemotypes. Two unsaturated amino-sugars, quinovosamine (Suzuki *et al.*, 1970) and fucosamine (Fensom and Gray, 1969; Suzuki, 1969) have also been, demonstrated in *P. aeruginosa*. All pseudomonas lipopolysaccharide complexes, regardless of serogroup, contained the same fatty acids, specially 3-OH 10:0, 2-OH 12:0, 3-OH 12:0, and 12:0 (Chester *et al.*, 1973). In pseudomonas, according to Homma (1968), there is also a proteinous endotoxin, but this is readily separable from the O-antigen.

8. *Cross-reactions between O-antigens of* P. aeruginosa *and other organisms*

Widermann and Flamm (1961) observed that *P. aeruginosa* colonies on plates seeded with faecal specimens frequently agglutinated in *Escherichia coli* O: 26: B6 serum. Horch (1969), studying the serology of *Pseudomonas aureofaciens*, showed that the four antigenic groups of the organism were

5

TABLE IX

Relationship between the O-antigens of *P. aeruginosa* and *Enterobacteriaceae*

P. aeruginosa†	*Salmonella*	*Citrobacter*	*Escherichia* and *Shigella*	*Proteae*
2				*R. rettgeri* 1, 17
(2)	(21, 63)	(32, 35)		*P. hauseri* (20)
(4)	(64)	(16, 22)	*S. flexneri* (1a, 1b, 4aB, 5, Y)	
6			*E. coli* 26	
(6)	(45)	(8a, 8b)	*S. dysenteriae* (7), *S. flexneri* (1b, 4aB, 6), *S. boydii* (4, 6, 9)	
9			*S. boydii* 7	
(9)				*P. hauseri* (39)
(10)				*P. hauseri* (22)
11	59			
(11)	(60)			*P. hauseri* (2)
(12)	(61)	(39)		*M. morganii* (4)
Strain 170017			*S. flexneri* (1b, 4aB), *S. boydii* (5, 9)	
Strain 170018		(6, 4b, 5b)		

† Arabic–Latin system, see Table II.

‡ Bracketed figures indicate unilateral relationship.

serologically unrelated to the *P. aeruginosa* type strains of Habs. Systematic studies on antigenic relationships between *P. aeruginosa* and *Enterobacteriaceae* have been reported by Lányi *et al.* (1972, 1973) and Lányi and Ádám (1973) with only minor unilateral and a few bilateral reactions (Table IX). Høiby (1975d) studied the cross-reactivity of various species by crossed immunoelectrophoresis and obtained the results shown in Table X.

C. Characteristics of H-antigens

1. *Existence of thermolabile antigens*

Sera prepared against organisms that have not been exposed to heat contain antibodies against heat-labile bacterial constituents. Attempts to construct serotyping schemes on that basis have given varying results (Aoki, 1926; Christie, 1948; van den Ende, 1952; Gaby, 1946; Lányi, 1970; Matsui, 1959; Mayr-Harting, 1948; Verder and Evans, 1961).

Christie (1948) and Matsui (1959) have recognized several heat labile

TABLE X

Cross-reaction between *Pseudomonas aeruginosa* and other bacterial species. The numbers signify the cross-reactive antigens in the reference system. The number of strains tested and the group, type or collective numbers are given in parentheses (Høiby, 1975d)

Species	Cross-reactive antigens and percentage of cross-reactivity			
	100%	100%–75%	75%–50%	50%–25%
Staphylococcus aureus (5, from the 4 phage groups)				24
Streptococcus pyogenes (1, group A)				24
Streptococcus faecalis (1)				24
Diplococcus pneumoniae (1, type 19A)				10-24-36
Bacillus cereus var. *mycoides* (1, ATCC 11778)			10	24-36
Corynebacterium spp. (1)				24-36
Clostridium welchii (1)				24
Neisseria meningitidis (1, group A)			36	
Haemophilus influenzae (2, non-capsulate and type b)	14		10-17-24	35
Bordetella pertussis (4, St. 3803-3825-3843-3860)			10-24-36	
Pasteurella multocida (1)			10-24	
Escherichia coli (2, O21 : H27 and rough)	14-36		10-24-35	
Salmonella typhosa (1)	14-17-34-36		10	35
Shigella sonnei (1)	14-36		10-17-24-35	
Citrobacter intermedius (1)	36		10-14-17-24-35	
Enterobacter cloacae (1)	14-36		10-17	24
Klebsiella pneumoniae (2, type 35 and 38)	14-36		10-24-35	
Serratia marcescens (1)	36		10-24-35	17
Proteus mirabilis (1)	14-36		10-17-24-35	
Yersinia enterocolitica (1, type 3)			10-17-24	35
Flavobacterium meningosepticum (1)				10
Bacteroides fragilis spp. *thetaiotaomicron* (1, VPI 5)			36	
Vibro cholerae (1, classical Inaba)	14		10	17-24

antigens, but the two most elaborate systems have been those of Lányi (1970) and Verder and Evans (1961).

Heat labile antigens are found on both flagella and fimbriae (Pitt and Bradley, 1975). It has been observed that an antiserum prepared against formalinized bacteria and exhausted of O-antibody by appropriate absorption might agglutinate two different strains, although the motility could thereby be inhibited only for one of them (Parker, 1976). Pitt and Bradley (1975) have prepared H-antisera with fimbria-less motile variants selected on the basis of their resistance to fimbria-specific phages. By special labelling technique and electron microscopy, Bradley (1973) has shown that anti-flagellar antibodies adsorb only to flagella. The anti-fimbrial titres appear to be low compared to those against the flagella. Thus, agglutination with suitably diluted antisera will provide agglutination on the basis of flagellar antigens, i.e. true H-antigens, only. The system of heat labile antigens described by Lányi (1970) is accordingly referred to as a flagellar, H-typing system in the following.

2. *Immunogenicity of H-antigens*

Living and formalinized cultures of motile *P. aeruginosa* strains produce H-agglutinins in high titres. Immunogenicity remains unaffected after heating at 60°C for 1 hour and after exposure to saturated sodium chloride, but is lost after alcohol and acid treatment, or heating above 75°C (Lányi, 1976) (Table XI). The maximum H-antibody titre is reached on the 20th day of immunization. In contrast to the sharp fall of O-antibody level, usually during the 3rd week after the end of immunization, the H-titre shows but a slight decrease even 30 days after immunization (Pitt and Bradley, 1975).

3. *Antibody-binding capacity*

As seen in Table XI, in resistance to heat and chemical agents, the immunogenicity and antibody-binding capacity of *P. aeruginosa* H-antigens are similar (Lányi, 1970).

4. *Agglutinability*

Living or formalinized suspensions of motile cultures agglutinate readily in homologous H-serum from which O-agglutinins have been removed. Agglutination is also good in unabsorbed OH-serum prepared with a strain of identical H-antigen, but an O-antigen which differs from the culture under investigation (Kleinmaier *et al.*, 1958; Kleinmaier *et al.*, 1959; Lányi, 1970; Verder and Evans, 1961). Cells reacting with H-antibodies are held apart by entangled flagella resulting in a fluffy type of agglutination which is easily dispersed upon shaking. In the presence of O-antibodies, especially with non-formalinized cultures, the flagellar reaction is masked by a high titred and rapidly proceeding O-agglutination. Heating at 60°C to abolish the thermolabile antigens or suspending in saturated sodium chloride, due to interference, renders the bacteria weakly agglutinable in H-sera. Cultures heated to a minimum of 70°C or treated with either alcohol or acid lose their H-agglutinability (Lányi, 1970; Pitt and Bradley, 1975) (Table XI).

TABLE XI

Characteristics of the H-antigens of *P. aeruginosa*

Antigen	Agglutin- ability	Immuno- genicity	Agglutinin- binding capacity
Living	+ + + +	+ + + +	+ + + +
60°C 1 h	+	+ + + +	+ + + +
70°C or above 1 h	−	−	−
Saturated NaCl	+	+ + + +	+ + + +
Ethanol, 50%	−	+	+ +
HCl, N	−	−	−
Formaldehyde, 0·5%	+ + + +	+ + + +	+ + +

5. *Specific immobilization*

The motility of *P. aeruginosa* cells is inhibited by the addition of specific H-serum (Lányi, 1970; Pitt and Bradley, 1975). The effect of H-serum is demonstrable both under the microscope and in semisolid agar in which migration is inhibited (see Section V, B).

6. *Classification by H-antigens*

Verder and Evans (1961) were the first to subdivide *P. aeruginosa* serogroups into serotypes by thermolabile antigens. They demonstrated 10 factors in different combinations forming complex antigens; only one of the serotypes contained a single thermolabile factor. On the basis of different combinations of O- and H-antigens, they distinguished 29 serotypes.

Lányi (1970) brought evidence that serologically reactive thermolabile antigens in formalinized motile cultures are referable to the flagella. He elaborated another scheme, distinguishing two serologically unrelated main H-antigen complexes, H: 1 and H: 2. The former is subdivisible into H: 1a (which is the main factor present in all H: 1 strains) and into

H: 1b (which is a minor partial antigen present only in a few strains).
The H: 2 complex is divisible into 6 different combinations of well-defined
partial antigens, H: 2a, 2b, 2c, 2d, 2e and 2f. Based on the combination
of 27 O- and the 8 H-antigens, Lányi (1970) divided his strains into 53
serotypes. The antigenic scheme showing the structure of H-antigens and
type strains for the serotypes is presented in Table XII.

7. H-antigen variation

The occurrence of non-flagellated strains of *P. aeruginosa* is extremely
rare. Out of 541 isolates, Lányi (1970) found only one non-flagellated

TABLE XII

Complete antigenic scheme of *Pseudomonas aeruginosa*

Group	O-antigen	H-antigen	Type strain
1	1	1	171350
		2a, 2b	Habs 1
		2a, 2c	171365
2	2a, 2b	1	170003[1]
	(2a), 2c†	1	Habs 2
	2a, 2d	1	170005[2]
		2a, 2b, 2f	171175
	2a, 2d, 2e	1	170006
		2a, 2c	171188
	(2a), 2d, 2f	1	170007[3]
		2a, 2b, 2f	171192
3	3	1	Habs 3
		2a, 2b	171059
		2a, 2c	171031
4	4a, 4b	1	Habs 4
		2a, 2c	171492
		2a, 2c, 2f	170021
	4a, 4c	2a, 2c	170040
6	6a	2a‡	Habs 6
	6a, 6b	2a, 2b	170008
	6a, 6c	—	170009
		1	171230
		2a, 2b, 2f	171252
		2a, 2c	171269
		2a, 2c, 2f	171248
	6a, 6d	2a, 2b, 2f	170010[4]
		2a, 2c, 2f	171272

TABLE XII (*continued*)

Group	O-antigen	H-antigen	Type strain
7	7a, 7b, 7c	1	170011[5]
		2a, 2d	171304
	7a, 7b, 7d	1	171312
		2a, 2d	170012[6]
	7a, 7d	1	170013
		2a, 2c	171348
		2a, 2d	171338
9	9a	1	170019[7]
		2a, 2b, 2f	171464
		2a, 2c	171455
	9a, 9b	1	171478
		2a, 2c	170020
10	10a, 10b	1	Habs 10
	10a, 10c	2a, 2b	170002
		2a, 2c	171074
11	11a, 11b	1	Habs 11
		2a, 2c	170015
		2a, 2d	171420
	11a, 11c	1	171447
		2a, 2b	171445
		2a, 2c	170016
12	12	1	Habs 12
13	13a, 13b	2a‡	Sandvik II
	13a, 13c	2a‡	Verder & Evans 1M-1 (group V)
14	14	2a, 2d	Meitert X
15	15	1	170022
		2a, 2c	171518

† Figures in brackets indicate antigens that are frequently weakly developed.
‡ Further heat labile antigens present.
Strains to be examined for H-antigens and for equivalence to define subgroup antigens versus Lányi's strains:
[1] Homma YS-74 *vs.* 170003.
[2] Véron 2(b) and Habs 5 *vs.* 170005.
[3] Véron 5(d) *vs.* 170007.
[4] Wahba 14 *vs.* 170010.
[5] Habs 7 *vs.* 170011.
[6] Habs 8 *vs.* 170012.
[7] O-group 10 strains cross-react with Habs 9 but not with 170019; thus the type strain for the subgroup should be 170019.

strain and even this had probably lost its motility in the course of maintenance in the laboratory. Artificial induction of a non-flagellated mutant was described by Bradley (1973).

Phase variation, that is, the presence of two serologically different H-antigens in the same strain, a characteristic feature of most *Salmonella* serotypes, has not been demonstrated in *P. aeruginosa*. Attempts to induce suppressed H-antigen phases by using semisolid phase reversal medium with homologous H-antiserum, have been unsuccessful (Lányi, 1970).

D. Other antigenic factors

1. *R-antigens*

Although *P. aeruginosa* produces several morphological types of colonies, rough forms are rarely encountered among freshly isolated strains. Characteristic, small, rough colonies may appear during serial passage of the culture in broth or may be induced by ultra-violet-irradiation or phage action. These forms are unstable in suspensions and have so far not been analysed by serological methods.

Another type of R-variant has a normal smooth colonial form, is stable in living suspensions, but tends to produce aggregates when heated at 120°C. Such strains were described by Lányi (1966/67) as representatives of his antigenic groups O: 8 and O: 9 (strains 170017 and 170018, respectively). Later, the antigens of these cultures have been shown to differ in many respects from other *P. aeruginosa* O-antigens: (i) they are weakly immunogenic, (ii) extracts from these cultures give low titres in passive haemagglutination, (iii) extracts fail to precipitate readily, and (iv) they show an unusual immunoelectrophoretic pattern (Ádám *et al.*, 1971; Lányi and Ádám, 1973; Lányi *et al.*, 1975).

Smooth forms of *P. aeruginosa* contain basal somatic factors ("R-antigens") which are serologically distinct from the O-antigens. When heated to 130°C, *P. aeruginosa* cultures of different O-groups usually show cross-agglutination which can be absorbed out by practically any heterologous cultures. Antibodies against the common antigens fail to agglutinate living strains (Lányi, 1966/67) and do not precipitate with lipopolysaccharide extracts, whereas erythrocytes coated with *P. aeruginosa* lipopolysaccharides often show cross-reactions not attributable to O-antigen relationships (Ádám *et al.*, 1971; Jones and Roe, 1975).

The fact that *P. aeruginosa* contains a large number of different antigenic factors has been shown by Høiby (1975a, b). He used a sonicated polyvalent *P. aeruginosa* antigen as reference system derived from four strains of the Habs serogroups O: 3, 5a, 6, 11, produced serum against it, and detected no less than 55 different precipitates by crossed-immunoelectrophoresis. Fifty-one of the 55 antigen specificities were present in all strains representing the 13 antigenic groups of Habs (1957) and O: II of Sandvik (1960a, b).

2. *Slime layer*

Slime production can be induced in non-mucoid strains of *P. aeruginosa* by culturing them in the presence of glucuronate (Haynes, 1951) or desoxycholate (Lányi, 1968) or by exposing suspensions to the effect of alcohol, saturated sodium chloride, or moderate heat (see Section IV.B.3 of this Chapter).

Liu *et al.* (1961) prepared a purified slime from strains exhibiting the usual smooth colony forms and showed that the anti-slime serum agglutinated the cells and protected animals against infection. The protective capacity was verified by Dimitracopoulos *et al.* (1974). Alms and Bass (1967a, b) have found evidence that protection may be elicited by a highly active carbohydrate moiety of the ethanol-precipitable layer. The serological heterogeneity of, and the specificity of protection by, the slime polysaccharides have been shown by Young *et al.* (1969) and by Mates and Zand (1974). The relationship between the slime layer and the O-antigens has not yet been elucidated; according to Sensakovic and Bartell (1974) the slime polysaccharides differ in sedimentation rate and serological properties from lipopolysaccharide extracted by the phenol water method.

Using the acetone-alcohol technique (cf. Section V.E), two distinct fractions may be separated from mucoid strains of *P. aeruginosa*. Precipitate fraction A is a stringy material which contains 17–27% uronic acid. Precipitate fraction B is floccular, contains O-antigen and consists of less than 2·5% uronic acid (Martin, 1973).

3. *Mucoid substance*

Strains of *P. aeruginosa* with mucoid colonies occur frequently in chronic disease of the respiratory tract, especially in cystic fibrosis, as derivatives of non-mucoid organisms colonizing the patient after admission to hospital. Their appearance is probably associated with the specific immune response of the host (Dogget and Harrison, 1972; Høiby, 1974a, b). Mucoid colonies may appear around areas of phage lysis (Martin, 1973). Upon maintenance in the laboratory, mucoid strains tend to split off non-mucoid colonies (e.g. Bergan and Høiby, 1975). The non-mucoid colonies are real dissociants from the mucoid variants since it has been demonstrated that both the mucoid parent strains and their non-mucoid derivatives are identical in serogroup, phage type, and pyocine type (Bergan and Høiby, 1975).

To prevent complete reversion to the non-mucoid state, successive streakings with intervals of only a few days and single colony isolation are necessary.

The behaviour of live mucoid strains of *P. aeruginosa* differ from mucoid strains of *Klebsiella* or *Escherichia* in several respects. Serological comparisons of the antigenic specificity of capsular material and O-antigens have not been carried out. From our knowledge of the chemical structure of the mucoid substance as compared to the lipopolysaccharide in the O-antigen, it is not likely that the two will show antigenic identity. Linker and Jones (1966) have isolated mucoid material from isolates derived from the air passages of patients with cystic fibrosis. Thus mucoid material resembles alginic acid (found only in seaweed) and, like that, contains only D-mannuronic and L-glucuronic acid. The pseudomonas polysaccharide contains O-acetyl groups, which have not been identified in alginate. The LPS composition is mentioned in Section IV.B.7.

Of practical significance, though, is the fact that mucoid strains of *P. aeruginosa* agglutinate in O-sera. In some instances, the mucoid substance seems to inhibit O-agglutination (Bergan and Høiby, 1975) and in some cases there seems to be inagglutinability with an occasional isolate from a patient when other serial isolates from the same patient have the same pyocine type and phage type as the non-agglutinated culture. Such a pattern is explainable on the basis of O-antigen inhibition and the experience refers to agglutination with live cells. After boiling, there is no difference between the mucoid and the non-mucoid variant of the same epidemiological type (Lányi, 1966/67). In cases where the cells do agglutinate, the O-reaction is as accurate for mucoid strains as for their non-mucoid counterparts.

4. Fimbriae

In *P. aeruginosa*, two types of fimbriae (pili) have been shown: (i) thin, polar, filamentous appendages constituting one class of heat-labile antigens of the organism (Bradley, 1966; Bradley and Pitt, 1975), and (ii) thicker, non-polar pili with drug resistance plasmids (Bradley, 1974).

The fimbrial antigenicity is due to polymerized pilus protein (pilin), but native antigen is only present in living cells. Consequently, for immunization, living suspensions must be employed. The binding of antibodies to the fimbriae can be detected by electron microscopy (Lawn, 1967). Fimbrial antigen is also demonstrable by ordinary agglutination with living organisms. The fimbrial antigen of *P. aeruginosa* is heat labile, but little is known about the tolerance of pilous antigens to chemical agents. Under certain conditions, such as after formaldehyde treatment or bacteriophage action, the filaments apparently (Pitt and Bradley, 1975) withdraw into the cell, the pilin becoming depolymerized. Some mutants of *P. aeruginosa* lack the ability to retract their fimbriae and retraction in other cultures can be inhibited by osmium-tetroxide fixation (Bradley, 1972a, b; Bradley and Pitt, 1975).

To determine fimbrial antigens, the immune sera should be absorbed with homologous O- and H-antigens. O-agglutinins are removable with boiled cultures, whereas H-agglutinins are absorbed with formalinized suspensions of flagellated strains. With non-fimbriated flagellated mutants one may differentiate between fimbrial and flagellar heat-labile antigens. Non-fimbriated strains can be selected by their resistance to fimbria-specific phages (Bradley and Pitt, 1974).

Fimbrial antigens are serologically heterogeneous (Bradley and Pitt, 1975), such that their determination may be useful for epidemiological tracing.

5. *Enzyme antigens*

Enzyme antigenicity generally has taxonomic significance, since their structure reflects genetic nucleotide sequences. Proteins, in addition, are good immunogens. A number of enzyme activities could be studied, but it is simplest to focus attention on extracellularly liberated products that can easily be separated from cellular structures. Examples of such enzymes are alkaline phosphatase, elastase, phosphatase, phospholipase (lecithinase C), or protease, which have been subject to some studies. Because the enzymes may be labile, substrates expensive, or assay complicated, all possible enzymes have not been studied thus far.

V. METHODS OF EXAMINING *P. AERUGINOSA* ANTIGENS

A. Determination of O-antigens

1. *Preparation of O-antisera*

(a) *General comments*. The immunization must yield specific sera with high titres and limited cross-reactions. A short course of immunization is preferable, since IgM immunoglobulins are most efficient in agglutinating bacteria (Homma *et al.*, 1971). The IgG titre is low. Addition of anti-antibody to the system implements a doubling of the titre caused by IgM and that due to IgG by a factor of eight (e.g. from 1/40 to 1/320) (Homma *et al.*, 1971). This shows that IgG is bound to the cells, but that their ability to bring two adjoining cells together is less than that of IgM. This is a parallel to the situation in blood typing where IgM is responsible for the ordinary agglutination reactions and IgG functions as an incomplete antibody which is detected only with the Coombs technique. The explanation is that the negative charge of the erythrocyte surfaces cause the cells to be pulled away from each other. The gap between two cells is never reduced sufficiently so that the width between the two antigen binding sites on the same IgG immunoglobulin molecule can possibly reach the antigens of two neighbouring cells simultaneously. IgM, however, which has elements of five immunoglobulin basic structures bound together with a J-piece (J=joining) has a larger distance between binding sites such that the same antibody molecule is able to cover the minimum distance between two blood cells and bind them together. The explanation for the observations in bacterial somatic agglutination is undoubtedly the same, i.e. a consequence of mutual repulsion by adjoining bacteria with the same net charge.

The only published systematic studies on immunization with pseudomonas antigen has been carried out by Mikkelsen (1968, 1970). The methods described below are based on procedures used by Verder and Evans (1961), Lányi (1966/67) and Mikkelsen (1968, 1970).

(b) *Preparation of antigens.* Colonies showing characteristic, specific O-agglutination are selected and saline suspensions tested for smoothness and lack of spontaneous clumping after treating at 100°C for $2\frac{1}{2}$ h. To produce sufficient quantities of antigen, one may use either of two alternatives:

(i) Nutrient agar cultures grown at 37°C for 18–20 h (Lányi, 1966/67), or

(ii) Cultures in aerated infusion broth at 37°C for 18 h (Mikkelsen, 1968, 1970).

This is followed by boiling for $2\frac{1}{2}$ h and subsequently two washings in physiological saline (Mikkelsen, 1968, 1970). Lányi (1966/67) prefers to heat the cell suspension at 75–100°C for 1–2 h, and wash once in saline.

A suspension of 5×10^{10} cells per ml is suitable for immunization (Mikkelsen, 1968, 1970).

(c) *Immunization and preservation of sera.* Rabbits are injected at 4-day intervals with graded intravenous doses of 0·25, 0·5, 1·0, 1·5 and 2·0 ml of the antigen suspension described above. The optimal time for bleeding is 3–4 days after the last injection. Then a titre against the homologous antigen strain will usually be 1/800 or more (Mikkelsen, 1970). Nine volumes of the serum are mixed with one volume of 5% aqueous phenol solution. This acts as a preservative. The sera may alternatively be preserved with merthiolate (1 in 10,000 w/v), or by the addition of an equal volume of glycerol. Mikkelsen (1970) recommended that sera from 2–7 rabbits immunized with the same antigen be pooled. However, we would like to emphasize that this procedure applies to the production of sera for routine typing only. For work which is aimed at studies of the antigenic mosaic, of the antigens, e.g. when comparing typing schemes or the possibility that one has isolated a novel O-subgroup, it is imperative that only sera from individual animals, i.e. non-pooled sera, be used.

(d) *Absorption of sera.* The bacteria to be used as antigen are suspended in saline, steamed at 100°C for 1–2½ h, and centrifuged. During the absorption, the deposit is resuspended in diluted serum. For tube agglutination, the serum to be absorbed should be diluted 1:5 to 1:10, for slide agglutination serum should be 3 to 4 times more concentrated than the working dilution of unabsorbed sera. The mixture of serum and bacteria is incubated first for 2 h at 37°C and then overnight at 4°C. After centrifugation, the supernatant serum is preserved with phenol or merthiolate. The bacteria remaining in the deposit may be used for a repeated absorption after resuspension, heating at 100°C for 1 h, centrifugation and mixture with a fresh aliquot of unabsorbed serum. Suitable type strains for immunization and absorption of sera are listed in Table XIII.

(e) *Determination of the working dilution.* Routine serogrouping should be performed with sera adjusted to a dilution in which the homologous culture gives a distinct slide agglutination reaction within 1 to 4 seconds (+ + + + reaction). Major antigenic relationships indicated in the antigenic scheme are demonstrable as + + to + + + reactions, whereas agglutinations due to minor relationships are weak or absent (± or −).

(f) *Preparation of pooled O-sera.* In preparing pooled sera, minor relationships should also be considered, as the combined effect of different cross-reacting antibodies may lead to disturbing and unwanted reactions. For this reason, it is often unnecessary or even disadvantageous to add the single serum components to the pooled serum at amounts calculated on the basis of their working dilutions.

The ingredients of pooled O-sera are given in Table XIV, numbers and types of O-sera required are given in Table XV.

2. O-agglutination

These methods have been compiled on the basis of observations of several authors referred to in Section IV.B.3 of this Chapter.

(a) *Tube method.* Bacterial suspensions heated at 100°C for 2½ h give moderate agglutination titres. Suspensions autoclaved at 120°C for 1–2 h or bacteria steamed in saline for 2½ h, then centrifuged, homogenized in glycerol, heated at 130°C for 1 hour and resuspended in phenolized saline (9·5 g phenol in 1000 ml saline) are more reactive, i.e.

render higher titres. The suspension should be adjusted to contain approximately 5×10^9 bacteria per ml. To 0·5 ml amounts of twofold serial dilutions of the serum, 0·05 ml of bacterial suspension is added before the

TABLE XIII
Determination of the O-antigens of *P. aeruginosa*

O-antigen	Agglutination in	No. of Roux flasks†
1	Unabsorbed serum Habs 1	—
2a	Unabsorbed serum 170003 + unabsorbed serum 170005	—
2b	Serum 170003 absorbed by Habs 5	15
2c	Serum Habs 2 absorbed by 170006 + Habs 5	20 + 10
2d	Serum Habs 5 absorbed by 170003	30
2e	Serum 170006 absorbed by Habs 2 + Habs 5	20 + 25
2f	Serum 170007 absorbed by Habs 5	20
3	Unabsorbed serum Habs 3	—
4a	Unabsorbed serum Habs 4 + unabsorbed serum 170040	—
4b	Serum Habs 4 absorbed by 170040	20
4c	Serum 170040 absorbed by Habs 4	20
6a	Unabsorbed serum 170008 + unabsorbed serum 170009	—
6b	Serum 170008 absorbed by 170009	20
6c	Serum 170009 absorbed by 170008	30
6d	Serum 170010 absorbed by 170009 + Habs 6	20 + 10
7a	Unabsorbed serum 170011 + unabsorbed serum 170013	—
7b	Serum Habs 8 absorbed by 170013	30
7c	Serum 170011 absorbed by Habs 8	30
7d	Serum 170013 absorbed by 170011	30
9a	Unabsorbed serum 170019	—
9b	Serum 170020 absorbed by 170019	20
10a	Unabsorbed serum Habs 10 + unabsorbed serum 170002	—
10b	Serum Habs 10 absorbed by 170002	20
10c	Serum 170002 absorbed by Habs 10	20
11a	Unabsorbed serum Habs 11 + unabsorbed serum 170016	—
11b	Serum Habs 11 absorbed by 170016	30
11c	Serum 170016 absorbed by Habs 11	30
12	Unabsorbed serum Habs 12	—
13a	Unabsorbed serum Sandvik II + unabsorbed serum 1M-1	—
13b	Serum Sandvik II absorbed by 1M-1	20
13c	Serum 1m-1 absorbed by Sandvik II	20
14	Unabsorbed serum Meitert X	—
15	Unabsorbed serum 170022	—

† Amount of bacteria needed for the absorbtion of 10 ml diluted serum. Roux flasks are made with 150 ml nutrient agar (surface of each plate, approximately 220 cm²).

tubes are incubated in a water bath at 50°C for 20 h and read for the agglutination titre.

(b) *Slide method.* For routine serological grouping of *P. aeruginosa*, slide agglutination is the method of choice. It is performed by the usual technique using 18–20 h blood agar cultures and the working dilutions of O-sera. For subgroup determination, it is advisable to test the strain under investigation first in pooled O-sera, then in unabsorbed O-sera and, finally, in absorbed sera (Tables XIII, XIV).

3. Precipitation

(a) *Preparation of O-antigen extracts*

(i) *Heat extracts* (Lányi *et al.*, 1975). Approximately 1·5 g of bacteria

TABLE XIV
Ingredients of *P. aeruginosa* pooled sera

| Designation | Ingredients, O-sera prepared with | |
	Antigen†	Type strain
I	O: 3	Habs 3
	O: 4	Habs 4
	O: 6a, 6b	Lányi 170008
	O: 6a, 6c	Lányi 170009
	O: 6a, 6d	Lányi 170010
	O: 9a	Lányi 170019
	O: 9a, 9b	Lányi 170020
	O: 14	Meitert X
II	O: 11a, 11b	Habs 11
	O: 12	Habs 12
	O: 13a, 13b	Sandvik II
	O: 13a, 13c	Verder & Evans 1M-1
	O: 15	Lányi 170022
III	O: 2a, 2b	Lányi 170003
	O: (2a), 2c	Habs 2
	O: 2a, 2d, 2e	Lányi 170006
	O: (2a), 2d, 2f	Lányi 170007
IV	O: 1	Habs 1
	O: 7a, 7b, 7d	Habs 8
	O: 7a, 7d	Lányi 170013
	O: 10a, 10c	Lányi 170002

† Proposed scheme, see Tables IV and XII.

TABLE XV

Minimum number of sera for O-grouping of *Pseudomonas aeruginosa*

O-group	Habs strain or other cont. equivalent	Equivalent Lányi antigen (1966/67)
1	1	6
2a†		3a
2b	16	3b
2c	2	3c
2d	5	3d
2e		3e
2f		3f
3	3	1
4a†	4	
4b		11
4c		
6a†	6	4a
6b		4b
6c		4c
6d		4d
7a†		5a
7b		5b
7c	7	5c
7d	8	5d
9a†	9	10a
9b		10b
10a†		
10b	10	
10c		2
11a†		7a
11b	11	7b
11c		7c
12	12	13
13a†		
13b	13 (Sandvik O: II)	
13c	14 (Verder and Evans 1M-1)	
14	17 (Meitert O: X)	
15	15 (Lányi O: 12)	12

† Group antigens, i.e. antigens common to group.

(moist weight) are suspended in 50 ml physiological saline, heated at 100°C for $2\frac{1}{2}$ h and centifuged before the supernatant is pipetted off.

(ii) *Trichloroacetic acid extract* (Lányi et al., 1975). Ten grams of moist bacteria are suspended in 50 ml of ice-cold trichloroacetic acid (10% w/v), refrigerated at 4–6°C for 24–48 h, centrifuged, dialysed, concentrated by evaporation, freeze-dried and dissolved in saline (2 mg/ml).

(iii) *Purified lipopolysaccharide extract* (Westphal and Jann, 1965). Twenty grams of freeze-dried bacteria are suspended in 350 ml water at 65–68°C. Then an equal amount of 90% phenol, preheated to 65–80°C, is added during vigorous stirring. After 10–15 min, heating at 65–68°C, the mixture is cooled to 10°C and centrifuged at 3,000 rpm for 30–40 min. The water phase is sucked off and the extraction of the remainder repeated with 350 ml water. The water extracts are pooled, dialysed against water for 3–4 days, concentrated by evaporation at 35–40°C, and centrifuged. The supernatant is freeze-dried. To remove ribonucleic acid, the crude extract is dissolved in water to give a 3% solution, centrifuged three times at 105,000 g for 3 h each, freeze dried, and redissolved in water or saline (5 mg/ml). The use of ribonuclease will also remove RNA, leaving solubilized nucleotides.

(iv) L_1 *fraction.* The supernatant of ultracentrifuged phenol–water extracts are freeze dried and redissolved in water or saline (5 mg/ml).

(v) *Alkali extracts* (Lányi et al., 1975). Approximately 1·5 g of washed bacteria (moist weight) are suspended in 50 ml of 0·5 M sodium hydroxide. Half of the suspension is heated at 80°C for 1 h, the other half at 80°C for 24 h. The extracts are neutralized with hydrochloric acid or dialysed. All extracts may be preserved with merthiolate (1:10,000 w/v).

(b) *Double agar gel diffusion* (Lányi and Ádám, 1973). *Agar gel.* The following composition of gel for immunodiffusion is recommended: Agar Noble (Difco), 8·5 g; K_2HPO_4, 9·2 g; KH_2PO_4, 1·8 g; NaCl, 6·0 g; merthiolate, 0·1 g; water, 1000 ml; 100°C 1 h. Alternatively Agar No. 1 (Oxoid) may be used.

Procedure. Aliquots of 3·5 ml melted agar are poured on to clean glass slides (25 × 75 mm), holes of 3 mm diameter made by means of a cutter to make a pattern of six peripheral wells arranged hexagonally around a central well. The distance between the centres of each should be 9 mm. Into the central well, 10 μl of undiluted immune serum, and into the peripheral wells 10 μl of antigen extracts are pipetted. The slides are incubated in moist chambers at 37°C for 2 days. Positive reactions are observed as one or more precipitation lines between the antigen and antiserum wells.

(c) *Immunoelectrophoresis* (Lányi *et al.*, 1975). *Agar gel.* Agar Noble (Difco), 9 g; K_2HPO_4, 2·61 g; KH_2PO_4, 2·04 g; merthiolate, 0·1 g; water, 1000 ml. Alternatively, Agar No. 1 (Oxoid) may be used.

Procedure. Each glass slide (25 × 75 mm) is covered with 3·5 ml agar gel. Ten microlitre amounts of the extracts are pipetted into wells which are 3 mm in diameter. Electrophoresis may proceed with potassium phosphate buffer (0·03 M, pH 6·9) at 3–4 mA per slide for 2 h. Then, a median trench is cut parallel to the direction of the current and filled with 50 μl of undiluted antiserum. After incubation in moist chambers at 37°C for 24 h, precipitation lines appear as illustrated, for example, by Lányi *et al.* (1975), Figs. 1–7. On the basis of the pattern of the precipitation lines, the cultures may be classified into distinct immunoelectrophoretic groups according to the scheme outlined in Table XVI.

(d) *Passive haemagglutination.*

(i) *General.* High-titred, group-specific reactions are obtained when erythrocytes sensitized with purified O-antigens are mixed with specific immune sera. The method is suitable for the detection of *P. aeruginosa* antibodies in human and animal sera (Ádám *et al.*, 1971; Jones and Roe, 1975). The reactions of lipopolysaccharide coated erythrocytes parallel O-agglutination with bacterial cells. The passive haemagglutination (HA) reaction is sensitive and detects a few additional minor cross-reactions that are not revealed by bacterial O-agglutination (cf. Table II in Ádám *et al.*, 1971, and Tables V and VIIa in Lányi, 1966/67), but the converse is also true for cell agglutination and HA.

(ii) *Extracts* are prepared as described for precipitating antigens (*vide supra*).

(iii) *Coating of erythrocytes.* Sheep erythrocytes are washed three times in saline or in HB (haemagglutination buffer: NaCl, 9·0 g; Na_2HPO_4, 13·7 g; $NaH_2PO_4 \cdot 2H_2O$, 2.4 g in 1000 ml of water, pH 7·2). The washed erythrocytes are resuspended in 9 volumes of purified lipopolysaccharide dissolved in saline or HB (20 μg/ml) and heated previously at 100°C for 1 h. The mixture is incubated at 37°C for 2 h, the erythrocytes are washed three times and resuspended in 100 volumes of saline or HB. If tanned erythrocytes are used to prepare the antigen, good adsorption of antigen is achieved and the antigen-coated cells keep longer.

(iv) *Procedure.* Serial dilutions of the sera are made in tubes and transferred in 0·025 ml amounts to wells in plastic trays. Subsequently, an equal volume of a 1% suspension of sensitized erythrocytes is added. (The sera may be diluted in the plastic trays by the spiral loop or diluter method.) The plates are then incubated at 37°C for 1 hour before reading. A smooth

TABLE XVI

Immunoelectrophoretic characteristics of *P. aeruginosa* antigens

Immuno-electrophoretic group	Precipitation arcs, in tests with homologous antiserum, given by						O-antigens†
	Saline extract	L_1 fraction	LPS fraction	TCA extract	Alkali extract NaOH 1 h	Alkali extract NaOH 24 h	
Ia	A, B	A, B	A, B, C_x	A, B, C_x	A^+	—	O: 2a, 2b; O: 2a, 2c; O: 2a, 2d; O: 2a, 2d, 2e; O: 2a, 2d, 2f; O: 10a, 10b; O: 10a, 10c
Ib	A, B	A, B	A, B, C_x	A, B, C_x	A	—	O: 3; O: 1
Ic	A, B	A, B	A, B, C_x	A, B, C_x	—	—	O: 6a, 6c; O: 7a, 7b, 7c; O: 7a, 7b, 7d; O: 7a, 7d; O: 9a; O: 9a, 9b
II	B_x, C_1, C_2	C_1, C_2	C_1, C_2, C_x	C_1, C_2, C_x	—	—	O: 6a, 6b; O: 6a, 6d
IIIa	C_1, C_2, D_x	C_1, C_2	C_1, C_2, C_x	C_1, C_2, C_x	C	C	O: 15
IIIb	C_1, C_2, D_x	—	C_x	C_1, C_2, C_x	A	A	O: 12
IV	D_1, D_2, D_x	—	C_x	D_1, D_2, C_x	D	D	O: 4; O: 11a, 11b; O: 11a, 11c
V	A_x	—	A_x, C_x	—	—	—	Strains 170017, 170018

† Arabic–Latin system, see Tables III and IV.

button of erythrocytes in the centre of the bottom of a microtube indicates a negative reaction, whereas an evenly spread out deposit which upon careful agitation resuspends into agglutinated erythrocytes is recorded as a positive reaction.

(e) *Immunofluorescence.*

(i) *General.* Detection of pseudomonas in mixture with other species such as in pus, sputum or faeces, or in tissue maybe desirable. Generally, the fluorescent antibody (FA) technique is suitable for such situations. It has been used successfully for many species and under suitable circumstances enables a rapid and easy identification of specific antigens. The indirect FA-technique has been explored by Nishimura *et al.* (1973), who used O-sera produced against the type strains of the scheme published by Homma *et al.* (1971).

(ii) *Sera.* Ordinary O-grouping sera prepared according to Section V.A.1 of this Chapter are suitable for detection of specific somatic antigens of *P. aeruginosa.* These may be used singly but more conveniently in order to save time pooled sera are used, e.g. the pools defined in Table XIV of this Chapter (Section V.2). To detect rabbit antibody which has been bound to the bacterial cells, commercial fluorescent antibody, FITC-labelled anti-rabbit immune serum (from, e.g., BBL, Behringwerke, Difco, or Wellcome) is suitable. Nishimura *et al.* (1973) used the BBL variety. This must be absorbed with an emulsion or homogenate of normal human or animal kidney and liver if used to detect pseudomonas in tissues. (Absorption to be done with normal tissue of the same species as the tissue to be examined.)

(iii) *Tissue sections or smears.* Tissues may be fixed in 95% ethanol or 10% formaldehyde, followed by embedding in paraffin wax in the conventional manner for preparation of tissue sections. Sections of suitable thickness are 4–5 μm. Smears are made in the usual manner, not too thin. Smears must be fixed by drawing through a flame 3–4 times.

(iv) *Antibody reaction.* To treat the section or smear with serum a layer of specific antiserum is placed on top of the material. The slides are incubated in moist chambers, e.g. made *ad hoc* from large Petri-dishes, at room temperature for 1 h. Subsequently, the preparations are washed thoroughly with phosphate buffer. After this stage, only specific immunoglobulins which have reacted with cellular components remain.

(v) *Anti-antibody* bound to the bacterial cells is detected by subsequently flooding the preparations with antibodies against the O-specific immunoglobulins. Since rabbit O-antisera are usual, fluorescent anti-rabbit sera are normally suitable. The preparations are left in moist chambers for a further 1 h, when non-bound immunoglobulins are again washed off with phosphate buffer.

(vi) *Microscopy.* Nishimura *et al.* (1973) used a drop of buffered glycerol saline as mounting medium for study under the UV-microscope. Specific coloration is found corresponding to the antigenically homologous bacterial cell walls. Nishimura *et al.* (1973) could not detect any FA-cross-reactivity between *P. aeruginosa* and *Escherichia coli, Proteus* sp., or *Staphylococcus aureus.*

(vii) *Evaluation.* As is usual with the FA procedure, meticulous controls are necessary to differentiate between background staining and specific antigen–antibody reactions.

It is likely that the FA procedure for pseudomonas will have only limited use, since once a pure culture is obtained agglutination is easy to set up and easy to read. The greatest asset of the method is the possibility of rapid diagnosis on primary material. Since cross-reactions are found between pseudomonas and other species by other methods like agglutination, immunoelectrophoresis and cross-immunoelectrophoresis (*vide* Section V.A.), identification by FA-technique is only tentative in nature. Identification of *P. aeruginosa* by subsequent isolation from pathological material therefore, is mandatory whenever possible to verify the FA procedure diagnosis.

(viii) *Other antigens in immunofluorescence.* In addition to antibodies against the somatic antigens, the possibility of using immunoglobulins directed against a protein moiety, called OEP, produced by pseudomonas has been investigated (Homma, 1975).

(f) *Commercial sources of O-sera.* Commercial serogrouping antisera are produced according to the scheme of Habs (1957) modified by Véron (1961) and supplemented by O: 13 (Sandvik O: II) by API Products Ltd in collaboration with the Pasteur Institute, Paris, France (Al-Dujaili and Harris, 1974). Parke Davis and Co., Detroit, Michigan, USA, has a limited range of sera for 7 serogroups (Young and Moody, 1974) according to the scheme of Fischer *et al.* (1969) based on the protective effect of O antigens. In Japan, the Toshiba Kagaku Kogyo Co. Ltd, Niigata, and the Institute of Medical Science, University of Tokyo, Tokyo, Japan (Homma, 1974) produce sera according to the scheme of Homma (1974). Difco, Detroit, Michigan, USA, has produced sera corresponding to the O-group scheme of the continuous numbering system developed by the international collaborative study and has agreed to start distributing sera when a serogrouping subdivision O-scheme has been agreed upon in the international collaborative study.

B. Determination of H-Antigens

1. *Preparation of H-antisera* (Lányi, 1970; Pitt and Bradley, 1975)

(a) *Preparation of antigens.* Fimbria-less motile mutants are preferable, since antibodies to the fimbriae may disturb the flagellar agglutination test. Such mutants may be obtained by treating the cultures with pilus-attacking phage (Bradley and Pitt, 1974) and selecting the resistant colonies.

To increase the number of motile cells, the culture is seeded into U-tubes containing semisolid nitrate agar (agar, 4 g; sodium or potassium nitrate, 2 g; nutrient broth, 1000 ml) and incubated at 37°C. After growth appears in the opposite branch of the U-tube, subcultures are made on soft agar plates (swarm plate) (agar, 6–8 g; sodium or potassium nitrate, 2 g; nutrient broth, 1000 ml). After incubation at 37°C for 18 h, about 10 ml of a 0·42% sodium chloride solution is pipetted onto each swarm plate. The Petri-dishes are left at room temperature for about 1 h, when the suspensions are transferred to Erlenmeyer flasks and left at room temperature for 3–4 h. Finally the bacteria are killed with formaldehyde (0·2%) and the suspension adjusted to approximately 5×10^9 bacteria/ml.

(b) *Immunization and preservation.* Rabbits are immunized at 3–4-day intervals with intravenous doses of 0·5, 1·0, 2·0, 3·0 and 4·0 ml of the antigen suspension. Bleeding is performed 3–4 days after the last injection. Preservation of sera is achieved by phenol (0·5% w/v) or with merthiolate (1 part in 10,000 w/v).

(c) *Absorption.* O-agglutinins are first removed by absorbing the sera with the homologous strain which has been heated at 100°C for 1–2½ h.

Cultures for the absorption of H-antibodies are prepared as follows: Motile bacteria (selected by U-tubes) are transferred to broth and after incubation at 37°C for 4–6 h, 1 ml of the culture is seeded into Roux flasks, in which the nutrient agar medium has been overlayered with 5 ml nutrient broth. After incubating at 37°C for 18 h the culture is harvested and centrifuged. Finally, the bacteria are resuspended in diluted H-serum which previously has been depleted of O-antibodies. The mixture of serum and bacteria is incubated at 37°C for 2 h, then at 4°C overnight, centrifuged and preserved with phenol or merthiolate.

(d) *Determination of the working dilution.* The single tube agglutination technique or the single tube migration-inhibition test is suitable for routine examination of H-antigens. The H-sera should be diluted, but still give a + + + +-reaction by tube agglutination with the homologous H-antigens and a negative result with unrelated antigens.

For the migration-inhibition test, antibody should be incorporated in the soft agar medium in amounts completely abolishing motility of homologous cultures, but without interfering with the migration of strains with different H-antigens. The absence of O-agglutinins should be checked by testing the sera with the homologous heated culture.

Type strains used for the preparation and absorption of H-sera are presented in Table XVII.

TABLE XVII
Determination of the H-antigens of *P. aeruginosa*

H-antigen	Tube agglutination in
1	Serum 170001 absorbed by 170001 1 h 100°C culture
2 complex	Polyvalent serum pool "H2" (mixture of H-sera 170002, 170016, 170012, 170018 and 170021, each absorbed by heated homologous culture)
2a	Serum 170016 absorbed by 170016 1 h 100°C culture and serum 170012 absorbed by 170012 1 h 100°C culture
2b	Serum 170002 absorbed by 170002 1 h 100°C + 170012 living + 170018 living culture
2c	Serum 170016 absorbed by 170016 1 h 100°C + 170002 living culture
2d	Serum 170012 absorbed by 170012 1 h 100°C + 170002 living culture
2e	Serum 170018 absorbed by 170018 1 h 100°C + 170021 living culture
2f	Serum 170021 absorbed by 170021 1 h 100°C + 170016 living culture

One ml of H-serum is diluted with 39 ml of sodium chloride solution (0·85%) and absorbed first with heated homologous culture (5 Roux flasks), then with the appropriate living culture (20–40 Roux flasks). Roux flasks are made with 150 ml of nutrient agar (surface of each plate, approx. 220 cm^2).

2. H-agglutination (Lányi, 1970; Pitt and Bradley, 1975)

(a) *Tube agglutination*. The bacterial suspensions are prepared in the same way as for immunization, except that they are preserved with 0·5% formaldehyde and adjusted to contain approximately 5×10^8 bacteria/ml. Single tube agglutination is performed with an equal amount of serum at its working dilution and bacterial suspension (0·5 or 0·25 ml each). Readings are made after incubating the tubes at 37°C for 18–20 h. Each strain under examination is first tested in two tubes, one containing serum H:1, the other pooled serum against the H:2 factors. If agglutination occurs, the suspensions are examined in absorbed H:2 factor sera to determine the partial antigen constitution (Table XVII).

(b) *Migration inhibition*. Although the specific inhibitory effect of diluted H-serum on the motility of *P. aeruginosa* cells can be demonstrated by dark-field (Lányi, 1970) or phase-contrast microscopy (Pitt and Bradley, 1975), the soft agar method is recommended as a routine test.

Tubes $(100 \times 7$–8 mm) are filled with nitrate soft agar (see Section V.B.1.a) containing the H-sera at previously determined dilutions. The strains to be tested are stab-inoculated to a depth of 10 mm and incubated overnight. The absence of gas bubbles and opacity in the medium is read as a specific inhibition of migration.

C. Detection of common heat-stable antigens

O-sera prepared in the usual manner contain common antibodies which agglutinate at low titres against cultures not related in major group-specific O-antigens to the homologous type strain used for immunization (Bergan, 1973a; Habs, 1957; Wahba, 1965a, b). To detect such antibodies cell suspensions heated first at $100°C$ for $2\frac{1}{2}$ h in saline and then at $130°C$ for 1 h in glycerol may be used. Tube agglutination is set up with two or more sera prepared with strains which differ in O-groups and from the strain to be examined. The presence of common antibodies is proved if a low titre, fine granular agglutination appears in all sera and, after absorption with any, O-antigenically heterologous strain, the serum fails to agglutinate the culture under investigation. Common heat-stable antibodies can also be shown by passive haemagglutination using erythrocytes coated with lipopolysaccharide extract.

D. Detection of slime layer antigens

P. aeruginosa produces extracellular polysaccharides that mostly do not remain adherent to the cell wall to form capsules. When these associate with nucleic acids and protein from autolysed cells the substance acquires an increased viscosity and is often called slime. Often, however, the term slime is used nebulously without reference to chemistry. Various meanings of the term have been discussed by Liu (1969). Linker and Jones (1966), for instance, used the word slime to characterize the capsular material of mucoid strains isolated from patients with cystic fibrosis.

Of the several methods described, the simple technique of Mates and Zand (1974) based on the procedure of Alms and Bass (1967a, b) yields easily detectable precipitates.

The bacterial culture is first centrifuged at $7300\ g$ for 1 h. Then the supernatant is centrifuged at $27,000\ g$ for 1 h. To the supernatant, which now contains the slime substance, sodium acetate (10% w/v) and glacial acetic acid (1% w/v) are added. This is followed by precipitation of the slime substance at $4°C$ with an equal volume of ethanol and centrifugation at $27,000\ g$ for 1 h. After rinsing the precipitate with water, saline is added and the substance is allowed to dissolve at $4°C$ for 72 h. The solution is dialysed against distilled water for 48 h and freeze-dried.

E. Detection of mucoid substance antigens (Martin, 1973)

To the supernatant of the mucoid culture an acetone–ethanol mixture (3:1 v/v) is added slowly. After the addition of 1–3 volumes of the reagent, a stringy precipitate is formed. This can be removed with a bent glass rod (precipitate A). Upon further addition of the reagent, a floccular precipitate containing most of the O-antigen fraction forms. This precipitate is best recovered by centrifugation (precipitate B).

F. Detection of enzyme antigens

Enzymes may be examined by immune neutralization or by more standard immunological techniques once the antigen has been purified, and is available for immunization in rabbits or other suitable animals. Choice methods would be the Ouchterlony double diffusion technique which would require extracts or preparations of whole cells, or the method of Elek. The latter procedure would entail placing porous paper impregnated with specific antiserum on top of a nutrient agar plate of high transparency with a streak of the strain growing perpendicularly to it. Both antibodies and extracellular products diffuse out into the agar. Precipitin lines form between homologous or cross-reacting antigen–antibody systems. Such studies have been carried out both within *P. aeruginosa* and for the purpose of elucidating its taxonomic relationships to other bacterial groups (Liu, 1969). Generally, enzyme antigens show less antigenic variation within species, indeed, many extracellular antigens in the bacterial world are species specific.

Some further enzymes will be discussed in Section V.G and V.H.

G. Detection of protective substances

1. *Protective moieties*

In mice and mink, prior immunization with a proteinous fraction of liquid cultures of a strain of *P. aeruginosa* has protective effect against infectious challenge with *P. aeruginosa* (Homma, 1974, 1975). The protective moiety is rich in protein and has been interpreted as a portion of the endotoxin. The fraction containing this material also contains lipopolysaccharide (LPS); it has been termed "original endotoxic protein" (OEP). The OEP in contrast to LPS is weak in its ability to elicit the dermal Shwartzman reaction, pyrogenic response, and bone marrow haemorrhages and necrosis (the bone marrow reaction) (Homma and Abe, 1972). On the other hand, OEP induces more interferon production and has an antitumour effect that is not seen with LPS (Homma and Abe, 1972). Whereas LPS is protective only against infection caused by strains of the same serogroup from which it has been derived, OEP is protective against infection with *P. aeruginosa* regardless of serotype (Homma, 1975) (cf. Table XVIII). A serological cross-reactivity has been found between OEP on the one hand and LPS from strains of all *P. aeruginosa* serogroups (according to the scheme of Homma (1974), but probably also against serogroup specificities not represented there) on the other. There are also cross-reactions between *P. aeruginosa* OEP and strains of *P. aureofaciens*, *P. fluorescens* and *P. putida*.

TABLE XVIII

Biological and chemical properties of fractions derived from cultures of *P. aeruginosa* (Homma, 1975)†

	OEP	LPS
Biological properties (μg/kg)		
Pyrogenicity	0·3	0·003
Limulus test	10	10^{-5}
Dermal Shwartzman	No	Yes
Non-specific protective property	1·5	9·8
Anti-tumour activity	1·0	700
Interferon induction	0·01	1·0
Chemical properties (%)		
Nitrogen	13·8	0·05
Phosphorus	1·1	3·9
Protein	85·0	0·3
Hexosamine	0·03	0·9
Total sugars	0·01‡	40·0
2-heto-3-deoxyoctonate (K O)	0·3	2·0

† OEP = original endotoxic protein; LPS = lipopolysaccharide.
‡ By another method the sugar content was determined to be 4·1%.

The degree of protective effect is manifested by the circumstance that the lethal dose killing 50% of the mice (LD_{50}) is usually raised by 10^2–10^3 (10^1–10^6) in OEP immunized mice compared to untreated controls as tested by all serogroup type strains of the schemes of Fisher *et al.* (1969) and of Homma (1974) (Homma, 1975).

Liu (1973c) has shown a protective effect of neutralizing antibody against his exotoxin A, and has detected three different antigenic specificities of that toxin, by double immuno-diffusion, but it is not known how universal the protective effect would be against strains producing antigenically different exotoxin A.

2. *Preparation of OEP*

The material designated OEP may be isolated in the following manner:

(i) *Inoculation*. *P. aeruginosa* grown on nutrient agar overnight at 37°C is rinsed off the agar and washed three times with the following sterile synthetic medium:

20 g sodium glutamate, 5 g glycerol, 0·1 g $MgSO_4 . 7H_2O$, 0·25 g KH_2PO_4, 5·6 g $Na_2HPO_4 . 12H_2O$, 10 mg $Ca(NO_3)_2 . 4H_2O$, 50 μg $FeSO_4 . 7H_2O$. The pH is adjusted to 7·6.

Cells thus grown and washed are used for inoculating large quantities of the medium (quantity depending upon desired OEP yield).

(ii) *Growth*. The culture is grown for several hours after reaching the stationary phase (time not specified, probably not critical).

(iii) *Autolysis*. When taken out of the growth system (e.g. a fermenter), 1N NaOH is added until pH 8·5 is reached. Then toluene is added to the culture which is then left at 37°C for 2 days. During this period, autolysis occurs.

(iv) *OEP precipitation*. The OEP is precipitated out from the culture supernatant as a Zn-complex (add 1/20 volume of a 1M Zn-acetate solution). After 4 h at 4°C the precipitate is collected by centrifugation.

(v) *Elution*. The OEP material is eluted from the Zn-precipitate with a solution of $Na_2HPO_4 . 12H_2O$.

(vi) *Dialysis*. The eluate is dialysed against phosphate buffer.

(vii) *Reprecipitation*. The dialysate is reprecipitated with acetone. If the equipment is available, the precipitate may be subjected to electrodialysis before final acetone precipitation. This moiety has been designated "original endotoxin" and is equivalent to the original endotoxic protein, OEP.

It is entirely possible from the way the OEP is procured that the material contains a number of extracellular products and probably also intracellular protein.

3. *Preparation of lipopolysaccharide (LPS)*

The preparation of LPS may be carried out by the phenol–water method described in Section V.A.3.a.iii of this Chapter.

4. *Method of determining immune protection*

The protective substances may be studied by general immunological procedures like double agar immunodiffusion, single or crossed immuno-electrophoresis, passive haemagglutination (cf. Section V.A.3 of this Chapter). For proper infectious models, preparation of bacterial suspensions in, for example, 2·5% mucin solution for intraperitoneal challenge, animal handling and the statistics of LD_{50}, the reader is referred to other literature (Homma, 1975; Liu, 1973b, c).

H. Detection of antibody in patient sera

1. Precipitation

In some instances, one may wish to study antibody formation against *P. aeruginosa*. Immunoprecipitation by double diffusion, single or double immunoelectrophoresis may be performed (Høiby, 1975a, b, c, d).

2. Bacterial agglutination

Agglutination with bacterial cells will mainly detect IgM. If it is desired to monitor total antibody production, the Coombs technique will have to be employed, i.e. by adding anti-human gamma globulin produced in a heterogeneous species like goat, sheep or horse. However, this will be laborious, since each patient serum will have to be examined in a whole battery of bacterial suspensions such that all O-groups are represented. Agglutination, consequently, is mostly impractical for routine use.

3. Passive haemagglutination

(a) *Somatic antigens.* Passive haemagglutination (HA) may be used for the detection of patient antibodies (see Section V.A.3.d). When coated erythrocytes are prepared with lipopolysaccharide extracts, the method detects antibody against the corresponding homologous O-antigens. This is simpler than using the Coombs technique. Presumably, IgG and IgM both participate in these reactions, at least when tanninized erythrocytes are used. This technique has been applied on both human and animal sera (Ádám *et al.*, 1971; Jones and Roe, 1975). Since HA with LPS-coated erythrocytes give the same pattern of homologous and cross-reactions as O-agglutination, several coated cell antigen suspensions have to be set up with each patient serum.

(b) *Protective protein antigen of Homma and Abe* (1972), *OEP.* In comparison to LPS-HA, the reaction with OEP, OEP-HA has been used by Tomiyama *et al.* (1973) and appears to have a more universal application. This uses an antigen that is common to all (or at least a great majority of) strains of *P. aeruginosa*. The antigen is proteinaceous and heat labile.

Here formalinized tanned sheep erythrocytes coated with OEP (*vide* Section V.G.2) are used. After the coating (sensitization), the cells are lyophilized and kept as such until use. Lyophilized unsensitized cells of sheep are used as negative controls. These may easily be prepared in the laboratory or procured from Homma (Department of Bacteriology, Institute of Medical Science, University of Tokyo, PO Takanawa, Tokyo 108, Japan) (Homma, 1974).

The serum to be tested is first treated at 56°C for 30 min (to destroy complement activity). Then patient serum is diluted 1 : 10 with a diluent consisting of phosphate buffered saline with rabbit serum and bovine plus sheep erythrocyte stroma (suitably 0·05 ml serum + 0·45 ml diluent). The mixture is left at room temperature for an hour, or in the refrigerator overnight before use—to absorb heterophilic antibodies (e.g. Forssman antigen).

The set-up itself is best made in microtitre transparent plastic trays with which dropper and microdiluters of 0·025 ml are used. The reaction mixture consists of one 0·025 ml drop each of (1) diluent, (2) diluted serum, (3) tanninized, coated or uncoated cells.

Two parallel tests are set up, one with OEP-coated cells and one with unsensitized sheep red cells. After agitation of the trays to mix reagents, they are left at room temperature overnight. The reactions are recorded according to their macroscopic appearance. Reactions due to specific antibody in the patient serum appear as an even cell layer on the bottom of the micro-tubes. To read, it may be helpful to raise the tray upright upon which negative reactions are easily spotted by the cellular buttons running downwards along the plastic tube walls. In positive reactions, the lattice of cells and antibodies is kept in place and remains unchanged and stationary on the bottom of the tubes. It is critical for proper assessment of the tests that the reactions in the control with unsensitized sheep cells are definitely negative. If the negative controls are reactive, the serum contains non-specific antibody against sheep cells. The patient serum must then be absorbed with sheep erythrocytes. An aliquot of 0·1 ml sheep cells (washed three times) is mixed with 0·05 ml inactivated patient serum and 0·45 ml diluent. Absorption takes place under conditions as specified (*vide supra*) before the supernatant (diluted serum) is used in the HA test as above. With the OEP-HA, only one antigen is sufficient to examine each serum. Thereby, the test is faster to set up. According to Homma (1974), the test is dependable.

(c) *Extracellular enzymes and toxins.* The work on pathogenicity factors and vaccines of *P. aeruginosa* has led to isolation and characterization also of pseudomonas elastase and protease which cause tissue haemorrhage and necrosis upon subcutaneous injections, and corneal ulcers upon application to the eye. These enzymes have also been used in HA assays, to follow antibody production. Distinct increases also in elastase-HA and protease-HA titres have been observed in severe cases of cow mastitis and in some patients with chronic bronchitis (Homma, 1975). Methodology and results have not yet been published to our knowledge.

According to the experience of Homma (1975), prior immunization with elastase and protease does not elicit a protective effect against infectious challenge with strains producing antigenically homologous enzymes. However, Liu (1969) has observed that rabbits which have anti-protease are protected from the appearance of typical haemorrhagic lesions upon intracutaneous injection of live *P. aeruginosa*.

Pollack *et al.* (1976) have identified anti-exotoxin in human sera by a cytotoxicity neutralizing assay. Mouse fibroblasts or L-cells in cell cultures were used. The toxin is heat labile and proteinaceous, and appears identical to the exotoxin A of Liu. The MW is 54,000 (Liu, 1966a, b, c). It elicits antibody production (titre increases by four or even more steps compared with those detected at the start) during infections (Pollack *et al.*, 1976). It is not known whether the three different antigenic specificities described by Liu (1973c) can be paralleled by the neutralizing assay system using cell cultures. Pollack *et al.* (1976) describe only one serospecific entity.

The methods for isolation of exotoxin have been described by Callahan (1974, 1976) and Liu (1973a, b), the techniques for the detection of exotoxin activity and specific immune neutralizing of cytotoxic effect by Pollack *et al.* (1976).

In most adult sera, antibodies against lecithinase are found (Liu, 1969).

VI. APPLICATION OF SEROTYPING OF *P. AERUGINOSA*

A. Routine serological grouping and typing

1. *Methodological difficulties*

(a) *Quality of sera.* It is well known that some immunized rabbits have antibodies in their sera which, even when considerably diluted, give non-specific reactions. Consequently, it is imperative that O-sera be carefully checked with at least one type strain for each group and subgroup of the antigenic scheme. Similarly, H-antisera should be checked with all kinds of H-antigens and H-antigen complexes. Sera giving cross-reactions which do not conform to antigenic relationships set out in the antigenic scheme and which cannot be abolished by proper dilution of serum, should be discarded. Preparation of absorbed sera against *P. aeruginosa* is as laborious as the production of, for example, *Shigella flexneri* typing sera. Accordingly, the task requires a well-equipped central laboratory and trained staff.

Antisera, especially diluted sera, tend to show a decrease in agglutinating titre during long-term storage. Thus, the sera should be checked for the homologous titre every 9–12 months. Absorbed sera, because of a release of antibodies bound to soluble antigens, occasionally may become reactive with strains they had agglutinated before absorption.

(b) *O-antigens.* Although slide agglutination may be accurate when the bacteria have been grown on nutrient agar, blood agar is the medium of choice. Cultures incubated for more than 24 hours should be avoided, since this increases a tendency towards spontaneous clumping and may possibly lead to production of envelope material interfering with the O-agglutination.

For tube agglutination, the time and temperature of heating as well as the density of the bacterial suspensions should be carefully standardized.

The lower the temperature and the shorter the time of heating, the lower the titre of agglutination. Overheating of the antigen usually results in instability. Suspensions too dense or too dilute tend to give respectively lower and higher titres than expected.

(c) *H-antigens.* Unless one uses actively swarming cultures which have been washed off soft agar plates and killed with formaldehyde, accurately readable reactions may fail to develop in tube agglutination.

For the migration inhibition technique, cultures previously passed through antiserum-free nitrate semisolid agar in U-tubes are recommended. Many strains exhibit a weak migration activity. Typing and demonstration of partial H-antigens, in such strains, is best done by agglutination.

B. Indications for serogrouping and serotyping

Serotyping of *P. aeruginosa* is performed in order to follow nosocomial spreading of the microbe for the purpose of elucidating an outbreak of hospital infections or aid in effective hospital infection control. The organism is easily recognized on the basis of cultural characteristics so that serology has no significance for the bacteriological diagnosis. Since no type may be regarded as apathogenic, as particularly pathogenic, or as associated with characteristic antibiotic sensitivity, serogrouping or serotyping has no direct clinical or prognostic function.

It is recommended that central reference laboratories receiving a substantial number of strains and thus having adequate controls, should be appointed to perform typing for smaller laboratories. In order to avoid waste of time and resources, before sending the cultures for typing, the clinicians and microbiologists should carefully consider whether the results will contribute to the elucidation of a given problem or will help in recommending effective preventive measures.

C. Frequency of serogroups and serotypes†

1. *Distribution of groupable and typable strains*

(a) *Comparison of typing schemes.* The frequency of each antigen group

† Serogroups and serotypes are expressed with symbols of the compiled Arabic–Latin system (see Tables IV and XII) and of the H-antigens of Lányi (1970).

varies with the nosocomial situation at the source of the strains, and to some extent with the antigenic scheme used. In examining strains derived from a wide variety of sources within a single hospital unit, the incidence of groupable strains has been found to be 62–99·7% for the Habs scheme, 84·9–94·8% for the Lányi scheme, 83·1–94·0% for the Fisher scheme, and 71·7–81% for the Homma scheme (cf. Bergan, 1975, Table; Lányi, 1966/67, unpublished data). When every single strain of a collection was considered for the purpose of elaborating an antigenic scheme, only unstable cultures represented the ungroupable percentage (Sandvik, 1960; Verder and Evans, 1961; Meitert and Meitert, 1966; Lányi, 1966/67).

(b) *Non-faecal pathological specimens* (Table XIX). The most frequently encountered serogroup in extra-intestinal pathological processes all over the world is O: 2 (18·6–37·1%, average 29·9%). Low values described by Wretlind *et al.* (1973) (15·9%), and by Homma *et al.* (1970) (11·6%), as well as the very high incidence shown by Meitert and Meitert (1966) (66·6%) may have a nosocomial association. Serogroup O: 6, next in order, occurred in 7·8–32·2% (average 17·1%). Serogroup O: 6 is more frequent than O:2 in Norway (Bergan, 1972b), whereas O:2a, 2c constitutes 1/4 and O:2a, 2d of the strains in a Polish material (Bergan, 1972), a relatively low incidence of O: 6 has been seen in India and in Japan. Serogroup O: 11, in turn, has been found considerably more frequently in India 23–24·1% (Agarwal and Talwar, 1976; Agarwal *et al.*, 1972b), in Japan (16·3%) and in the USA (8·9–17·7%) than in Europe (3·7–7·1%). Epidemiological reasons are suggestive; the incidence in certain provinces in India, for instance, has reached 35 and 45% (Agarwal and Talwar, 1976). Among the rest, serogroups O: 1, O: 3 and O: 7 occur with an average frequency of not more than 5%.

Serogroup O: 2 has frequently been isolated from blood cultures: in 13 out of 26 patients with *P. aeruginosa* septicaemia Lányi (1966/67) showed O: 2 strains, whereas Moody *et al.* (1972) reported the incidence of O: 2 strains in 28·1% of *P. aeruginosa* positive blood cultures. All six cases of *P. aeruginosa* meningitis examined by Lányi (1966/67) were caused by strains belonging to different subgroups of O:2 (O:2a, 2b, O:2a, 2d, O:2a, 2d, 2f).

In miscellaneous non-faecal pathological specimens, the subgroup distribution of serogroup O: 2 strains was as follows (Lányi, 1966/67): O: 2a, 2b 39·2%, O: (2a), 2c 12·7%, O: 2a, 2d 20·3%, O: 2a, 2d, 2e 5·9%, O: (2a), 2d, 2f 21·9%. Within serogroup O: 6, subgroup O: 6a, 6d predominates: O: 6a, 6b 12·0%, O: 6a, 6c 31·6%, O: 6a, 6d 56·4%.

In addition to the above two groups, subgrouping is valuable for strains of group O: 7, the isolates of which are fairly evenly distributed between

TABLE XIX

Incidence (%) of *P. aeruginosa* serogroups in miscellaneous non-faecal human specimens

Country and reference	No. of strains	Distribution according to serogroups† (%)															
		1	2	3	4	6	7	9	10	11	12	13	14	15	SA	PA	ND
German Federal Republic (Kleinmaier) and Quincke, 1959)	301	10·6	18·6	5·6	13·0	16·6	8·0	0·7	2·0	3·7	2·3	.	.	.	6·3	0	12·6
U.S.A. (Verder & Evans, 1961)	90	12·2	36·8	3·3	.	24·4	2·2	3·3	.	8·9	6·7	12·0	.	.	0	0	0
Roumania (Meitert and Meitert, 1966)	364	.	66·6	12·9	2·5	12·7	2·7	.	.	.	0·5	.	0·5	.	0	0	1·6
Hungary (Lányi, 1966/67)	827	3·5	37·1	9·4	1·5	14·1	12·9	2·3	0·6	7·1	0	.	.	0	0·7	10·2	0·6
U.S.A. (Fisher et al., 1969)‡	342	10·3	30·1	.	.	21·8	5·5	.	8·6	17·7	.	.	.	.	.	.	6·0
Denmark (Mikkelsen, 1970)	767	5·0	28·3	6·6	0·5	15·4	3·1	2·9	4·7	6·4	0	0·1	.	.	12·1	.	14·9
Japan (Hamma et al., 1970)§	915	10·9	11·6	6·6	2·5	9·6	1·6	4·5	8·1	16·3	.	.	.	.	1·0	15·5	11·8
U.S.A. (Adler & Finland, 1971)	83	12·0	36·1	.	.	14·5	4·8	.	2·4	13·3	.	.	.	.	.	.	16·9
India (Agarwal et al., 1972)‡	526	4·9	26·2	5·7	.	7·8	7·9	1·0	0·8	23·0	6·0	0·2	.	.	0	0	16·5
U.S.A. (Moody et al., 1972)	742	4·6	28·1	.	.	25·2	19·9	.	6·6	15·1	.	.	.	.	0	0	0·5
Poland (Bergan, 1972a)	302	1·7	23·5	3·3	1·0	11·9	1·0	2·6	1·7	2·0	0	0·7	1·7	18·9	13·6	0	15·2
Sweden (Wretlind et al., 1973)	189	7·9	15·9	7·9	3·7	32·2	4·2	1·1	4·8	6·9	1·1	7·4	.	.	0	3·2	3·7

† Expressed in serogroup symbols of the compiled Arabic–Latin systems (see Tables III and IV).

‡ Source of strains not stated.

§ Including faecal strains.

Abbreviations: SA = self-agglutinable, PA = polyagglutinable, ND = not determined or non-groupable according to the compiled scheme, . = not tested.

the three subgroups. In contrast, within groups O:9 and O:11, the dominating subgroups are O:9a and O:11a, 11b. There are no data for the subgroup distribution of isolates within the groups O:10 and O:13.

Typing of isolates according to their H-antigens is particularly valuable for group O:1 strains which all have identical O-antigen constitution. The group is subdivisible into three approximately evenly distributed serotypes (1:1, 1:2a, 2b and 1:2a, 2c). Similarly, group O:4a, 4b strains are subdivided in the types 4a, 4b:1, 4a, 4b:2a, 2c, and 4a, 4b:2a, 2c, 2f and subgroup O:9a strains into the types 9a:1, 9a:2a, 2b, 2f, and 9a:2a, 2c. For the remaining isolates, the value of differentiation by individual serotypes is more limited as the majority of strains in each group or subgroup possess only one kind of H-antigen specificity (Lányi, 1970).

(c) *Faecal specimens* (Table XX). In contrast to strains from extraintestinal pathological processes, isolates from human faeces usually belong to group O:6 (21·3–34·7%, average 27·4%). Group O:2 strains are next in order, but in faecal specimens these are much less uniform than O:6 in incidence (4·5–41·8%, average 20·7%). In subgroup and type distribution, faecal and non-faecal strains O:6 and O:2 are similar. Also for other serogroups there is on the whole no conspicuous difference between faecal and non-faecal specimens. National or regional differences in serogroups distribution is incidental.

(d) *Animal sources* (Table XX). From the limited data available, it seems that there are no particular animal serogroups of *P. aeruginosa*. The incidence of each serogroup apparently varies with the herd examined (Wokatsch, 1964; Bergan, 1972a).

(e) *Water*

(i) *Drinking water* (Table XXI). Similarly to faecal specimens, in drinking water obtained from a wide variety of sources in Hungary, serogroup O:6 strains were uniformly the most frequent (average, 24·1% of all serogroups). Gross contamination of the municipal water supply of Szeged city was due to subgroup O:6a, 6c (Lantos *et al.*, 1969). Other serogroups frequent in human sources, including O:2, were fairly uniformly distributed in drinking water.

(ii) *Surface water* (Table XXI). Isolates of *P. aeruginosa* from specimens of surface water have had a similar serogroup distribution to those derived from human faeces and drinking water. Strains of group O:6 have been most frequent (average, 24·2%).

TABLE XX

Incidence of *P. aeruginosa* serogroups in human faeces and in animals

Source of strains, country and reference	No. of strains	Distribution according to serogroups, %															
		1	2	3	4	6	7	9	10	11	12	13	14	15	SA	PA	ND
Human faeces, G.F.R. (Kleinmaier and Quincke, 1959)	199	23.6	4.5	15.6	1.0	24.1	2.0	10.6	2.5	3.0	0.5	.	.	.	4.0	0	8.6
Human faeces, U.S.A. (Verder and Evans, 1961)	210	4.3	41.8	0.5	.	28.1	1.0	1.4	.	15.7	2.4	4.8	.	.	0	0	0
Norman adults' faeces Hungary (Lányi et al., 1966/67)	118	11.0	12.7	16.2	4.2	21.3	9.3	7.6	1.7	5.9	0	.	.	0.8	0	5.9	3.4
Hospitalized infants' faeces, Hungary (Lányi et al., 1966/67)	208	1.9	18.8	1.9	4.3	34.7	9.1	1.4	1.9	10.1	0	.	.	0	0	13.0	2.9
Human faeces, Denmark (Mikkelsen, 1970)	53	13.2	22.6	13.2	0	22.6	0	1.9	3.8	7.6	0	0	.	.	1.9	0	13.2
Cattle, milk and milking equipment, Norway (Bergan, 1972a)	256	6.4	0	24.2	1.9	32.0	5.5	3.2	0	0.8	0	23.7	.	.	2.3	0	0
Various animals, G.F.R. (Wokatsch, 1964)	230	10.1	15.2	21.3	0.9	3.5	0.8	3.0	0.9	0	0	.	.	.	0	6.1	38.2

For abbreviations see Table XIX.

TABLE XXI

Incidence of *P. aeruginosa* serogroups in water and sewage

Source of strains, country and reference	No. of strains	Distribution according to serotypes, %															
		1	2	3	4	6	7	9	10	11	12	13	14	15	SA	PA	ND
Drinking water, Hungary (Lányi *et al.*, 1966/67; Némedi and Lányi, 1971)	212	12·3	4·7	24·1	2·8	22·6	10·8	7·1	6·1	3·8	0	.	.	0·5	0	0	5·2
Surface water, Hungary (Lányi *et al.*, 1966/67; Némedi and Lányi, 1971)	360	10·6	10·0	13·8	1·1	24·2	7·2	2·5	3·9	13·1	0·3	.	.	0·3	0	3·6	9·4
Surface water, Denmark (Mikkelsen, 1970)	21	14·3	14·3	23·7	0	9·5	4·8	0	9·5	4·8	0	4·8	.	.	0	0	14·3
Swimming pools, Hungary (Némedi and Lányi, 1971)	285	10·9	15·8	8·4	0·7	10·2	9·5	9·5	6·3	13·6	0	.	.	0	0	2·5	12·6
Sewage, Hungary (Lányi *et al.*, 1966/67; Némedi and Lányi, 1971)	204	16·2	6·9	8·3	3·4	18·6	12·3	3·4	7·8	7·8	1·0	.	.	0	0	2·5	11·8

For abbreviations see Table XIX.

(iii) *Swimming pools* (Table XXI). Compared to drinking and surface water, group O: 6 strains have been less frequent in swimming pools (10·2%). The frequency of individual serogroups has essentially corresponded to that found in human specimens.

(iv) *Sewage* (Table XXI). In sewage serogroup O: 6 strains were met with in 18·6% of cases. The distribution of other serogroups was also similar to that in drinking water, surface water and faecal isolates.

2. *Frequency of polyagglutinable and self-agglutinable strains*

(a) *Polyagglutinability (multiple agglutinability)* is relatively frequent. Literary data indicate that several authors have not distinguished it from spontaneous agglutinability in saline. "Polyagglutinable" strains are characterized by smooth colony forms and reactivity in a number of sera prepared with serologically unrelated strains. With slide agglutination in O-sera, these cultures frequently show a special kind of loose, flaky aggregation of bacteria, instead of the granular clumping characteristic of group-specific O-agglutination. Such cultures are often met with in certain hospital units or communities. Homma *et al.* (1970) described their incidence as 15·5% (tested with heated cultures) whereas in various specimens examined by Lányi (1966/67), Lányi *et al.* (1966/67) and Némedi and Lányi (1971) they occurred in 0–13·0% of isolates (living cultures tested with slide agglutination). Lányi and Lantos (1976), for example, have observed strains which react simultaneously in different O sera (O:3, O:4, O:6, O:9) and in the Lányi group O:8 serum, but it is to be noted that antigen O:8 is an R-like factor. Bergan (unpublished) has observed strains which have had factors of two unrelated serogroups, but only to a frequency of some 0·1%.

(b) *Spontaneous agglutinability.* Certain isolates of *P. aeruginosa*, especially when heated cultures are used, show more or less definite granular clumping of the cells in physiological saline. The incidence of unstable (or self-agglutinable) cultures among fresh isolates has been determined to be 1.0% if tested with heated antigens (Homma *et al.*, 1970) or 0–0·7% for living cultures examined by the slide method (Lányi, 1966/67; Lányi *et al.*, 1966/67; Némedi and Lányi, 1971).

D. Clinical achievements of serological characterization

Epidemiological typing methods have special uses such as differentiation between relapse and reinfection of urinary tract infection (Neussel, 1971), but their chief merit is the elucidation of nosocomical outbreaks of infection, determination of sources, reservoirs and vectors, and surveillance of general hygiene in health institutions.

A constant source of pseudomonas are healthy people of the general public who have a faecal carrier rate of 4–6% (Shooter et al., 1966; Stoodley and Thom, 1970). The frequencies of individual serogroups of P. aeruginosa in surface and sewage water reflect their incidence in healthy people living in the same area (Lányi et al., 1966/67). Usually, a large number of bacteria are needed (more than 10^6 bacteria) for colonization, and the duration of excretion is short. Buck and Cooke (1969) recovered pseudomonas from faeces for a maximum of 6 days, and only when more than 10^6 bacteria were ingested. The interplay between microbe and host is such that disease favours colonization. Healthy hospital personnel had a sixfold lesser frequency in stool than hospitalized patients (Shooter et al., 1966) in the same environment, this in spite of the close contact between nursing staff and a large number of patients. Whereas pseudomonas is rapidly eliminated from the bowel of healthy adults (Buck and Cooke, 1969) excretion of pseudomonas may continue for more than 2 months in infants. Clearing is more efficient in full-term normal babies than in premature or sick infants.

Eleven to 14% of patients have pseudomonas in the stool at admission and an additional 10–17% acquire it during the course of their hospitalization (Arseni and Doxiadis, 1967; Shooter et al., 1966). Among leukaemia patients, one quarter exhibit pseudomonas in the bowel at admission; again, approximately the same number acquires the organism during their stay in hospital. The influence of the hospital milieu on disease is also reflected in the finding that out-patients have a three-fold lesser probability of faecal pseudomonas carriage than warded patients (Shooter et al., 1966). Previous hospitalization, antibiotic treatment, and enterostomias in addition to reduced immune response were some factors associated with increased occurrence. Shooter et al. (1966) used phage, pyocine and serological typing to substantiate that pseudomonas may spread from the bowel of one patient to another. Strains were only considered related when there were similar phage patterns, identity in serogroup, and pyocine type.

In a number of instances colonization of the gut is often antecedent and followed by auto-infection (Deighton et al., 1971; Shooter et al., 1971). Pseudomonas in the bowel may derive from ingested foods. Clinical isolates have been traced by pyocine typing to vegetables in hospital kitchens (Kominos et al., 1972b; Shooter et al., 1971). Even pharmaceutical products have been incriminated (Shooter et al., 1971). Lantos et al. (1969) observed an episode where grossly polluted municipal drinking water would increase colonization in the region serviced by the water supply.

Nosocomial pseudomonas infections usually spread in one of three ways:

1. They may be transmitted directly between patients such as is frequent in burn units, surgical wards, and urology departments.
2. An inanimate object may be involved as reservoir or vector.
3. In a number of cases, autoinfection follows colonization of the bowel.

Spread from the bowel to the hospital environment is inevitable both among adults and newborns (Shooter *et al.*, 1966; Maruyama *et al.*, 1971). Shooter *et al.* recovered patient strains from water jugs, draw sheets, table tops and floors; sluices and bathrooms were frequent sources. Whitby and Rampling (1972) made an interesting comparison of the level of pseudomonas contamination in hospital and the domestic milieu. Although only hospital staff were involved, pseudomonas was rarely observed in their private homes. None of the domestic strains by typing were identical to simultaneous isolates from the hospital.

Staff probably constitute a rare *source* of pseudomonas infections, but nurses and physicians play an important role in the spread of microbes. This has been amply documented by epidemiological typing (Bergan, 1967; Deighton *et al.*, 1971; Jellard and Churcher, 1967; Kominos *et al.*, 1972a; Lowbury *et al.*, 1970). A study of Deighton *et al.* (1971) demonstrated many typical aspects of nosocomial pseudomonas infections. By pyocine typing, serogrouping and phage typing, the recognition of isolates was easy. Objects and persons were contaminated or infected from patients disseminating pseudomonas; several instances of cross-infection were demonstrated. Infected hands of healthy personnel contributed decisively to the spread of infection. In one instance, a healthy nurse who became contaminated while bathing a child subsequently passed on the organism to another child.

Whereas hands are very important for the spread of microbes, inanimate objects have often been involved. Ayliffe *et al.* (1965), in a series of cases of pseudomonas meningitis after neurosurgery, recovered the same phage pattern, pyocine type and serogroup on a shaving brush used for depilation prior to surgery. The typing methods were instrumental in establishing the causative relationship and in eliminating a number of sources such as staff, hand creams, sinks, soaps, trays, aseptic bottles, urine bottles, and another depilation brush. Similarly, intraocular pseudomonas infections arising after eye operations were caused by a contaminated saline solution used to moisten the cornea during operations (Ayliffe *et al.*, 1966). The saline had been contaminated from a sink during washing.

Rouques *et al.* (1969) studied a series of pseudomonas infections in patients on haemodialysis. The same phage type was recovered from a benzalkonium solution used with the intent of sterilizing (*sic!*) the parts of the equipment which had contact with the blood.

Bodey (1970) found that the frequency of pseudomonas septicaemia was particularly high in leukaemia reflecting a high faecal carrier rate (54%) of this particular group. Simultaneous isolates from blood, stool and throat of the same individual always had the same pyocine types, but in some instances the pyocine type was not reproducible. In the inanimate milieu, pseudomonas was found in sinks, in the air, and on the floors. Sixty-eight per cent of the strains belonged to p1. When cross-infections are common, the number of predominant epidemiological types may be small. Grogan (1966) demonstrated 3 dominant phage types among surgical patients where environment isolates only reflected the patient strains to a minor sero-grouping degree. Serotyping using both O- and H-antigens would be equally effective in establishing such relationships.

Typing methods have been instrumental in the elucidation of nosocomial patterns of infection in paediatric departments. Knights et al. (1968) employed all three typing methods to characterize the epidemiology within a neonatal unit. The typing methods enabled an analysis of the identification of the reservoirs of infection and pathways of nosocomial spread. Cross-infection of four strains implicated several wards and inanimate sources such as nursery washbasins, sinks, sluices and cleaning equipment. In contrast to all too common experience in nurseries, humidifiers, resuscitation equipment and suction tubes were not involved. Measures instituted to eradicate pseudomonas were so successful that no milieu or patient yielded pseudomonas for a subsequent 8-month period. Dexter (personal communication, 1973) eliminated cross-infection by eliminating pseudomonas from moist areas.

Jellard and Churcher (1967) studied a baby unit for $1\frac{1}{2}$ years when pseudomonas isolates of a uniform phage pattern repeatedly appeared in routine stool cultures (65 of 66 cultures). In various simultaneous infections many other epidemic types occurred. Episodes of a possible nosocomial nature were followed, but the patient types were never obtained from healthy personnel, inanimate objects, or the milieu of an operating theatre. The main reservoir and source of infection were the babies themselves. In burns with large areas presenting excellent growth conditions pseudomonas is a serious problem. Colonization may follow autoinfection from the bowel (Sutter and Hurst, 1966), but usually cross-infection is involved. Liljedahl et al. (1972) found a single phage type (1214, 109/F8) in one-third of a group of burn patients, so that a nosocomial pattern was clearly indicated.

Cross-infection may be effectively reduced by segregation between infected and non-infected patients and when nurses tend to only one group of patients (Dexter, 1971). Epidemic types may be found on the hands of staff and parents visiting their children (Bergan, 1967), occasionally derived from contaminated towels. Respirators and/or their humidifier units may carry organisms from one patient to another. By serogrouping and lyso-typing it has been shown that bronchial infections may be derived from infected lubrication fluid for bronchoscopes or suction tubes (Meitert *et al.*, 1967; Phillips, 1966; Rubbo *et al.*, 1966). Autoinfection usually pre-ceded by bowel colonization has been demonstrated in a number of cases (Darrell and Wahba, 1964; Lowbury *et al.*, 1970).

Faecal carriers among the staff may also be a hazard to the patients as was shown in a nursery where a staff strain was recovered from a number of infants with diarrhoea caused by the same pyocine type (Falcao *et al.*, 1972).

Besides staff and patients, the role of fomites and the inanimate environ-ment is important (Losonczy *et al.*, 1971). Organisms may also remain long after discharge of the patients (Liljedhal *et al.*, 1972; Malmborg *et al.*, 1969). Hurst and Sutter (1966) thus recovered patient phage types from a floor for more than 8 weeks. In many instances, modern technology may enhance the spread of infection. In one instance, pseudomonas from infected burns was carried to remote parts of a burns unit by positive pressure ventilation. This spread was eliminated only after negative and positive air pressure had been applied to various parts of the ward (Dexter, 1971).

Pseudomonas infections are also a prominent problem of the respiratory tract in respirator treated and tracheostomized patients (Grieble *et al.*, 1970). Mucoid strains of *P. aeruginosa* have been noted particularly fre-quently in cystic fibrosis (Høiby, 1974a, b). When mucoid and non-mucoid strains occurred at the same time they often belong to identical pyocine types, indicating that they are, indeed, variants of the same strain (Bergan and Høiby, 1975; Williams and Govan, 1973). Mucoid variation may be due to lysogenization (Martin, 1973).

Important to the elimination of pseudomonas infections is adherence to rigorous aseptic techniques and good nursing procedures (Lowbury *et al.*, 1970). Pharmaceuticals, instruments, utilities and the environment (sinks, and other objects) must be free from pseudomonas. Good hand hygiene is perhaps the single most decisive factor.

VII. BIOLOGICAL PROPERTIES OF EPIDEMIOLOGICAL TYPES

One may ask whether epidemiological typing methods can do more than aid in the elucidation of spread of infection. Are certain serotypes, for instance, more pathogenic, produce exotoxin A, or resistant to anti-biotics? Is there any preference for particular sites or types of infection?

On the whole, it appears that no distinct biological properties are concordant with given serogroups. The deviations from overall frequency data found in some instances are very difficult to interpret with confidence.

Nord et al. (1972) reported that a single strain of serogroup Habs O:1, and phage type (21, 44, 1214, 109, F8) dominated in oral infections associated with poor oral hygiene. Fifteen out of 29 patients had O:1; a higher frequency of O:1 than usual. In comparison, Bergan (1972b) reported that O:1 occurred in 32% of isolates, few of which had oral infections. The rate differences were most likely incidental. On this basis, it is difficult to pinpoint any fundamental biological properties for given pseudomonas serotypes. There is always the possibility of a nosocomial reason for preponderance of a certain type. In the study by Nord et al. (1972) this was considered possible only for two of the 29 strains. Similar evidence has been observed for a correlation between Meitert serogroup II and low pathogenicity and serogroup VIII and low pathogenicity (Meitert, E., personal communication, 1976).

Moody et al. (1972) studied cancer patients and concluded that particular foci show predominance of certain serogroups. The Fisher et al. serogroups O:1 and O:2 were retrieved from blood cultures more often than from other sources. Groups O:4 and O:5 occurred more often in wounds. It was concluded that a particular serogroup was more "capable of establishing persisting colonization" than others.

The group frequencies were evaluated statistically. It is, however, doubtful whether evaluation of a small portion of the data in such a large table can proceed by standard statistical procedures, since they would be constrained by all the other data. It is obvious that, for example, an epidemic of O:7 wound infections will make O:7 more frequent in wounds than in urine and thus influence the apparent frequency of any other group.

A predilection of a certain epidemiological type among patients with similar clinical picture from the same environment may also have a nosocomial explanation. Although differences in the relative frequencies of different types may be obvious, these are not per se indicative of fundamental biological differences between certain types. In the study of Moody et al. (1972), the types from wounds were also encountered in the general environment, although it is open to speculation which preceded the other. No data are available to suggest whether, for example, most of the septicaemic patients came from the same hospital environment which had a distinct nosocomial predominance of the O:1 or O:2 strains from blood. At present, it is best to regard the question of biological differences between epidemiological types with an open mind.

Edmonds et al. (1972a) found no difference between serogroup, pyocine type or phage type for burn wound septicaemia compared to non-fatal infections from the same environment. Bergan (1967, 1973c, unpublished results) has isolated the same phage and serological O-types from various clinical manifestations within the same departments. The types have varied from one ward to another. Since a department often specializes in certain diseases, a higher frequency of the local epidemic types in a particular type of infection may be merely incidental and reflect the local morbidity panorama.

Southern *et al.* (1970) differentiated *P. aeruginosa* according to rapidity with which they vanished from mouse lungs, but noted no relationship between kinetics of disappearance and serogroup, pyocine type or bacteriophage type. Likewise, Meitert and Meitert (1971) found no association between virulence and lysotype or serogroup. Kobayashi (1971a, b) found virulence distinctions for particular serogroups, but a higher virulence was noted for non-typable isolates. Wretlind *et al.* (1973) could not detect any correlation between serogroups of phage type and the production of enzymes or toxins. Baltimore *et al.* (1974) found that there was no significant association between individual immunotypes and either

(a) pathogenicity or commensal state,
(b) specific sites of infection or colonization,
(c) underyling disease,
(d) subspeciality of wards within hospital,
(e) antibiotic treatment before the isolation of pseudomonas,

although the mortality appeared to be lower among non-typable strains.

Sato and Diena (1974a, b) found no apparent relationship between serogroups and either source of specimen or characteristics such as mucoid appearance and pigment production.

In bovine mastitis, predominance of certain serogroups has been noted, but this has been due to epidemic spread of the strains (Bergan, 1972a; Sandvik, 1960a, b; Thörne and Kyrkjebø, 1966).

Denis and Godeau (1972) and Yoshioka *et al.* (1970) found some serotypes to be somewhat more resistant to antibiotics. Others have revealed that there is no association between serogroups and susceptibility to antibiotics, pathogenicity, site of infection, or biochemical or cultural characteristics (Adler and Finland, 1971; Bergan, 1972a, b; Klyhn and Gorrill, 1967; Köhler, 1957; Lányi, 1968, 1969; Michel-Briand *et al.*, 1975).

VIII. REPRODUCIBILITY OF SEROGROUPING

The reproducibility of serogrouping is fairly high compared to the notable instability of phage typing and the variation seen with pyocine typing (e.g. Bergan, 1973a, b, c).

In the history of *P. aeruginosa* serology, the problem of specificity and reproducibility has arisen again and again. Today, when serogrouping and serotyping can be performed on the basis of well elaborated and established antigenic schemes, it may still present difficulties.

Isolates obtained over a period of time from the same patients cannot adequately elucidate this point. Quite often, several strains of different serogroups are present simultaneously, particularly in chronic diseases like respiratory tract disease (e.g. chronic bronchitis or cystic fibrosis). Since cross-infection is to be reckoned with clinically, appearance with time of strains with new serogroups is to be expected. Urinary tract isolates, however, tend to maintain their serogroup characteristics (Matsumoto *et al.*, 1968). For instance, a number of cases have been described in which isolates which appeared to be the same organism acquired new antigens, in predominant nosocomial organisms involving changes from one O-subgroup to another (Lányi, 1966/67). These involved O:7a, 7b → O:7a, 7c alteration.† Lányi and Lantos (1976) similarly observed a change from O:11a, 11b → O:11a, 11c.† Changes which occur fairly commonly in patients consist of the appearance of a more complex antigenic structure. The culture retains its smooth colonial form and its original antigen(s), but, in addition, becomes agglutinable in one or more specific antisera with which the parent strain does not react. A number of changes which are interpreted as degradation or loss of antigens occur both *in vivo* and after lysogenization *in vitro*, and have been reported by Lányi and Lantos (1976).

In some instances, there have been documented cases where the possibility of antigenic change is indicated by type identity in two independent typing systems like pyocine typing and lysotyping between early and subsequent isolates from the same individuals. For instance, Bergan (1973c) observed one such instance of change from O: 6 to O: 1.

More conclusive information is derivable from *in vitro* data—although even such experience seems rather conflicting from different centres. It is the long experience of both authors, and others, that the serogroup is a stable characteristic, during usual laboratory maintenance conditions (unpublished data; Bergan, 1973a; Kleinmaier, 1957/58). However, antigen changes have been reported on subcultivation and storage of cultures at room temperature (Homma, 1971, 1974; Homma *et al.*, 1972). For instance, 11 strains of different serogroups were maintained for a long time (not specified), and multiple subculture in four instances yielded progeny of different serogroup specificities (Homma, 1971; Homma *et al.*, 1972). Kawaharajo (1973) subcultured his strains three times during 85 days and stored them at room temperature between periods of incubation

† Serogroup designation system of Lányi (1966/67) O: 11a, 11b → O: 11a, 11c and O: 4a, 4b → O: 4a, 4c.

at 37°C and found that only 94·1% (of 405 strains) maintained their serogroup specificity. Of the remainder, 1·5% changed to reaction with one other serogroup serum, 2·7% started to react with more than one serogrouping serum, 1% started to react with one instead of with two grouping sera, and 0·7% developed spontaneous agglutination.

When a culture agglutinates in more than one grouping serum, the reaction may under certain circumstances be due to colony dissociation (Shionoya and Homma, 1968). This is a similar phenomenon to that observed in phage typing (Zierdt and Smith, 1964). Differences among different colonies of the same culture, as have repeatedly been noted, may be due to co-infection by several strains simultaneously. Variations in conditions of strain cultivation may influence results, particularly if the cultures are old before they are used in agglutination, when the reactions may be erratic. It is possible—although not systematically studied—that longer incubation times allow for the formation of envelope substance that can interfere with the somatic antigens of the cell wall. For instance, mucoid substance in a number of instances has made individual clones inagglutinable in O-sera, although identity in pyocine type and phage type has shown that the clones derived from single clones of the same strain were all identical (Bergan and Høiby, 1975). Perhaps simple differences in the media used and variation in the age of cultures, which have consistently been less than 24 h in the laboratories of the present authors, can serve to explain some of the apparently conflicting experience of stability of antigen specificity. We therefore recommend 16–18 h blood agar cultures for live slide agglutination. For tube agglutination using 1–2½ h boiled cells (100°C), the growth conditions are probably not so crucial, but controlled growth conditions within limits which usually give satisfactory results still appear advisable.

Another explanation could be that the genetics of the cell become modified.

O-antigen specificity is determined at least in part by a gene (or genes) located very near the *leu* locus on the linkage map of Holloway *et al.* (1971) (Matsumoto and Tazaki, 1975) as evidenced by both conjugation and transduction. Spontaneous changes certainly may occur in the genes controlling the specificity of antigen determinants, as occurs with other characteristics. In a few instances, genetic change has even been the result of planned experiments.

Thus, change has been effected *in vitro* by lysogenization (Bergan and Midtvedt, 1975; Holloway and Cooper, 1962; Lányi and Lantos, 1976; Liu, 1969). Such change has been labelled seroconversion. Modification of serogroup by pseudolysogeny and a carrier state have been discussed by Bergan and Midtvedt (1975), but such changes are only temporary. The stability of seroconversion must be sustained after serial subculture. Stable seroconversion *in vitro*, in principle from O: a, b to O: a, c, was induced by Holloway and Cooper (1962). Liu (1969) reported on a number of conversions. Bergan and Midtvedt (1975) induced changes from Habs group O: 5 to groups O: 6 and O: 9. Lányi and Lantos (1976) observed the following (using the terminology of Lányi, 1966/67):

Serogroup antigens before	Serogroup antigens after
O: 1	O: 1, (O: 8)
O: 4a, 4b	O: 1, O: 4a, 4b, O: 8, (O: 10a), O: 11
O: 4a, 4b	O: 1, O: 4a, 4b, O: 8, O: 10a, O: 11
O: 4a, 4c	O: 1, O: 4a, 4c, (O: 8), (O: 10a), (O: 11)

It is interesting to note that in the hands of Bergan and Midtvedt (1975) the Habs O:5† (Lányi O:3a, 3d in which Lányi and Lantos (1976) failed to induce seroconversion) changed to O: 6 and O: 9, which were also present (as Lányi O: 4a and O: 10a) in the derivates of Lányi and Lantos (1976). The two groups of investigators both observed simultaneous changes in phage types.

Similar changes have been proven to occur *in vivo*. Bergan and Midtvedt (1975) used gnotobiotic rats contaminated by only one strain of *P. aeruginosa* and controlled phage strains. A change from Habs O: 5 to O: 9 was obtained, parallel to the *in vitro* results. These findings *in vivo* imply a basis for serogroup changes in patients and consequently have considerable importance and implications for the reliability of epidemiological typing and its use in nosocomial tracing. Lányi and Lantos (1976) substantiated the changes by both tube and slide agglutination, and in the latter described some of the new reactions as a loose, flaky aggregation of bacteria instead of the smaller granular clumping characteristic of usual group specific O-agglutination. Because the derived strains retained their smooth colonial form and the antigens thereof remained heat stable, the changes could be interpreted as a kind of serological R-antigen variation— or degradation. The assumption is made likely by the circumstance that all secondary strains possessed the Lányi (1966/67) factor O: 8 not included in the O-scheme presented here because it is an R-like factor (Ádám *et al.*, 1971; Lányi and Ádám, 1973; Lányi *et al.*, 1975). One interesting observation is a difference in the stability of the seroconversion in the Hungarian and Norwegian studies. After maintenance in the lyophilized state at +4°C for 1½ years the latter had reverted to their original

† The strains used were not the same. In Budapest, strain 170005, in Oslo, the well known strain IC of Holloway, which has been particularly useful in extensive successful genetic studies, was employed.

O: 5 and no prophage could be induced to enter a lytic cycle. Nutrient broth was used as lyophilizing medium. The Hungarian study, using *P. aeruginosa* strains which differed from those of the other study could maintain the seroconverted antigen specificities for one year at 18–20°C in rabbit serum–cysteine-inositol suspending fluid.

Beumer *et al.* (1972) observed that lyophilization had a dramatic effect upon the phage type of pseudomonas which, subsequent to freeze drying, was changed in 40% of the strains. The fact that a frequency of lysogeny of 90–100%, even polylysogeny in some strains, has been detected in *P. aeruginosa* (*vide* Bergan and Midtvedt, 1975), provides a key for the development of a molecular biology mechanism to explain such instability. An extrachromosomal factor may easily be lost. It is important to have these mechanisms of antigenic change in mind. However, although changes due to cultivation on artificial media can readily be elucidated, clinically it will usually be more than a trivial matter to differentiate between stable seroconversion or simple bacterial superinfection.

IX. INTERRELATIONSHIP BETWEEN TYPING METHODS

The interrelationships between different typing methods are of practical importance. Gould and McLeod (1960) and Gould (1963) combined serogrouping and lysotyping on a small number of nosocomially related strains. Eighty-five per cent of the 286 isolates examined constituted only three phage sensitivity patterns. This explains why in those studies only a few serogroups were identified, and a relationship between serological and phage typing was suggested. The experience of Meitert and Meitert (1966) based on 364 isolates was quite different. Each of their lysotypes could be divided into several serogroups. Accordingly, their combination of serology with phage typing rendered a differentiation which is adequate for detailed assessment of a nosocomial situation.

Recently, the possibility of a correlation between serogroups and pyocine types has been studied (Bergan, 1973a). Few strains were epidemiologically related. Still, there was a tendency for a few combinations of pyocine types and serogroups to occur with a slightly higher frequency. Thus, whereas pyocine type 1 occurred in one-third of the total material, two-thirds of the strains of serogroups O: 2 and O: 6 were all of p1. Fourteen per cent of the total material was p5,† but p5 contributed 54% of the group O: 3 strains. Whereas group O: 6 contributed 18% of the total, among the p3 strains 57% were O: 6. Similarly, 18% of the total were O: 3, but among the p5 strains three-quarters were O: 3. Wahba (1965a, b), who combined

† p5 Indicates pyocine type 5, other pyocines referred to similarly.

the Darrel and Wahba pyocine typing system with the Habs serogrouping scheme, and Csiszár and Lányi (1970) with the Gillies and Govan pyocine system and Lányi serogrouping scheme, all concluded that some relationship exists between pyocine type and serogroup.

It may seem surprising that serogroup and phage susceptibility do not show more overlapping, since both are determined by surface structures. The existence of a relationship between lysotype and serogroup was assumed in *S. aureus* until Oeding and Williams (1958) found that there was no absolute interdependence between the two. Also, in *P. aeruginosa* phages do not appear to have a preference for certain serogroups (Bergan, 1973b; Meitert and Meitert, 1966; Edmonds *et al.*, 1972b). Lantos *et al.* (1969) on pseudomonas isolates from a water supply found many lysotypes among each serogroup. In one instance, the pseudomonas isolates from a particular water supply were all of the same serogroup and phage type indicating that pollution originated from one single source. Such a relationship (Bergan, 1973b) was only demonstrated for a few phages, and the tendency was so feeble that generally no relationship exists between lysosensitivity and serogroup. Jedlićková and Pillich (1968) thought that there might be a slight tendency towards a relationship between serogroups and lysosensitivity, but the results show that serogroups are efficiently subdivided by phages and that individual phages lyse strains of several serogroups. Yamada (1960) with 6 phages and 6 O-sera typed a very limited series of only 34 strains and concluded that the two methods gave almost the same subdivision.

Similarly, pyocine (indicator strain streaking technique) and phage typing are not correlated (Bergan, 1973b; Sjöberg and Lindberg, 1968; Farmer and Herman, 1969). Since pyocine typing examines the ability to *produce* a substance and phage typing the *sensitivity* to an agent produced elsewhere, this is not surprising.

It is interesting to note, in this connection, that Homma and Suzuki (1961) found pyocine activity to be associated with the protein component of the cell wall lipopolysaccharide-protein complex. Such results would, of course, be obtained if the immunizing antigens contained both pyocines and phages. Purifications were carried out by various procedures and checked by electron microscopy which showed that the antigen preparations were pure, consisting either of phages or of pyocines. Still, it is difficult to exclude completely the possibility that there could have been impurities in concentrations below the sensitivity level of the control methods. The relationship also concerns the function of the two agents. Sensitivity to certain phages was accompanied by sensitivity to given pyocines (Ito and Kageyama, 1970). Indeed, Ito and Kageyama concluded that phage and pyocine receptors were identical.

There is a definite relationship, however, between pyocines and phages, i.e. between the agents which interfere with the bacteria (Homma and Shionoya, 1967; Ito and Kageyama, 1970). Antisera against bacteriophages also inhibit the activity of pyocines and anti-pyocine sera neutralize phage activity.

X. PREFERENCE OF TYPING METHODS

The serology of *P. aeruginosa* has been important ever since epidemiological tracing of bacteria started. Serological methods have now reached a level of refinement which makes serotyping well suited to the characterization and subdivision of epidemic types.

If suitable agglutinating sera and the corresponding control cultures are available, grouping by O-antigens offers a simple, reliable, and rapid method. By slide agglutination from 18 to 20-h blood agar cultures, first in pooled sera and then in single, unabsorbed O-sera or factor sera, a skilled person is able to examine 20–40 strains an hour. Determination of subgroup antigens by slide agglutination in absorbed sera only represents a small amount of additional work. It also gives valuable information in excess of using unabsorbed grouping sera, since strains belonging to two or more different subgroups of the same O-group may frequently be encountered in the same hospital unit. Due to the lack of suitably absorbed antisera, subgrouping has not yet gained wide recognition.

Typing according to H-antigens is not being used routinely even in laboratories where H-sera are available. This is partly due to the fact that the methods (agglutination test or migration-inhibition technique) are more laborious and time consuming than O-agglutination. Moreover, the majority of isolates in many frequent serogroups bear within each group only one kind of H-antigen. Therefore, the value of additional H-typing is often more limited.

Other serological methods (precipitation, passive haemagglutination, immunoelectrophoretic grouping, immunofluorescence, and identification of extracellular products' antigens) although giving reliable and reproducible results, are too laborious for the routine laboratory.

An alternative to H-typing, if subdivision of serogroup or subgroups is desired, are phage typing or pyocine typing. With the subdivision of frequently occurring O-complexes such as O: 2 and O: 6, as described in this article, it is not quite as necessary to supplement serotyping with other procedures as before, but previously recommendations for combining two methods have often been given. Thus Bergan (1973c), on the basis of in-depth analysis of epidemiological typing patterns, concordance of types and reproducibility and ease of maintenance of methods, has preferred

7

combined serogrouping and pyocine typing. The pyocine typing method of Gillies and Govan (1966) would be recommended for this purpose. In many centres, combined use of serogrouping and phage typing is used (Asheshov, 1974; Parker, 1976; Meitert and Meitert, 1966; Meitert and Meitert, personal communication, 1976).

These conclusions, however, were based upon experience with serogrouping systems which are not as differentiating in important O-groups as the scheme presented here (Table IV). Also, some laboratories which prefer a combination of sero-grouping and phage typing in their published work have published on pyocine typing systems that are less satisfactory than that of Gillies and Govan (1966). Other laboratories have not yet published on pyocine typing, but have good experience with their own high quality typing methods. Comparative experience indicates that the best pyocine typing method is that of Gillies and Govan (1966), which is recommended (Bergan, 1973b, c, 1975). Some of the laboratories which have reached the conclusion that phage typing is more practical, have most experience with the pyocine typing method of Wahba (1965a, b).

Phage typing provides the possibility of a better differentiation within each serogroup than does pyocine typing. At the same time, however, phage typing of *P. aeruginosa* is troubled to some extent with unsatisfactory reproducibility. Consequently, it is considered that phage typing, if used, should be combined with serogrouping. This, in effect, resembles the place of phage typing in *Salmonella*, although the reasons for this combined approach are widely different. Phage typing would be useful for possible subdivision within each serological subgroup or subtype.

REFERENCES

Ádám, M. M., Kontrohr, T. and Horváth, E. (1971). *Acta microbiol. Acad. Sci. Hung.* **18**, 307–317.

Adler, J. L. and Finland, M. (1971). *Appl. Microbiol.* **22**, 870–875.

Agarwal, K. C., Talwar, P. and Chitkara, N. L. (1972). *Bull. P.G.I. Chandigarh* **6**, 30–32.

Agarwal, K. C. and Talwar, P. (1976). *Indian J. med. Res.* **64**, 248–259.

Al-Dujaili, A. H. and Harris, D. M. (1974). *J. clin. Path.* **27**, 569–571.

Alms, T. H. and Bass, J. A. (1967a). *J. infect. Dis.* **117**, 249–256.

Alms, T. H. and Bass, J. A. (1967b). *J. infect. Dis.* **117**, 257–264.

Aoki, K. (1926). *Zbl. Bakt., I. Abt. Orig.* **98**, 186–195.

Arseni, A. E. and Doxiadis, S. A. (1967). *Lancet* **1**, p. 787.

Asheshov, E. (1974). "An Assessment of the Methods used for Typing Strains of *Pseudomonas aeruginosa*". Proceedings 6th Greek National Symposium on Microbiology, Athens, pp. 9–22.

Ayliffe, G. A. J., Lowbury, E. J. L., Hamilton, J. G., Small, J. M. Asheshov, E. A. and Parker, M. T. (1965). *Lancet* **2**, 365–369.

Ayliffe, G. A. J., Barry, D. R., Lowbury, E. J. L., Roper-Hall, M. J. and Walker, W. M. (1966). *Lancet* 1, 1113–1117.

Baltimore, R. S., Dobek, A. S., Stark, F. R. and Artenstein, M. S. (1974). *J. infect. Dis.* 130, Suppl. ad Nov., 53–59.

Bergan, T. (1967). *Farmakoterapi (Oslo)*, 23, 72–86.

Bergan, T. (1968). *Nord. Med.* 79, 505–509.

Bergan, T. (1972a). *Acta path. microbiol. scand.* 80B, 351–361.

Bergan, T. (1972b). "Bacteriophage typing of *Pseudomonas aeruginosa*". Universitetsforlaget, Oslo.

Bergan, T. (1973a). *Acta path. microbiol. scand.* 81B, 70–80.

Bergan, T. (1973b). *Acta path. microbiol. scand.* 81B, 81–90.

Bergan, T. (1973c). *Acta path. microbiol. scand.* 81B, 91–101.

Bergan, T. (1975). *In* "Resistance of *Pseudomonas aeruginosa*" (Ed. Brown, M. R. W.), pp. 189–235. John Wiley and Sons, London.

Bergan, T. and Høiby, N. (1975). *Acta path. microbiol. scand.* 83B, 553–560.

Bergan, T. and Midtvedt, T. (1975). *Acta path. microbiol. scand.* 83B, 1–9.

Beumer, J., Cotton, E., Delmotte, A., Millet, M., von Grüningen, W. and Yourassowsky, E. (1972). *Ann. Inst. Pasteur* 122, 415–423.

Bodey, G. P. (1970). *Am. J. med. Sci.* 260, 82–89.

Boivin, A. and Mesrobeanu, L. (1937). *C. r. Séanc. Soc. Biol.*, 125, 273–275.

Borst, J. and de Jong, J. H. L. (1970). *Antonie v. Leeuwenhoek* 36, 190.

Bradley, D. E. (1966). *J. gen. Microbiol.* 45, 83–96.

Bradley, D. E. (1972a). *Biochem. Biophys. Res. Commun.* 47, 142–149.

Bradley, D. E. (1972b). *J. gen. Microbiol.* 72, 303–319.

Bradley, D. E. (1973). *J. Virol.* 12, 1139–1148.

Bradley, D. E. (1974). *Virology* 58, 149–163.

Bradley, D. E. and Pitt, T. L. (1974). *J. gen. Virol.* 23, 1–15.

Bradley, D. E. and Pitt, T. L. (1975). *J. Hyg. (Lond.)*, 74, 419–430.

Buck, A. C. and Cooke, E. M. (1969). *J. med. Microbiol.* 2, 521–525.

Callahan, L. T. (1974). *Infect. Immun.* 9, 113–118.

Callahan, L. T. (1976). *Infect. Immun.* 14, 55–61.

Caselitz, F.-H. (1966). "Pseudomonas-Aeromonas und ihre human-medizinische Bedeutung". G. Fischer, Jena.

Chester, I. R., Gray, G. W. and Wilkinson, S. G. (1972). *Biochem. J.* 126, 395–407.

Chester, I. R., Meadow, P. M. and Pitt, T. L. (1973). *J. gen. Microbiol.* 78, 305–318.

Chia-Ying, W. (1963). *Chinese med. J.* 82, 358–362.

Christie, R. (1948). *Aust. J. exp. Biol.* 26, 425–437.

Csiszár, K. and Lányi, B. (1970). *Acta microbiol. Acad. Sci. hung.* 17, 361–370.

Darrell, J. H. and Wahba, A. H. (1964). *J. clin. Path.* 17, 236–242.

Deighton, M. A., Tagg, J. R. and Mushin, R. (1971). *Med. J. Aust.* 1, 892–896.

Denis, F. and Godeau, C. (1972). *C. r. Séanc. Soc. Biol.* 166, 1535–1538.

Dexter, F. (1971). *J. Hyg.* 69, 179–186.

Dimitracopoulos, G., Sensakovic, J. W. and Bartell, P. F. (1974). *Infect. Immun.* 10, 152–156.

Dogget, R. G. and Harrison, G. M. (1972). *Infect. Immun.* 6, 628–635.

Drewry, D. T., Gray, G. W. and Wilkinson, S. G. (1971). *Europ. J. Biochem.* 21, 400–403.

Drewry, D. T., Gray, G. W. and Wilkinson, S. G. (1972a). *Biochem. J.* 130, 289–295.

Drewry, D. T., Gray, G. W. and Wilkinson, S. G. (1972b). *J. gen. Microbiol.* 73, viii.

Editorial (1975). *Lancet* 1, p. 168.

Edmonds, P., Suskind, R. R., MacMillan, B. G. and Holder, I. A. (1972a). *Appl. Microbiol.* 24, 213–218.

Edmonds, P., Suskind, R. R., MacMillan, B. G. and Holder, I. A. (1972b). *Appl. Microbiol.* 24, 219–225.

Eeden, D. van (1967). *J. gen. Microbiol.* 48, 95–105.

Ende, M. van den (1952). *J. Hyg. (Lond.)* 50, 405–414.

Falcao, D. P., Mendonça, C. P., Scrassolo, A. and de Almeida, B. B. (1972). *Lancet* 2, 38–40.

Farmer, J. J. and Herman, L. G. (1969). *Appl. Microbiol.* 18, 760–765.

Feller, I. and Pierson, C. (1968). *Arch. Surg.* 97, 225–229.

Fensom, A. H. and Gray, G. W. (1969). *Biochem. J.* 114, 185–196.

Fensom, A. H. and Meadow, P. M. (1970). *FEBS Letters* 9, 81–84.

Finland, M. (1971). *In* "Bacterial Infections. Changes in their Causative Agents, Trends and Possible Basis" (Eds. Finland, M., Marget, W. and Bartmann, K.), pp. 4–18. Springer Verlag, Berlin-Heidelberg-New York.

Fisher, M. W., Devlin, H. B. and Gnabasik, F. J. (1969). *J. Bact.* 98, 835–836.

Forkner, C. E. (1960). *"Pseudomonas aeruginosa* Infections". Modern Medical Monographs, Grune and Stratton, New York, London.

Gaby, W. L. (1946). *J. Bact.* 51, 217.

Gillies, R. R. and Govan, J. R. W. (1966). *J. Path. Bact.* 91, 339–345.

Gould, J. C. and McLeod, J. W. (1960). *J. Path. Bact.* 79, 295–311.

Gould, J. C. (1963). *In* "Infection in Hospitals. Epidemiology and Control" (Eds. Williams, R. E. O. and Shooter, R. A.), pp. 119–130. Blackwell Scientific Publications, Oxford.

Govan, J. R. W. (1968). "The Pyocines of *Pseudomonas pyocyanea*". Department of Bacteriology, University of Edinburgh. Thesis presented for the Degree of Doctor of Philosophy, Edinburgh.

Grieble, H. G., Colton, F. R., Bird, T. J., Toigo, A. and Griffith, L. G. (1970). *New Engl. J. Med.* 282, 531–535.

Grogan, J. B. (1966). *J. Trauma* 6, 639–643.

Habs, I. (1957). *Z. Hyg. Infekt.-Kr.* 144, 218–228.

Haynes, W. C. (1951). *J. gen. Microbiol.* 5, 939–950.

Hobbs, G., Cann, D. C., Gowland, G. and Byers, H. D. (1964). *J. appl. Bact.* 27, 83–92.

Høiby, N. (1974a). *Acta path. microbiol. scand.* 82B, 541–550.

Høiby, N. (1974b). *Acta path. microbiol. scand.* 82B, 551–558.

Høiby, N. (1975a). *Acta path. microbiol. scand.* 83B, 321–327.

Høiby, N. (1975b). *Acta ath. microbiol. scand.* 83B, 433–442.

Høiby, N. (1975c). *Scand. J. Immunol.* 4, Suppl. 2, 197–202.

Høiby, N. (1975d). *Scand. J. Immunol.* 4, Suppl. 2, 187–196.

Høiby, N. and Wiik, A. (1975). *Scand. J. resp. Dis.* 56, 38–46.

Holloway, B. W. and Cooper, G. N. (1962). *J. Bact.* 84, 1321–1324.

Holloway, B. W., Krishnapillai, V. and Stanisich, V. (1971). *Ann. Rev. Genet.* 5, 425–446.

Homma, J. Y. (1968). *Z. allg. Mikrobiol.* 8, 227–248.

Homma, J. Y. (1971). *Jap. J. exp. Med.* 41, 387–400.

Homma, J. Y. (1974). *Jap. J. exp. Med.* 44, 1–12.

Homma, J. Y. (1975). *In* "Microbial Drug Resistance" (Eds. Mitsuhashi, S. and Hashimoto, H.), pp. 267–279. University Park Press, Baltimore-London-Tokyo.

Homma, J. Y., Sagehashi, K. and Hosoya, S. (1951). *Jap. J. exp. Med.* 21, 375–379.

Homma, J. Y. and Suzuki, N. (1961). *Jap. J. exp. Med.* 31, 209–213.

Homma, J. Y. and Shionoya, H. (1967). *Jap. J. exp. Med.* 37, 395–421.

Homma, J. Y., Kim, K. S., Yamada, H., Ito, M., Shionoya, H. and Kawabe, Y. (1970). *Jap. J. exp. Med.* 40, 347–359.

Homma, J. Y., Shionoya, H., Yamada, H. and Kawabe, Y. (1971). *Jap. J. exp. Med.* 41, 89–94.

Homma, J. Y. and Abe, C. (1972). *Jap. J. exp. Med.* 42, 23–34.

Homma, J. Y., Shionoya, H., Yamada, H., Enomoto, M. and Miyao, K. (1972). *Jap. J. exp. Med.* 42, 171–172.

Horch, H. H. (1969). *Zbl. Bakt., I. Abt. Orig.* 211, 52–57.

Hosoya, S., Homma, J. Y., Egami, F. and Yagi, Y. (1949). *Jap. J. exp. Med.* 20, 55–68.

Hurst, V. and Sutter, V. L. (1966). *J. infect. Dis.* 116, 151–154.

Ito, S. and Kageyama, M. (1970). *J. gen. appl. Microbiol. (Tokyo)* 16, 231–240.

Jacobsthal, E. (1912). *Münch. Med. Wschr.*, p. 1247.

Jedlićková, Z. and Pillich, J. (1968). *Zschr. inn. Med.* 23, 21–25.

Jellard, C. H. and Churcher, G. M. (1967). *J. Hyg. (Lond.)* 65, 219–228.

Jessen, O. (1965). "*Pseudomonas aeruginosa* and other Green Fluorescent Pseudomonads. A Taxonomic Study". Munksgaard, Copenhagen.

Jones, R. J. and Roe, E. A. (1975). *Br. J. exp. Path.* 56, 34–43.

Kanzaki, K. (1934). *Zbl. Bakt., I. Abt. Orig.* 133, 89–94.

Kawaharajo, K. (1973). *Jap. J. exp. Med.* 43, 225–226.

Kleimaier, H. (1957/1958). *Zbl. Bakt., I. Abt. Orig.* 170, 570–583.

Kleinmaier, H. and Müller, H. (1958). *Zbl. Bakt., I. Abt. Orig.* 172, 54–65.

Kleinmaier, H. and Quincke, G. (1959). *Arch. Hyg. (Berlin)* 143, 125–134.

Kleinmaier, H., Schreil, W. and Quincke, G. (1959). *Zbl. Bakt., I. Abt. Orig.* 174, 229–241.

Kleinmaier, H., Schreiner, E. and Graeff, H. (1958). *Z. Immun.-Forsch.* 115, 492–508.

Klyhn, K. M and Gorril, R. H. (1967). *J. gen. Microbiol.* 47, 227–235.

Knights, H. T., France, D. R. and Harding, S. (1968). *N.Z. med. J.* 67, 617–620.

Kobayashi, F. (1971a). *Jap. J. Microbiol.* 15, 295–300.

Kobayashi, F. (1971b). *Jap. J. Microbiol.* 15, 301–307.

Köhler, W. (1957). *Z. Immun.-Forsch.* 114, 282–302.

Köhler, W. (1957/1958). *Wissenschaft. Z. der Universität Rostock* 7, 25–79.

Kominos, S. D., Copeland, C. E. and Grosiak, B. (1972a). *Appl. Microbiol.* 23, 309–312.

Kominos, S. D., Copeland, C. E., Grosiak, B. and Postic, B. (1972b). *Appl. Microbiol.* 24, 567–570.

Koval, S. F. and Meadow, P. M. (1975). *J. gen. Microbiol.* 91, 437–440.

Kumari, S., Bhatia, S. L. and Agarwal, D. S. (1974). *Indian J. med. Res.* 62, 484–490.

Lantos, J., Kiss, M., Lányi, B. and Völgyesi, J. (1969). *Acta microbiol. Acad. Sci. hung.* 16, 333–336.

Lányi, B. (1966/1967). *Acta microbiol. Acad. Sci. hung.* 13, 295–318.

Lányi, B. (1968). *Acta microbiol. Acad. Sci. hung.* 15, 337–355.

Lányi, B. (1969). *Acta microbiol. Acad. Sci. hung.* 16, 357–361.

Lányi, B. (1970). *Acta microbiol. Acad. Sci. hung.* **17**, 35–48.
Lányi, B. and Ádám, M. M. (1973). *Acta microbiol. Acad. Sci. hung.* **20**, 337–346.
Lányi, B., Ádám, M. M. and Szentmihályi, A. (1975). *J. med. Microbiol.* **8**, 225–233.
Lányi, B., Ádám, M. M. and Vörös, S. (1972). *Acta microbiol. Acad. Sci. hung.* **19**, 259–265.
Lányi, B., Gregács, M. and Ádám, M. M. (1966/1967). *Acta microbiol. Acad. Sci. hung.* **13**, 319–326.
Lányi, B. and Lantos, J. (1976). *Acta microbiol. Acad. Sci. hung.* **23**, 337–351.
Lányi, B., Vörös, S. and Ádám, M. M. (1973). *Acta microbiol. Acad. Sci. hung.* **20**, 249–254.
Lawn, A. M. (1967). *Nature (Lond.)* **214**, 1151–1152.
Liljedahl, S.-O., Malmborg, A.-S., Nyström, B. and Sjöberg, L. (1972). *J. med. Microbiol.* **5**, 473–481.
Linker, A. and Jones, R. S. (1966). *J. biol. Chem.* **241**, 3845–3851.
Liu, P. V. (1966a). *J. infect. Dis.* **116**, 112–116.
Liu, P. V. (1966b). *J. infect. Dis.* **116**, 237–246.
Liu, P. V. (1966c). *J. infect. Dis.* **116**, 481–489.
Liu, P. V. (1969). *In* "Analytical Serology of Microorganisms" (Ed. Kwapinski, J. B. G.), Vol. 2, pp. 1–44. John Wiley and Sons, Inc., New York.
Liu, P. V. (1973a). *J. infect. Dis.* **128**, 506–513.
Liu, P. V. (1973b). *J. infect. Dis.* **128**, 514–519.
Liu, P. V. (1973c). *J. infect. Dis.* **128**, 520–526.
Liu, P. V., Abe, Y. and Bates, J. C. (1961). *J. infect. Dis.* **108**, 218–228.
Losonczy, G., Tóth, L., Petrás, G., Bognár, S., Lányi, B. and Csekes, J. (1971). *Acta microbiol. Acad. Sci. hung.*, **18**, 261–269.
Lowbury, E. J. L. (1974). *In* ."Genetics and Biochemistry of *Pseudomonas*". (Eds. Clarke, P. H. and Richmond, M. H.), pp. 37–65. John Wiley, London.
Lowbury, E. J. L., Thom, B. T., Lilly, H. A., Babb, J. R. and Whittall, K. (1970). *J. med. Microbiol.* **3**, 39–56.
Malmborg, A.-S., Liljedahl, S.-O., Nystrøm, B., Seim, S. and Sjöberg, L. (1969). *Acta path. microbiol. scand.* **76**, 329–336.
Martin, D. R. (1973). *J. med. Microbiol.* **6**, 111–118.
Maruyama, S., Takimoto, M., Suehiro, T., Kawamura, S., Iwata, T., Ono, H., Murayama, T. and Yoshioka, H. (1971). *Acta neonat. Jap.* **7**, 146–150.
Mates, A. and Zand, P. (1974). *J. Hyg. (Lond.)* **73**, 75–84.
Matsui, N. (1959). *Kansai Med. School.* **11**, 287–296.
Matsumoto, H. and Tazaki, T. (1969). *Jap. J. Microbiol.* **13**, 209–211.
Matsumoto, H. and Tazaki, T. (1975). *In* "Microbial Drug Resistance" Eds. Mitsuhashi, S. and Hashimoto, H.), pp. 281–290. University Park Press, Baltimore–London–Tokyo.
Matsumoto, H., Tazaki, T. and Kato, T. (1968). *Jap. J. Microbiol.* **12**, 111–119.
Mayr-Harting, A. (1948). *J. gen. Microbiol.* **2**, 31–39.
Meitert, T. (1964). *Arch. roum. Path. exp.* **23**, 679–688.
Meitert, T. and Meitert, E. (1960). *Arch. roum. Path. exp.* **19**, 623–634.
Meitert, T. and Meitert, E. (1966). *Arch. roum. Path. exp.* **25**, 427–434.
Meitert, T. and Meitert, E. (1971). *Arch. roum. Path. exp.* **30**, 37–43.
Meitert, E., Meitert, T., Cazacu, E. and Moscuna, M. (1967). *Microbiologia, Parazitol., Epidemiol.* **12**, 329–338.
Michel-Briand, Y., Jouvenot, M. and Roche, J. (1975). *C. r. Séanc. Acad. Sci.*, **280**, 2397–2400.

Mikkelsen, O. S. (1968). *Acta path. microbiol. scand.* **73**, 373–390.
Mikkelsen, O. S. (1970). *Acta path. microbiol. scand.* **78B**, 163–175.
Mlynarcik, D. and Muszyński, Z. (1974). *J. Hyg. Epidem.* **18**, 425–428.
Moody, M. R., Young, V. M., Kenton, D. M. and Vermeulen, G. D. (1972). *J. infect. Dis.* **125**, 95–101.
Müller, H. and Kleinmaier, H. (1958). *Z. Hyg. Infekt.-Kr.* **145**, 85–91.
Müller, H., Kleinmaier, H. and Pech, H. (1973). *Zbl. Bakt., I. Abt. Orig.* **225**, 487–503.
Munoz, J., Scherago, M. and Weaver, R. H. (1949). *J. Bact.* **57**, 269–278.
Muraschi, T. F., Miller, J. K., Bolles, D. M. and Hedberg, M. (1966a). *N.Y. St. J. Med.* **66**, 3033–3035.
Muraschi, T. F., Bolles, D. M., Moczulski, C. and Lindsay, M. (1966b). *J. infect. Dis.* **116**, 84–88.
Némedi, L. and Lányi, B. (1971). *Acta microbiol. Acad. Sci. hung.* **18**, 319–326.
Neussel, H. (1971). *Arzneimittel-Forsch.* **21**, 333–335.
Nishimura, T., Takagi, M. and Kotani, Y. (1973). *Jap. J. exp. Med.* **43**, 43–45.
Nord, C.-E., Sjöberg, L. and Wadström, T. (1972). *Acta odont. scand.* **30**, 371–381.
Oeding, P. and Williams, R. E. O. (1958). *J. Hyg. (Lond.)* **56**, 445–454.
Parker, M. T. (1976). *In* "Diagnosis and Management of Gram-Negative Nosocomial Disease" (Eds. Duncan, I. B. R., Hinton, N. A. and Godden, J. D.), pp. 13–24. Toronto.
Pennington, J. E., Reynolds, H. Y., Wood, R. E., Robinson, R. A. and Levine, A. S. (1975). *Am. J. Med.* **58**, 629–636.
Phillips, I. (1966). *Lancet* **1**, 903–904.
Pitt, T. L. and Bradley, D. E. (1975). *J. med. Microbiol.* **8**, 97–106.
Plehn, M. and Trommsdorff, R. (1916). *Zbl. Bakt., I. Abt. Orig.* **78**, 142–157.
Pollack, M., Callahan, L. T. and Taylor, N. S. (1976). *Infect. Immun.* **14**, 942–947.
Rouques, R., Vieu, J.-F., Mignon, F. and Leroux-Robert, C. (1969). *Presse med.* **77**, 509–511.
Rubbo, S. D., Gardner, J. F. and Franklin, J. C. (1966). *J. Hyg. (Lond.)* **64**, 121–128.
Sandvik, O. (1960a). *Acta vet. scand.* **1**, 221–228.
Sandvik, O. (1960b). *Acta path. microbiol. scand.* **48**, 56–60.
Sato, H. and Diena, B. B. (1974a). *Can. J. Microbiol.* **20**, 477–482.
Sato, H. and Diena, B. B. (1974b). *Rev. Can. Biol.* **33**, 93–97.
Sensakovic, J. W. and Bartell, P. F. (1974). *J. infect. Dis.* **129**, 101–109.
Shionoya, H. and Homma, J. Y. (1968). *Jap. J. exp. Med.* **38**, 81–94.
Shooter, R. A. (1971). *In* "Bacterial Infections. Changes in their Causative Agents. Trends and Possible Basis" (Eds. Finland, M., Marget, W. and Bartmann, K.), pp. 125–130. Springer-Verlag, Stuttgart.
Shooter, R. A. (1973). *In* "Brit. Encycl. med. Pract. Medical Progress 1972–73", pp. 47–53. Butterworths, London.
Shooter, R. A., Walker, K. A., Williams, V. R., Horgan, G. M., Parker, M. T., Asheshov, E. H. and Bullimore, J. F. (1966). *Lancet* **2**, 1331–1334.
Shooter, R. A., Faiers, M. C., Cooke, E. M., Breaden, A. L. and O'Farrell, S. M. (1971). *Lancet* **2**, 390–392.
Sjöberg, L. and Lindberg, A. A. (1968). *Acta path. microbiol. scand.* **74**, 61–68.
St. John-Brooks, R., Nain, K. and Rhodes, M. (1925). *J. Path. Bact.* **28**, 203–209.
Southern, P. M., Mays, B. B., Pierce, A. K. and Sanford, J. P. (1970). *J. Lab. clin. Med.* **76**, 548–559.

Stoodley, B. J. and Thom, B. T. (1970). *J. med. Microbiol.* **3**, 367–375.

Sutter, V. L. and Hurst, V. (1966) *Ann. Surg.* **163**, 597–602.

Suzuki, N. (1969). *Biochem. biophys. Acta* **177**, 371–373.

Suzuki, N., Suzuki, A. and Fukasawa, K. (1970). *J. Jap. Biochem. Soc.* **42**, 130–134.

Tchernomordik, A. B. (1956). *Zh. Mikrobiol. Epidemiol. Immunol.* **27** (4), p. 116.

Thörne, H. and Kyrkjebø, A. (1966). *Acta vet. scand.* **7**, 289–295.

Tomiyama, T., Homma, J. Y., Abe, C. and Yoichi, M. (1973). *Jap. J. exp. Med.* **43**, 185–189.

Trommsdorff, R. (1916). *Zbl. Bakt., I. Abt. Orig.* **78**, 493–502.

Verder, E. and Evans, J. (1961). *J. infect. Dis.* **109**, 183–193.

Véron, M. (1961). *Ann. Inst. Pasteur* **101**, 456–460.

Wahba, A. H. (1965a). *Zbl. Bakt., I. Abt. Orig.* **196**, 389–394.

Wahba, A. H. (1965b) *Br. med. J.* **1**, 96–89.

Westphal, O. and Jann, K. (1965). *In* "Methods of Carbohydrate Chemistry" (Ed. Whistler, R. H.), Vol. 5, pp. 83–91. Academic Press, New York.

Whitby, J. L. and Rampling, A. (1972). *Lancet* **1**, 15–17.

Wiedermann, G. and Flamm, H. (1961). *Zbl. Bakt., I. Abt. Orig.* **182**, 67–70.

Williams, R. J. and Govan, J. R. W. (1973). *J. med. Microbiol.* **6**, 409–412.

Wokatsch, R. (1964). *Zbl. Bakt., I. Abt. Orig.* **192**, 468–476.

Wretlind, B., Hedén, L., Sjöberg, L. and Wadström, T. (1973). *J. med. Microbiol.* **6**, 91–100.

Yamada, K. (1960). *Mie. med. J.* **10**, 359–365.

Yoshioka, H., Takimoto, M., Maruyama, S., Furuyama, M. and Murayama, T. (1970). *J. Jap. Ass. infect. Dis.* **44**, 340–344.

Young, L. S. and Armstrong, D. (1972). *CRC Crit. Rev. clin. Lab. Sci.* **3**, 291–347.

Young, V. M. and Moody, M. R. (1974). *J. infect. Dis.* **301**, Suppl. ad Nov., 47–52.

Young, V. M., Moody, R., Kenton, D. M. and Vermeulen, G. (1969). *Bact. Proc.* p. 87.

Zierdt, C. H. and Schmidt, P. J. (1964). *J. Bact.* **87**, 1003–1010.

CHAPTER V

Phage Typing of *Pseudomonas aeruginosa*

Tom Bergan

Department of Microbiology, Institute of Pharmacy,
and Department of Microbiology, Aker Hospital,
University of Oslo, Oslo, Norway

I. INTRODUCTION

Phage typing is one of the standard methods for epidemiological typing. For *P. aeruginosa*, various phage typing procedures have been developed (Table I). These phage typing sets have mostly been developed locally. The phage typing sets of Sutter *et al.* (1965) and that of Bergan (1972) were based on several other previous typing sets. This Chapter will discuss the basic mechanisms involved for phage–host-interaction, and the methods used for phage typing of *P. aeruginosa*.

II. GENERAL CHARACTERISTICS OF
P. AERUGINOSA PHAGES

A. Existence of phages

Phages of P. aeruginosa may be isolated from sewage or from lysogenic isolates. Such strains are fairly common. Alföldi (1957a, b) and others (Feary et al., 1963; Hamon et al., 1961; Holloway et al., 1960; Meitert and Meitert, 1961; Paterson, 1965) have shown that up to 90–100% of the isolates of P. aeruginosa may turn out to be lysogenic. That means that a large number of strains may liberate phages upon proper induction. This also means that it is fairly easy to obtain phages, e.g. for the purpose of constructing a typing scheme. Indeed, one single bacterial strain may even simultaneously contain, i.e. be lysogenic to, several different types of P. aeruginosa phage. If a single isolate yields phage plaques of different morphology, that in itself is not a proof that there are several different phages present; polylysogeny is indicated by the occurrence of several phage strains (isolated from single plaques) of individually different serological specificity in a single bacterial culture (Holloway et al., 1960; Feary et al., 1963).

Sewage specimens may give pseudomonas phages at a farily high frequency.

If the properties of phages from lysogenic strains and from sewage are compared, the former tend to have turbid plaques, whereas the latter exhibit plaques with clear centres and relatively larger diameters.

B. Structure and biology of P. aeruginosa phages

The nucleic acid of the bacteriophages of P. aeruginosa may contain either DNA or RNA (Feary et al., 1963, 1964).

The former are best known. They contain double stranded DNA. The mole % (G+C) ratio of such phages has been reported as falling in the range 46–55% (Chow and Yamamoto, 1969; Grogan and Johnson, 1964; Yamamoto and Chow, 1968). O'Callaghan et al. (1969) found the % (G+C) for 12 phages to vary between 47 and 63%. This is lower than the % (G+C) of ca. 67 obtained for the host, P. aeruginosa (Grogan and Johnson, 1964; Doudoroff and Palleroni, 1974). The latent time has been reported as 35–65 min (O'Callaghan et al., 1969), and burst size 10–200 phages per host cell (Chow and Yamamoto, 1969; O'Callaghan et al., 1969). Part of the phage DNA may be derived from the host, as evidenced by incorporation of radioactively labelled host DNA into the phage genome (Chow and Yamamoto, 1969). Most phages attach randomly to any region of the cell surface, but some seem to have affinity only for the polar ends of the cells (Chow and Yamamoto, 1969) and others to be specific for flagellae.

The morphology of the phages vary. The DNA-phages resemble the T-even phages of *Escherichia coli* in having a head and tail (Chow and Yamamoto, 1969). Most have a morphology corresponding to group A of Bradley and Kay (1960), but group B phage morphology has also been encountered. The tail lengths vary; upon contact with specific bacterial receptors, the sheath of the tails contracts. Some may have a curved tail (Feary *et al.*, 1964). The phage heads vary from 60–70 to 140 nm in diameter (Birdsell and Drake, 1964).

RNA phages with only a spherical structure—and no tail—have been observed (Feary *et al.*, 1964). RNA phages may attach only to fimbriae (Lin and Schmidt, 1972).

Fibrous phages have also been isolated (Minamishima *et al.*, 1968). These have proved to be serologically homogeneous, and production of phages is not affected by Acridine orange. Takeya *et al.* (1959) described a *P. aeruginosa* phage which had a rod-shaped head and a long tail. This had a very narrow host spectrum, minute plaques, heat inactivation at 60°C, latent period of 35 min, and a burst size of 130. In contrast to fibrous *E. coli* phages, the fibrous phages of *P. aeruginosa* have no activity against male strains. The phages probably contain DNA, as evidenced by the fact that recombinants may be formed (Minamishima *et al.*, 1968). A series of papers by Jacob (1952a, b, c) on induction and development of *P. aeruginosa* phages are classic, and provide essential base reading for anyone interested in the subject.

C. Sensitivity of phages

The resistance of *P. aeruginosa* phages to chemical and physical agents has been investigated. The phages usually resist a temperature of 60°C fairly well, but are inactivated at 65°C. They are stable at pH 6·5–10·0, but not below 6·5 (Dickinson, 1948). Some phages also withstand exposure to 70°C (O'Callaghan *et al.*, 1969).

A number of chemicals have been tested for their ability to inhibit phage production. Some 500 substances have no effect in concentrations allowing bacterial multiplication. A virus-inhibitory effect is obtained by Proflavine, acridines (5-aminoacridine, 2:7-diaminoacridine, 2-chloro-5-amino-7-methoxyacridine), phenol, hexylresorcinol, whereas Notatin and H_2O_2 only act antivirally in a chemically defined mineral medium, not in broth (Dickinson, 1948).

D. Phage serology

Serologically, the phages of *P. aeruginosa* have been separated into a number of types. Dickinson (1952) found two serologically distinct categories. Feary *et al.* (1964) found a difference between three phages (one a RNA-virus). O'Callaghan (1969) found five serotypes among 12 typing phages.

Lantos (1971) grouped 20 phages belonging to the phage typing set of Lindberg *et al.* (1964) (supplemented by 3 phages). She had 17 antisera and grouped the phages in 10 serogroups.

E. Genetics of *P. aeruginosa* phages

Since a large proportion of *P. aeruginosa* strains are lysogenic, and some temperate phages have been included in phage typing sets, the type of association between a phage and its host cell is of significance. Generally, phages may be incorporated into the continuity of the bacterial genome, usually at one integration site, occasionally a phage is capable of only attaching itself without integration. There is also the possibility that phage may attach to a membrane site (e.g. P.1 of *E. coli*). Krishnapillai and Carey (1972) showed that there is a stable association between a given phage and the bacterial genome close to the *his*-locus.

F. Relationship between phages and pyocins

Since phages and pyocins both interfere with structures on the bacterial cell surface, and there are pyocins which have a morphology reminiscent of phage tails, it has been suggested that the two are in some way related. Ito and Kageyama (1970) and Kageyama (1975) have demonstrated serological cross-reactivity between a few pyocins and *P. aeruginosa* phages.

The relationships must be rather remote, since a large number of phages have been tested for cross-reactivity to pyocins without result. Antibodies prepared against the 5 serotypes of pyocins characterized by Kageyama (sera produced by him) failed to inactivate phages from various typing sets (Bergan, unpublished data).

G. Relationship between phages and autoplaques

P. aeruginosa tends to exhibit plaque-like changes of the surface on densely growing agar cultures. These are called autoplaques and the phenomenon is frequently associated with a metallic sheen. Because the autoplaques are morphologically reminiscent of phage plaques, the two have regularly been confused for each other in the older literature (Lode, 1923; Hauduroy and Peyre, 1923; Pesch and Sonnenschein, 1925; Pons, 1923).

Early reports on filtrates which produced plaques and thus appear to have concerned genuine phages have been published by Okuda (1923), Quiroga (1923), Lisch (1924), Hadley (1924), Asheshova (1926), Gaté and Gardère (1927), Jadin (1932), Rabinowitz (1934), Linz (1938), and Fastier (1945).

Warner studied the phages (1950a) and the iridescent phenomenon—the autoplaques—thoroughly (1950b). His conclusion was that the cause of the autolytic phenomenon could not be explained, although it was observed that crystals of lipid material formed within the autoplaques. They have been the subject of several lucid studies (Berk, 1963, 1965, 1966; Berk and Gronkowski, 1964; Coleman *et al.*, 1969; Conge, 1948; Döll and Freytag, 1964; Fedorko *et al.*, 1967; Pillich *et al.*, 1974; Sierra and Zagt, 1959; Sonnenschein, 1925; Wahba, 1964; Zierdt, 1971), but without any real breakthrough on etiology or formation. The frequency of strains showing the autolytic phenomenon is around 65%. The composition of the medium may influence plaque formation. Plaque-forming strains tend to be more haemolytic against human erythrocytes. No relationship has been found to either clinical source or pathogenicity (Pillich *et al.*, 1976). The ability to undergo autolysis is not mediated by cell-free filtrates of autolytic strains such that the iridescent phenomenon/autolysis is not associated with the production of bacteriophages (Pillich *et al.*, 1976).

H. Phage receptors

The interaction between phage and bacterium is dependent upon attachment to a specific site, a receptor, on the surface of the bacterial cell. The receptor site chemistry is not known in detail, but trichloroacetic acid extracts of the cell wall inhibit phage action (Mead and van den Ende, 1953), presumably because of attachment of the receptor molecule (contained in the trichloroacetic acid extract) to the attachment locus on the phage. Since phages and pyocin both attach to the bacterial surface, it is interesting to note that Homma and Shionoya (1967) concluded that specificity of the receptor sites of phages and of pyocins were related. Ito and Kageyama (1970) felt that the receptor sites for the two agents were identical.

III. HISTORICAL PERSPECTIVE ON PHAGE TYPING OF *P. AERUGINOSA*

The possibility of differentiating different strains of *P. aeruginosa* by the action of standardized sets of phage preparations was demonstrated in principle by Warner (1950a), Don and van den Ende (1950), and Holloway (1960).

Phage typing† in a more systematic fashion appears first to have been developed by Terry (1952), later followed Potel (1957), Yamada (1960), Grogan and Artz (1961), Hoff and Drake (1961), Postic and Finland (1961), and Grün et al. (1967), all with separate, independent phage sets. Some of these merely examined the possibility of differentiating isolates by means of phages.

The 1960's and beginning of the 1970's saw the development of more elaborate phage sets (Table I): Gould and McLeod (1960), Pavlatou and Kaklamani (1961), Graber et al. (1962), Lindberg et al. (1963, 1964), Feary et al. (1963), Zanen and van den Berge (1963), Meitert (1965), Sutter et al. (1965), Jedličková and Pillich (1968), Herrmann (1970), and Bergan (1972b). Sutter et al. and Bergan attempted to obtain better sets by studying previous sets and selecting those phages which together seemed most suitable. Lindberg et al. employed some phages of Graber et al. and several of those used by Hoff and Drake.

The most widely distributed set appears to be the one developed by Lindberg et al., in places supplemented by a few phages. This set as well as the set of Meitert (1965) and of Bergan (1972c) will be discussed in the following. No set has received wide recognition and all are at present used at different centres. Since the sets differ both in phages and in methodology, they will be presented separately, but first common techniques will be described.

IV. TYPING METHODS

A. General procedures

1. *Culture medium*

A number of cultivation media may be suitable both for propagation and typing. Meitert (1965) used 1% peptone water for growth of the bacteria to be typed and supplemented it with 2% agar (pH 7·8) for the typing medium. Sutter et al. (1965) used a chemically defined medium, sodium lactate medium: NaCl, 5 g; $MgSO_4 \cdot 7H_2O$, 0·2 g; $(NH_4)H_2PO_4$, 1 g; K_2HPO_4, 1 g; sodium lactate (60% syrup), 2 ml. The sodium lactate medium was supplemented with 1·5% agar for plates and with gelatin (50 μg/ml) for harvesting phages. Bergan (1972c) used a medium which (i) was rich to ensure good growth of all bacterial strains, (ii) was buffered to better maintain pH at the optimal level, and (iii) was supplemented with bivalent ions to ensure phage attachment. Tryptone (Difco), 10 g; yeast extract (Difco), 5 g; NaCl, 5 g; CaCl, 0·4 g; $MgSO_4 \cdot 7H_2O$, 0·2 g; glucose, 4 g; 0·2 M tris, 250 ml; 0·2 M HCl, 225 ml; distilled water to

† Phage typing and lysotyping are used interchangeably in this Chapter.

TABLE I

Key characteristics and performance of phage typing sets as reported by first authors

	No. of phages	No. of bacteria used for testing set	% Typable	% Lysed by phage	Reproducibility	No. of patterns
Potel (1957)	7	150	—	—	—	—
Yamada (1960)	6	34	—	—	—	6
Grogan & Artz (1961)	8	—	—	—	Same focus yields same strain in 72%. Cultures from more foci of same patient are same in 59%	—
Hoff & Drake (1961)	20	ca. 300	—	—		—
Postic & Finland (1961)	13	161	89	—	Satisfactory	—
Feary et al. (1963)	12	95	70	1–37	—	—
Grün et al. (1967)	10	130	97	19–87	—	19
Gould & McLeod (1960)	16	286	92	—	Little smaller for phage typing of S. aureus	—
Meitert (1965)	13	652	93	—	—	64
Pavlatou & Kaklamani (1961)	12	174	79	—	10% change sensitivity pattern after 6 months	12
Graber et al. (1962)	21	508	88	—	—	6
Lindberg et al. (1963)	15	1100	92	—	—	—
Zanen & van den Berge (1963)	13	—	—	—	—	—
Sutter et al. (1965)	18	317	86	0·3–65	Studied	87
Jedličková & Pillich (1968)	9	—	67	—	—	15
Herrmann (1970)	11	372	67	—	—	—
Bergan (1972d)	24	486	96	1–44	Ca. 90% showed difference in only one or no reaction upon retyping within a week	240

1000 ml; pH 7·1 prior to autoclaving at 121°C for 15 min. Plates contained 1·4% agar (Difco).

2. *Propagation*

Propagation of phages is preferably carried out in Roux flasks or flat-bottomed, 2-litre Erlenmeyer flasks with 250 ml broth. The initial number of bacteria should be 10^7 cells/ml of an overnight liquid culture. Sufficient phages should be added to give 10^5 plaque forming units (PFU) per ml cell suspension. Flasks are incubated in a gyratory shaker for 5 h at 37°C. The sloppy agar technique used for *Staphylococcus* (Blair and Williams, 1961) may also be used, but has resulted in lower titres for some phages (unpublished results). After centrifugation, the filtrates are filtered through Millipore membranes of pore size 0·45 μm. Filtrates are stored at 4°C. Work with the phage suspensions should be carried out in laminar air flow benches to reduce the risk of contamination. The addition of chloroform has been used by several workers to prevent growth of bacteria or moulds. The practice does not seem to harm the phages.

3. *Typing procedure*

Each phage typing set consists of a number of phages. A suitable dilution of each is applied as a calibrated drop (0·01 ml) by multiple inoculator (or other device) to a particular position on the plate.

To determine what dilution of phage is suitable for typing, calibrated aliquots (loopfulls) of a series of ten-fold dilutions in propagating medium (liquid) are applied to a plate seeded with the host propagating strain.[†]

The strength of the phage suspension in all typing schemes should be standardized to correspond to the routine test dilution (RTD). RTD is that dilution of the phage suspension which gives semiconfluent plaques (more than 50 plaques) corresponding to the zone covered by the drop applied. The results are as follows:

[†] Bacterial strain grown for 3–4 h in broth, suitably diluted, seeded on plates, dried at room temperature for 15–20 min after application of the phage drops. Plates are dried until the viscal liquid of the aliquots disappears before incubating overnight at 37°C. The same procedure is used for typing with the only modification that strains are usually taken from overnight blood agar cultures and suspended in liquid before inoculation.

It is important that the bacterial suspensions are not too dense. Suspensions should be even (use mixers or shakers such as Vortex or Whirlmixer). Suitable density is an optical density (O.D.) of 0·1–0·2 as measured on a Beckman Colorimeter D.B.

Reaction score	Plaques
+ +	semiconfluent; more than 50 plaques; corresponds to RTD
+	20–50 plaques
±	20 plaques

Quantitation of plaque forming units (PFU) is performed by the soft agar overlay method of Adams (1959). The bottom agar (20 ml per 9 cm diameter plates) consists of the usual typing medium with 1·4% agar (Difco), whereas the top layer contains 0·6% agar (5 ml). One drop of the bacterial culture is added per tube of melted soft agar at 50°C and 0·1 ml aliquots of the appropriate dilutions of the phage suspension are added immediately before it is poured as an even layer on top of the agar. Triplicate counts should be made to improve accuracy of quantitation. After incubation (37°C, 18–20 h) each phage (given appropriate dilution of phages) will have given rise to a single plaque.

Usually, typing is carried out with phage at RTD. Vieu (1971) with 100× RTD, has been able to type some strains which were non-typable at RTD. Bernstein-Ziv *et al.* (1973) compared the results of typing with RTD; 10× RTD, 100× RTD and 1000× RTD. They found that 100× RTD gave a better differentiation of strains than did RTD. Sjöberg and Lindberg (1968) found 100× RTD to give good results and improve the percentage of typable strains.

4. *Determination of lytic spectra*

In order to ensure that the host range of the phage after propagation remains unchanged from time to time, the lytic spectrum of each phage should be determined on the propagating strains. For *P. aeruginosa*, it is admittedly difficult to obtain identical results each time, but identity in host spectrum is important for an acceptable reproducibility of results.

Determining the lytic spectrum of a phage consists of finding out for each bacterial strain which phage dilution in 10-log steps (1/10, 1/100, 1/1000, etc.) gives a + + reaction. This is compared to the dilution which corresponds to RTD, i.e. gives a + + reaction in the homologous host-propagating strain. The degree of difference is scored as follows:

5 = same as RTD
$4 = 10^1$ to 10^2 more concentrated than RTD
$3 = 10^3$ to 10^4 more concentrated than RTD

2 = 10^5 to 10^6 more concentrated than RTD
1 = very weak lysis
− = no reaction
( ) = growth inhibition.

B. Phage typing set of Lindberg *et al.* (1963a, b, c)

1. *Introduction*

The phage typing set of Lindberg *et al.* is based upon studies with a number of phages ($n = 75$) including 10 strains from Texas, 12 from the Hoff and Drake (1961) phage typing set, 12 from the set of Postic and Finland (1961), 9 from Minnesota, 6 from California, 2 from Australia, and 24 from England. All phages were tested on each of the propagating strains. The selection for the final typing set was based on the 75 × 75-data matrix (i.e. 5625 reactions) and trials carried out which were designed to provide data on the consistency of reactions and ease of reading.

For a decade, details of the phage typing set of Lindberg *et al.* were only presented at meetings and published as summaries (1963a, b, 1964) and reports for private circulation (e.g. 1963c). This has now been changed with an excellent extensive presentation (Lindberg and Latta, 1974).

2. *Phages*

The phages included in the phage typing set are designated 2, 7, 16, 21, 24, 31, 44, 68, 73, 109, 119×, 352, 1214, F7, F8, F10, M4 and M6 (Lindberg and Latta, 1974). At various centres, these are supplemented by, for example, 11, 18, 21 and 188/1 (Asheshov, 1974). The host-propagating bacterial strains have identical labels. The phages are presented in more detail in Table II. At the Institut Pasteur, the phages have been supplemented by 13 phages isolated in Paris (Vieu, 1969). The latter group are applied to bacteria resistant to the first set (Vieu, 1971).

3. *Handling of strains to be typed*

The procedures used correspond to those employed for *Staphylococcus aureus* (Blair and Williams, 1961) and are outlined in Section IV.A of this Chapter. The host-propagating strains have the same designation as their homologous phages.

Lindberg and Latta (1974) propagated their phages on semi-solid agar overlay plates (150 mm in diameter). Phages are harvested by disruption of agar gel by freezing followed by centrifugation. The typing phages are found to be stable at 4°C for at least a year.

After counting of phage preparations, and determination of their spectra (Table III), the phages are ready to be used in phage typing. The procedures used by Lindberg *et al.* have been described in detail for the bench worker (Lindberg, pers. comm., 1967).

To obtain optimal results, all procedures should be carefully standar-

TABLE II

Characteristics of phage strains included in the set of Lindberg *et al.* (1963a, b, c, 1964) and strains used in association with it

Phage designation	Source	Used in other phage typing set*	% Strains lysed				
			Asheshov (1974)	Bergan (1972a)	Piguet & Kékessy (1972)†	Sjöberg & Lindberg (1968)†	Vieu (1971)†
2	Sewage	HD, G	20	37		47	
7	Sewage	HD, G	28	39	38	46	
16	Sewage	HD, G	10	10	20	12	
21	Sewage	HD, G	38	40, 44	59	31	
24	Sewage	HD, G	10	12	11	11	3
31	Sewage	HD, G	18	19, 17	17	13	13
44	Sewage	HD, G	32	27	28	21	
68	Sewage	HD, G	54	36	48	36	
73	Sewage	HD, G	11	5	12	25	2
109	Sewage	HD, G	34	23	38	32	
119x	Sewage		40	26	42	36	
352	Lysogenic strain	G	20	16	15	45	
1214	Sewage	HD, G	35	35	39	38	11
F7	?		11	7	12	12	3
F8	?		27	25	25	21	12
F10	?		2	0·4	2	2	1
M4	?		12	11	23	26	
M6	?		8	4	5	11	0·2
Col11	Sewage	PK	20	26	20		
Col18	Lysogenic strain		7	30	23		
Col21	Lysogenic strain		8	3	62		
188/1‡	Lysogenic strain		16	27			

* HD = Hoff and Drake (1961); G = Graber *et al.* (1962); PK = Pavlatov and Kaklamani (1961).

† The strain has been derived from Piguet, Geneva, Switzerland.

‡ Extrapolated from graphs.

dized. The procedures are applicable also to other typing sets for *P. aeruginosa*, and for this reason, they have been included in the Appendix.

4. *Interpretation of results*

The phages of Lindberg *et al.* (1963a, b, 1964) have considerable bac-

TABLE III
Characteristics of phage typing set of Bergan (1972a)

Phage designation	Source	Plaque morphology	% of bacteria lysed, Bergan (1972a)
Primary set			
73	L	clear centre, 2 mm$\varnothing$ + wide halo	36
F7	L	clear centre, 1 mm$\varnothing$ + halo	7
M6	L	opaque, 1–2 mm$\varnothing$	4
Me13	M	pin point, halo, 1 mm$\varnothing$	23
113	H	clear, 1 mm$\varnothing$	8
F116	H	opaque, 1–2 mm$\varnothing$	5
Px3	O	clear, 2–3 mm$\varnothing$ + halo	17
C1c	S	clear, 2–3 mm$\varnothing$ + halo	29
C4	S	pin point	7
C13	S	pin point	6
C21	S	pin point	25
H249	S	clear, 2–3 mm$\varnothing$	21
P10	S	pin point	16
VII	Z	pin point	7
XVI	Z	clear centre, 1–2 mm$\varnothing$ + halo	14
Z2	Z	clear centre, 1 mm$\varnothing$ + halo	22
Z3	Z	clear, 1 mm$\varnothing$	3
Z19	Z	opaque, 1–2 mm$\varnothing$	9
Z20	Z	pin point	5
Auxiliary set			
21B	L	pin point to 1 mm clear$\varnothing$ + halo	44
68	L	opaque, 3–5 mm$\varnothing$	36
Col11	A	clear, 2–3 mm$\varnothing$	26
K9	PK	pin point + halo	23
C15	S	opaque, 1–3 mm$\varnothing$	19

L = Lindberg *et al.* (1963).
M = Meitert (1965).
H = Dr B. W. Holloway, Department of Genetics, Monash University, Clayton, Victoria, Australia.
O = Dr R. H. Olsen, Department of Microbiology, Medical School, The University of Michigan, Ann Arbor, Michigan 48104, USA.
S = Sutter *et al.* (1965).
Z = Zanen and van den Berge (1963).
A = Asheshov (1974).
PK = Pavlatou and Kaklamani (1961).
$\varnothing$ = Diameter.

terial avidity. Eight of the phages attack more than one-quarter of the *P. aeruginosa* isolates, 4 more than one-third, and one more than half of the bacteria. Consequently, the pattern codes are long. Although phage patterns were initially indicated by enumeration of each phage active on a bacterial strain (Ayliffe *et al.*, 1966; Bergan and Kozaczek, in press; Bernstein-Ziv *et al.*, 1973; Edmonds *et al.*, 1972; Lantos *et al.*, 1969; Lindberg *et al.*, 1963c; Vieu, 1971), due to the long codes, the phage patterns have more recently been identified by letters and numerals similar to the procedure employed by Meitert (1966) (cf. Table V). Type A-strains react with phage no. 2, and have different patterns with the remaining phages, each pattern denoted by index numbers. Type B-strains are sensitive to phage 7, resistant to phage 2, and give several different patterns with the remaining phages, again each characterized by index numbers. Eleven type groups have been designated, and some 400 different pattern types recognized (Lindberg and Latta, 1974).

The phage types of strains from a given source tend to differ from time to time (Lindberg, 1963c; Lindberg *et al.*, 1966). The phage set has typed 82% of the bacteria studied (Lindberg *et al.*, 1963c).

5. *Stability of lysotypes*

No special report has appeared in writing on the reproducibility of the patterns of the set developed by Lindberg *et al.* Phage typing has been described as a precise and valuable tool for tracing of "nosocomial episodes" (Lindberg and Latta, 1974). It has also been mentioned that there is a lability of phage behaviour with difficulty in interpretation, "so that the identity of two strains may not be determined with certainty" (Lindberg and Latta, 1974).

C. Phage typing set of Meitert (1965)

1. *Introduction*

The phage typing set published in 1965 was an extension of work started in 1958 (Meitert and Meitert, 1958, 1960, 1961). The set has been further refined since its first publication. The phages used originally were obtained by induction from lysogenic strains of *P. aeruginosa*. With these an instability of phage type pattern was noted.

In the new set, phages from pus and other infectious material were included.

2. *Phages*

The phages used are designated by Arabic numerals 1–13. Further details of the typing set are shown in Table IV, which shows the source of

TABLE IV

Characteristics of phage typing set of Meitert (1965)

Phage designation	Source	Host propagating strain	Plaque morphology	% of bacteria lysed, Bergan (1972c)
1	UTI*	72	clear, 1·5 mm∅†	24
2	UTI	79	clear, 1·5 mm∅	29
3	Meningitis	Do.	pin point, <1 mm∅	27 & 16
4	UTI	237	clear, 2 mm∅	31
5	Biliary infection	406	clear with halo, 2 mm∅	34
6	Abscess	1660	clear, 1·5 mm∅	26
7	Septicaemia	184	clear, 1·5 mm∅	28
8	UTI	280	clear, 1·5 mm∅	34
9	Arthritis	95	clear with halo, 2 mm∅	26
10	Septicaemia	502	clear with halo, 1·5 mm∅	26
11	Septicaemia	D	opaque, 1 mm∅	40
12	Faeces	100	opaque, 1 mm∅	32
13	Peritonitis	411	pin point, opaque <1 mm∅	23

* UTI = urinary tract infection.
† ∅ = Diameter.

the phages, the designations of the propagating strains, and plaque morphology.

The lytic activities of the phages as tested on strains from outside Romania are also listed in Table IV.

3. *Handling of strains to be typed*

Meitert (1965) grew the strains to be typed in 1% peptone water for 24 h at 37°C. Five to 6 ml of the culture were suspended in 10 ml of peptone and incubated a further $1\frac{1}{2}$–2 h before inoculation by flooding the typing agar.

4. *Interpretation of results*

The principle used for the interpretation of results by the Meitert typing set is quite unusual compared to that employed for other typing sets of *P. aeruginosa* and for other species like *Staphylococcus aureus* (Blair and Williams, 1961), *Salmonella*, *Shigella* and others (*vide infra*).

A special type designation is attached to every single pattern of lytic reactions encountered. The first ten phages (nos. 1–10) are used to define ten lysogroups as shown in Table V. The bacterial strains of lysogroup 1 are all characterized by sensitivity to phage no. 1. The bacteria belonging to lysogroup 2 are all resistant to phage no. 1, but sensitive to phage no. 2. Analogous patterns are defined for each lysogroup, such that, for example, lysogroup no. 5 has no reaction with phages of lower numerical designations (1–4) and all are sensitive to phage no. 5. There are varying sensitivities to phages with numbers higher than that of the designated group number. Each phage pattern defines a single lysotype. Each phage typing pattern thus is designated not by enumeration of the phages which show lytic activity, as is the case for most other phage typing systems, but with a code consisting of an Arabic numeral for the lysogroup and a Latin letter for the lysotype, e.g. 5d. The key to the various types is shown in Table V (issued by private circulation, September 1973).

By virtue of the fact that there are more phages which contribute to the differentiation of the pattern within lysogroup 1, that inevitably becomes subdivided into more categories, i.e. lyso*types*, than any of the other lysogroups.

Phages 11, 12 and 13 are not utilized in the key at all once there is sensitivity to any of the phages 1–10. The last three phages are only considered when there is resistance to the first 10 phages. The reason is that phages 11, 12 and 13 show more variable reactions. According to the patterns with phages 11–13, 8 different lysotype variants are discerned—in addition to 87 lysotypes differentiated by the first 10 phages.

The frequency of the most important lysotypes are (Meitert, 1966):

4a	34%
1a	18%
1b, 3f, 4b each	5%
9a, 10 each	3%
3, 3a each	2%
2, 4i each	1%
4f	0·3%

5. *Stability of lysotypes*

After three subcultures during the course of one year's storage on agar slants, 16% of 624 strains exhibited a changed lysotype (Meitert, 1966)—mostly within the same lysogroup. Changes were most frequent within groups 1, 2 and 3.

Notwithstanding *in vitro* instability, clinical experience with serial isolates from the same individuals and passages in mice, have indicated satisfactory reproducibility of results (Meitert, 1966).

D. Phage typing set of Bergan (1972a)

1. *Introduction*

The phage typing set of Bergan (1972a) was developed on the basis of five previous typing sets (Lindberg *et al.*, 1963a; Meitert, 1965; Pavlatou and Kaklamani, 1961; Sutter *et al.*, 1965; Zanen and van den Berge, 1963) and a few additional phages (Bergan, 1972a).

Because some of the previous sets had also been based partly or entirely

TABLE V

Lysotyping of *Pseudomonas aeruginosa*

Lysotype	Phage group	1	2	3	4	5	6	7	8	9	10	11	12	13
1a	1	•	•	•	•	•	•	•	•	•	•		v *)	
1b		•	•		•	•	•	•	•	•	•		v	
1c		•	•	•	•	•	•	•	•		•		v	
1d		•	•	•	•	•	•		•	•	•		v	
1e		•		•	•	•	•		•	•	•	•	v	
1f		•	•			•		•	•	•	•		v	
1g		•	•	•		•				•	•		v	
1h		•										•	v	
1i		•	•		•	•	•	•	•	•			v	
1j		•	•		•	•	•		•	•			v	
1k		•		•	•	•		•	•	•			v	
1l		•	•	•	•								v	
1m		•	•										v	
1n		•	•	•	•	•			•	•		•	v	
1o		•	•	•	•	•			•	•	•		v	
1p		•	•	•	•	•	•	•	•				v	
1r		•	•	•	•	•	•	•	•	•			v	
1s		•	•	•	•	•		•	•	•	•		v	
1t		•	•	•	•	•	•	•			•	•	v	
1u		•	•	•	•	•		•	•				v	
1v		•	•		•	•		•		•	•		v	
1w		•	•						•	•	•		v	
1x		•	•		•	•			•	•	•		v	
1z		•			•	•	•	•	•	•	•		v	
1y		•	•			•	•		•	•	•		v	
2a	2		•	•	•	•	•	•	•	•	•		v	
2b			•		•	•	•	•	•		•		v	
2c			•		•	•	•	•	•	•	•		v	
2d			•	•		•			•	•			v	
2e			•			•			•	•			v	
2f			•	•	•	•	•	•	•				v	
2g			•		•	•	•	•	•				v	
2h			•		•			•	•				v	
2i			•	•		•							v	
2j			•			•							v	
2k			•										v	
2l			•	•	•	•	•	•	•	•			v	
2m			•		•		•	•	•	•	•		v	
2n			•	•	•	•			•	•	•		v	
2o			•	•	•			•	•	•	•		v	

TABLE V (*continued*)

													V			
3a					●	●	●	●	●	●	●	●	V			
3b					●	●	●	●	●	●		●	V			
3c					●		●	●				●	V			
3d					●		●				●	●	V			
3e					●			●				●	V			
3f					●					●	●	●	V			
3g					●					●	●	●	V			
3h					●							●	V			
3i	**3**				●	●		●	●	●			V			
3j					●				●			V			
3k					●		●	●	●				V			
3l					●								V			
3m					●			●			●	●	V			
3n					●	●		●	●	●	●	●	V			
3o					●	●			●	●	●	●	V			
3p					●						●		V			
3r					●						●	●	V			
4a						●	●	●	●	●	●	●	V			
4b						●	●	●	●	●	●	●	V			
4c						●	●	●	●	●		●	V			
4d						●	●	●	●		●	●	V			
4e						●	●	●	●			●	V			
4f	**4**					●	●	●	●	●			V			
4g						●	●	●		●			V			
4h						●		●	●	●			V			
4i						●				●			V			
4j						●							V			
4k						●		●		●	●	●	V			
4l						●	●	●					V			
4m						●		●					V			
5a							●	●	●	●	●	●	V			
5b							●	●			●	●	V			
5c	**5**						●				●	●	V			
5d							●					●	V			
5e							●	●				●	V			
5f							●			●		●	V			
6a								●	●	●	●	●	V			
6b	**6**							●			●	●	V			
6c								●					V			
7a									●				V			
7b	**7**								●	●	●	●	V			
7c									●	●	●		V			
7d									●			●	V			
8a	**8**									●	●	●	V			
9a	**9**										●	●	V			
9b											●		V			
10a	**10**											●	V			
Variant	0																
"	1													●	●	●
"	2													●	●	
"	3													●		●
"	4													●		
"	5														●	
"	6															●
"	7														●	●

* = Phages 11–13 give various reactions corresponding to variants 0–7 and allow lysotopes to be divided into sublysotypes.

● = Phage lysis of intensities CL, OL, SCL, $3+n$, $2+n$ and $1+n$.

on other preceding typing sets, actually eight other phage typing sets were included in the study in one way or another.

In all, 113 phages were candidates for inclusion in the new set. In order to assess their suitability for inclusion, these were tested on 486 bacterial strains. This rendered a data matrix with 54,918 reactions. This data mass was too big for simultaneous evaluation by straightforward human methods. Consequently, clustering techniques as developed for numerical taxonomy were employed. This enabled a sorting out and lumping into groups of phages according to similarity in their lytic spectra. By selecting phages with individually different spectra, taking into consideration the quality of the phage reactions and leaving out phages with the highest avidity, several alternative combinations of phages were selected. These were tested against each other and the most efficient set established as the final typing set.

2. Phages

The new set consists of 19 phages with a lower percentage of lysis (lytic to a mean of $12 \cdot 0 \pm 8 \cdot 6\%$ of the bacteria used for the development of the set). These phages are labelled 73, F7, M6, Me13, 113, F116, Px3, C1c, C4, C13, C21, H249, P10, VII, XVI, Z2, Z3, Z19 and Z20. These are used and evaluated as a primary set. In addition, for the bacterial strains resistant to the primary set, is a set of five phages with higher avidity. This is called the auxiliary set and consists of the phages 21B, 68, Col11, K9 and C15. Host-propagating strains have the same designations. Some properties of the phages are shown in Table III. In operation, all 24 phages are applied to the unknown simultaneously. We do not type first with the primary set and only thereafter with the auxiliary set for bacteria left untyped by the primary set since that would take longer. But by evaluating results in this two-step fashion, we (i) avoid long pattern codes as one would obtain when including phages of considerable avidity, and (ii) reach an acceptable percentage of typable strains (Bergan, 1972a, b).

Propagation of phages, analysis of lytic spectra and determination of RTD have been outlined in Section III.A of this Chapter. Typing is only carried out at RTD.

3. Handling of strains to be typed

Bacterial strains to be typed are taken from 37°C, overnight blood agar cultures and processed as indicated in Section III.A of this Chapter. The typing medium has been described in Section III.A, 1.

4. Interpretation of results

Interpretation of the results with this set is as outlined by Blair and Williams (1961) for *Staphylococcus aureus*. The individual reactions are scored as shown in Section III.A, 3 of this Chapter. The pattern reactions are reported by enumerating all phages which exhibit a reaction with the unknown *P. aeruginosa*. The phage codes for this purpose may conveniently be translated into numbers by the order of their listing in, for example Table III.

5. *Stability of lysotypes*

One definitely weak point in phage typing of *P. aeruginosa*, which is repeatedly mentioned in the relevant literature, is lack of reproducibility. The set (Bergan and Lystad, 1972) was studied specially with this in mind by:

- (i) duplicate typing of the same strains (within a couple of days),
- (ii) comparing the recordings made on the very same plates by two independent observers,
- (iii) letting both observers act as their own reference control by reading all plates twice.

The results are shown in Table VI. It is seen that the variation really is unacceptable—in spite of the utmost care being exercised to use standardized procedures during handling of strains and typing.

E. Typing by phage liberation (Farmer and Herman, 1969, 1974)

Since such a large proportion of strains of *P. aeruginosa* are lysogenic, they may be characterized by the phages they liberate. This technique is the reverse of the classical procedure. A very interesting procedure for this purpose has been developed by Farmer and Herman (1969), who used Mitomycin C to liberate the phages.

The cultures to be tested were streaked on trypticase soy agar (TSA) and incubated at 32°C for 24 h. Then, an isolated colony was chosen, subcultured and grown at 32°C for 16 h. This growth was used to make a 10 ml suspension (in trypticase soy broth—TSB) of standard density (O.D. = 0·4 at 550 nm, unknown instrument) which was mixed with 20 ml TSB and incubated in a 125 Erlenmayer flask with constant agitation for 2 h. Then, 1 ml of 30 μg/ml solution of Mitomycin C (Sigma Chemicals C., St Louis, Mo.) was added. After further shaking for 5–6 h, the fluid was mixed with 50 ml of chloroform (to kill bacteria), and centrifuged for 10 min (5000 g). The top layer was sucked off and placed in a sterile flask.

The bacterial indicators used to detect the activity of phage and/or pyocins in the Mitomycin C lysates were grown on TSA at 32°C for 16 h. A calibrated loop (0·01 ml) was used to transfer the indicator strain (O.D. adjusted to 0·4 at 550 nm) to 10 ml TSB. After mixing, the suspension was used to flood-inoculate a TSA.

TABLE VI

Results of reproducibility of phage typing patterns of *P. aeruginosa* (Bergan and Lystad, 1972)

Row	Class of discrepancy	No. of comparisons	Total no. of plates with differences	No. of plates with differences in recorded reactions 1	2	3	4	5	≧6	Sum ≧2	Total no. of reaction differences	Non-typable at only one of the recordings
A	Intra-observer discrepancy for person A	1004	105	84	17	2	1	1	1	21	133	10
B	Intra-observer discrepancy for person B	1004	204	116	21	10	3	4		38	220	16
C	Inter-observer discrepancy	1004	186	144	32	5	2	3		42	246	11
D	Differences in two typings as recorded by observer A	502	201	114	36	12	4	1	4	57	314	28

Intra-observer discrepancy has been noted when a + or a + + reaction (designations used in reference (1)) was recorded once and a negative reaction at the other reading.

In noting *inter-observer discrepancy*, two recordings of each observer were evaluated. Observer inconsistencies make several situations possible. The evaluation system is explained in the following example:

A_1: 73, F7, M6, Me13, 113, F116, (Px3)
A_2: 73, (F7), 113, F116, (Px3)
B_1: 73, Me13
B_2: 73, (113), F116

where A_1 and A_2 are the recordings made by observer A, and B_1 and B_2 the corresponding recordings made by observer B. Here a difference would be recorded only for phage F7, i.e. a + or a + + reaction observed only once or a ± reaction (figure in parentheses) is considered to represent an inconsistent reaction which must be interpreted more liberally.

This technique was used in two ways:

(a) *Production pattern*. Determination of the activity of pyocin/phage produced by the unknown as tested against a fixed set of 27 sensitive indicator strains.

(b) *Sensitivity pattern*. Detection of sensitivity of the unknown to a fixed set of 24 phage/pyocin preparations.

The activity of phage and pyocins was differentiated visually (Farmer and Herman, 1969). Pyocins produced zones of inhibition which were clear, whereas those resulting from the action of phage showed scattered, "deformed" colonies. The two were differentiated by replica plating by which phage lysis may be transferred, but not pyocin activity. Upon dilution of the preparation, pyocin activity tends to become increasingly weak (fade away), whereas phages show a transition from complete lysis to discrete plaques.

Pyocin activity appears to have been the most important criterion in the test described above (Farmer and Herman, 1969, 1974). By this is meant that more of the growth inhibitory reactions were caused by pyocins.

All strains of *P. aeruginosa* examined by the procedure have been typable. The patterns appear to have been stable (Farmer and Herman, 1969), although slight changes may be seen when retyping is carried out after storage for several months (Farmer and Herman, 1974).

The procedure is strongly reminiscent of pyocin typing methods using a fixed set of standard pyocins dropped on to the unknown strain (Osman, 1965; Rampling and Whitby, 1972).

TABLE VII

Key characteristics of 6 sets studied simultaneously (Bergan, 1972c). Performance on 486 pseudomonas strains

	% Typed	No. of patterns	Mean no. of reactions per plate
Pavlatou & Kaklamani (1961, 1962)	70	78	2·0
Lindberg *et al.* (1964)	86	224	3·9
Zanen & van den Berge (1963)	75	219	3·1
Meitert (1965)	74	158	4·0
Sutter *et al.* (1965)	86	278	3·9
Bergan (1972d)	96	240	2·6

The Pavlatou and Kaklamani set used lacked phage 11. The Sutter *et al.* set was modified by Sutter in relation to the set published, *vide* (Bergan, 1972d). The Lindberg *et al.* set comprised 2 more phages added by Lindberg after their first publication.

V. COMPARISON BETWEEN PHAGE TYPING SETS

During the elaboration leading to the phage typing set of Bergan (1972a, b), results on the bacteria included were as indicated in Table VII. The longest pattern codes were seen with the sets of Lindberg et al. (1963a, b, c) and Meitert (1965). Some of the isolates exhibited very long codes as is also apparent from published reports on, for example, the former set (Ayliffe et al., 1966; Kozaczek, 1972; Lindberg and Latta, 1974).

The percentage of typable strains may vary from one location to another. Thus, the number of non-typable strains have often been lowest on the collection of bacteria on which the phage sets have been developed, or in the location where the phage typing sets have been developed. For example, whereas 96% of the bacteria were reported to be typed originally, only 83% were typed among strains isolated from Poland (Bergan and Kozaczek, unpublished results; Kozaczek et al., 1973; Kozaczek, 1972). The results are comparable, because the typing was carried out in the same laboratory. Similarly, whereas Lindberg and Latta (1974) reported that their set typed 96% of the strains, Bergan (1975) found a typability of 86%, whereas only 66% of the Polish strains mentioned above were typed. Edmonds et al. (1972) found 75% to be typable, Sjöberg and Lindberg (1968) found variations between 79 and 93% depending on geographical source. Such differences reflect the local domination of nosocomially important P. aeruginosa strains. On the Polish strains a better reproducibility was seen for the set of Bergan (1972a, b) than for that of Lindberg (1963a, b, c), but both showed variable results, and the typing with the two sets was carried out in two different laboratories, so the results should be interpreted with caution.

Apart from the studies mentioned, several investigations have compared previous sets in the process of establishing their own, but explicit written reports on this very valuable information have not appeared. Comparisons, consequently, must largely be based upon reports of experience with single sets. This allows of only limited conclusions. The comparative assessment of several typing sets at more centres carried out in a collaborative fashion would seem indicated. Such a study is necessary if a full or semi-international agreement to use only a single set is to be reached.

VI. ASSESSMENT OF PHAGE TYPING

It is perhaps necessary to discuss the reproducibility of phage typing of P. aeruginosa. This seems to leave something to be desired. Meitert (1966) with her set experienced an instability both upon storage under good laboratory conditions and to a lesser extent when strains from the same patient or endemic outbreak were typed soon after isolation. She pointed out that interpretation of results is facilitated by combination with another typing method such as serology or pyocin typing. In later work, the Romanian group has always combined phage typing and serogrouping (Meitert and Meitert, 1966, 1971, 1972; Meitert *et al.*, 1967, 1976). Bergan and Lystad (1972) have presented data showing the variability of phage typing patterns when patterns are read by independent observers and the typing repeated within days. The findings of the reproducibility of the set of Bergan (Bergan and Lystad, 1972) are paralleled by the stability of the results with the phage typing set of Sutter *et al.* (1965). Among 50 bacteria, 70% showed the same pattern upon duplicate typing on the same day, and 58% when retyped on successive days. The variation increased after storage for 1–3 months before retyping. The difference, though, was only in one reaction. After 4 months' storage, Sjöberg and Lindberg (1968) found the phage type patterns to vary for 27% of the strains in one phage reaction, 6% in two reactions, and 3% in three reactions. Changes in lysotypes after 6–12 months' storage were seen in 16% of the strains in the Meitert (1965) system. Pavlatou and Kaklamani (1962) found 89·7% of their strains to retain their phage type after 6 months (storage at 4°C on slants without subculture). Bernstein-Ziv *et al.* (1973) found seven of their 22 patterns to have changed upon typing.

The variability is also mentioned by a number of other authors, although not quantitated. Lindberg and Latta (1974) said that an inherent difficulty in phage typing "is a degree of lability in phage behaviour . . . so that the identity of two strains may not be determined with certainty". Edmonds *et al.* (1972) stated that it was difficult to interpret the significance of specific variations in pattern reactions. The instability is mentioned by Herrmann (1970), who commented that reproducibility often presented considerable difficulties. Vieu (1969) reports similar experience. Grün and Heyn specifically (1969) studied the variability and found that the kind of peptone in the medium influenced the results. Their conclusion was that a chemically defined medium is preferable—such as was the standard recommended method of Sutter *et al.* (1965). They also considered that some of the variability reported may be due to mixed infections. By starting from single colonies, reproducibility could be improved.

Development of the autolytic phenomenon and production of mucoid substance (e.g. strains from cystic fibrosis) represent difficulties for phage typing. In such instances, reactions should be read after 6 h. This will improve results for the strains in question, but has not been studied specifically with a view to using it as general procedure for all strains of *P. aeruginosa*.

The reason that *P. aeruginosa* apparently has a higher variability in phage reactions than other species may be associated with the high degree of lysogenicity in this species. Vieu (1969) and Lindberg and Latta (1974) felt that hypogenicity could increase the variability of typing results. This correlates well with the observation that lysogenization may induce change in phage type (Bergan and Midtvedt, 1975; Lányi and Lantos, 1976). Such a change has been accompanied by change in serogroup (lysogenic seroconversion). A few additional reports on seroconversion have appeared (Holloway and Cooper, 1962; Liu, 1969; Phelps and Kurtz, 1964).

Due to the variability, phage typing results should be interpreted with great caution. Bergan and Lystad (1972) proposed that only differences in three reactions could be accepted as definitely indicative of a type difference. This is more than the permissible variability in *Staphylococcus aureus* (Blair and Williams, 1961). Bernstein-Ziv *et al.* (1973) considered differences in two or more lytic reactions as indicative of a significant difference between strains.

At any rate, it would seem preferable to carry out phage typing of *P. aeruginosa* mainly at central reference laboratories which may have an adequate, large number of isolates (a) to justify maintenance of such a method, and (b) to enable those involved to acquire sufficient experience of the pitfalls and limitations of the method.

VII. COMBINATIONS OF PHAGE TYPING WITH OTHER TYPING METHODS

As is apparent from the above, this author would advise phage typing only for very limited situations, and never alone. The use of two methods simultaneously has often been recommended (Asheshov, 1974; Bergan 1973b; Parker, 1976). Serology is often used with phage typing (Asheshov, 1974; Edmonds *et al.*, 1972; Gould and McLeod, 1960; Graber *et al.*, 1962; Jedlickova and Pillich, 1968; Meitert and Meitert, 1966, 1971, 1972; Parker, 1976).

The combination of phage and serotyping is rational in that both detect differences in bacterial surface structure, phage typing monitoring the finer surface structures.

Bergan (1973a, b) recommends serogrouping as a supplement to phage typing, but prefers the combination of pyocin typing and serogrouping (Bergan, 1973b), and would probably not use phage typing at all due to the variability of results.

APPENDIX
(adapted from description of Lindberg, private communication)

Propagation of phage

Materials (all equipment must be sterile)	Per phage
Peptone agar, in Petri dishes (140 mm), incubated overnight for sterility check	2
Semi-solid agar (0·7%) in tubes, 10 ml	2
(Prepared by adding 0·7% agar to trypticase soy broth (TSB) or 500 ml peptone agar to 500 ml TSB will yield approximately 0·7%)	
Trypticase soy broth (TSB) in tubes, 5 and 10 ml	2
Glass scrapers (6 mm) (solid glass tubing bent at right angle)	1
50 ml round-bottom autoclavable plastic centrifuge tube	1
Sintered glass or Selas filter with flask, 50 ml volume	1
Screw cap tube	2

Methods

1. First, transfer the propagating strain (PS) from a fresh agar slant culture to a tube of 5 ml TSB.
2. Incubate at 37°C for 4–6 h. If screw cap tubes are used, leave cap fairly loose.
3. After incubation use Vortex mixer to make an even suspension of the cells.
4. Concentrate by centrifuging and pour off TSB. Homogenize the button with, e.g., a Vortex mixer.
5. Melt tubes of semi-solid agar.
6. Label two agar plates with the phage number.
7. Cool the two tubes of 10 ml semi-solid agar until 45–47°C.
8. Add 1 ml of phage to the homogenized suspension of its homologous propagating strains.
9. Mix and distribute equally into the two tubes of semi-solid agar. Mix.
10. Overlay by pouring the phage–PS mixture on the top of each agar plate.
11. Distribute the semi-solid agar evenly by slowly rotating the dish.
12. Allow to solidify before inverting.
13. Incubate at 37°C overnight.
14. Remove plates from incubator. Most will be clear although certain phages, particularly 16, 21, 119x, F7, consistently exhibit turbidity.
15. Use a sterile scraper to break up the semi-solid layer, scrape it off into a 50 ml centrifuge tube.
16. Add a tube of TSB, 10 ml, to wash off remaining semi-solid agar into tube. Repeat for the second plate of phage and collect in same centrifuge tube.
17. The supernatant after centrifugation at high speed (refrigerated) is filtered (e.g. Millipore 0·22 μm).

Assay of phage preparations

Determination of titre of phage stock solutions using the semi-solid layer method

The titre of a phage solution is the number of plaque-forming units per millilitre of stock solution.

Materials	Per phage
TSB in tubes, 9·9 ml	5
Peptone agar in Petri dishes (90 mm)	3
Semi-solid agar in tubes, 10 ml	1
Wassermann tubes	3
TSB in tubes, 5 ml	1

Methods

1. Inoculate a loopful of fresh propagating strain from a peptone agar slant into a tube of 5 ml TSB.
2. Incubate at 37°C for 4–6 h.
3. Using tubes of 9·9 ml TSB, prepare dilutions of the phage to be assayed: 10^{-2}, 10^{-4}, 10^{-6}, 10^{-8}, 10^{-10}. Label each tube with phage number and dilution. Refrigerate.
4. Remove 4–6 h cultures from incubator and concentrate growth by centrifugation.
5. Pour off all but about 1 ml of the broth. Mix to obtain an even suspension (Vortex).
6. Melt semi-solid agar.
7. Measure 2 ml amounts into sterile Wassermann tubes in a 47°C water bath, three tubes/phage to be assayed.
8. Label three peptone agar plates with phage number and dilution factors, 10^{-6}, 10^{-8}, 10^{-10}.
9. Add 0·2 ml of the propagating strain to each of the three tubes of semi-solid agar. Mix gently.
10. To the first tube, add 0·1 ml of 10^{-6} dilution of phage; to the second, add 0·1 ml of 10^{-8} dilution; and to the third, add 0·1 ml of 10^{-10} dilution of phage. Mix each thoroughly.
11. Overlay each plate with the contents of the proper tube.
12. Allow to solidify, and incubate at 37°C overnight.
13. Examine each plate and count plaques.

Determination of the routine test dilution (RTD) of a phage

The RTD is the highest dilution of a phage which under standard conditions will yield confluent lysis of its own propagating strain. This dilution is used during typing.

Materials	Per phage
Peptone agar in Petri dishes (90 mm) incubated overnight and dried	1
TSB in flasks or bottles, 50 ml amounts	1
Wassermann tubes for dilution	7
Replicator apparatus when available	1

Methods

1. Inoculate a tube of TSB, 5 ml, with each propagating strain and incubate overnight at 37°C.
2. Prepare dilution tubes by adding 3·6 ml TSB to a series of sterile Wassermann tubes (seven tubes per phage).

3. Label each tube with phage number and appropriate dilution factor.
4. Prepare ten-fold dilutions of each phage by adding 0·4 ml of the concentrated stock phage solution to the first tube, mixing and transferring 0·4 ml to second tube, mixing, etc. Dilutions will be 1:10, 1:100, 1:1000, 1:10,000, etc. Once phage has been diluted, keep tubes refrigerated when not in use.
5. Remove overnight cultures of the propagating strains from the incubator. Mix to obtain an even suspension (Vortex).
6. Label a peptone agar plate with phage number and the dilution factors.
7. Seed the peptone agar plate evenly in order to obtain confluent growth, either with cotton-tipped applicator or by flooding with appropriate dilution of bacterium.
8. Using a 1 ml syringe or calibrated loops start with the highest dilution and proceed to the lowest, and place a drop of each dilution in its proper place on the seeded plate.
9. Allow drops to absorb before inverting plates.
10. Incubate at 37°C overnight.
11. Remove and record degree of lysis at each dilution of phage. Record degree of lysis as follows:

   4+ confluent lysis
   3+ semi-confluent lysis.
   2+ a number of isolated plaques with some semi-confluent lysis
   1+ a number of isolated plaques.

For each phage, the RTD is the highest dilution yielding 4+ or very nearly 4+. This tube is removed for use in the phage typing procedure.

This dilution should remain stable at refrigerator temperature for two weeks. At the end of two weeks, however, it should be checked against its propagating strain to ensure a continued 4+ lytic reaction.

Phage typing procedure

Materials	Per *Pseudomonas*
Peptone agar in Petri dishes, 90 mm, which has been incubated and *dry*	1
Tubes of TSB, 5·0 ml	1

Methods

1. Each *Pseudomonas* strain is inoculated into a tube of TSB and incubated overnight at 37°C.
2. Using a cotton-tipped applicator or a suitable suspension of the unknown by flooding, seed a sterile peptone agar Petri dish evenly with the *Pseudomonas* strain. Label dish with identifying number of *Pseudomonas*. Refrigerate plates as seeded in order that the *Pseudomonas* does not start growing before the phage is applied.
3. Fill the replicator apparatus with each of the phage suspensions at their respective RTD.
4. Remove inoculated dishes from refrigerator and using phage dropping apparatus, place one drop of each phage on to the seeded surface. Keep the lid off until the

drops have disappeared before inverting the plates, and incubate dishes at 37°C overnight.

5. Examine each plate for lysis by phage and record degree of lysis as stated previously where it occurs. If the strain is not lysed by any of the phages, it is recorded as being non-typable (NT). A note is made as to whether or not the strain is actually a *Pseudomonas*, or if some other organism is suspected.

Storage of *Pseudomonas* propagating strains, phages, typed *Pseudomonas* strains

In order to maintain stable propagating strains, a large batch of each strain should be held either frozen at −70°C or lyophilized. The stability of the strain is very important.

Phages are quite stable when stored in the refrigerator. It is suggested, however, that several containers of each phage are kept. Phages remain stable when frozen, but lyophilization lower the titres of some of the phages.

REFERENCES

Alföldi, L. (1957a). *Acta microbiol. Acad. Sci. hung.* **4**, 107–118.

Alföldo, L. (1957b). *Acta microbiol. Acad. Sci. hung.* **4**, 119–122.

Asheshov, E. (1974). An assessment of the method used for typing strains of *Pseudomonas aeruginosa*. Proceedings 6th Greek National Symposium on Microbiology, Athens, pp. 9–22.

Asheshova, I. (1926). *C.R. Soc. Biol.* **95**, 1029–1031.

Ayliffe, G. A. J., Lowbury, E. J. L., Hamilton, J. G., Small, J. M., Asheshov, E. A. and Parker, M. T. (1965). *Lancet* **2**, 365–369.

Ayliffe, G. A. J., Barry, D. R., Lowbury, E. J. L., Roper-Hall, M. J. and Walker, W. M. (1966). *Lancet* **1**, 1113-1117.

Bergan, T. (1972a). *Acta path. microbiol. scand.* **80B**, 177–188.

Bergan, T. (1972b). *Acta path. microbiol. scand.* **80B**, 189–201.

Bergan, T. (1973a). *Acta path. microbiol. scand.* **81B**, 81–90.

Bergan, T. (1973b). *Acta path. microbiol. scand.* **81B**, 91–101.

Bergan, T. (1975). *In* "Resistance of *Pseudomonas aeruginosa*" (Ed. M. R. W.), Brown, pp. 189–235. John Wiley and Sons, London–New York–Sydney–Toronto.

Bergan, T. and Lystad, A. (1972). *Acta path. microbiol. scand.* **80B**, 345–350.

Bergan, T. and Midvedt, T. (1975). *Acta path. microbiol. scand.* **83B**, 1–9.

Berk, R. S. (1963). *J. Bact.* **86**, 728–734.

Berk, R. S. (1965). *Can. J. Microbiol.* **11**, 213–219.

Berk, R. S. (1966). *Can. J. Microbiol.* **12**, 371–375.

Berk, R. S. and Gronkowski, L. (1964). *Antonie van Leeuwenhoek* **30**, 141–153.

Berk, R. S. and Morris, J. M. (1966). *Proc. Soc. exp. Biol. Med.* **122**, 1075–1079.

Bernstein-Ziv, R., Mushin, R. and Rabinowitz, K. (1973). *J. Hyg.* **71**, 403–410.

Birdsell, D. C. and Drake, C. H. (1964). *Bact. Proc.*, p. 120.

Blair, J. E. and Williams, R. E. O. (1961). *Bull. Wld Hlth Org.* **24**, 771–784.

Bradley, D. E. and Robertson, D. (1968). *J. gen. Virol.* **3**, 247–254.

Chow, C. T. and Yamamoto, T. (1969). *Can. J. Microbiol.* **15**, 1179–1186.

Coleman, R. G., Janssen, R. J. and Ludovici, P. P. (1969). *Proc. Soc. exp. Biol. Med.* **131**, 311–315.

Conge, G. C. (1948). *Ann. Inst. Pasteur* (Paris) **75**, 368–376.

Dickinson, L. (1948). *J. gen. Microbiol.* **2**, 154–161.
Dickinson, L. (1952). *J. gen. Microbiol.* **6**, 1–18.
Döll, W. and Freytag, K. (1964). *Arch. Mikrobiol.* **48**, 332–338.
Don, P. A. and van den Ende, M. (1950). *J. Hyg.* **48**, 196–214.
Doudoroff, M. and Palleroni, N. J. (1974). *In* "Bergey's Manual of Determinative Bacteriology" (Eds. Buchanan, R. E. and Gibbons, N. E.), 8th edn, p. 222. The Williams & Wilkins Company, Baltimore, Md.
Edmonds, P., Suskind, R. R., Macmillan, B. G. and Holder, I. A. (1972). *Appl. Microbiol.* **24**, 213–218.
Farmer, J. J. and Herman, L. G. (1969). *Appl. Microbiol.* **18**, 760–765.
Farmer, J. J. and Herman, L. G. (1974). *J. infect. Dis.* **130** (Suppl. ad Nov.), 43–46.
Fastier, L. D. (1945). *J. Bact.* **50**, 301–303.
Feary, T. W., Fisher, E. and Fisher, T. N. (1963). *Proc. Soc. exp. Biol. (N.Y.)* **113**, 426–430.
Feary, T. W., Fisher, E. and Fisher, T. N. (1963). *Biochem. biophys. Res. Commun.* **10**, 359–365.
Feary, T. W., Visher, E. and Fisher, T. N. (1964). *J. Bact.* **87**, 196–208.
Fedorko, J., Katz, S. and Allnoch, H. (1967). *J. Bact.* **94**, 1251–1252.
Gaté, J. and Gardère, H. (1927). *C. r. Séanc. Soc. Biol.* **96**, 545–546.
Gould, J. C. and McLeod, J. W. (1960). *J. Path. Bact.* **79**, 295–311.
Graber, C. D., Latta, R., Vogel, E. H. and Brame, R. (1962). *Am. J. clin. Path.* **37**, 54–62.
Grogan, J. B. and Artz, C. P. (1961). *Surg. Forum* **12**, 26–28.
Grogan, J. B. and Johnson, E. J. (1964). *Virology* **24**, 235–237.
Grün, L. and Heyn, U. (1969). *Arch. Hyg. Bakt.* **153**, 86–89.
Grün, L., Pillich, J. and Heyn, U. (1967). *Arch. Hyg.* (Berl.) **151**, 640–646.
Hadley, P. (1924). *J. infect. Dis.* **34**, 260.
Hauduroy, P. and Peyre, E. (1923). *C. r. Séanc. Soc. Biol.* **88**, 688–689.
Herrmann, H. (1970). *Z. ges. Hyg.* **16**, 876–879.
Hoff, J. C. and Drake, C. H. (1961). *Am. J. publ. Hlth.* **51**, 918.
Holloway, B. W. (1960). *J. Path. Bact.* **80**, 448–450.
Holloway, B. W. and Cooper, G. N. (1962). *J. Bact.* **84**, 1321–1324.
Holloway, B. W., Egan, J. B. and Monk, M. (1960). *Aust. J. exp. Biol. med. Sci.* **38**, 321–329.
Jacob, F. (1952a). *Ann. Inst. Pasteur* (Paris) **82**, 433–457.
Jacob, F. (1952b). *Ann. Inst. Pasteur* (Paris) **82**, 578–602.
Jacob, F. (1952c). *Ann. Inst. Pasteur* (Paris) **83**, 671–692.
Jadin, J. (1932). *C.r. Séanc. Soc. Biol.* **109**, 556.
Jedličková, Z. and Pillich, J. (1968). *Zschr. inn. Med.* **23**, 21–25.
Kabinowitz, G. (1934). *J. Bact.* **28**, 237–247.
Kageyama, M. (1975). *In* "Microbial Drug Resistance" (Eds. Mitsuhashi, S. and Hashimoto, H.), pp. 291–305. University Park Press, Baltimore–London–Tokyo.
Kozaczek, W. (1972). *Rocznik Wojskowego Instytutu Higieny i Epidemiologii im. Gen. Karola Kaczkowskiego* **12**, 61–96.
Kozaczek, W., Bergan, T., Lachowicz, T. and Szczepánski, K. (1973). *Przeg. Epid.* **26**, 37–44.
Krishnapillai, V. and Carey, K. E. (1972). *Genet. Res.* (Camb.) **20**, 137–140.
Lantos, J. (1971). *Acta microbiol. Acad. Sci. hung.* **18**, 207–211.
Lantos, J., Kiss, M., Lányi, B. and Völgyesi, J. (1969). *Acta microbiol. Acad. Sci. hung.* **16**, 333–336.

Lányi, B. and Lantos, J. (1976). *Acta microbiol. Acad. Sci. hung.* **23**, 337–351.

Lin, L. and Schmidt, J. (1972). *Arch. Mikrobiol.* **83**, 120–128.

Lindberg, R. B., Latta, R. L., Brame, R. and Moncrief, J. A. (1963a). Bacteriophage typing of *Pseudomonas aeruginosa*: epidemiological observations based on type distribution. Progress Report. U.S. Army Surgical Research Unit. Brooke Army Medical Center, Fort Sam, Houston, Texas, pp. 1–19. Unpublished.

Lindberg, R. B., Brame, R., Latta, R. L., Mason, A. D. and Moncrief, J. A. (1963b). *Fed. Proc. Abstract*, no. 276.

Lindberg, R. B., Latta, R., Brame, R. and Moncrief, J. A. (1963c). *Bact. Proc.*, p. 72.

Lindberg, R. B., Latta, R. L., Brame, R. E. and Moncrief, J. A. (1964). *Bact. Proc.*, p. 81.

Lindberg, R. B., Latta, R. L., Brame, R. E. and Moncrief, J. A. (1966). *Bact. Proc.*, p. 65.

Lindberg, R. B. and Latta, R. L. (1974). *J. infect. Dis.* **130** (Suppl. ad Nov.), 33–42.

Linz, R. (1938). *C.r. Séanc. Soc. Biol.* **129**, 24.

Lisch, H. (1924). *Zbl. Bakt., I. Abt. Orig.* **93**, 421–424.

Liu, P. V. (1969). *J. infect. Dis.* **119**, 237–246.

Lode, A. (1923). *Arch. Hyg.* **93**, 267–279.

Mead, T. H. and van den Ende, M. (1953). *J. Hyg.* **51**, 108–124.

Meitert, E. (1965). *Arch. Roum. Path. exp.* **24**, 439–458.

Meitert, E. and Meitert, T. (1958). *Microbiologia, Parazitologia, Epidemiologia* (Bucuresti) **6**, 535–545.

Meitert, E. and Meitert, T. (1972). *Arch. Roum. Path. exp. Microbiol.* **31**, 443–448.

Meitert, E., Meitert, T., Sima, F., Savulian, C. and Mihalache, V. (1976). *Arch. Roum. Path. exp. Microbiol.* **35**, 1–10.

Meitert, T. and Meitert, E. (1960). IVe Colloquium Lysotypie, Wernigerode Tagungsbericht, p. 179. Cited Meitert (1960).

Meitert, T. and Meitert, E. (1966). *Arch. Roum. Path. exp. Microbiol.* **25**, 427–434.

Meitert, T. and Meitert, E. (1971). *Arch. Roum. Path. exp. Microbiol.* **30**, 37–44.

Meitert, E., Meitert, T., Cazacu, E. and Moscuna, M. (1967). *Microbiologia, Parazitologia, Epidemiologia* (Bucuresti) **12**, 329–338.

Minamishima, Y., Takeya, K., Ohnishi, Y. and Amako, K. (1968). *J. Virol.* **2**, 208–213.

Okuda, S. (1923). *Wien. klin. Wschr.* **36**, 638–639.

O'Callaghan, R. J., O'Mara, W. and Grogan, J. B. (1969). *Virology* **37**, 642–648.

Osman, M. A. M. (1965). *J. clin. Path.* **18**, 200–202.

Parker, M. T. (1976). In "Diagnosis and Management of Gram-Negative Nosocomial Disease" (Eds. Duncan, I. B. R., Hinton, N. A. and Godden, J. D.), pp. 13–24. Toronto.

Pavlatou, M. and Kaklamani, E. (1961). *Ann. Inst. Pasteur* (Paris) **101**, 914–927.

Pavlatou, M. and Kaklamani, E. (1962). *Ann. Inst. Pasteur* (Paris) **102**, 300–308.

Pesch, K. L. and Sonnenschein, C. (1925). *Klin. Wschr.* **4**, 1585–1586.

Phelps, L. N. and Kurtz, H. M. (1964). *Bact. Proc.*, p. 81.

Piguet, J. D. and Kékessy, D. A. (1972). *Progr. immunobiol. Standard* **5**, 406–409.

Pillich, J., Kazdová, A. and Pulverer, G. (1974). *Path. Microbiol.* **40**, 79–88.

Pons, R. (1923). *C.R. Soc. Biol.* (Paris) **89**, 77–78.

Postic, B. and Finland, M. (1961). *J. clin. Invest.* **40**, 2064–2075.

Potel, J. (1957). *Naturwissenschaften* **44**, 332–333.

Quiroga, R. (1923). *C.r. Séanc. Soc. Biol.* **88**, p. 363.

Rampling, A. and Whitby, J. L. (1972). *J. med. Microbiol.* **5**, 305–312.

Sierra, G. and Zagt, R. (1959). *Antonie van Leeuwenhoek* **26**, 193–208.

Sjöberg, L. and Lindberg, A. A. (1968). *Acta path. microbiol. scand.* **74**, 61–68.

Sonnenschein, C. (1925). *Zbl. Bakt., I. Abt. Orig.* **95**, 257.

Sutter, V. L., Hurst, V. and Fennell, J. (1965). *Hlth Lab. Sci.* **2**, 7–16.

Takeya, K., Mori, R., Ueda, S. and Toda, T. (1959). *J. Bact.* **78**, 332–335.

Vieu, J. F. (1969). *Bull. Inst. Pasteur* **67**, 1231–1249.

Vieu, J. F. (1971). *Arch. Roum. exp. Microbiol.* **30**, 227–334.

Wahba, A. H. (1964). *Nature* **204**, 502.

Warner, P. T. J. C. P. (1950a). *Br. J. exp. Path.* **31**, 112–129.

Warner, P. T. J. C. P. (1950b). *Br. J. exp. Path.* **31**, 242–257.

Yamada, K. (1960). *Mie. med. J.* **10**, 359–365.

Yamamoto, T. and Chow, C. T. (1968). *Can. J. Microbiol.* **14**, 667–673.

Zanen, H. C. and van den Berge, M. (1963). *Nederl. T. Geneesk.* **107**, 1700–1703.

Zierdt, C. H. (1971). *Antonie van Leeuwenhoek* **37**, 319–337.

CHAPTER VI

Identification of the Species and Biotypes Within the Genus *Brucella*

NORMAN B. McCULLOUGH

Departments of Microbiology and Public Health and of Medicine,
Michigan State University, East Lansing, Michigan 48824

I. CHARACTERISTICS OF THE GENUS

Members of the genus *Brucella* are mammalian facultatively intracellular parasites and pathogens, with a relatively wide host range including man. They cause infection and notably epizootic abortion in a variety of domestic animals, i.e. cattle, swine, sheep, goats, reindeer and dogs.

These micro-organisms are coccobacilli or short Gram-negative rods measuring $0\cdot5$–$0\cdot7$ by $0\cdot6$–$1\cdot5$ μm, occurring singly or more rarely in short chains. They are non-motile and do not form endospores or capsules.

Brucellas are strict aerobes. Some strains require 5–10% added CO_2 for growth, particularly on initial isolation. The optimum temperature for growth is 37°C. They are catalase positive, oxidase positive (with the exception of B. *ovis* and B. *neotomae*), and do not require either hematin (X factor) or NAD (nicotinamide adenine dinucleotide, V factor). Urea is hydrolysed to a variable extent; nitrates are reduced to nitrites (except for B. *ovis*); citrate is not utilized for growth; indole is not produced; Methyl red and Voges–Proskauer tests are negative.

The $G + C$ content of the DNA ranges from 56 to 58 mol%. As defined by DNA hybridization studies (Hoyer and McCullough, 1968) the members of the genus comprise a very closely related and sharply demarcated group of micro-organisms.

The genus is also fairly sharply delineated from other genera by the immunological relationship among the members. With the exception of B. *ovis* and B. *canis* which occur in nature as rough (R) or rough, mucoid forms, all the other species and biotypes of *Brucella* occur as smooth (S) forms and exhibit A and M surface antigens in varying amounts. In the agglutination test the S members of the genus cannot be distinguished from one another; similarly with the R members, or the S members in the R form. Further, antisera against an S form of *Brucella* does not agglutinate an R form or vice versa. In either instance there is no extensive cross-agglutination with members of other genera. Thus, agglutination to known endpoint titre in one of two appropriate sera, one for the S and one for the R members of the genus, provides presumptive evidence that an organism having the morphological, staining and biochemical attributes enumerated above is probably a member of the genus.

II. HISTORICAL INTRODUCTION

A knowledge of the evolution of the taxonomic principles applied in the classification of this group of micro-organisms over the last 60 years is almost essential to an understanding and intelligent use of the current classification schema. Accordingly, a brief history is presented.

The first member of the genus (B. *melitensis*) was isolated by Bruce, in 1887, from patients dying of Malta fever. He described the organism as a micrococcus. Hughes, in his monograph (1897), also considered this organism to be a coccus. Bang, in 1897, isolated the agent of infectious abortion in cattle (B. *abortus*) and described it as a bacillus. The relationship between these two bacteria was revealed some 20 years later by the careful studies of Alice Evans, published in 1918. Similarity was demonstrated in morphology, staining reactions, cultural characteristics and biochemical reactions. Confirming and extending this work, Meyer and Shaw (1920) suggested the creation of a new genus, *Brucella*, to accommodate these organisms. A main distinguishing difference between them was that the natural host of *B. melitensis* was the goat and of *B. abortus*, the cow. The third classical member of the genus (*B. suis*) was first isolated by Traum in 1914 from the fetus of an aborting sow and described as similar to *B. abortus*. Only later was it adequately differentiated from *B. abortus*.

In the 15 years commencing with 1920, a number of characteristics were described and tests developed which are still in use for classification of these bacteria. In 1921, Huddleson noted that *B. abortus* needed an increased carbon dioxide atmosphere, particularly on initial isolation. For the cultures then available this characteristic separated *B. abortus* from *B. melitensis* and later from *B. suis* when that species was recognized. In 1927, Huddleson and Abell reported that the ability to produce hydrogen sulphide distinguished *B. abortus* from *B. melitensis*. Later studies revealed that porcine (*B. suis*) and bovine (*B. abortus*) strains differed quantitatively in the production of this gas. The use of differential dye media containing Thionin or Basic fuchsin in appropriate concentrations was developed by Huddleson in 1929 and strengthened the separation of the genus into three species (Huddleson, 1931). In the concentrations used, *B. abortus* could grow on media containing Basic fuchsin, but not on media containing Thionin, while the reverse was true of *B. suis*. *B. melitensis* was able to grow on both media. Growth on these dye media was dependent on the organism's ability to reduce the O–R potential in the presence of the dye.

A number of workers had investigated the agglutinin–absorption test as a possible aid in differentiating the species. Feusier and Meyer (1920) found that the *B. melitensis* strains were not antigenically homogeneous in structure. The studies of Evans (1923) and Francis (1931) confirmed this finding. Huddleson, in 1929, concluded that this procedure did not distinguish all strains of *B. melitensis* from *B. abortus* or *B. suis* which were mutually indistinguishable from one another. The studies of Wilson and Miles (1932) and Wilson (1933) clarified the antigenic relationship within the genus. They found that all members of the genus then known shared two surface antigens, A and M, in varying proportions. By careful reciprocal absorption, typing sera could be prepared such that one serum would agglutinate only organisms with M antigen predominating (*B. melitensis*) and the other serum only strains with A antigen predominating (*B. abortus* and *B. suis*). It was recognized early by critical workers in the field that antigenic typing did not always yield results concordant with the other tests.

The tests discussed in the preceding paragraphs provided the basis for speciation within the genus for many years. It is to be noted that all of the tests yielded data primarily quantitative in nature, rather than revealing qualitative differences between the organisms. Nevertheless, they served to properly speciate the greater proportion of all strains of *Brucella* then available, regardless of source.

Over the years, commencing soon after the creation of the genus, there were occasional reports of strains, isolated mostly from the principal hosts mentioned above, which, when tested, yielded one or more test results not in conformity with the usual reactions of a particular species. As the years passed and the number of these aberrant strains increased, it became apparent that some of them were stable variants occurring in particular geographical areas. The more common of these strains were often referred to by such terms as "British melitensis" (*B. abortus*, biotype 5), "American melitensis" (*B. suis*, biotype 3), "Danish or Thomsen suis" (*B. suis*, biotype 2) and *B. abortus*, Wilson type 2 (*B. abortus*, biotype 2).

Obviously, some of these strains were being relegated to the wrong species. In the account of the genus *Brucella* in *Bergey's Manual of Determinative Bacteriology*, 7th edition, published in 1957, and prepared by Dr I. F. Huddleson, there was an attempt to provide for some of these aberrant strains. Each of the species, *B. abortus* and *B. suis*, was divided into three types. However, a residue of unclassified or improperly classified strains remained.

In addition, new species were being proposed. *B. ovis* was isolated by Buddle (1956) and established as the causative agent of ram epididymitis. In 1957, Stoenner and Lackman described *B. neotomae* isolated from the desert wood rat in the western U.S.A. Later, in 1966, *B. canis* was isolated and described as the major cause of canine brucellosis by Carmichael (1966) and Carmichael and Bruner (1968). In addition, cultures obtained in considerable numbers from infected reindeer and caribou did not fit the description of any of the established species or types.

At this juncture, two new tools for use in speciation of *Brucella* became available. Meyer and Cameron (1961) and Meyer (1961) reported the use of oxidative metabolic patterns in determination of species allocation of doubtful strains of *Brucella* and the utility of *Brucella* bacteriophage (Tbilisi phage) in taxonomy was recognized (Stableforth and Jones, 1963). This bacteriophage replicates only on smooth cultures of *B. abortus*. In comparing the results of the oxidative tests and phage typing, it was apparent that they were in agreement in regard to species designation, not only on classically conforming strains of *Brucella*, but also on the aberrant strains studied. Further, assignment of strains to species on this basis conformed with epidemiological evidence of host preference, i.e. those strains isolated predominately from cattle (bovines) fell to the *B. abortus* species and "American *melitensis*" from swine to the *B. suis* species.

Accordingly, in 1962, the subcommittee on the taxonomy of *Brucella* of the International Committee on Bacteriological Nomenclature established the current taxonomic schema (Stableforth and Jones, 1963). The aberrant strains were allocated to species on the basis of their oxidative metabolic patterns. Biotypes were established within each classical species: three for *B. melitensis*, nine for *B. abortus* and four for *B. suis*. In each species, strains classified as such by the conventional tests and recognized as most typical of the species were assigned to biotype 1 of the respective species.

III. CHARACTERIZATION OF BRUCELLAS

A. Dissociation in the genus *Brucella*

When grown in laboratory media, the *Brucella* are prone to dissociation. This is accompanied by antigenic change, loss in virulence, change in susceptibility to bacteriophage, colonial and other changes. This tendency is so pronounced that it must be taken into consideration in any discussion of differential characteristics. Cultures dissociate more rapidly in liquid media than on solid media. If initial isolation is accomplished in liquid media, the culture may be highly dissociated when first examined. Prompt subculture to solid medium is recommended.

Prior to applying the typing procedures to any culture, it should be examined for purity and colonial morphology. If dissociants are present, the S phase should be isolated by colonial selection prior to typing. This, of course, applies equally to reference strains.

Colonial S→R change in the *Brucella* is largely inapparent to the unaided eye. Cultures grown on trypticase-soy agar, or tryptose agar plates and incubated for four days should be viewed through a low power stereoscopic microscope with reflected 45° incident transmitted light (a mirror is placed between the light source and the microscope) (Henry, 1933). Using this arrangement, numerous graded colonial types may be distinguished in the S→R progression (Huddleson, 1952). S colonies are a blue-green colour throughout. The first detectable change is the appearance of larger colonies with a yellowish cast in the centre (SI_1). No colonial type beyond this stage is satisfactory for typing and particularly for antigenic or phage typing. Dissociants further removed show progressively greater change in colour value and appear granular.

Dissociants beyond the SI_1 range will usually agglutinate in neutral acriflavine (trypaflavine) 1:1000 (aqueous solution) (Braun and Bonestell, 1947). This test can be used to confirm the visual selection of S or SI_1 colonies. A portion of a colony is emulsified in a drop of the acriflavine solution on a glass slide. It may be examined immediately. If no agglutination is visible, the preparation should be checked under a low power microscope. If agglutination occurs, that colony should not be used as seed in the typing procedures.

B. Media

In the following typing procedures, any suitable medium that adequately supports the growth of *Brucella* may be used, except as expressly specified. The more commonly recommended media are: potato infusion agar, trypticase-soy agar, tryptose agar and serum dextrose agar (Alton and Jones, 1967). Liver infusion agar (Huddleson, 1943) has advantages in some tests. "Brucella agar" (Albimi) has given variable results. Dissociation proceeds more rapidly in this medium than in the other media mentioned. The author routinely uses trypticase-soy medium, except where specified otherwise in this Chapter. *B. abortus*, biotype 2, requires serum for growth. Five per cent serum of any species may be added to any of the above media not already containing serum. It should be checked and found negative for antibodies to *Brucella* prior to use. Medium containing serum should be used for initial isolation and subculture in areas where *B. abortus*, biotype 2, is expected.

C. Standard inoculum

In determining carbon dioxide requirement, hydrogen sulphide production, and dye sensitivity, the size of inoculum is somewhat important. However, an experienced technician should be able to carry out these determinations dependably, in accordance with the general methods presented under the separate headings. If more rigid standardization becomes necessary, to yield consistent results, it may be accomplished by referring to an opacity or density standard.

A dependable and simple method of quantitation is provided by spectrophotometric measurement of light transmission of a bacterial suspension and reference to a predrawn graph. Using a standard reference strain of *Brucella*, a suspension of cells is prepared in physiological saline containing 0·1% peptone. A series of dilutions is made. The number of viable organisms per millilitre is determined by triplicate plating and the light transmission at a wave length of 650 nm is measured for each of the suspensions. Using these data, a graph is constructed relating number of organisms to percentage light transmission. (For dense suspensions, dilutions are made for measurement of light transmission.) The approximate cell count of an unknown suspension can be determined by measuring the percentage light transmission and extrapolation from the graph.

There will be some deviation among the various species and strains in accuracy of estimates made by this method, but it compares favourably with other methods of quantitation.

For use in the tests mentioned above, a suspension containing 1×10^8 to 10^{10} cells/ml is prepared. A 2 mm loopful (0·02ml) of the suspension is used for inoculum.

General reviews of the conventional tests are available (Alton and Jones, 1967; Huddleson, 1943; FAO/WHO Comm. Rep., 1953). The detailed reactions of the various species and biotypes are presented in Table I.

D. Carbon dioxide requirement

Most strains of *B. abortus* require an atmosphere with increased CO_2 tension for initial isolation. The amount is quite variable. Some strains require from 5 to 10%. (This concentration cannot be obtained by burning a candle in a closed container.) This is a stable indicator on initial isolation. Cultures can be kept for months and years in the CO_2-requiring state, if they are always kept under an increased CO_2 tension during periods of growth. However, there is usually a small percentage of cells in a culture which will adapt quickly and grow out in a normal atmosphere. Subcultures from this growth no longer require an increased CO_2 tension. Accordingly, the CO_2 requirement should be determined promptly after isolation unless steps are taken to preserve this characteristic.

The CO_2 requirement of an unknown culture is determined by use of any of the recommended solid media prepared as test-tube slants. As seed, a 24–48 h culture (which of course is derived from a culture, or series of cultures, which has been maintained in an increased CO_2 atmosphere for growth continuously since isolation) grown on solid medium is used. The growth is suspended in a few millilitres of broth medium or physiological saline and a 2 mm loopful is transferred to an agar slant. A second slant is similarly inoculated.

One of these tubes is incubated in an atmosphere of air with 10% CO_2 added, the other in a normal atmosphere. As a check on technique, a known CO_2-requiring *B. abortus* is similarly inoculated in duplicate on the same medium as used for the unknown. These two slants are incubated at 37°C, one under each of the atmospheric conditions specified above, along with the unknown. The cultures are inspected for growth after 48 h. Carbon dioxide-requiring strains should show optimum growth in the tube incubated in the 10% CO_2-enriched atmosphere. The tube incubated in a normal atmosphere should show no growth or only a few scattered colonies.

A source of error in the past has been flaming of cotton plugs. In some laboratories cotton plugs removed from test-tubes containing medium are flamed (set afire) before being replaced in the tubes. This produces enough CO_2 to allow growth of some strains of *B. abortus*. Cultures so prepared and incubated in a normal atmosphere can yield erroneous results.

E. Hydrogen sulphide production

Hydrogen sulphide production varies with the medium used and the

TABLE I

Differential reactions of the species and biotypes of the genus *Brucella* in the conventional tests

Species	Biotype	CO_2 req.	H_2S† prod.	Growth on dye media‡		Agglutination in monospecific sera	
				Basic fuchsin	Thionin	A	M
B. melitensis	1	–	–	+	+	–	+
	2	–	–	+	+	+	–
	3	–	–	+	+	+	+
B. abortus	1	+(–)§	+	+	–	+	–
	2	+(–)	+	–	–	+	–
	3	+(–)	+	+	+	+	–
	4	+(–)	+	+	–	–	+
	5	–	–	+	+	–	+
	6	–	–	+	+	+	–
	7	–	+(–)	+	+	+	+
	8	+	–	+	+	–	+
	9	–	+	+	+	–	+
B. suis	1	–	++	–	+	+	–
	2	–	–	–	+	+	–
	3	–	–	++	+	+	–
	4	–	–	++	+	+	+
B. neotomae	1	–	+	–	+	+	–
B. ovis	1	+	–	+	+	–	–
B. canis	1	–	–	–	+	–	–

† A trace, or inconsistent production of small amounts is regarded as negative.
‡ Both dyes used in a concentration of 1/50,000.
§ Usually positive; negative varieties occur.

kind and content of sulphur-containing compounds in the medium, as well as with the enzymatic characteristics of the *Brucella* strains. Although tryptose agar and trypticase-soy agar are often used for this test, potato infusion agar and liver infusion agar are more suitable. The author prefers liver infusion agar and believes that more clear-cut results are obtained with it. The medium must be made carefully and not overheated to avoid inhibited growth of *Brucella* and less hydrogen sulphide production.

The test is conducted on agar slants of this medium. A 48 h culture of the unknown on solid medium is used for seed. A transfer loop is used to inoculate the slant heavily by spreading the seed culture over the entire surface. A strip of lead acetate paper, completely dry, is inserted into the mouth of the tube, positioned so as not to touch the medium directly and held in place by insertion of the cotton stopper. (Lead acetate paper is prepared by soaking absorbent filter paper in an aqueous solution of 10% lead acetate. The paper is then dried and cut into strips.) Cultures, including a known positive reference strain, are incubated at 37°C with CO_2 supplementation if required. In this case the reference strain likewise should be chosen for having this requirement. The cultures are inspected daily and the lead acetate papers replaced with fresh strips. A typical strain of *B. suis*, biotype 1, should produce moderate to heavy discoloration of the strips for four or five days; typical *B. abortus*, biotype 1, should produce a lesser amount of discoloration for the same or fewer days; *B. melitensis*, biotype 1, produces none, or only a trace of discoloration.

F. Inhibition by dyes

This procedure tests the ability of a culture to grow in the presence of certain aniline dyes. To grow, a micro-organism must be able to lower the O–R potential of the medium in the presence of the dye. Inhibition of growth is concentration dependent. Any of the recommended solid media are satisfactory for this test; however, the activity of the dyes is determined partly by the medium used. There is no single concentration of dye which can be used in all media and give the same results. In the author's experience, more uniform results are obtained between different batches of media using the commercially prepared products, trytose agar and trypticase-soy agar. The latter provides for better growth of some strains. If *B. abortus*, biotype 2, is suspected, 5% serum should be added to the medium.

The two standard dyes are Basic fuchsin and Thionin. Only certified dyes (National Aniline Division, Allied Chemical and Dye Co., New York) should be used. The concentration should be calculated on the basis of the dye content of the sample. A 0·1% aqueous (distilled water) stock solution may be prepared and used for several weeks. A portion of the stock solution should be heated in flowing steam for 20 min and an appropriate amount while still hot added to a flask of sterile melted medium. The medium and dye are thoroughly mixed and poured into Petri plates. The plates are allowed to cool and may be stored in the refrigerator for several days if desired. When used, the surface should be free of excess moisture. If moisture is visible, and particularly if used shortly after preparation, the plates should be incubated at 37°C until the moisture disappears.

Even within a biotype there is strain variation in dye tolerance. When testing an unknown, it is preferable to use several dilutions of each dye, Basic fuchsin 1/50,000 and 1/100,000, and Thionin 1/25,000, 1/50,000 and 1/100,000. With experience from a given geographic area, it is often possible to reduce the number of dilutions tested. Other dilutions may prove more appropriate. In any event, known reference strains should always be included in the procedure. By using more than one dilution of the dyes and by comparison with reference strains, it should be possible to place most isolates in the proper niche of the classification schema as far as dye sensitivity is concerned.

In doing the test, 48 h cultures, grown on solid media and without any history of prior dye exposure, are used. A loopful of culture is suspended in a small amount of saline, 1 ml, or less, and a 2 mm loopful of this suspension is streaked over the agar surface. Plates may be divided and several tests carried out on a single plate. The plates are incubated for 72 h at 37°C. Carbon dioxide-requiring cultures should be incubated in an atmosphere supplemented by 10% added CO_2; all other cultures should be incubated in a normal atmosphere.

At dye dilutions of 1/50,000 or 1/100,000, *B. abortus*, biotype 1, should grow on Basic fuchsin, but not Thionin; *B. suis*, biotype 1, should grow on Thionin, but not Basic fuchsin; *B. melitensis*, biotype 1, should grow on both media.

G. Oxidative metabolic tests

Comparative oxidative metabolic rates on a variety of amino-acid and sugar substrates (Cameron and Meyer, 1954; Meyer and Cameron, 1957) are determined using resting cell suspensions and conventional Warburg techniques (Umbreit et al., 1957). Oxygen uptake per hour per milligram of cell nitrogen $[O_2(N)]$ provides a standardized means of comparing different species and biotypes (Meyer and Cameron, 1961; Meyer, 1961). This methodology allows detection of both qualitative and quantitative differences in oxidative metabolism.

Brucella cells are grown on appropriate solid media. After 48 h incubation at 37°C, the cells are harvested in Sørensen's 0·06M phosphate buffer with a pH of 7·0. They are washed with phosphate buffer and collected by centrifugation three times. After the last wash, they are resuspended in buffer and the suspension standardized for density. It is adjusted so that when diluted 1 to 20, the resulting suspension gives a reading between 15 and 20% light transmission as determined with a spectrophotometer at a wavelength of 650 nm. The nitrogen content per millilitre of the adjusted suspension is determined by a micro-Kjeldahl technique. (Shake the suspension well before taking the specimen.) The results usually range from 2·0 to 2·3 mg/ml. The cell suspension should be held at 4°C until used.

Substrates are dissolved in the phosphate buffer at a concentration of 10 mg/ml and adjusted to pH 7·0 with sodium hydroxide. Standard Warburg vessels are loaded with 1·0 ml of cell suspension and 1·4 ml of buffer; 0·5 ml of substrate is placed in the sidearm and 0·1 ml of 20% KOH in the centre well. Endogenous controls and known reference strains are included in each run. All vessels are run in duplicate. The water bath is set at 37°C and final readings taken at the end of 60 min. The endogenous values are subtracted from these figures and oxygen uptake per milligram of cell nitrogen is calculated. The values for the unknown are now available for comparison with those of the reference strains.

It should be emphasized that the taxonomic value of this method of examining *Brucella* strains stems from determination of the metabolic pattern on a battery of substrates, rather than emphasizing test results with a single substrate. Currently, the recommended battery consists of L-alanine, L-asparagine, L-glutamic acid, L-arabinose, D-galactose, D-ribose, D-glucose, L-erythritol, D-xylose, L-arginine and L-lysine.

All biotypes of *B. melitensis* oxidatively metabolize L-alanine, L-asparagine, L-glutamic acid, D-glucose and L-erythritol. All biotypes of *B. abortus* oxidatively metabolize the above five substrates and, in addition, L-arabinose, D-galactose and D-ribose. The biotypes of *B. suis* are more variable. None metabolize L-alanine. They all oxidatively metabolize D-xylose and L-arginine (also DL-citrulline and DL-ornithine, the other members of the urea cycle) which are not metabolized by *B. melitensis* or *B. abortus* biotypes.

The detailed reactions for all species and biotypes are listed in Table II.

H. Serological typing

Reciprocally absorbed monospecific sera are prepared and used to determine whether either A or M antigen is predominant on the surface of *Brucella* cells, or that both are present, but neither predominating. Since both antigens are present in all smooth cultures of *Brucella*, to obtain differential antisera, the absorption must be carried out critically. One should approach the task as an experiment on an aliquot of serum. Having

TABLE II

Oxidative metabolic patterns of the species and biotypes of the genus *Brucella*

Species	Biotype	L-Alanine	L-Aspara-gine	L-Glutamic acid	L-Arabi-nose	D-Galac-tose	D-Ribose	D-Glucose	L-Ery-thritol	D-Xylose	L-Argi-nine†	L-Lysine
B. melitensis	All	+	+	+	−	−	−	+	+	−	−	−
B. abortus	All	+	+	+	+	+	+	+	+	−	−	−
B. suis	1	−	−	−	+	+	+	+	+	+	+	+
	2	−	+	−	+	+	+	+	+	+	+	−
	3	−	−	+	−	−	+	+	+	+	+	+
	4	−	−	+	−	−	+	+	+	+	+	+
B. neotomae	1	−	+	+	+	+	+(−)‡	+	+	+	−	−
B. ovis	1	+	+	+	−	−	−	−	+	+	−	−
B. canis	1	−	−	−	−	−	+	+	+(−)	−	+	+

† Same reactions with DL-citrulline and DL-ornithine.
‡ Usually positive; negative varieties occur.

determined a procedure which yields a satisfactory product with the aliquot, it can be applied to the entire lot of a serum.

It is imperative that the cultures used for production of antisera and for the absorptions be entirely in the smooth phase. If dissociants are present, satisfactory sera cannot be prepared. Theoretically, any pair of cultures, one with A antigen predominant and the other with M antigen predominant, can be used. In the interests of uniformity, it is preferable to use the recognized reference strains, *B. melitensis*, biotype 1, reference strain 16M and *B. abortus*, biotype 1, reference strain 544. Antisera are prepared in rabbits against these two strains. It is important to test the rabbits for agglutinins against *Brucella* prior to use. Rabbits with positive tests should not be used.

Forty-eight hour slant cultures of the selected strains are used to actively infect the rabbits. The growth from each culture is suspended in 10 ml of physiological saline. One millilitre suspension (approximately 1×10^8 cells) is injected intravenously using an ear vein. The rabbits should be caged separately and housed so that cross-infection cannot occur. Adequate titres are usually raised in 10–14 days. The animals should be trial bled and titres determined every few days. When a titre of at least 1/640 or higher is reached, the rabbits are bled out by cannulation of the carotid arteries. The serum is preserved with 0·5% phenol.

Small aliquots of each serum are absorbed with the heterologous organism using 48 h cultures. The cells are suspended in physiological saline, recovered by centrifugation and the packed cells added in measured amounts to the serum aliquots with thorough mixing. For initial absorption 1 ml of packed cells is added to 10 ml of antiserum. The suspensions are incubated at 37°C for 2 h with frequent mixing. The bacterial cells are removed from the sera by centrifugation and each absorbed aliquot tested for agglutination against each of the reference strains. A satisfactory typing serum should show a four tube difference (doubling dilution series) in the titres against the two organisms. If this degree of differentiation is not obtained, the absorbing process is repeated. The amount of absorbing cells and the number of absorptions necessary to yield satisfactory typing sera is determined. Extrapolating from these results, the procedure is applied to the entire lot of each serum.

The procedure above employs live bacteria for absorption. There is some chance of workers becoming infected, particularly as a result of aerosols formed during centrifugation, and appropriate precautions should be observed. To reduce the risk, some workers prefer to use heat-killed cells for absorption. However, heat-killed cells are not as effective in removing agglutinins as live cells. With live cells and repeated absorptions, all agglutinins may be removed from a serum. With heat-killed cells a residue of non-absorbable agglutinins remains. Further, it is the author's impression that one is more often successful in preparing satisfactory typing sera if live cells are used.

Prior to using a newly prepared batch of typing serum routinely, it should be tested against several appropriate reference strains. If the results are other than those expected, the preparation should be discarded.

To conserve sera, at the time of testing, appropriate dilutions of the typing sera in phenolized saline may be made so that the end-point titre of each against the appropriate reference strain is 1/20 (complete agglutination). In typing an unknown culture, a single tube is set up with each typing serum using 0·5 ml of serum diluted as above and 0·5 ml of antigen made from the unknown organism. To prepare the antigen, growth of a 48 h culture on solid medium is suspended in physiological saline containing 0·5% phenol and adjusted by further addition of organisms, or phenolized saline, to yield a suspension giving 78% light transmission as measured in a spectrophotometer at a wavelength of 650 nm. The suspensions are mixed by shaking and incubated at 37°C for 48 h. The reference strains are included as controls each time tests are done.

Using absorbed typing sera with higher titres, a spot slide test may be employed. A drop of typing serum is placed on a glass slide, a loopful of culture from solid medium is emulsified in the serum and the slide rotated gently. Agglutination is usually prompt and can be read immediately. The author prefers to check all such results with the standard tube test.

I. Bacteriophage typing

A number of bacteriophages specific for members of the genus *Brucella* have been described. The phages appear to be related. The majority replicate only on smooth or near smooth strains of *B. abortus*. As soon as these agents became available, their possible use in the taxonomy of *Brucella* was considered (Drozhevkina, 1957; Vershilova, 1957; Parnas *et al.*, 1958; van Drimmelin, 1959; Stinebring and Braun, 1959; Jones, 1960; Morgan *et al.*, 1960; Parnas, 1962).

When the Subcommittee on the Taxonomy of *Brucella* met in 1962, all the phage strains then available were regarded as similar if not identical. A strain from Russia designated Tb (Tbilisi) was recognized as the prototype for taxonomic purposes. This phage replicates effectively only on *B. abortus* including all of the biotypes. (Cultures of biotype 8 are not available.) When used at routine test dilution (RTD) it lyses only *B. abortus*. It produces tiny plaques and some replication occurs on *B. neotomae*, but there is no increase in amount of phage (Jones *et al.*, 1968). When used at 10,000 × RTD, both *B. neotomae* and *B. suis* are "lysed". This effect has been shown to be lysis from without, a bacteriocin-like effect. No plaques are produced on *B. suis* and phage does not replicate.

The use of phage Tb has served to confirm the allocation of biotypes to the respective species on the basis of oxidative metabolism.

More recently *Brucella*-phages with different host ranges have been reported. Moreira-Jacob (1968) described three phage strains with extended host ranges. These reactions were clarified (Morris *et al.*, 1973) later. One of the strains was identical with phage Tb. The other two were immunologically distinct and each lysed all four biotypes of *B. suis* and *B. neotomae* in addition to *B. abortus* biotypes at RTD. In 1973, Morris and Corbel reported on a phage, immunologically distinct from the above strains, which also lyses *B. abortus*, *B. suis* and *B. neotomae*. A phage isolated from *B. ovis* has been reported from the Soviet Union. It is said to lyse most strains of *B. abortus* and some strains of *B. melitensis*. It does not lyse *B. ovis*. A phage under study in the U.S.A. is said to have a broad host range including all smooth species of *Brucella*. The significance of these new phages in taxonomy cannot be assessed at this time.

With further acquaintance with these new phages and perhaps with others to be discovered or developed, the role of phage typing in *Brucella* taxonomy will probably expand.

The following description of the characteristics of *Brucella*-phage and the technology of its use applies particularly to the Tbilisi phage.

1. Characteristics of Brucella-phage

Morphology. By electron microscopy (McDuff *et al.*, 1962; Calderone and Pickett, 1965) the phage exhibits a polygonal (icosahedral) head measuring approximately 65 nm in diameter with a wedge-shaped tail about 23 nm long. (Reported measurements of *Brucella*-phages range from 59 to 70 nm in diameter for the head and 16 to 30 nm in length for the tail.)

Heat stability. The phage is stable at 50°C for at least 1 h, but partially inactivated at 60°C and completely inactivated at 70°C for 1 h.

pH. The phage is stable in broth for at least 24 h at 37°C and pH values between 6·2 and 8·1. Below pH 6·0, there is progressive loss of titre until the loss is complete at pH 3·1. Above pH 8·1 progressive inactivation also occurs.

Solvents. Toluene and diethyl ether have little effect, but chloroform causes a marked reduction in titre.

Chemical stability. The ionic detergents are destructive of phage activity, particularly the cationic detergents. Proteolytic enzymes produce marked lowering of the titre and M/50 periodate completely inactivates the agent.

Broth preparations are stable at 5°C and at -20°C for at least 20 months. They can be lyphilized and reconstituted without loss.

Plaque characteristics. Both large and small plaques are produced. The large plaques, 0·5–2·5 mm in diameter, are usually clear; the smaller ones, 0·1–0·5 mm in diameter, may be clear or turbid. Plaques which are turbid at 24 h may become clear by 48 h. Plaque size has no significance. *Brucella*-phage is very slowly adsorbed on the host cell. This may, in part, explain the variation in plaque size. If cultures are not entirely in the smooth phase, turbid plaques which do not clear may result from the presence of insensitive cells.

Propagation strain. The phage titres produced may vary considerably among host strains of *Brucella*. Theoretically, any smooth culture of *B. abortus* can be used to propagate *Brucella*-phage Tb. When the phage was first distributed years ago a propagation strain, *B. abortus* R 19, was supplied. This strain yields high titres and is still used by many workers. The culture does not require added CO_2 for growth. It produces smooth-intermediate colony types and is rather unstable. Colonial selection is necessary to maintain the culture in a satisfactory state. Some workers prefer *B. abortus*, biotype 1, reference strain 544.

In the interests of uniformity, predictability and possibly phage stability, a standard recognized strain should be used for propagation.

A variety of media and techniques give satisfactory results. Serum dextrose broth and agar, *Brucella* (Albimi) broth and agar, and trypticase-soy broth and agar have all been used extensively. Using trypticase-soy media as an example, two methods are described.

The propagation strain, *B. abortus* R 19, is examined carefully for colonial morphology prior to use. Approximately 10^5 phage particles (plaque forming units) are added to each ml of a 6 h trypticase-soy broth culture of the host strain. Incubation is continued at 37°C for 36 h on a rotary shaker. The bacterial lysate is then centrifuged at $2000 \times g$ for 10 min to remove cellular debris. The supernatant is filtered through a membrane filter (type HA, pore size 0·45 μm, Millipore Corp., Bedford, Mass., U.S.A.) to remove all bacterial cells and stored at 4°C.

The phage titre is determined by the agar layer technique (Adams, 1959). An 18 h culture of the propagation strain of *B. abortus* grown on trypticase-soy agar is harvested in physiological saline containing 0·1% peptone. The suspension is adjusted to contain approximately 10^7–10^8 cells/ml. Appropriate dilutions of the phage preparation are prepared in trypticase-soy broth anticipating a titre of approximately 5×10^9–10^{10} ml. One ml of cell suspension and 1 ml of phage dilution are added to 2 ml of melted trypticase-soy agar (47°C), gently mixed and poured over the surface of trypticase-soy agar plates. Plaques are counted after 48 h incubation at 37°C. The RTD (routine test dilution) of the phage preparation is represented by the highest dilution producing complete lysis.

As an alternative, propagation may be performed on a solid medium. *B. abortus*, biotype 1, reference strain 544, is used for propagation. The organism is grown on trypticase-soy agar for 18–24 h at 37°C. The growth is suspended in physiological saline containing 0·1% peptone and adjusted to contain approximately 10^{10} cells/ml. Semi-solid agar, prepared by adding 0·7% agar to trypticase-soy broth, is melted and cooled by 45°C. A previously determined amount of phage in 0·25 ml and 0·25 ml of the bacterial suspension is added to 3 ml of the semi-solid agar. The suspension is mixed well and poured over the surface of a trypticase-soy agar plate. The amount of phage to be used should be determined in a preliminary trial with the same system. The proper amount is that which will cause almost complete lysis. The inoculated plate is incubated at 37°C for 24–48 h. When lysis is nearly complete, the phage is harvested by scraping off the semi-solid agar layer and suspending it in trypticase-soy broth. The suspension is held overnight at 4°C and centrifuged to remove the agar and cells. The supernatant is passed through a Millipore filter and stored at 4°C. One-tenth % toluene may be added as a preservative.

The titre and RTD may be determined using the same semi-solid agar overlay technique as above. Serial ten-fold dilutions of the phage preparation are made in trypticase-soy broth. Separate plates are prepared for each phage dilution tested. To 3 ml of melted semi-solid agar is added 0·25 ml of a phage dilution and 0·25 ml of a suspension of the propagation strain. The combination is mixed and poured over the surface of a trypticase-soy agar plate. The plates are incubated at 37°C for 48 h. The plaque count (titre) is determined and the RTD discerned.

The RTD may be determined more simply by preparing a bacterial lawn by direct flooding of the surface of a trypticase-soy agar plate with a suspension (see above) of the propagation strain. The plate is placed at 37°C for 1 or 2 h to allow the excess moisture to disappear. Using a calibrated dropper, or pipette, one drop (0·02 ml) of each phage dilution is spotted on the agar surface of the inoculated plate. The plate is inspected after incubation for 48 h at 37°C. The highest phage dilution causing complete lysis represents the RTD.

2. *Determination of phage sensitivity*

Prior to testing for phage sensitivity, a new isolate should be examined critically for colonial type. If necessary, an S phase is isolated by colony selection. The culture should be grown on a solid medium for 18 to 24 h. The growth is then suspended in physiological saline containing 0·1% peptone and adjusted to approximately 5×10^8–10^{10} cells/ml. There are a variety of ways to prepare a bacterial lawn. It may be done by simply streaking the surface of a trypticase-soy agar plate. Alternatives are to flood the surface of the plate with the bacterial suspension, or to add it to melted semi-solid agar and pour the mixture over the surface of the agar. If consistent results are not obtained with simple streaking, the other alternatives should be tried. In all cases, the lawn surface is allowed to dry before application of phage. Drops of Tb phage at RTD and $10,000 \times$ RTD are placed on the culture. The results are read after incubation at 37°C for 48 h.

For both propagation and sensitivity testing the soft agar overlay technique appears to be superior. Whenever tests are carried out the three reference strains, *B. melitensis* 16M, *B. abortus* 544 and *B. suis* 1330 should be tested concurrently as controls on the method and technique.

J. Other epidemiologic markers

In addition to Basic fuchsin and Thionin, a number of other dyes have been used as discriminating agents for *Brucella*. The use of Safranin O (Moreira-Jacob, 1963) deserves mention. Although not judged useful in taxonomy of the genus at present, it provides an epidemiologic marker that might on occasion be helpful. Likewise, the urease test (Bauer, 1949; Hoyer, 1950) has limited value in *Brucella* taxonomy and is no longer included as a definitive test. However, this characteristic is stable and might under some circumstances be useful for epidemiologic studies.

Vershilova *et al.* (1973) have found cytochrome absorption spectra to be valuable in delimiting the genus. Likewise, Morris (1973) reports that poly-acrylamide gel electrophoresis provides an additional aid in taxonomy at the generic level. The significance of both of these latter proposals must await their application and evaluation in other laboratories.

IV. DISTRIBUTION OF BRUCELLAS

B. abortus occurs world-wide in domestic cattle (bovines). Biotype 1 is the most common biotype and accounts for the greater proportion of all infections due to *B. abortus*. Biotype 2 has been reported from England, Europe, the United States, Japan, and elsewhere. The higher numbered biotypes have been reported mainly from the Mediterranean littoral, Europe, Africa and the Far East. They should all be looked for wherever

B. abortus infection is found. There are no known differences in virulence between biotypes.

B. melitensis is found world-wide in goats and milking sheep. Biotype 1 is the most common. The other biotypes have been reported mainly in the Mediterranean littoral and elsewhere in Europe, Africa and Asia. These biotypes differ only in their reactions to the absorbed typing sera. They are not known to differ in virulence.

B. suis is more limited in distribution. It occurs in swine in North and South America, Europe, the Orient and elsewhere. Biotype 1 is the most common. Biotype 2 occurs in Denmark and elsewhere in Europe. It has been reported from Russia and occasionally from other locations. In Europe the hare is a reservoir of this biotype. Only a few human cases have been reported. It is believed to have low virulence for man. *B. suis*, biotype 3, is found mainly in the mid-western portion of the U.S.A. in swine (and man). There is no known difference in virulence for swine of these biotypes. Biotypes 1 and 3 appear equally virulent for man. *B. suis*, biotype 4, does not occur naturally in swine. It is found in reindeer and caribou (and in man) in the Arctic regions.

B. ovis, the cause of ram epididymitis, has been reported from New Zealand, Australia, North America, Europe, South Africa and elsewhere. It has not been reported to cause disease in man.

B. neotomae is found in the desert wood rat, *Neotoma lepida*, of the western U.S.A. Human cases or natural infections of domestic animals have not been reported. Limited experimental infections have been produced in cattle and hogs.

B. canis is the major cause of brucellosis in dogs. It has been reported in the U.S.A., Japan, Europe and elsewhere. Beagles appear to be particularly susceptible. However, it has been isolated from many different breeds. A dozen or more human cases have been reported.

Brucellosis is primarily a disease of domestic animals. The three classical species are found mainly in the hosts mentioned. However, they are not entirely confined to these hosts and any one of them may be found occasionally in any of the other animal species. The host range is wide and a variety of wild animals may become infected. These infections, with the exception of those due to *B. suis*, biotype 4, in caribou, seldom provide human exposure and when the domestic animal focus is removed, infection of wild-life does not usually persist.

V. EPIDEMIOLOGY

Man contracts brucellosis mainly through direct contact with infected animals or their tissues or by ingestion of unpasteurized dairy products derived from infected animals. The organisms can penetrate the apparently unbroken skin and mucosa. Where pasteurization is practised widely, brucellosis has become largely an occupational disease of those who raise and care for livestock, or are employed in the slaughter of meat animals and processing of the product. A minor epidemiological pathway is by inhalation of aerosols (produced in abattoirs, or the laboratory centrifuge) or dust laden with the organisms.

VI. USE OF EPIDEMIOLOGICAL MARKERS

In the initial investigation of the population (man or animal) of a geographical area for the presence of *Brucella* infection, there are two main screening procedures available. These are the detection of delayed hypersensitivity to the organism, or fractions thereof, and the determination of the presence of circulating antibody against the organism.

Delayed hypersensitivity is usually determined by the intracutaneous injection of a suspension of dead *Brucella* organisms, or preferably a refined extract of the organisms. A variety of preparations have been used. These have been reviewed by Huddleson (1943) and Alton and Jones (1967). The author prefers Brucellergen, a nucleoprotein fraction of the organism, developed by Huddleson (1943). This preparation can be well standardized and has a long history of use. It is no longer available commercially but can be prepared and standardized without great difficulty.

The Brucellergen test, and similar tests, when applied to domestic animals have failed to detect a significant percentage of infected animals. The utility of this test is limited to man. One-tenth ml of the material is injected intradermally on the volar surface of the forearm. The test is read at 48 h. A positive reaction consists of erythema, oedema and induration. A reaction of less than 0·5 cm in diameter is considered negative. A positive reaction denotes delayed hypersensitivity to brucellar antigens. It does not distinguish between present and past infection. It is highly specific for members of the genus *Brucella*.

For the detection of circulating antibodies, the agglutination test is the simplest and most used test. It is performed in the usual fashion, using a standard antigen prepared from a species which occurs naturally in the S phase. To detect antibody against *B. ovis* and *B. canis*, a different antigen prepared from one of these species, must be used. In interpreting the results of serological surveys for antibody to the S phase members of the genus, one must consider the known significant cross reactions. These occur with *Francisella tularensis*, *Yersinia enterocolitica* and *Vibrio cholerae*. Differential homologous and heterologous titres and the clinical aspects of the various diseases usually provide clarification of the significance of the titres. In considering titres against R phase *Brucella*, readings of less than 1/50 should be given little weight. Our knowledge of cross reactions is still incomplete for these organisms.

The determination of species and biotypes requires isolation of the infecting organism and typing by the procedures already described. Within the limits of the usual understanding of the term "biological stability", the various markers used in *Brucella* taxonomy are stable (McCullough and Beal, 1958) and hence dependable for epidemiological purposes.

For successful isolation of *Brucella*, a knowledge of the pathogenesis of the disease is helpful in selecting tissues and procedures for culture. It should be remembered that *B. abortus*, biotype 2, requires serum for growth.

An isolate having the morphological, staining and biochemical properties of the genus and which agglutinates to end-point titre in a known antiserum is presumably a member of the genus. It should be submitted to the differential tests for speciation and determination of biotype if any.

All microbiological laboratories should be capable of performing the traditional tests. Whether a particular laboratory should be expected to perform phage typing and determine the oxidative metabolism should depend on the volume of *Brucella* cultures handled. If there is only an occasional call for identification of a *Brucella* biotype, the culture should be sent to a reference laboratory for definitive typing. If the demand is frequent, then local competence should be developed. Any well-trained technician can learn to perform these tests dependably.

As an aid in solving epidemiological problems arising in programmes for the control or eradication of brucellosis, and to increase our knowledge of the distribution of the various species and biotypes of *Brucella*, WHO/FAO have designated certain national and regional laboratories as Brucellosis Centres. Some of these centres serve as reference laboratories for *Brucella* typing, or for supply of materials for such tests. In a particular country, the national laboratory system should be able to provide advice on the availability of typing services, typing sera, bacteriophages, reference strains and other aids. An appendix to this Chapter provides information on the availability of reference strains of all the species and biotypes of *Brucella* in the NCTC and ATCC with their identifying numbers.

The determination of oxidative metabolism is the basis of speciation. Phage typing is confirmatory. However, once the occurrence of the various biotypes within a region has been determined, if the isolate is from a host where the species predilection is known, then the traditional tests are still quite adequate for the presumptive determination of the species (and biotype if any) of most isolates. If absolute certainty is desired the complete typing procedure must be employed. It is recommended that all isolates of *Brucella* from unusual hosts, or those that seemingly deviate in any manner from the established species and biotypes, be sent to reference centres for study.

APPENDIX

Reference cultures

Reference cultures of the various species and biotypes (with the exception of *B. abortus* biotype 8) are available from standard collections. The following tabulation presents the species or biotype reference strain designations and the number under which each is carried in the NCTC and the ATCC, if available from these sources.

B. melitensis

B. melitensis biotype 1. The neotype strain of the species and biotype reference strain: 16M; NCTC 10094; ATCC 23456.
B. melitensis biotype 2. Reference strain: 63/9; NCTC 10508; ATCC 23457.
B. melitensis biotype 3. Reference strain: Ether; NCTC 10509; ATCC 23458.

B. abortus

B. abortus biotype 1. The neotype strain of the species and biotype reference strain: 544; NCTC 10093; ATCC 23448.
B. abortus biotype 2. Reference strain: 86/8/59; NCTC 10501; ATCC 23449.
B. abortus biotype 3. Reference strain: TULYA; NCTC 10502; ATCC 23450.
B. abortus biotype 4. Reference strain: 292; NCTC 10503; ATCC 23451.
B. abortus biotype 5. Reference strain: B3196; NCTC 10504; ATCC 23452.
B. abortus biotype 6. Reference strain: 870; NCTC 10505; ATCC 23453.
B. abortus biotype 7. Reference strain: 63/75; NCTC 10506; ATCC 23454.
B. abortus biotype 8. No cultures available.
B. abortus biotype 9. Reference strain: C68; NCTC 10507; ATCC 23455.

B. suis

B. suis biotype 1. The neotype strain of the species and biotype reference strain: 1330; NCTC 10316; ATCC 23444.

B. suis biotype 2. Reference strain: Thomsen; NCTC 10510; ATCC 23445.
B. suis biotype 3. Reference strain: 686; NCTC 10511; ATCC 23446.
B. suis biotype 4. Reference strain: 40; ATCC 23447.

B. neotomae. Type strain of the species and reference strain: 5K33; NCTC 10084; ATCC 23459.
B. ovis. The neotype strain of the species and reference strain: 63/290; NCTC 10512; ATCC 25840.
B. canis. Reference strain: RM 6/66; ATCC 23365.

REFERENCES

Adams, M. H. (1959). "Bacteriophages". Interscience Publishers, Inc., New York.
Alton, G. G., and Jones, L. M. (1967). "Laboratory Techniques in Brucellosis", World Health Organization Monograph Series No. 55. World Health Organization, Geneva, Switzerland.
Bang, B. (1897). Die Aetiologie des seuchenhaften (infectiosen) Verwerfens. *Zr. Tier-med.*, **1**, 241–278.
Bauer, H. (1949). A study of *Brucella* and *Proteus* urease, Minneapolis. Thesis, University of Minnesota.
Braun, W., and Bonestell, A. (1947). Independent variation of characteristics in *Brucella abortus* variants and their detection. *Am. J. Vet. Res.*, **8**, 386–390.
Bruce, D. (1887). Note on the discovery of a microorganism in Malta fever. *Practitioner*, **39**, 161–170.
Buddle, M. B. (1956). Studies on *Brucella ovis* (N. Sp.). A cause of genital disease of sheep in New Zealand and Australia. *J. Hyg. (Camb.)*, **54**, 351–364.
Calderone, J. G., and Pickett, M. J. (1965). Characterization of brucella-phage. *J. gen. Microbiol.*, **39**, 1–10.
Cameron, H. S., and Meyer, M. E. (1954). Comparative metabolic studies on the genus Brucella. II. Metabolism of amino acids that occur in the urea cycle. *J. Bactl.*, **67**, 34–37.
Carmichael, L. E. (1966). Abortions in 200 beagles. *J. Am. vet. med. Ass.*, **149**, 1126.
Carmichael, L. E. and Bruner, D. W. (1968). Characteristics of a newly recognized species of *Brucella* responsible for infectious canine abortions. *Cornell Vet.*, **58**, 579–592.
Drozhevkina, M. S. (1957). *Brucella* bacteriophage and the prospects of its utilization. *J. Microbiol. Epidemiol. Immunobiol. (U.S.S.R.)*, **28**, 1221–1225.
Evans, A. C. (1918). Further studies on *Bacterium abortus* and related bacteria. II. A comparison of *Bacterium abortus* with *Bacterium bronchisepticus* and with the organism which causes Malta fever. *J. infect. Dis.*, **22**, 581–593.
Evans, A. C. (1923). The serological classification of *Brucella melitensis* from human, bovine, caprine, porcine and equine sources. *Publ. Hlth Rep. (Wash.)*, **38**, 1948–1963.
Feusier, M. L., and Meyer, K. F. (1920). Principles in serologic grouping of *B. abortus* and *B. melitensis*: correlation between absorption and agglutination tests. *J. infect. Dis.*, **27**, 185–206.

Francis, E. (1931). Agglutinin absorption in undulant fever (Brucellosis). *Publ. Hlth Rep. (Wash.)*, **46**, 2416–2437.

Henry, B. S. (1933). Dissociation in the genus *Brucella*. *J. infect. Dis.*, **52**, 374–402.

Hoyer, B. H. (1950). Some aspects of the physiology of *Brucella* organisms. *In* "Symposium on Brucellosis", Bethesda, Md., 1949, p. 20. Washington, D.C.

Hoyer, B. H., and McCullough, N. B. (1968). Homologies of deoxyribonucleic acids from *Brucella ovis*, canine abortion organisms and other *Brucella* species. *J. Bact.*, **96**, 1783–1790.

Hoyer, B. H., and McCullough, N. B. (1968). Polynucleotide homologies of *Brucella* deoxyribonucleic acids. *J. Bact.*, **95**, 444–448.

Huddleson, I. F. (1921). The importance of an increased carbon dioxide tension in growing *Bact. abortum* (Bang). *Cornell Vet.*, **11**, 210–215.

Huddleson, I. F., and Abell, E. (1927). A biochemical method of differentiating *Brucella abortus* from *Brucella melitensis-paramelitensis*. *J. Bact.*, **13**, 13.

Huddleson, I. F. (1929). The differentiation of the species of the genus *Brucella*. *Mich. State College Agr. Exp. Sta. Bull.*, **100**, 1–16.

Huddleson, I. F. (1931). Differentiation of the species of the genus *Brucella*. *Am. J. Pub. Hlth*, **21**, 491–498.

Huddleson, I. F. (1943). "Brucellosis in Man and Animals". The Commonwealth Fund, New York.

Huddleson, I. F. 1952. The dissociation pattern in the species of the genus *Brucella*. *In* "Studies in Brucellosis III". Michigan Agr. Exp. Sta., Mem. No. 6, pp. 7–63.

Hughes, M. L. (1897). "Mediterranean, Malta or Undulant Fever". Macmillan and Co. Ltd, London.

Joint FAO/WHO Expert Committee on Brucellosis: Second Report (1953). Tech. Rep. Series, No. 67. World Health Organization, Geneva.

Jones, L. M. (1960). Comparison of phage typing with standard methods of species differentiation in brucellae. *Bull. Wld Hlth Org.*, **23**, 130–133.

Jones, L. M., Merz, G., and Wilson, J. B. (1968). A lytic factor associated with brucellaphage causing "lysis from without". *Experientia*, **24**, 20–22.

Jones, L. M., Merz, G. and Wilson, J. B. (1968). Phage typing reactions on *Brucella* species. *Appl. Microbiol.*, **16**, 1179–1190.

McCullough, N. B., and Beal, G. A. (1958). The biological stability of the genus *Brucella*. *Bull. Wld Hlth Org.*, **19**, 725–737.

McDuff, C. R., Jones, L. M., and Wilson, J. B. (1962). Characteristics of *Brucella-phage*. *J. Bact.*, **83**, 324–329.

Meyer, K. F., and Shaw, E. B. (1920). A comparison of the morphologic, cultural and biochemical characteristics of *B. abortus* and *B. melitensis*. Studies on the genus *Brucella* nov. gen. I. *J. infect. Dis.*, **27**, 173–184.

Meyer, M. E., and Cameron, H. S. (1957). Species metabolic patterns in morphologically similar Gram-negative pathogens. *J. Bact.*, **73**, 158–161.

Meyer, M. E., and Cameron, H. S. (1961). Metabolic characterization of the genus *Brucella*. I. Statistical evaluation of the oxidative rates by which type 1 of each species can be identified. *J. Bact.*, **82**, 387–395.

Meyer, M. E., and Cameron, H. S. (1961). Metabolic characterization of the genus *Brucella*. II. Oxidative metabolic patterns of the described biotypes. *J. Bact.*, **82**, 396–400.

Meyer, M. E. (1961). Metabolic characterization of the genus *Brucella*. III. Oxidative metabolism of strains that show anomalous characteristics by conventional determinative methods. *J. Bact.*, **82**, 401–410.

Meyer, M. E. (1961). Metabolic characterization of the genus *Brucella*. IV. Correlation of oxidative metabolic patterns and susceptibility to *Brucella* bacteriophage, type *abortus*, strain 3. *J. Bact.* **82**, 950–953.

Moreira-Jacob, M. (1963). Safranine O: reliable selective dye for characterization of *Brucella suis*. *J. Bact.* **86**, 599–600.

Moreira-Jacob, M. (1968). New group of virulent bacteriophages showing differential affinity for *Brucella* species. *Nature (Lond.)*, **219**, 752–753.

Morgan, W. J. B., Kay, D., and Bradley, D. E. (1960). *Brucella* bacteriophage. *Nature (Lond.)*, **188**, 74–75.

Morris, J. A., Corbel, M. J., and Phillip, J. I. H. (1973). Characterization of three phages lytic for *Brucella* species. *J. gen. Virol.*, **20**, 63–73.

Morris, J. A., and Corbel, M. J. (1973). Properties of a new phage lytic for *Brucella suis*. *J. gen. Virol.*, **21**, 539–544.

Morris, J. (1973). The use of polyacrylamide gel electrophoresis in taxonomy of *Brucella*. *J. gen. Microbiol.*, **76**, 231–237.

Parnas, J., Feltynowski, A., and Bulikowski, W. (1958). Anti-*Brucella* phage. *Nature (Lond.)*, **182**, 1610–1611.

Parnas, J. (1961). Differentiation of Brucellae by the aid of phages. *J. Bact.*, **82**, 319–325.

Stableforth, A. W., and Jones, L. M. (1963). Report of the Subcommittee on Taxonomy of the genus *Brucella*. Speciation in the genus *Brucella*. *Int. Bull. Bactl. Nomen. Taxon.*, **13**, 145–158.

Stinebring, W. R., and Braun, W. (1959). *Brucella* phage. *J. Bactl.*, **78**, 736–737.

Stoenner, H. G., and Lackman, D. B. (1957). A new species of *Brucella* isolated from the desert wood rat, *Neotoma lepida*, Thomas. *Am. J. vet. Res.*, **18**, 947–951.

Traum, J. (1914). Annual Report of the Chief, Bureau of Animal Industry, U.S. Dept. of Agr., p. 86.

Umbreit, W. W., Burris, R. H., and Stauffer, J. F. (1957). "Manometric Techniques and Related Methods for the Study of Tissue Metabolism", 2nd Edition. Burgess Publishing Company, Minneapolis.

van Drimmelen, G. C. (1959). Bacteriophage typing applied to strains of *Brucella* organisms. *Nature (Lond.)*, **184**, 1079.

Vershilova, P. A. (1957). Some results of practical scientific experience in the struggle against brucellosis. *J. Microbiol. Epidemiol. Immunobiol. (U.S.S.R.)*, **28**, 1397–1402.

Vershilova, P. A., Dranovskaya, E. A. and Kushnarev, V. M. (1973). An additional method of determining the relationship of bacteria to the genus *Brucella*. *Zh. Microbiol. Epidemiol. Immunobiol.*, **12**, 98–101.

Wilson, G. S., and Miles, A. A. (1932). The serological differentiation of smooth strains of the *Brucella* group. *Br. J. exp. Path.*, **13**, 1–13.

Wilson, G. S. (1933). The classification of the *Brucella* group: a systematic study. *J. Hyg. (Camb.)*, **33**, 516–541.

CHAPTER VII

Identification of *Francisella tularensis*

KARL-AXEL KARLSSON

Department of Biological Products, National Veterinary Institute,
Stockholm, Sweden

I. INTRODUCTION

In 1910, McCoy discovered among ground squirrels shot or found dead in Tulare Country, California, a disease characterized by lesions similar to those of plague. McCoy and Chapin named the causative organism *Bacterium tularense*. Francis (1919) investigated rabbit fever in Utah and discovered that the blood of an infected rancher bitten on the neck by a deer-fly produced a plague-like disease in guinea-pigs. In rapid succession, Francis reported the isolation of *B. tularense* from jack rabbits, the transmission of the infection by bites of the deer-fly and the rabbit louse, the cultivation of the organism on a new medium and a method of serodiagnosis.

According to the 8th edition of *Bergey's Manual*, the genus *Francisella* comprises two species, viz. *Francisella tularensis* and *F. novicida*.

F. tularensis is Gram-negative, non-motile without capsules or spores. Grown on agar media, it tends to be pleomorphic; coccoid, ovoid, bacillary, bean-shaped, dumb-bell 0·2–0·7 μm in length, even filamentous forms may be seen. *F. tularensis* is aerobic and does not grow on ordinary media without enrichment. It grows well on glucose-cystine-blood agar, less well on glucose-cystine agar and coagulated hen's egg yolk medium. Growth occurs also on glucose-blood agar, glucose-serum agar, and blood agar slants provided that a piece of rabbit's spleen is rubbed over the surface. Glucose-cystine-blood agar inoculated with infective tissue may show discrete growth within 2–7 days, but subcultures show confluent growth within 24–48 h. The colonies are viscous grey and may attain 4 mm in diameter. Glucose, glycerol, maltose, mannose, fructose and dextrin may be fermented with production of acid, but no gas. However, these reactions are not essential for routine identification. Olsufjev and Emelyanova (1962) found that most American strains fermented glycerol and were highly pathogenic for the rabbit, whereas European and Asiatic strains did not ferment glycerol and were only mildly pathogenic for the rabbit.

F. tularensis is very susceptible to antimicrobial agents, including Chloramphenicol and the tetracyclines and is killed by moist heat at 55–60°C within 10 min. *F. tularensis* appears antigenically homogenous. It shows a weak serological cross-reaction by agglutination with organisms of the genus *Brucella* and by immunofluorescence with *Pseudomonas aeruginosa* (Yager *et al.*, 1960; Franék and Procházka, 1965).

Under natural conditions, *F. tularensis* gives rise to tularaemia in rodents and occasionally in man. It causes a latent infection in a wide variety of mammals and birds (Burroughs *et al.*, 1945). Significant vectors include a number of ticks, deer-flies and mosquitoes. Experimentally the disease can be reproduced in ground-squirrels, gophers, guinea-pigs, rabbits, mice, hamsters, cotton-rats, and monkeys. Rats are relatively resistant (Dieter and Rhodes, 1926), cats, dogs, chickens and pigeons practically immune (Downs *et al.*, 1947).

According to differences in virulence and biochemical reactions, two basic varieties of tularaemia organisms occur in nature (Olsufjev, Emelyanova and Dunaeva, 1959). One variety termed *F. tularensis* is thought to be restricted to the New World. This is highly virulent for laboratory animals including laboratory rabbits producing a high fatality rate in untreated human cases (5–7%), ferments glycerol and produces citrulline ureidase. The second variety termed *F. tularensis holearctica* occurs both in the Old and the New World. This is relatively avirulent for laboratory rabbits, producing fatal disease in less than 1% of untreated human cases, and neither ferments glycerol nor produces citrulline ureidase.

II. COLLECTION AND HANDLING OF SPECIMENS

In man, the onset of illness is sudden and associated with septicaemia, continuing for 7–10 days. Thereafter, the micro-organisms become localized. Thus, attempts to isolate *F. tularensis* from blood should be limited to the first 7–10 days after onset, except in cases with signs and symptoms indicating the presence of secondary septicaemia, as indicated by remittent or continuous high fever. It is best to look for micro-organisms in specimens from diseased sites. Conjunctival scrapings readily yield the micro-organisms in cases of oculoglandular tularaemia. The local lesions contain large numbers of micro-organisms in the ulceroglandular type of illness as does sputum or pleural fluid in cases of typhoidal or pulmonary tularaemia. Exhudate or scrapings from lymph nodes draining the site of the initial infection may be employed for isolation. In untreated patients, organisms may persist in these areas for months. Since the procedure for isolating and identifying *F. tularensis* is fraught with real danger to the technician, reasonable precautions must be employed to minimize the risk. Such precautions include attempts to decrease the probability of producing aerial contamination. Animals to be autopsied should first be immersed in a strong solution of a disinfecting agent. Inoculating loops should be heated gradually rather than thrust into a flame to sterilize them, because the droplets of infected material dispersed in the air when loops are heated too quickly may be a source of infection.

III. BACTERIOLOGICAL EXAMINATION

F. tularensis may be isolated directly on culture media from infected materials, but often these materials may contain so many contaminating agents that the procedure is rendered extremely difficult or even impossible. The most suitable medium for general laboratory procedures is glucose-cystine-blood agar. This may be made from infusion agar prepared in the laboratory but commercial preparations are also adequate. The medium is removed from the autoclave and brought to a temperature of 60°C in a water bath. Sterile defibrinated rabbit blood is added to a concentration of 8–10%. Absence of growth on medium without cystine is a significant differentiating characteristic of *F. tularensis*. In general, attempts to isolate the microbes by direct inoculation of culture media are very often unsuccessful. The use of laboratory animals is recommended. The animals of choice are guinea-pigs, mice, or hamsters. These may be inoculated either subcutaneously or intraperitoneally. If the material is grossly contaminated, it may be rubbed into the broken skin of the laboratory animal. The method of scarifying the skin is simple and may be employed with confidence. Animals usually survive 5–7 days, but may succumb as early as 48 h after inoculation. Guinea-pigs injected subcutaneously show enlarged caseous lymph nodes at the site of injections, enlarged spleen, and necrotic foci on the liver and spleen. The lesions are typical in guinea-pigs, less typical in mice and hamsters.

For inoculation into animals, suspend specimens in physiological salt solution, using in the case of sputum about 10 to 20 volumes of the solution. When making the suspension, use a syringe fitted with a 20 gauge needle. Inoculate amounts varying from 0·1 to 0·5 ml subcutaneously into 4–6 white mice and one or two guinea-pigs. Kill one or two mice after guinea-pigs have developed enlarged lymph nodes. Enlargement of the regional lymph nodes in inoculated guinea-pigs indicate when the number of micro-organisms in the mice has become sufficiently large to make detection relatively easy. Then culture heart blood and fragments of liver and spleen on plates of glucose-cystine-blood agar. Rub the cut surface of liver and spleen fragments vigorously over the entire agar surface, using forceps to grip the tissue. Frequently, *F. tularensis* may be isolated in cultures made from tissues of mice killed early in the course of experimental infection, thus obviating examination of animals which die subsequently. The isolated organisms are identified by agglutination. For the test to be of diagnostic value, the micro-organisms should be agglutinated to the same end point as an established strain of *F. tularensis*.

IV. SEROLOGICAL TECHNIQUES IN IDENTIFICATION

Serologically, the agglutination test is of greatest value for the identification of *F. tularensis*. The precipitin test employing thermostable antigens and the immunofluorescence technique will also be discussed in view of their value in establishing an early diagnosis of tularaemia.

Specific immune sera may be obtained from humans who have recovered from tularaemia or from animals immunized with killed suspensions of live vaccine strains. Rabbits serve as a good source of serum when immunized with suspensions of killed organisms. A suspension of formalin-killed *F. tularensis* employed as antigen in the agglutination test is suitable for immunizing rabbits for the preparation of antiserum. The rabbits are given 1·0 ml of the antigen intravenously on three successive days each week for two weeks. After a resting period of a week, the animals are bled and the serum separated and examined for the presence of agglutinins. If these are present in sufficiently high titre, the animals are exsanguinated and the serum stored at −20°C.

Hyperimmunization of rabbits with the live vaccine strain (Eigelsbach and Down, 1961) by three intravenous injections of 10^8 viable cells at weekly intervals has been efficient for increasing antibody levels (Nutter, 1968).

Also chicken may give specific immune sera. One single dose of 5×10^6 viable organisms given intravenously in 0·1 ml, has given sufficient titre even after nine days (Yager *et al.*, 1960; Karlsson and Söderlind, 1973).

A. Agglutination

Preparation of antigen

Micro-organisms suspended in physiological saline are transferred to glucose-cystine-rabbit blood agar plates and incubated at 37°C for 48–72 h. The cultures are harvested in saline to which a final concentration of 0·5% formalin is added. The suspension is centrifuged to sediment micro-organisms and the deposit washed twice with saline containing 0·5% formalin. The final sediment is suspended in 15–20 volumes of salt solution with formalin and stored as stock suspension at 4°C in a tightly stoppered container. For use in agglutination tests, the stock antigen is diluted with saline to a turbidity corresponding to the Wellcome opacity tube No. 2.

Tube agglutination technique. Nine agglutination tubes are placed in a rack. The dilution procedure is as follows: Pipette 0·8 ml of a physiological salt solution into the first tube and 0·5 ml into each of the others. Pipette 0·2 ml of the serum under test into the first tube and mix thoroughly (serum dilution in Tube 1 = 1:5). Transfer 0·5 ml of the diluted serum from Tube 1 to Tube 2, mix, and repeat through Tube 9. Add 0·5 ml of diluted antigen to each tube and shake vigorously. An antigen control of 0·5 ml physiological salt solution and 0·5 ml antigen is included in the tests. After incubating at 37°C for 18–20 h, the results are read by the naked eye against a dark background. The results are graded 1+ to 4+ for each tube. A water-clear supernatant with a compact sediment consti-tutes a 4+ reaction, a slightly turbid supernatant with a compact sediment a 3+ reaction, a turbid supernatant with a relatively easily dispersed sedi-ment a 2+ reaction, and the presence of floccules only, a 1+ reaction. The highest serum dilution yielding a 4+ or 3+ reaction is regarded as titre value.

Slide agglutination

A slide agglutination procedure dispersing the cells as customary in suitable serum dilutions directly on glass slides has been developed. The results obtained by this technique correlate well with the results obtained by tube agglutination (Haug and Pearsson, 1972).

B. Precipitin test (modified Ascoli)

Antigens are prepared from liver and spleen of infected animals by ex-traction by heating or by the addition of diethyl ether.

Antigen extraction by heat is an effective procedure achieved by grinding tissues in a mortar with sterile sand and adding 2–3 volumes of physio-logical saline. This is placed in an autoclave at 100°C with flowing steam for 15 min or boiled gently for 5 min. The heated suspension is then centrifuged at 4200 rev/min for 30 min and the clear fluid retained.

To extract antigen with dethyl ether, add two volumes to the suspension of tissues in physiological salt solution. Use either a separating funnel or a cork-stoppered tube, depending on the quantity of material to be handled. Shake vigorously and keep at room temperature for at least 1 h. The aqueous phase is harvested and centrifuged at 4200 rev/min for 30 min and the clear fluid retained.

The precipitation test is most easily performed by the capillary tube method. Two-fold saline dilutions of the antigen are prepared. Serum is then drawn into capillary tubes to about one-third the length of the tubes followed by a similar amount of antigen. The tubes are inverted and the ends inserted into a rack containing plasticine or modelling clay. After incubation at 37°C for 2 h, the tubes are kept in a refrigerator over-night before examining for the presence of precipitate.

This procedure is used for the titration of antigen contained in tissues of animals. The tests are read as positive or negative, depending upon whether or not a precipitate is formed. The relative amount of precipitate in positive tubes is not considered. The precipitin titre of extracts from animal tissues may be as high as 1:256, but ordinarily titres of 1:32 are encountered. However, even titres of 1:2 or 1:4 are of diagnostic significance.

The precipitin test is confirmed by isolation of *F. tularensis* either by inoculating laboratory animals or culture media.

C. Immunofluorescent technique

To detect *F. tularensis* in infected materials, the *direct immunofluorescent technique* has been shown to be very useful (Franék and Procházka, 1965; Karlsson et al., 1970). Imprints on microscope slides are prepared from infected material and after the preparations have been air-dried and heat-fixed, they are treated with a drop of a conjugated anti-*F. tularensis* immunoglobulin. After incubation in a moist chamber at 37°C for 30 min, the preparations are rinsed and washed for about 15 min in phosphate buffered saline (PBS). Finally, the slides are mounted under cover glasses in a mixture of one part glycerol and nine parts of PBS before observation in a fluorescent light microscope.

Appropriate controls with negative and positive smears are set up.

Specific anti-*F. tularensis* sera from man, rabbits or chickens may be used for the preparation of conjugates (for technical details see Walker et al., this Series, Volume 5A).

In our experience, the *indirect immunofluorescent* test has also rendered specific results. The specific immune serum has been prepared in rabbits and fluorescent dye labelled anti-rabbit globulin is used to visualize the reaction. The working-dilutions of the reagents are determined by chessboard titrations (Beutner *et al.*, 1968). The smears are treated with one drop of the unlabelled antiserum, incubated and rinsed as described for the direct technique. After excess moisture has been blotted from the slides the smears are stained with the conjugate and treated as described above.

In our experience, cross-reactive positive staining reactions with bacteria of other genera have not been serious complications.

V. EVALUATION

Valuable guides for the laboratory identification of *F. tularensis* include the following differential criteria: absence of growth on ordinary media, little or no growth on blood-enriched media that lack added cysteine or cystine, relatively slow growth on special media, distinctive bacteriological morphology and staining properties. Specific immunofluorescent reactions and agglutination occur with specific antisera. If the isolate meets the cultural and morphological criteria indicated above and the organisms are agglutinated by specific antiserum, it should be considered as *F. tularensis*.

All work with potentially infectious clinical materials and cultures of *F. tularensis* should be performed in a suction vented hood. Surgical gloves should be worn to prevent skin contact with the organism. Also, special care must be observed in housing animals inoculated with clinical specimens and in examination of their tissues.

An innocuous, but highly effective live vaccine may be used for immunizing individuals at risk of being infected, including laboratory animal caretaker personnel (Eigelsbach *et al.*, 1967). The live vaccine is not directly available commercially, but can be obtained from the Center for Disease Control, Attention Immunobiologics Activity, Atlanta, Ga. 30333, U.S.A.

REFERENCES

Beutner, E. H., Sepulveda, M. R., and Barnett, E. V. (1968). *Bull. Wld Hlth Org.*, **39**, 587–606.

Burroughs, A. L., Holdenried, R., Longanecker, D. S., and Meyer, K. F. (1945). *J. infect. Dis.*, **76**, 115.

Dieter, L. V., and Rhodes, B. (1926). *J. infect. Dis.*, **38**, 541.

Downs, C. M., Coriell, L. L., Pinchot, G. B., Maumenee, E., Klauber, A., Chapman, S. S., and Owen, B. (1947). *J. Immunol.*, **56**, 217.

Eigelsbach, H. T., and Downs, C. M. (1961). *J. Immunol.*, **87**, 415–425.

Eigelsbach, H. T., Hornick, R. B., and Tulis, J. J. (1967). *Med. Ann. D.C.*, **36**, 282–286.

Francis, E. (1919). *Publ. Hlth Rep.*, **12**, 2061–2062.

Franék, J., and Procházka, O. (1965). *Folia Microbiol.*, **10**, 77–84.

Haug, R. H., and Pearson, A. D. (1972). *Acta path. microbiol. scand. Section B,*
    80, 273–280.
Karlsson, K.-A., and Söderlind, O. (1973). *In* "Contributions to Microbiology and
    Immunology" (Ed. S. Winblad), pp. 224–230. Karger, Basel.
Karlsson, K.-A., Dahlstrand, S., Hanko, E., and Söderlind, O. (1970). *Acta path.
    microbiol. scand.,* **78,** 647–651.
Nutter, J. E. (1969). *Appl. Microbiol.,* **17,** 355–359.
Olsufjev, N. G., Emelyanova, O. S., and Dunaeva, T. N. (1959). *J. Hyg. Epidemiol.
    Microbiol. Immunol.* (Prague), **3,** 138–149.
Olsufjev, N. G., and Emelyanova, O. S. (1962). *J. Hyg. Epidemiol. Microbiol.
    Immunol.* (Prague), **6,** 193.
Yager, R. H., Spertzel, O. R., Jaeger, R. F., and Tigerit, W. D. (1960). *Proc. Soc.
    exp. Biol. Med.,* **105,** 651–654.

CHAPTER VIII

Serotyping of *Haemophilus influenzae*

Tov OMLAND

*Norwegian Defence Microbiological Laboratory, National Institute of Public Health,
Oslo, Norway*

I. INTRODUCTION

A. Taxonomy. Classification. Methods for isolation and identification

For a detailed taxonomic description of the species *Haemophilus influenzae* (Haemophilus, from Greek: haima, blood and filos, lover) the reader is referred to *Bergey's Manual of Determinative Bacteriology*, 8th edition (Buchanan and Gibbons, 1974).

In clinical laboratory work as well as for most research purposes, the classification is based on properties and procedures reviewed in literature especially devoted to this species (Alexander, 1965). The isolation and identification rests mainly on properties such as the characteristic odour of the culture, often called seminal, on colonial and cellular morphology, and on nutritional requirements (Omland, 1963a).

Six serotypes are recognized based on capsular polysaccharide antigens.

1. *Colonial morphology*

Dome shaped, opaque to translucent colonies with entire edges and more or less dense centres are seen. Distinction is made between mucoid (M), smooth (S), and rough (R) colonies (Chandler *et al.*, 1939). A smooth colony is often splayed-out and the centre a little raised. Under good growth conditions, the colonies, after 18–20 h incubation at 37°C, have a diameter up to 2 mm. Mucoid colonies are usually somewhat larger and often confluent. The culture medium of choice is blood agar prepared from horse or rabbit blood, either in the ordinary non-heated form or as heated or digested blood agar (chocolate agar), possibly with the addition of antibiotics, such as Bacitracin (Hovig and Aandahl, 1969) for selective media. When non-heated blood agar is used, it is necessary to apply a streak of *Staphylococcus aureus* perpendicularly to the streaking of the inoculum, thereby producing the so-called satellite growth phenomenon, a characteristic and useful feature, particularly in primary isolation and tentative identification of the organism. Heated or digested blood agar (chocolate agar) allows uniform, rich growth and is useful when much cellular material is needed, e.g. for antigen production. In the author's experience it is advantageous to employ an enrichment of yeast concentrate, e.g. in the form of Supplement B (Difco). For such purposes, selective media should be avoided.

The presence or absence of iridescence may be studied in a translucent mediun such as Levinthal agar (Alexander, 1965). The phenomenon is present only in strains possessing capsules of considerable thickness, and is observed by viewing the plate in transmitted light at an oblique angle.

2. *Cellular morphology*

H. influenzae may show considerable polymorphism. In young cultures, short, coccobacillary forms with dimensions $0.2–0.3 \times 0.5–2.0$ μm are common. In some S or R strains, filamentous forms may be prevalent. The varying tendency to denser colouring at the ends of the cells may sometimes be difficult to distinguish from polar staining seen, e.g. in pasteurellae. The distribution pattern of single cells in smears may, to the trained observer, be suggestive of *Haemophilus* although not readily definable in exact terms. For satisfactory results, Gram-staining with dilute Carbol fuchsin as counter stain, is recommended.

3. *Nutritional requirements*

H. influenzae grows well under atmospheric oxygen tension. It requires two growth factors, the so-called X-factor (haematin or related compounds) and the V-factor (nicotine-amide adenine di-nucleotide (NAD) or related compounds) (Davis, 1921; Fildes, 1921, 1922, 1924; Thjøtta and Avery, 1921; Lwoff and Lwoff, 1937).

In practical work, the nutritional requirements may be examined by using a medium devoid of the growth factors, e.g. Heart Infusion Broth (Difco) with the addition of 1·5% (w/v) agar. After inoculation from a pure culture, X-, V-, and X+V-factor paper discs (Oxoid or equivalent) are applied on the medium. Alternatively, the factors may be supplied in the form of streak growth of an X- and V-factor producing microbe such as *Micrococcus luteus* (*Sarcina lutea*) and a V-factor producing microbe such as *Streptococcus faecalis* (Pickett and Stewart, 1953).

II. BIOLOGICAL BASIS OF SEROTYPING

According to traditional use, the term "serotyping" of *H. influenzae* means serological typing based on immunochemical differences in capsular polysaccharides. Serotyping is thus only applicable to encapsulated strains. Non-encapsulated strains are serologically heterogeneous. Serotyping must, however, in practice be performed indiscriminately on all strains of *H. influenzae*, because no reliable procedure exists for the *a priori* exclusion of non-encapsulated isolates. Even the phenomenon of iridescence, which is attributed exclusively to encapsulated strains, is not sufficiently distinctive.

Encapsulated strains are, however, considered the most important in clinical illness. In clinical and epidemiological investigations such strains usually constitute $\frac{1}{4}-\frac{1}{3}$ of all strains. For the remaining $\frac{2}{3}-\frac{3}{4}$ non-encapsulated strains no satisfactory serological classification has yet been established. An example of the degree of typability and of the type distribution in a clinical material is given by Omland (1963d). He found 54 typable strains out of 163 (33%). The most frequent type was *b*, followed by the types *f*, *a*, *d*, *e*, in that order. Type *c* did not occur.

A. Historical

Early studies on the serology of *H. influenzae* showed that the serological procedures used at that time, i.e. agglutination, yielded inconsistent results (Park *et al.*, 1918 (cit. Wilson and Miles, 1966); Anderson and

Schultz, 1921; Yabe, 1921; Krah, 1930; Yagi (=Iizuka), 1935, 1938; Platt, 1937). These studies were relevant for what are customarily called R-strains. The S-strains (in this review called M-strains) presented a more orderly picture as first noted by Margaret Pittman (1929, 1931). Subsequent studies are all largely based upon Pittman's classical findings (Fothergill and Chandler, 1936; Wilkes-Weiss, 1937; Engbæk, 1949, 1950; Tunevall, 1952, 1953; Omland, 1963d, 1964c; Branefors-Helander, 1972a, b).

During the last three decades the chemical composition of the different type specific capsular substances has been largely elucidated (Alexander and Heidelberger, 1940; MacPherson et al., 1946; MacPherson, 1948; Williamson and Zinnemann, 1951, 1954; Zamenhof et al., 1953; Zamenhof and Leidy, 1954; Rosenberg et al., 1961; Williamson and Zamenhof, 1963).

The capsular substance of H. influenzae type b was shown to belong to a new class of immunologically active compounds, the phosphopolysaccharides (Zamenhof et al., 1953). The type b substance is a polyribophosphate, in which the sugar and the phosphoric acid alternate, linked by ester bridges, forming a chain, to which other chains are linked in $1:1'$-glycosidic linkages as it exists in pentose nucleic acids.

Subsequent work has shown that the types a, c, and f substances are also sugar phosphates, the sugar in type a probably being glucose, in type c galactose, and in type f N-acetylgalactosamine.

The types d and e substances differ from a, c or f in not containing phosphoric acid and having a more complex sugar composition. Thus, the type d substance contains N-acetylglucosamine uronic acid and N-acetylglucosamine in a 2:1 molar ratio, while the type e substance contains glucosamine and a not yet conclusively identified hexose. Accordingly, only type b contains pentose, all others having a hexose or a hexose derivative.

B. Antigenic structural schema

The six recognized serotypes are labelled by letters. This system, established in principle by Pittman (1929, 1931), became somewhat more complex after the findings of Williamson and Zinnemann (1951, 1954) that type e encompasses two subtypes, one corresponding to the formula e_1e_2 and the other to the formula e_2. This has been confirmed by later studies (Omland, 1964a; Branefors-Helander, 1972b). A spatial arrangement of the two e-antigens has been proposed by Williamson and Zinnemann (1954) on the basis of agglutination experiments using absorbed sera. Some of their conclusions have been disputed by Branefors-Helander (1972b).

Leidy et al. (1953) have shown that genetic transformation may yield strains possessing two type-specific capsular antigens. Branefors-Helander (1972a), in many instances, besides the major antigens was able to detect small amounts of type-specific polysaccharides belonging to other types. This demonstrates the existence of hybrid encapsulated strains also in nature. The amount of additional type-specific capsular antigen was, however, always much less than that of the main type-specific antigen. Accordingly, this would not usually lead to difficulties in the labelling of strains. It does, nevertheless, illustrate the complexity inherent in *H. influenzae* serotyping and underlines the necessity for further studies.

III. TECHNIQUES

A review is presented of some of the techniques employed in the serotyping of *H. influenzae*, together with details of recommended procedures for techniques of particular practical importance.

A. Production of antisera

The following procedure for the production of antisera has proved satisfactory (Omland, 1963b).

Albino rabbits weighing about 2 kg are chosen for inoculation. Care is taken that the antigen to be used has undergone as little denaturation as possible. This is achieved by using live organisms in the logarithmic phase of growth. Freeze-dried organisms are plated directly, or after one subculture on blood agar with a *Staphylococcus* streak, on to a plate of heated blood agar (chocolate agar) prepared from rabbit blood with Supplement B (Difco). The plate is incubated for 6–8 h at 37°C in a moist chamber. A Gram-stained smear is examined as a control against contaminants. If found satisfactory, the growth is harvested into about 2 ml of sterile physiological saline. For the first few inoculations of the series, the density of the suspension is measured colorimetrically and adjusted to the equivalent of about 10^9 organisms/ml. If the inoculations are well tolerated, this adjustment may later be omitted. The dose schedule may be from 0·10 to 0·50 ml with a gradual increase during the series. If the animal reacts untowardly to the first inoculation of 0·10 ml, it is recommended that the dose be reduced to one-tenth by dilution. It is important to keep the animal under close observation during the hole inoculation period and to lower the doses if not well tolerated. The intervals between inoculations are, as a rule, from two days to one week and the total immunization course usually includes from 10 to 15 injections.

During immunization, control tests for antibody production are carried out on samples of blood from the animal's ear.

The final bleeding (e.g. by heart puncture) is ordinarily started after eight to ten injections. During the period of bleeding, the animals should receive one injection weekly and the bleeding should be performed four to five days after each injection. A weight record is kept for each animal as a simple check on its condition. Serum is inactivated at 56°C for 30 min and all satisfactory specimens from each animal are mixed into a serum pool which is distributed in small quantities (e.g. 1 ml) and kept in the frozen state to avoid repeated freezing and thawing during the work.

A final control of the potency and specificity of the typing sera may be carried out by double diffusion in agar (cf. Section III. C, Immunoprecipitation, and Fig. 1). It is essential that commercial sera be subjected to similar control.

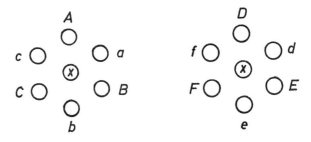

A, B, C, D, E, F: type reference antiserum
a, b, c, d, e, f : type reference antigen
x : antigen from unknown strain

FIG. 1. Immunoprecipitation (double diffusion). Arrangement and filling of wells.

B. Preparation of antigen for immunoprecipitation and immunoelectrophoresis

1. *Reference antigen*

The following procedure is a modification of the method described by MacPherson (1948) (Omland, 1963c).

Heated blood agar plates (chocolate agar) (horse or rabbit blood with Supplement B (Difco)) are inoculated heavily with a pure culture of the type strain. After 18 h incubation in a moist chamber at 37°C, the culture is harvested into a minimum (about 1·5 ml per plate) of 1M sodium acetate and precipitated by five volumes of ethanol (95% v/v). The mixture is left in the refrigerator (+4°C) for 4–5 h or until the following day and is then centrifuged at the same temperature and moderate speed (1000–1500 × *g*) for 30 min. The supernatant is discarded and the precipitate dissolved in 90% (w/v) phenol (1 ml per harvested plate) and left at room temperature for 15 min. Twenty per cent (w/v) sodium acetate (0·1 ml per harvested plate) is added and thereafter five volumes of 95% (v/v) ethanol for re-precipitation. The mixture is placed in ice water for a minimum of 1 h. After centrifugation at the same speed and temperature as described above, the supernatant is discarded and the precipitate washed three times in 95% (v/v) ethanol. Finally, the precipitate is extracted overnight in distilled water or physiological saline at room temperature (1 ml per harvested plate). The antigen solution thus obtained, is the type reference antigen. It may be kept in solution at +4°C for many weeks, but for longer preservation it is preferable to freeze-dry the reference antigen. Dried antigen in tightly sealed screw-cap bottles keeps well for many years in a desiccator at +4°C.

The advantage of the MacPherson method as compared to more gentle extraction procedures is that the capsular type substances are immunologically preserved, whereas other antigens, e.g. from the medium, are denatured.

Control of newly prepared type antigens is performed in a double diffusion system by testing each single antigen as an "unknown" antigen (central well, Fig. 1), and by immunoelectrophoresis.

2. *Antigen from unknown strains*

The same method may be used as for type antigens (cf. above). However, for most purposes, the more simple and rapid technique of ultrasonic disintegration may be employed. The same cultivation procedure is used as the one described above. Harvesting is carried out in physiological saline instead of sodium acetate (cf. above), or in the case of immunoelectrophoresis in a salt-buffer mixture of the same composition as is used in the gel. Ultrasonic treatment is performed in volumes down to about 2 ml, cooling the sample in ice water during the treatment. Time of treatment: 1 min (MSE 100W ultrasonic disintegrator at maximal output or equivalent treatment). In most cases, the antigen prepared in this way may be used directly in immunoprecipitation or immunoelectrophoresis. If preferred, the antigen preparation may be centrifuged at high speed (10,000–12,000 × *g*) for 30 min and the supernatants used instead (Omland, 1964b).

C. Immunoprecipitation (double diffusion)

Since the studies by Pittman in the early 1930s, immunoprecipitation has been the most important technique in the serotyping of *H. influenzae*. Particularly gel precipitation in the form of double diffusion systems (Ouchterlony, 1949, 1958), has proved advantageous. It is thereby possible to compare unknown and reference antigens. By the use of miniature modifications, it is furthermore possible to economize on reagents (Omland, 1963c, d).

10

1. *Procedure*

A 2–3 mm thick gel layer is poured on to a clean 25 × 75 mm microscope slide. The gel is prepared from highly purified agar (Special Agar Noble Difco or equivalent quality) in phosphate buffer pH 6·8 with an ionic strength of 0·01M. This is preferable instead of the alternative phosphate buffered saline (pH 7–7·5) with an ionic strength of 0·15M, as it usually yields stronger and sharper precipitation lines (Omland, 1963c). Soon after the agar layer is solidified, a hexagonal well pattern with a central seventh well is punched into the agar, one pattern on each half of the slide. Recommended dimensions are the following: well diameter, 2–3 mm; distance between neighbouring wells, 3–5 mm. Suitable punching devices are commercially available. Before filling reactants into the wells, it is important to empty them thoroughly by suction. The wells are subsequently filled according to the arrangement shown in Fig. 1. The slides are then left at room temperature (about 20°C) and results recorded after 20–24 h. In the case of an emergency, it may be worth while to scrutinize the slide as early as after about 6 h, but precipitation lines at that stage are usually faint and should be judged with caution. It is sometimes useful to observe the precipitate also after two days.

The reaction is considered positive when definite fusion of precipitation lines show immunological identity between the antigen preparation from an unknown strain and the type reference antigen (Fig. 2). Difficulties in interpretation may occur through interference with somatic and other antigens. Problems caused by such non-type-specific antigens are well known in *H. influenzae* work (Platt, 1937; Engbæk, 1950).

D. Immunoelectrophoresis

Conventional immunoelectrophoresis is an accessory technique in the serotyping of *H. influenzae*. The introduction of a new dimension, i.e. electrophoretic mobility, may be of assistance in determining certain special characteristics, such as the acidic properties of the capsular polysaccharides. The technique is indispensable as a control during the preparation of type reference antigens. It may occasionally be useful also for the examination of capsular preparations of unknown strains.

1. *Procedure*

Immunoelectrophoresis is performed on microscope slides (25 × 75 mm) in an electrophoresis apparatus of any recognized manufacture. One per cent (w/v) highly purified agar is used for the preparation of the gel (Special Agar Noble Difco, Agarose Behringwerke, or equivalent). The agar is prepared in a buffer of pH 8–8·6. A commonly used system is 0·10–0·15M Veronal buffer pH 8·6. This buffer is commercially available

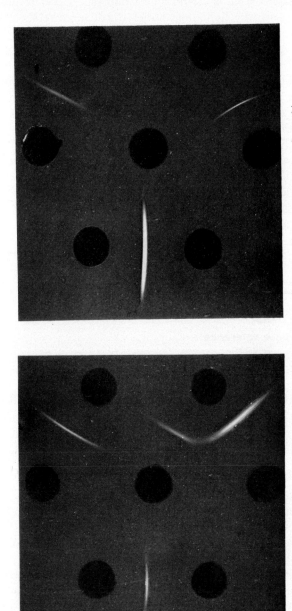

Fig. 2. Immunoprecipitation (double diffusion). Positive result of serotyping (type b).

in the dried state for blood serum electrophoresis. Good results are also obtained by a markedly hypotonic buffered salt mixture such as 0·005M NaCl + 0·005M phosphate buffer pH 8. The composition of the buffer salt mixture must allow for a suitable voltage and current. At 250 V, the current should be about 20 mA for each slide. The desired system of reservoirs is cut into the gel by means of a special gel punching device (LKB or other make) (Fig. 3). After having filled the antigens to be examined into the reservoirs, the electrophoresis is run for 1 h. It is important to take precautions against excessive heat. However, under the conditions described, gel heating usually is no problem. After the run, the slide is removed from the apparatus, the antiserum poured into its proper reservoir, and the slide is left at room temperature. A diffusion period of 20–24 h is usually adequate.

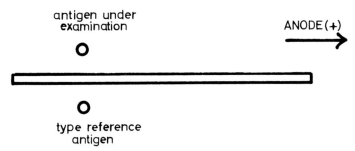

FIG. 3. Arrangement of reservoirs in immunoelectrophoresis.

The type specific capsular polysaccharides of *H. influenzae* all have acid properties and should yield precipitation lines pointing towards the anode. It is advisable to include a reference antigen for comparison (Omland, 1964c).

E. Countercurrent-immunoelectrophoresis

This variant of immunoelectrophoresis has proved of value when rapidity is essential. As a sensitive means of detecting small amounts of bacterial antigen, it has been employed in the rapid diagnosis of certain fulminant bacterial infections like meningitis (Myhre, 1974b). It may, however, also be used for serotyping purposes.

The enhanced sensitivity is attained by "guiding" the reactants towards each other by a combination of diffusion and electrophoresis, so speeding up the appearance of visible precipitation lines (Fig. 4).

1. *Procedure*

The procedure described is based on a recent study by Myhre (1974a).

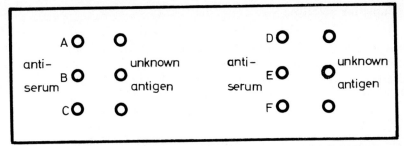

FIG. 4. Countercurrent-immunoelectrophoresis. Arrangement and filling of wells.

Microscope slides (25 × 75 mm) are covered with 2 ml 1% (w/v) agarose (Agarose Behringwerke or equivalent quality) in veronal buffer (pH 8·6, ionic strength 0·05M). Wells of 3 mm diameter are cut 5 mm apart, six pairs in two rows on each slide. The wells closest to the anode in each row are filled with type antisera *a–f* and in the opposing wells the supernatant of a 16 h culture of *H. influenzae* in Levinthal broth. Electrophoresis is performed at room temperature for 1 h using constant voltage (usually about 4 V/cm agarose). The slides are inspected immediately for precipitate with oblique lighting against dark background (Fig. 5).

Because of somatic and other antigens, similar interpretative difficulties may occur as in the double diffusion technique. Adjustments of the growth time of the organism in the broth may be necessary to reduce this problem (Myhre, 1974a).

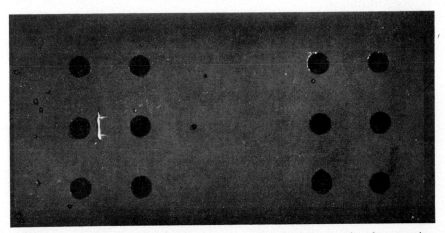

FIG. 5. Countercurrent-immunoelectrophoresis. Positive result of serotyping (type *b*).

F. Capsular swelling

The capsular swelling or "Quellung" reaction was first described by Neufeld (1902). For many purposes, this type of antigen–antibody reaction is unsurpassed, because it enables the investigator to observe the reaction microscopically in each single bacterial cell. The technique may be performed using a bacterial culture or directly in pathological specimens.

1. *Procedure*

Inoculation is made into Levinthal broth (Alexander, 1965) from a young, pure culture on solid medium. The broth tube is incubated at 37°C for 6–8 h in an oblique, nearly horizontal position with occasional shaking, so as to secure great surface/volume ratio and thereby better aeration. One drop of broth culture is mixed with one drop of adequately diluted type specific antiserum on a slide and examined microscopically with at least $400 \times$ magnification. Phase contrast illumination is most advantageous. It may be necessary to use magnifications up to $1000 \times$ (oil immersion), as *H. influenzae* is a small organism. The addition of methylene blue as described by Alexander (1965) may sometimes be advantageous.

If serotyping is required directly in pathological material, e.g. cerebrospinal fluid, it may be performed in the same way by mixing the material with the antiserum in equal parts.

It is important to realize that the reading of results must rest on comparisons with a positive and a negative reference system since it is difficult to assess dimensions accurately (Omland 1963b, e).

G. Agglutination

Although extensively used, agglutination tends to give inconsistent results, mainly because underlying somatic antigens may interfere (Platt, 1937; Engbæk, 1950). Consequently this technique is not recommended for ordinary use.

H. Growth in antibody containing media

Though not used for regular serotyping of *H. influenzae*, the principle has been well known for a long time (Fothergill and Chandler, 1936). Recently, there has been renewed interest in this technique especially for the detection of *H. influenzae* type *b* colonies on solid media (Michaels *et al.*, 1975).

I. Miscellaneous techniques

Of recent promising methods, the so-called coagglutination technique should be mentioned (Kronwall, 1972). By making use of an antibody preparation in which the immunoglobulins are bound to particles (e.g. protein-A carrying *Staphylococcus aureus* cells) a particularly high sensitivity is achieved. The technique may be used to detect antigen in solution or on the surface of particles, such as bacteria. It has, however, not yet been used to any extent for *H. influenzae*.

Techniques employing labelled antibody, i.e. immunofluorescence or radioimmunological methods have, so far, not found much application. (Sell *et al.*, 1963; Closs, 1968; Hambræus, 1969). In such techniques the use of highly purified and preferably monovalent antibody preparations is especially important and this requirement is not easily attainable.

J. Photographic recording of results of immunoprecipitation and immunoelectrophoresis

Technical problems concerning photography of immunoprecipitation lines have been dealt with by several authors (Hunter, 1959; Reed, 1960; Omland, 1963c). An arrangement suitable for most uses is oblique light from one lamp. Oblique light from several sources or in the shape of a light cone does not normally lead to better resolution of details. The use of only one lamp may sometimes cause undesired refraction effects at well rims, etc., but this may largely be prevented by filling all reservoirs immediately before photographing with fluid of the same composition as in the gel, or by submerging the whole slide in such fluid in a Petri dish with a faultlessly transparent bottom. It is of great importance to use high-contrast film (plate) and a contrast developer.

IV. SIGNIFICANCE OF SEROTYPING. APPLICATIONS

In order to evaluate the significance of serotyping of *H. influenzae*, it is necessary to review briefly what is at present known concerning pathogenicity, epidemiology, and reservoir.

A. Pathogenicity

H. influenzae is a human pathogen for which no good experimental animal model has been established. An exception is the mouse which acquires an infectious disease upon intraperitoneal injection of the organism mixed with porcine gastric mucin (Engbæk, 1949). This model, however, bears few similarities to natural infection in man, in which the portal of entry is almost exclusively the respiratory tract. In man respiratory tract infections with *H. influenzae* are often preceded by a viral infection, analogous to swine influenza, in which the bacterial pathogen is *H. suis*.

The respiratory tract with accessory organ systems, notably the middle ear, is the site of most infections with *H. influenzae*. Although numerically negligible, the septic infections, such as meningitis and epiglottitis are of particular significance because of their seriousness. A comprehensive review of the pathogenicity of *H. influenzae* has been presented by Turk and May (1967).

Whereas clinical experience has established that infections with *H. influenzae* in general cover the whole spectrum from extremely serious to quite benign illnesses, our understanding of the underlying factors is poor.

It is generally accepted that encapsulated strains are the most pathogenic, and that type *b* is responsible for practically all the serious septic infections. On the other hand, available evidence indicates that non-encapsulated strains are also pathogenic, although they mostly cause mild infections when alone.

Older as well as more recent studies point to cell wall antigens of the endotoxin type as pathogenicity factors (Branefors-Helander, 1973).

B. Reservoir. Epidemiology

Humans appear to be the exclusive reservoir of infection. Clinical infections are widespread, particularly among children. Of special interest is the occurrence of *H. influenzae* in adults or elderly individuals with an underlying state of lowered resistance associated with bronchiectasis or other anomalies of the lower respiratory tract.

The main epidemiological features of infections with *H. influenzae* follow the same trends as other respiratory infections regarding seasonal, geographical, and climatic variations.

C. Choice of technique

Of the methods suitable for routine use today, the immunoprecipitation (double diffusion) technique is the one yielding the most definite and unequivocal results. This is due to the readiness with which this method permits a direct comparison with standard reference antigens. Doubtful reactions are exceptional and may usually be clarified by simple repetition.

In the capsular swelling reaction, doubtful results are frequent because of difficulties inherent in microscopic visualization of the small dimensions in question. Although the problems may be reduced by frequent comparisons with reference systems, it is not possible entirely to eliminate these difficulties (Omland, 1963e).

In the case of countercurrent-immunoelectrophoresis, occasional doubtful results may also occur. Such results are partly related to the relatively high sensitivity of the method, but also to the fact that the technique in its normal modification does not readily permit direct comparison to reference systems (Myhre, 1974a).

Conventional immunoelectrophoresis must be considered merely an accessory method in the serological typing of *H. influenzae*. It is, however, valuable when further characterization of an antigen is needed.

The choice of technique, or combination of techniques, to some extent depends upon the reason for serotyping an isolate.

1. *Clinical microbiology*

For this type of work immunoprecipitation by double diffusion is the technique of choice, even though it may require two to three days, when a pure secondary culture has to be prepared. Serotyping may also be used in the rapid diagnosis of fulminant infections such as meningitis. In such situations, when speed is of vital importance, the capsular swelling method is of value, especially because it may also be used in primary pathological material such as cerebrospinal fluid or serum. Another promising rapid method is countercurrent-immunoelectrophoresis, which may give a definitive result within 1 h. This technique is equally suitable for primary pathological material and for pure cultures (Myhre, 1974a, b).

2. *Epidemiology*

For epidemiological purposes, speed is not important and immuno-precipitation by double diffusion is the method of choice. Countercurrent-immunoelectrophoresis is an alternative.

3. *Special purposes*

For special purposes, such as for research work, where rapidity is not essential but reliability and reproducibility are of the utmost importance, immunoprecipitation by double diffusion is recommended. Additional antigenic characterization may be achieved by conventional immunoelectrophoresis.

D. Limitations

The main limitation in serotyping *H. influenzae* is the circumstance that only a fraction of clinical isolates are typable, i.e. possess a type-specific capsule (Omland, 1963d, e). Exceptions are the fulminant septic infections (meningitis, epiglottis). In the literature, there has been speculation on the possible existence of strains containing only minimal amounts of type-specific polysaccharide. Practical experience indicates, however, that this problem, if it exists, is negligible provided satisfactory cultivation techniques are employed.

The significance of strains with a hybrid-type antigen make-up is still uncertain. Branefors-Helander (1972a) was the first to report the finding of two or more capsular antigens occurring naturally in *H. influenzae*.

Thus in one of her type *c* strains she demonstrated traces of the type-specific antigens *b*, *e*, and *f*. She made similar findings in the other type strains with the exception of type *a*. As pointed out by her, these findings may explain some of the cross-reactions experienced in *H. influenzae* serotyping by many workers.

In older literature, instability of serological type characteristics is frequently mentioned. The type-specific properties of a strain may apparently be lost upon subcultivation. In more recent experience, this problem seems less important. Although no definite explanation can be offered, it is probable that modern technical developments such as improved media and the avoidance of series of subcultures by the use of freeze-drying, are partly responsible for this improved situation.

REFERENCES

Alexander, H. E. (1965). The *Hemophilus* group. *In* "Bacterial and Mycotic Infections of Man" (Ed. R. J. Dubos), 4th edn, pp. 724–774. Pitman Medical Publishing Co. Ltd, London.

Alexander, H. E., and Heidelberger, M. (1940). *J. exp. Med.*, **71**, 1–11.

Anderson, R. A., and Schultz, O. T. (1921). *J. exp. Med.*, **33**, 653–666.

Branefors-Helander, P. (1972a). *Int. Archs Allergy appl. Immun.* **43**, 533–547.

Branefors-Helander, P. (1972b). *Int. Archs Allergy appl. Immun.*, **43**, 908–920.

Branefors-Helander, P. (1973). *Int. Archs Allergy appl. Immun.*, **44**, 585–600.

Buchanan, R. E., and Gibbons, N. E. (1974). "Bergey's Manual of Determinative Bacteriology", 8th edn, 1246 pp.

Chandler, C. A., Fothergill, L. D., and Dingle, J. H. (1939). *J. Bact.*, **37**, 415–425.

Closs, O. (1968). *Acta path. microbiol. scand.*, **72**, 412–420.

Davis, D. J. (1921). *J. infect. Dis.*, **29**, 171–177.

Engbæk, H. C. (1949). "Undersøgelser over Pfeiffers bacil". Nyt Nordisk Forlag–A. Busck, København (Copenhagen), pp. 245

Engbæk, H. C. (1950). *Acta path. microbiol. scand.*, **27**, 378–387.

Fildes, P. (1921). *Br. J. exp. Path.*, **2**, 16–25.

Fildes, P. (1922). *Br. J. exp. Path.*, **3**, 210–214.

Fildes, P. (1924). *Br. J. exp. Path.*, **5**, 69–74.

Fothergill, L. D., and Chandler, C. A. (1936). *J. Immun.*, **31**, 401–415.

Hambræus, A. (1969). *Nord. Med.*, **81**, 656–659.

Hovig, B., and Aandahl, E. H. (1969). *Acta path. microbiol. scand.*, **77**, 676–684.

Hunter, J. R. (1959). *Nature, Lond.*, **183**, 1283–1284.

Iizuka, A. (= Yagi, A.) (1938). *Z. ImmunForsch. exp. Ther.*, **94**, 312–318.

Krah, E. (1930). *Zentbl. Bakt. ParasitKde* Abt. I (Orig.), **116**, 101–113.

Kronwall, G. (1972). *J. med. Microbiol.*, **6**, 187–190.

Leidy, G., Hahn, E., and Alexander, H. E. (1953). *J. exp. Med.*, **97**, 467–482.

Lwoff, A., and Lwoff, M. (1937). *Annls Inst. Pasteur, Paris*, **59**, 129–136.

MacPherson, C. (1948). *Can. J. Res., E.*, **26**, 197–199.

MacPherson, C., Heidelberger, M., Alexander, H. E., and Leidy, G. (1946). *J. Immun.*, **52**, 207–219.

Michaels, R. H., Stonebraker, F. E., and Robbins, J. B. (1975). *Pediat. Res.*, **9**, 513–516.

Myhre, E. B. (1974a). *Acta path. microbiol. scand.* (Sect. B), **82**, 164–166.

Myhre, E. B. (1974b). *Scand. J. Infect. Dis.*, **6**, 237–239.

Neufeld, F. (1902). *Z. Hyg. InfektKrankh.*, **40**, 54–72.

Omland, T. (1963a). *Acta path. microbiol. scand.*, **57**, 268–278.

Omland, T. (1963b). *Acta path. microbiol. scand.*, **57**, 279–286.

Omland, T. (1963c). *Acta path. microbiol. scand.*, **59**, 341–356.

Omland, T. (1963d). *Acta path. microbiol. scand.*, **59**, 507–520.

Omland, T. (1963e). *Acta path. microbiol. scand.*, **59**, 521–525.

Omland, T. (1964a). *Acta path. microbiol. scand.*, **62**, 73–78.

Omland, T. (1964b). *Acta path. microbiol. scand.*, **62**, 79–88.

Omland, T. (1964c). *Acta path. microbiol. scand.*, **62**, 89–106.

Ouchterlony, Ø. (1949). *Acta path. microbiol. scand.*, **26**, 507–515.

Ouchterlony, Ø. (1958). Diffusion-in-gel methods for immunological analysis, pp. 1–78. *In* "Progress in Allergy" (Ed. P. Kallós), Vol. 5, 508 pp. S. Karger, Basel, New York.

Park, Williams, and Cooper (1918) cit. in: Wilson, G. S., and Miles, A. A. (1966) "Topley and Wilson's Principles of Bacteriology and Immunity", 5th edn, Vol. I, 970 pp. Edward Arnold Ltd, London.

Pittman, M. (1929). *Proc. Soc. exp. Biol. Med.*, **27**, 299–301.

Pittman, M. (1931). *J. exp. Med.*, **53**, 471–492.

Pickett, M. J., and Stewart, M. A. (1953). *Am. J. clin. Path.*, **23**, 713–715.

Platt, A. E. (1937). *J. Hyg. (Lond.)*, **37**, 98–107.

Reed, F. C. (1960). *Am. J. clin. Path.*, **33**, 364–366.

Rosenberg, E., Leidy, G., Jaffe, E., and Zamenhof, S. (1961). *J. biol. Chem.*, **236**, 2841–2844.

Sell, S. H. W., Cheatham, W. J., Young, B., and Welch, K. (1963). *Am. J. clin. Path.*, **23**, 713–715.

Thjøtta, T., and Avery, O. T. (1921). *J. exp. Med.*, **34**, 455–466.

Tunevall, G. (1952). *Acta path. microbiol. scand.*, **30**, 203–212.

Tunevall, G. (1953). *Acta path. microbiol. scand.*, **32**, 193–197.

Turk, D. C., and May, J. R. (1967). "*Heamophilus influenzae*. Its Clinical Importance", 140 pp. The English Universities Press Ltd, London.

Wilkes-Weiss, D. (1937). *J. infect. Dis.*, **60**, 213–222.

Williamson, A. R., and Zamenhof, S. (1963). *J. biol. Chem.*, **238**, 2255–2257.

Williamson, G. M., and Zinnemann, K. (1951). *J. Path. Bact.*, **63**, 695–698.

Williamson, G. M., and Zinnemann, K. (1954). *J. Path. Bact.*, **68**, 453–457.

Yabe, S. (1921). *Br. J. exp. Path.*, **2**, 197–204.

Yagi, A. (= Iizuka, A.) (1935). *Z. ImmunForsch. exp. Ther.*, **86**, 75–79.

Zamenhof, S., and Leidy, G. (1954). *Fedn Proc.*, **13**, p. 327.

Zamenhof, S., Leidy, G., Fitzgerald, P., Alexander, H. E., and Chargaff, E. (1953). *J. biol. Chem.*, **203**, 695–704.

CHAPTER IX

Biotyping and Serotyping of
Pasteurella haemolytica

E. L. BIBERSTEIN

School of Veterinary Medicine, University of California, Davis, California, U.S.A.

I. DEFINITION OF TAXON

The genus *Pasteurella* consists of pleomorphic, Gram-negative, non-motile rods, characterized by a fermentative carbohydrate metabolism. Being oxidase positive,† they are readily differentiated from members of *Enterobacteriaceae*, to which the same description applies. They grow poorly or not at all on the usual selective plating media for enteric organisms. In triple-sugar-iron agar (TSI), they produce acidity throughout, without gas or hydrogen sulphide formation, a reaction not typical of *Enterobacteriaceae*, except certain yersinias, which are further distinguishable from *Pasteurella* spp. by being motile and growing freely on MacConkey agar. The most tenuous delineation of *Pasteurella* is against the genus *Actinobacillus*, which resembles *Pasteurella* in all respects mentioned thus far. By current standards (J. E. Smith, 1974; Phillips, 1974), actinobacilli

---

† Tetramethylparaphenylenediamine-HCl on filter paper, using 10 sec of observation.

possess *beta*galactosidase and urease activity. *Pasteurella* spp. may have one or the other, rarely both. The suggestion has been made (Bohaček and Mráz, 1967) that *Pasteurella haemolytica* is more closely related to the genus *Actinobacillus*, as it is the only species of *Pasteurella* capable of some growth on MacConkey agar and harbouring subtypes with β-galactosidase capability. The diagnostically important characteristics of the species of *Pasteurella* and the genus *Actinobacillus* are summarized in Table I.

TABLE I

Differential characteristics of *Pasteurella* species and the genus *Actinobacillus* (After Frederiksen, 1973; Smith, 1974; Phillips, 1974)

	Haemolysis	Indole	Urease	ONPG	Growth on MacConkey agar
Pasteurella multocida	−	+	−	−	−
Pasteurella pneumotropica	−	+	+	d	−
Pasteurella ureae	d	−	+	−	−
Pasteurella haemolytica	+	−	−	d	+
Actinobacillus spp.	d	−	+	+	+

d = different reactions possible.

P. haemolytica is most readily distinguished from *P. multocida* by its failure to produce indole and its production of a usually narrow haemolytic zone, sometimes no bigger than the colony itself, on bovine or ovine blood agar. This haemolytic activity is not demonstrable in blood broth. *P. haemolytica* differs from *P. pneumotropica*, *P. ureae*, and *Actinobacillus* in being urease negative. Its ability to grow sparsely, but consistently, on MacConkey agar further separates it from the other *Pasteurella* species.

It should be emphasized that the typing procedures covered in this Chapter have been designed essentially for the classification of isolates from domestic ruminants. Organisms, described as *Pasteurella haemolytica* in the literature, but derived from other hosts, including horses, swine, chickens and humans, have only in exceptional cases been typable serologically, and, especially in the case of porcine and avian isolates that have reached us, have been unlike the ruminant strains in a number of cultural characteristics. These included growth rate, haemolytic activity, acidity produced in carbohydrates, and survival times on various media. Their assignment to the species, although defensible on the grounds of the usual qualitative criteria, is often questionable.

II. HISTORY OF TYPING

Two general approaches to typing of *P. haemolytica* have been taken. One, developed by G. R. Smith (1959, 1961), is biochemical and cultural and has resulted in the division of the species into two types, A. and T. The letters stand for arabinose and trehalose fermentation, respectively, which is characteristic of the members of the respective types. The other approach is serological, and, in its present form, was developed by E. L. Biberstein and co-workers (1960). It is based on type-specific soluble or extractable substances, the serological activity of which appears to reside in their polysaccharide component(s) (Cameron, 1966), and which can be adsorbed on red blood cells for use in an indirect haemagglutination procedure, or be employed in agar gel diffusion tests (Muraschi *et al.*, 1965).

Prior to the emergence of the present methods, attempts at sub-dividing the species have been more sporadic. Although some variation in biochemical reactions was noted early, most of the effort was directed toward serological differentiation and none toward correlating the two approaches. Serological studies prior to 1960 by agglutination (Carter, 1956; Florent and Godbille, 1950; Montgomerie *et al.*, 1938; Newsom and Cross, 1932; Tweed and Edington, 1930) and haemagglutination (Carter, 1956) suggested the existence of no more than three types. One of these was undoubtedly the present type 1, which predominates in bovine infections.

It is difficult to assign the cultures described in these older reports to one of the two biotypes A and T as the data are not completely consistent with either. In all likelihood the overwhelming majority were of type A. Only two cultures studied by Newsom and Cross (1932), the proponents of the species name, appear at all compatible with type T criteria.

In 1959 and 1961, Smith reported the occurrence of two types of *P. haemolytica* in sheep, distinguishable by a number of cultural traits. Moreover, there were pathogenic and epidemiologic differences between the two types, which Smith designated A and T, after their reactivity in arabinose and trehalose broth as previously noted.

A serological study by Carter (1956) of 61 strains, largely of bovine derivation, failed to disclose any type diversity by indirect haemagglutination and agglutination procedures. Subsequently, an investigation employing similar methods on 98 cultures of *P. haemolytica* from sheep and cattle and some other species revealed the existence of 10 capsular types, some of which showed some distinct biochemical, ecologic, and pathogenic patterns (Biberstein *et al.*, 1960). In 1962, an investigation (Biberstein and Gills, 1962) into the relationship of the A and T "biotypes" to the serotypes disclosed, in the sample studied, a consistent association between serotype and biotypes (see Section III.C below). Subsequently, two additional serotypes were identified (Biberstein and Gills, 1962; Biberstein and Thompson, 1966) so that at present twelve serological types are recognized. For the sake of clarity, the cultural types of Smith will be referred to as biotypes in distinction to serotypes. Table II sums up the most useful differential features of the types.

TABLE II

Useful differential characteristics of subtypes of *Pasteurella haemolytica* (For exceptions and qualifications see text)

Biotype	A	T
Fermentation of Arabinose	+	−
Trehalose	−	+
Salicin	−	+
Xylose	+	−
Lactose	d†	−
Susceptibility to Penicillin	High	Low
Serotypes	1, 2, 5, 6, 7, 8, 9, 11, 12	3, 4, 10
Principal localization in normal host	Nasopharynx	Tonsils
Principal disease association	Pneumonia of cattle and sheep Septicaemia of nursing lambs	Septicaemia of feeder lambs

† Serotype 2 negative, all others positive.

III. TYPING PROCEDURES

A. Determination of biotypes

1. *Basis*

Typing by differential biochemical reactions is based on G. R. Smith's observation that certain cultural characteristics went hand in hand with ecological and disease patterns associated with the isolates in question. These characteristics include colonial morphology on blood agar, fermentation of certain carbohydrates, growth curves, and susceptibility to antibiotics, particularly Penicillin. Of these, the carbohydrate fermentation pattern is the one most commonly used, but all characteristics will be described.

2. *Techniques*

(a) *Colonial morphology*. Medium used is nutrient agar at pH 7·2–7·4 containing 2·5% of Japanese agar fibre and 10% defibrinated or citrated sheep blood. The base of the medium is digest broth prepared according to the method of Brown (1948). The medium is poured in 10 ml volumes into Petri plates and inoculated so as to assure the growth of isolated colonies.

The plates are examined after incubation at 37°C for 18–24 h. At this time, type differences will be most marked and type A colonies have an even, greyish colour and sometimes a small, demarcated, central thickening. Type T colonies tend to be slightly larger, measuring up to 2 mm in diameter and possess large, dark, brownish centres, the colour fading peripherally (Smith, 1961). Haemolysis was described as similar for the two types, except that T strains were reported as being much less active on some lots of sheep blood agar.

(b) *Fermentation*. Smith used the Bromthymol blue medium of Bosworth and Lovell (1944). Subsequent workers have substituted Bromcresol purple broth (Biberstein and Gills, 1962) or Phenol red broth (Wessman and Hilker, 1968). As will be discussed later, it is difficult to make a confident pronouncement of the preferability of media as the same medium has given conflicting results in the hands of different investigators. The formulae of the two most widely used media, Bromthymol blue and Bromcresol purple broth, are as follows:

Bromthymol blue broth (Smith)
1% peptone water containing
10% brain heart infusion broth
7·5% Bromthymol blue (0·4% indicator solution, BDH)
1% fermentable substrate

Bromcresol purple broth
Bactopeptone (Difco) 10 g
Bacto beef extract (Difco) 4 g
Sodium chloride 5 g
Water 1,000 ml
Bromcresol purple (1·6% in 95% ethanol) 1 ml

An observation period of two weeks is generally followed, with daily readings on the first two or three days and periodic observation at two day intervals or longer, thereafter.

The most useful substrates by most accounts are arabinose, trehalose, lactose, and salicin. Arabinose is fermented only by type A strains, trehalose only by type T. Lactose is not fermented by type T. cultures, while salicin is usually attacked by type T, infrequently by type A. Some other substrates that have proved useful in soem studies were mannose and xylose.

Mannose has been reported to be more frequently fermented by T than A strains, while the opposite has been described for xylose (Fredriksen, 1973; Shreeve et al., 1970).

The following qualifications must be added. According to Smith, in the latter part of the observation period, i.e., after 10 days incubation, A strains may produce acidity in trehalose and T strains in arabinose. More importantly, a number of workers have reported absence of arabinose fermentation in cultures that by all other criteria were type A. An analogous difficulty with T strains has not been observed.

(c) *Growth curves.* Only Smith's data (1961) are available on the difference of growth and death patterns between types A and T. He established on the basis of testing 31 different isolates that through the accelerated growth phase, the growth curves of A and T strains were essentially indistinguishable, but that subsequently the T strains maintained a significantly higher viable population. This difference reached its maximum at about 24 h when T-type cultures exhibited on occasion a more than 40-fold population density compared to type A cultures. At that time a lower pH, by 0·2 to 0·3 units, was registered in the type T cultures.

(d) *Penicillin sensitivity.* Most of the data on antimicrobial sensitivity differences between A and T types are of a qualitative nature and, with one exception, are based on disc diffusion readings (Smith, 1961). They all agree that type A strains are more highly susceptible to Penicillin than type T. In the only quantitative tests on record the difference appeared to be about two-fold (Smith). In a recent study (Mwangota, 1975), this differential susceptibility, after having been confirmed by tests on 60 strains of known type, was used as the crucial test in assigning type specificities to a number of doubtful isolates.

3. *The meaning of biotypes*

Smith (1959) in his original description of the A and T types emphasized that all of his T types were derived from cases of septicaemia in feeder lambs (3–12 months old), while all the A types were obtained from pneumonic sheep. Subsequently (Smith, 1961), he reported septicaemia in infant lambs (less than three months old) to be associated with type A. Investigations on nasopharyngeal carriage of *P. haemolytica*, involving by this time, thousands of samplings and three continents, have established that type A strains predominate in this environment by a decisive margin of no less than 10 : 1. It has further been shown that type A strains are more common than type T strains in all infections associated with *P. haemolytica*, except the septicaemia of feeder lambs, in which type T enjoys an unchallenged monopoly. It was suggested at that point (Biberstein and Thompson, 1966) that type T strains, being (1) less frequent on the whole, (2) extremely rare in the normal nasopharynx, (3) usually associated with clinical infections, and (4) alone capable of causing septicaemic pasteurellosis in older lambs, was the type with greater pathogenic potential and lesser adaptation to a commensal existence.†

4. *Problems*

As should be evident from the description of the typing methods, determination of biotypes may not always be clear cut and straight-forward. Differences in colonial morphology are subtle and are identified with greatest reliability when large colonies of the two types occur side by side. The matter is complicated moreover by colonial dissociation within strains (Biberstein *et al.*, 1958), which occurs at varying frequencies and obscures the differences further.

Biochemical reactions have been relied on most heavily and are the single most dependable set of criteria presently available. As suggested earlier, they also have their limitations. Several workers have reported difficulties in obtaining positive arabinose reactions with strains expected to give them. The difficulties appeared independent of the fermentation medium employed. The identification then hinges on other biochemical reactions, mainly trehalose and lactose, which are the most consistent, and possibly salicin and xylose, or on serological types (see below). In several recent publications arabinose fermentation is given as a variable or even negative trait for type A *P. haemolytica* (Carter, 1975; Cowan, 1974; Frederiksen, 1973). The variability of fermentation tests according to the medium employed has been stressed by Wessman and Hilker (1968).

The differential growth rates of A and T strains have never been utilized for typing purposes and, judging from Smith's data, do not appear to lend themselves readily to the standardization that would be necessary for making this trait a reproducible criterion for typing. Susceptibility to Penicillin is a possible differential reaction and has been used as such on a qualitative basis. It would be highly desirable in this regard to establish the minimal inhibitory concentrations of A and T cultures with their tolerance limits by an accepted method (Ericsson and Sherris, 1972) and report them in metric units so that results can be compared between laboratories.

---

† A recent study (Gilmour *et al.*, 1974) of tonsillar infection by *P. haemolytica* in 50 clinically normal adult sheep revealed a 3 : 1 preponderance of T over A strains in contrast to the usual biotype distribution in the nasopharynx of the same animals (see Section IV below).

B. Serological typing

1. *Basis*

Present day serological typing of *P. haemolytica* is concerned entirely with soluble, presumably surface, antigens. These are polysaccharide (Cameron, 1956) or lipopolysaccharide (Carter, 1967, 1975) in nature. For their detection, the indirect haemagglutination (IHA) procedure in one of its several modifications is usually employed (Biberstein *et al.*, 1960; Biberstein and Thompson, 1966; Biberstein *et al.*, 1970).

Direct agglutination tests employing autoclaved cells as antigens are suitable for studies of somatic antigen factors.

2. *Methods*

(*a*) *Type strains.* Representative strains of the 12 types of *P. haemolytica* are being maintained in the Department of Veterinary Microbiology, University of California, Davis, California 95616, U.S.A. and Moredun Research Institute, 408 Gilmerton Road, Edinburgh, EH17 7JH, Scotland.

(*b*) *Production of typing sera.* Mucoid colonies of the respective strains are inoculated into infusion broth. Eighteen to 24 h cultures, live or killed with 3% formalin, constitute the immunizing antigen. The schedule used is that recommended for *Klebsiella pneumoniae* (Edwards and Ewing, 1955): 0·5 ml subcutaneously, then 1·0, 2·0, 3·0, 3·0, 3·0 ml intravenously at three to four day intervals. Six days after the final 3 ml dose, the rabbits are trial-bled. If the titres are satisfactory, i.e., better than 1 : 200, the serum is harvested on the following day. If not, three additional injections of 3·0 ml are given until a satisfactory titre is obtained or the attempt abandoned.

(*c*) *The IHA test.* (i) Propagation of cultures. The strain to be typed is grown in brain heart infusion broth overnight at 37°C. We find 15 × 150 mm tubes containing 5 ml of broth most convenient as they can be used throughout the procedure without any need for transfers until the actual test is set up.

(ii) Antigen preparation. The cultures are heated at 56°C for 30 min. This step kills the bacteria and is believed to liberate additional soluble antigen from the cells into the suspending medium.

Bovine red blood cells (RBC) are washed three times in phosphate-buffered neutral formalinized normal saline solution and packed after the third washing. One drop (roughly 0·05 ml or 1% by volume) of packed cells is added to each culture to be typed. After thorough mixing, the culture-RBC mixtures are incubated in a 37°C bath for 60 min and shaken periodically.

At the end of the incubation period, the cells are washed again three times in buffered formol saline. After the last washing, 10 ml of saline are added giving a 0·50% suspension of modified RBC.

(iii) Testing procedure. The test itself varies with the systems used.

a. When serological tubes (13 × 100 mm) are used 0·1 ml of typing serum at a dilution of 1 : 10 is mixed with 1 ml of modified RBC. The tests are incubated for 2 h at 37°C, read, and left at room temperature overnight. A final reading is then made.

b. With Perspex trays, the volumes are halved so that one drop (approximately 0·05 ml) of 1 : 10 typing serum is placed in each well followed by nine drops of RBC suspension.

c. With a microtitre set, microtitre pipettes delivering drops of 0·025 ml are used. One drop of serum (1 : 50 dilution) and one drop of modified RBC suspension are placed in each well and the mixture incubated at room temperature for 3 h before being examined for haemagglutination.

(vi) Reading of tests. The tests are read as positive or negative. At the dilution of the typing serum used, a positive test is indicated by a smooth uniform layer of RBC's evenly lining the bottom of the tubes or wells. Dense red buttons at the lowest point of the tubes or wells indicate a negative test. With sera of acceptable titre (above 1 : 200), these reactions are usually quite unequivocal and only one serum reacts. For occasional exceptions, see under 4, Problems.

(d) Somatic Agglutination Tests. For the study of somatic antigens, broth cultures are autoclaved for 15 min, the cells washed twice in neutral phosphate buffered formalinized saline. The test antigen is a cell suspension in such saline adjusted to compare with McFarland tube no. 2.

The test is set up in serological tubes 13 × 100 mm. To 0·1 ml of typing serum, diluted 1 : 10, is added 1 ml of test antigen. Tubes are incubated at 50°C overnight. Clumping of the cells with clearing of the supernatant constitutes a positive reaction.

Muraschi, *et al.*, (1965), reported extracting somatic antigens by the method of Ribi (1959) and using them as precipitinogens in an agar gel diffusion test against sera of homologous and heterologous types.

3. *The meaning of serotypes*

Since their first description, it has been clear that division into serotypes carries with it implications touching upon epidemiological, pathogenic and cultural aspects of the strains in question.

Type 1 appears to be the only type involved in epidemic respiratory disease of cattle and is in fact the only serotype of numerical prominence in that species. Type 2 plays a similar though not quite so exclusive role in sheep, at least in the United States and Great Britain. Types 3, 4, and 10 are the only types reported so far as involved in septicaemic pasteurellosis of feeder lambs, i.e., animals from 3 to 12 months of age. The term "septicaemic" is used here to describe the clinical and pathological entity reported from Britain and the United States (Stamp et al., 1955; Biberstein and Kennedy, 1959) rather than simply the haematogenous dissemination of the agent, a condition frequently encountered in the terminal stages of pneumonic pasteurellosis as well.

Type 11 appears to have little pathogenic association: although frequently recovered from normal nasal passages, it has rarely been isolated from pathological material.

The remaining serotypes, viz. 5–9 and 12, have been associated largely with sheep, both normal and abnormal. A recent survey in goats revealed all twelve serotypes in that species (Mwangota, 1975).

As untypable strains occur at rather high frequencies in the nasopharynx of normal animals while isolates from pathological conditions can usually be assigned to one of the twelve serotypes, typability in itself appears to be related to the pathogenicity.

Because subdivisions based on somatic antigens commonly encompassed several serotypes, they were designated as "groups" to distinguish them from the types, which are determined by the soluble surface antigens. In the only published study addressing itself to somatic antigens, it was found that group A included most of the strains of types, 1, 5, 6, 7, 8 and 9. Group B was composed mostly of type 2 strains. The remaining groups or types contained too few strains to permit any generalizations. It does appear, however, that the types associated with pneumonia of cattle and sheep tend to fall into one of two somatic groups, and that these groups are distinct from those harbouring types involved with septicaemia of feeder lambs.

Interestingly, Muraschi et al. (1965), obtained type- rather than group-specific reaction patterns with their ether-extracted "somatic" antigens.

4. Problems

The main limitation of serological typing is that not all isolates identifiable bacteriologically as P. haemolytica can be assigned to one of the 12 serotypes. In most cases where this problem has been investigated, it is found to be due, not to their belonging to an unrecognized type, but to their lack of the soluble antigen which forms the basis of typing. The vast majority of such untypable strains originate in the nasopharynx of healthy animals. Only in rare instances are they found in diseased tissues or exudates. It is noteworthy that the two strains recovered from human disease have both proved to be untypable. So have all isolates from horses and all but one culture from each of swine and poultry. The taxonomic relationship of strains obtained from these species to those of ruminants may well be questioned.

Some difficulty may arise from the fact that certain rare strains exhibit some degree of reactivity with more than one typing serum. Usually this cross reactivity occurred at titres 1 % or less of the homologous one. Dual reactions have been reported between types 1 and 6, 3 and 10, 4 and 10, 3 and 7, 7 and 8, and 7 and 12 (Biberstein, 1965). In most cases, it should be possible to eliminate the problem by using the typing sera at higher dilutions. In extremely rare cases, absorption of the reacting sera with the strain in question may be necessary to resolve the issue.

C. Relation of biotypes to serotypes

After the description of the A and T biotypes was published, a study was instituted to determine the distribution of these biotypes among representative strains of each of the 11 serotypes known at the time. This investigation (Biberstein and Gills, 1962) involving 37 isolates revealed that all strains of types 1, 2, 5 through 9, and 11 were of type A, while all cultures of types 3, 4, and 10 were of type T. When type 12 was identified, it was found to belong to biotype A. These relations between biotypes and serotypes were fully confirmed by a later investigation by Shreeve *et al.* (1970), on another 41 cultures and have been further borne out by extensive testing incidental to survey and diagnostic work in the United States and Great Britain, where many of Smith's cultures, used in the original work on A and T types, were typed serologically. The correlation has also been in perfect agreement with Smith's epidemiological characterization of A and T biotypes: types 3, 4, and 10 have remained the only serotypes associated with septicaemic pasteurellosis of feeder lambs, while types 1, 2, 5 through 9, and 12—the "A serotypes"—were the ones most frequently involved in enzootic pneumonia of sheep and infant lamb septicaemia.

In a recent report on *P. haemolytica* in domestic ruminants from Kenya, Mwangota (1975) recorded among 373 typable strains the occurrence of both A and T types within each of the serotypes 3, 4, 6, 10 and 12. That this observation, which conflicts so directly with the British and American experience, is not due merely to the large sample examined by Mwangota, is strongly suggested by the high frequency of the unexpected biotypes. Thus one-fifth of the type 3 strains were reportedly of biotype A, as were about one-third of the type 4 and 10 strains. Similarly 10% of the type 12, and 34% of the type 6 cultures were found to belong to biotype T. That this level of occurrence of "mixed" serotypes should have escaped notice during a decade of testing of hundreds of strains in Britain and the United States appears extremely unlikely on statistical grounds alone. It seems as though a special situation exists in Kenya, which must await further elucidation.

The question of biotype with regard to serologically untypable strains is an intriguing one. A study of 99 such cultures found in Scotland revealed that none attacked trehalose and 76% attacked arabinose. While this may suggest that they are biotype A, the fact that only 8% of serotypable biotype A cultures fermented salicin while fully 50% of the untypable ones did, should suggest some reservations. Further, if untypable strains are taken to be simply non-mucoid or non-smooth variants of typable ones, there is a disproportionately high prevalence of lactose fermenters among the untypable ones. In view of the prominence among typable strains in that area of serotype 2, a consistently lactose-negative group, prevalence of lactose fermenters would never be expected to reach 90% as it did among the untypable cultures. It may be that the biotype divisions do not legitimately apply to all non-typable strains (Aarsleff *et al.*, 1970).

IV. DISTRIBUTION AND PREVALENCE OF TYPES

A. Geographical

Both biotypes and all 12 serotypes have been identified wherever *P. haemolytica* has been studied extensively, viz. Great Britain (Biberstein and Thompson, 1966), Kenya (Mwangota, 1975) and the United States (Carter, 1956; Biberstein *et al.*, 1960; Wessman and Hilker, 1968). In the Republic of South Africa (Cameron and Smit, 1970), 50 strains from pneumonic sheep were found to represent ten serotypes: all except types 3 and 11. The absence of type 11 from this sample is not surprising as it is typically found in normal nasal passages of sheep and goats: of 293 strains of this type on record only one was obtained from pneumonia.

No published data on type prevalence in Australia are known to us, but we had an opportunity to culture pneumonic lungs from a large shipment of Australian sheep kept in quarantine at the Port of San Diego, i.e., before they came in contact with any American livestock. *P. haemolytica* was regularly isolated from lungs and pleura, and all strains were typable with the sera on hand. Only serotypes associated with biotype A were encountered (Biberstein and Gills, unpublished results).

B. Zoological

1. *Cattle*

(*a*) *Biotypes.* For practical purposes only biotype A needs to be considered in cattle. Although a few isolations of type T have been recorded in cattle, they appear to be extremely rare and play no part in epidemic disease.

Type A on the other hand is associated with a high proportion of cases of respiratory disease including shipping fever (Wessman and Hilker, 1968) and is also found frequently as part of the apparently normal nasopharyngeal population (Magwood *et al.*, 1969). Mastitis and septicaemia are other conditions in which *P. haemolytica*, type A, is occasionally seen.

(*b*) *Serotypes.* Within biotype A, it is serotype 1 which is most often encountered and apparently the only one associated with epidemic respiratory disease: of 39 isolates of *P. haemolytica* from bovine respiratory disease 36 were type 1, the other three type 2 (Wessmen and Hilker, 1968). Of the remaining types, 7 and 11 have been identified in cattle, while all of the three serotypes associated with biotype T, i.e. 3, 4, and 10, have been infrequently reported in that host (McDonald, 1974).

2. Sheep

(*a*) *Biotypes.* Both biotypes occur in sheep and play an important part in diseases of that species. As has been pointed out in the discussion on biotypes, type A far outnumbers type T in all situations examined except two: septicaemia of feeder lambs and the tonsils of normal sheep. These relations will be commented on further when type distribution under various conditions of health and disease is considered.

(*b*) *Serotypes.* All 12 serotypes occur in sheep (Biberstein and Thompson, 1966). The frequency distribution of the various types appears to be subject to significant variations according to geographical and pathological–anatomical origin, which are considered under these respective categories.

3. Goats

Only in Kenya has a survey of *P. haemolytica* in goats been carried out (Mwangota, 1975). It dealt largely with normal goats and revealed a picture much like that in sheep, with all serotypes present but type 11 clearly in the lead.

4. Other species

Haemolytic, fermentative, oxidase-positive, Gram-negative coccobacilli have been isolated from swine (Biberstein *et al.*, 1960), horses (Guerrero *et al.*, 1973), and poultry (Harbourne, 1962). Their growth and fermentation patterns raise doubts whether biotyping is applicable to them. Most strains have been untypable serologically. We have seen one poultry isolate of serotype 2 and one swine isolate, type 8 (Biberstein and Thompson, 1966). The strains recovered from these species should be compared in detail with typical ruminant cultures before they are accepted as *P. haemolytica* and typing procedures applied to them.

C. Pathological–anatomical

The distribution of the bio- and serotypes among various conditions of health and disease has been touched upon a number of times in this discussion. As has been pointed out, geography and/or host species appear to influence the occurrence of different types in different situations. To summarize, in cattle biotype A, serotype 1, dominates the picture in health and all forms of disease.

In sheep, biotype A is numerically the most abundant, occurring in the normal nasopharynx in the vast majority of enzootic and other forms of pneumonia and of most of the septicaemias of newborn lambs. However, a usually low but variable percentage of type T nasal carriers is present in many flocks (Biberstein et al., 1970). Gilmour et al. reported high prevalence of T strains within the tonsils of clinically normal sheep (1974). We may therefore assume that these type T strains are efficient, selective invaders of the tonsils, where they remain as a potential source of generalized infection. This hypothesis correlates well (1) with Smith's observation that septicaemia after the first three months of life is associated exclusively with biotype T cultures and (2) with the conclusion of Biberstein and Thompson (1965) that biotype T strains were more selectively pathogenic and potential tissue invaders compared to the A biotypes, which occur most frequently as commensals on the surface of mucous membranes. The alternate possibility, i.e. selective colonization of the tonsillar epithelium by type T strains, needs to be investigated.

Allowing for geographical variations we may state that all 12 serotypes except type 11 can be expected to occur in any of the locations or conditions described for biotype A. In addition, types 3, 4, and 10 are also found in the septicaemic pasteurellosis associated with type T. Type 11 must at this time be considered essentially non-pathogenic.

V. USES AND LIMITATIONS OF TYPING

A. Epidemiological studies

Typing, both in the cultural and serological sense has served as a useful tool in the search for an understanding of diseases related to P. haemolytica. The two main patterns of pasteurellosis in sheep, the pneumonic and septicaemic, are at least partially explained by the role played by the different types, A and T, in the two conditions.

Serotyping has further permitted insights into patterns of dissemination during an outbreak by providing a tracking device with which to follow the spread of infection through a population or establish the absence of such spread. It is often an open question whether a particular outbreak is purely endogenous or due to the spread of a virulent strain (Shreeve *et al.*, 1972). Serotyping may furnish important clues for the solution of such problems, especially when uncommon serotypes are involved.

Serotyping has been helpful in detailed tracing of the changes occurring in the nasopharyngeal flora with regard to *P. haemolytica* during critical time periods. Thus, it is possible to study the effect of seasonal change (Biberstein *et al.*, 1970), of exposure to animals carrying different types (Biberstein and Thompson, 1966), of passing through early infancy (Shreeve and Thompson, 1970) and of anatomic site (Gilmour *et al.*, 1974) on the composition of the *P. haemolytica* population in the nasal and pharyngeal area. The presence of only one significant serotype in cattle has made typing a much less important procedure for specimens from this host.

B. Immunological studies

The existence of a multiplicity of serological types explains in part the uneven track record so far of *P. haemolytica* bacterins as prophylactic measures against infection. One study points to the importance of serotype in determining the specificity of protection of mice by bacterins (Biberstein and Thompson, 1965). Subsequently, it was shown that bacterins made from cultures having no demonstrable serological relationship to the eventual infecting strain could protect mice effectively against this strain— better, in fact, than homologous bacterins (Knight *et al.*, 1969). This finding suggests important immunogenic determinants apart from, or perhaps in addition to, type-specific antigens. In cattle and sheep, largely because of the unavailability of a valid challenging technic, the importance of type specificity in immunogenesis is not understood. In cattle, where only one type requires attention, it would be of no great concern. In sheep and goats, until evidence to the contrary is presented, it would seem prudent to assume some influence of type specificity on the nature of immunity produced by bacterins.

REFERENCES

Aarsleff, B., Biberstein, E. L., Shreeve, B. J. and Thompson, D. A. (1970). *J. comp. Path.* **80**, 493–498.
Biberstein, E. L. (1965). *Cornell vet.* **55**, 495–499.
Biberstein, E. L. and Kennedy, P. C. (1959). *Am. J. vet. Res.* **20**, 94–101.
Biberstein, E. L. and Gills, M. G. (1962). *J. comp. Path.* **72**, 316–320.
Biberstein, E. L., Gills, M. G. and Knight, H. D. (1960). *Cornell vet.* **50**, 283–300.
Biberstein, E. L., Meyer, M. E. and Kennedy, P. C. (1958). *J. Bact.* **76**, 445–452.
Biberstein, E. L., Shreeve, B. J. and Thompson, D. A. (1970). *J. comp. Path.* **80**, 499–507.
Biberstein, E. L. and Thompson, D. A. (1965). *J. comp. Path.* **75**, 331–337.
Biberstein, E. L. and Thompson, D. A. (1966). *J. comp. Path.* **76**, 83–94.

Bohaček, J. and Mráz, O. (1967). *Zbl. f. Bakt., Parasitk., Infektkr. u. Hyg. I* (Orig.) **202**, 468–478.

Bosworth, T. J. and Lovell, R. (1944). *J. comp. Path.* **54**, 168–171.

Brown, J. H. (1948). *J. Bact.* **55**, 871–872.

Cameron, C. M. (1966). *J. South Afr. vet. med. Ass.* **37**, 165–170.

Cameron, C. M. and Smit, G. (1970). *Onderstepoort j. vet. Res.* **37**, 217–224.

Carter, G. R. (1956). *Can. J. Microbiol.* **2**, 483–488.

Carter, G. R. (1967). *Advances in veterinary Science* **11**, 321–379.

Carter, G. R. (1975). "Essentials of Veterinary Bacteriology and Mycology". Michigan State University Press, East Lansing.

Cowan, S. T. (1974). "Identification of Medical Bacteria", 2nd edn. University Press, Cambridge.

Edwards, P. R. and Ewing, W. H. (1955). "Identification of the Enterobacteriaceae". Burgess Publishing Co., Minneapolis.

Ericsson, H. and Sherris, J. C. (1971). Antibiotic Sensitivity Testing. *Acta path. microb. scand.*, Sec. B. Suppl., 217. Munksgaard, Copenhagen.

Florent, A. and Godbille, M. (1950). *Ann. méd. Vét.* **31**, 337–361.

Frederiksen, W. (1973). *In* "Contributions to Microbiology and Immunology", Vol. II, pp. 170–176.

Gilmour, N. J. L., Thompson, D. A. and Fraser, J. (1974). *Res. vet. Sci.* **17**, 413–414.

Guerrero, R. J., Biberstein, E. L. and Jang, S. (1973). *Anales del Congreso Nacional de Medicina Veterinaria y Zootecnia 17–23 de Mayo de 1970, Lima, Peru,* pp. 96–97.

Harbourne, J. F. (1962). *Vet. Rec.* **74**, 566–567.

Knight, H. D., Biberstein, E. L. and Allison, M. (1969). *Cornell Vet.* **59**, 55–64.

Magwood, S. E., Barnum, D. A. and Thomson, R. G. (1960). *Can. J. comp. Med.* **33**, 237–243.

McDonald, M. (1974). "A Study of *Pasteurella haemolytica* Isolated from Feedlot Cattle". M.A. Thesis, University of California, Davis.

Montgomerie, R. F., Bosworth, T. J. and Glover, R. E. (1938). *J. comp. Path.*, **51**, 87–107.

Muraschi, T. F., Lindsay, M. and Bolles, D. (1965). *J. inf. Dis.* **115**, 100–104.

Mwangota, A. U. (1975). "Serological Types of *Pasteurella haemolytica* in Kenya". M.Sc. Thesis, University of Nairobi, Kenya.

Newsom, I. E. and Cross, F. (1932). *J. Am. vet. med. Ass.* **80**, 711–719.

Phillips, J. E. (1974). *In* "Bergey's Manual of Determinative Bacteriology" (Eds. Buchanan, R. E. and Gibbons, N. E.), 8th edn, pp. 373–377. Williams and Wilkins, Baltimore.

Ribi, E., Milner, K. C. and Perrine, T. D. (1959). *J. Immunol.* **82**, 75–84.

Shreeve, B. J., Biberstein, E. L. and Thompson, D. A. (1972). *J. comp. Path.* **82**, 111–115.

Shreeve, B. J., Ivanov, I. N. and Thompson, D. A. (1970). *J. med. Microbiol.* **3**, 356–358.

Shreeve, B. J. and Thompson, D. A. (1970). *J. comp. Path.* **80**, 107–112.

Smith, G. R. (1959). *Nature* **183**, 1132–1133.

Smith, G. R. (1961). *J. Path. Bact.* **81**, 431–440.

Smith, J. E. (1974). *In* "Bergey's Manual of Determinative Bacteriology" (Eds. Buchanan, R. E. and Gibbons, N. E.), 8th edn, pp. 370–373. Williams and Wilkins, Baltimore.

Stamp, J. T., Watt, J. A. A. and Thomlinson, J. R. (1955). *J. comp. Path.* **65**, 183–196.

Tweed, W. and Edington, J. W. (1930). *J. comp. Path.* **43**, 234–252.

Wessman, G. E. and Hilker, G. (1968). *Can. J. comp. Med.* **32**, 498–504.

CHAPTER X

Pasteurella multocida—Biochemical Characteristics and Serotypes

SHIGEO NAMIOKA

Faculty of Veterinary Medicine, Hokkaido University, Sapporo, 060 Japan

I. INTRODUCTION

Pasteurella multocida, the organism which is pathogenic for various animals and fowls, can be divided into more than 15 serotypes. Certain serotypes are host specific while others are not. Consequently, different serotypes show different pathogenicity when tested in various hosts. The general and biochemical properties of the various strains are very similar, and from this point of view these organisms all belong to the single species, *P. multocida*.

The organisms can be divided into two pathogenic groups: those causing a haemorrhagic septicaemia and those causing non-haemorrhagic septicaemia. *Pasteurella multocida* and *P. haemolytica* show several biochemical properties in common but they differ with respect to indole production and haemolysis and there is no antigenic relationship between the two species.

II. TAXONOMY AND NOMENCLATURE
OF *PASTEURELLA MULTOCIDA*

According to Bergey's Manual of Determinative Bacteriology, 8th Edn, 1974, the name of the organism is *Pasteurella multocida* (Trevisan, 1887; Lehmann and Neumann 1889), Rosenbusch and Marchant 1939. In Table I, the history of the nomenclature of the organisms is summarized. Burril (1883) was the first to describe the organism as *Micrococcus gallicidus* which had been isolated from the blood of the domestic fowl suffering from "chicken cholera".

TABLE I

History of nomenclature of *Pasteurella multocida*

Name of scientist	Year	Name	Literature cited
Bollinger	1879	—	Microparasiten bei eine neue Wild und Rinderseuche, München, 1879.
Pasteur	1880	—	*C.R. Acad. Sci.*, Paris **90**, 230, 952, 1030, 1880.
Burril	1883	*Micrococcus gallicidus*	*Amer. Naturalist* **17**, 320, 1883; *J. Roy. Micro. Soc.*, London **3**, 339, 1883.
Zopf	1885	*Micrococcus cholerae-gallinarum*	*Die Spaltpilze* **3**, Aufl. 57, 1885.
Kitt	1885	*Bacterium bipolare multocidium*	*Sitz. Gesell. Morph. u. physiol.*, München **1**, 24, 1885.
Trevisan	1887	*Pasteurella cholerae-gallinarum*	*Rendiconti Reale Instituto Lombardo di Scienze e Lettere* **94**, 1887.
Lehmann & Neumann	1889	*Bacterium multocidum*	*Bact. Diag.*, 2. Aufl. **2**, 196, 1889.
Sternberg	1893	*Bacterium septicaemiae haemorrhagicae*	*Man. of Bact.* **408**, 1893.
Lignières	1900	Zoological classification: *Pasteurella aviseptica* *Pasteurella boviseptica* *Pasteurella oviseptica* etc.	*Ann. Inst. Pasteur* **15**, 734–736, 1900.
Topley & Wilson	1931	*Pasteurella septica*	*Princip. Bact. Immunol.*, 1st ed. **1**, 488, 1931.
Rosenbusch & Marchant	1939	*Pasteurella multocida*	*J. Bact.* **37**, 85, 1939.
Bergey's Manual	1948–	*Pasteurella multocida*	Since 6th Edn, 1948.

It therefore seems that the name *M. gallicidus* has priority over the other names proposed for the organism. The combination *Pasteurella gallicida* was first used by Buchanan: *Pasteurella gallicida* (Burril) Buchanan 1925 (Hugh, 1972, personal communication). In addition to the opinion of Hugh, there are other claims for the proper name of the type species of the organism, and the issue should be settled soon. There are, *Pasteurella gallicida* (Burril) Buchanan, 1925: General Systematic Bacteriology (Baltimore 1925); cited by Haupt: *Ergebn. Hyg. Bakt.* **17**, 220 (1935); used by Haupt: *Med. Bakt. Diagnostic* pp. 125ff (Stuttgart, 1964); used by Obreshkov *et al.*: *Vet. Sci., Sofia*, **2**, 687 (1965).

At the subcommittee on *Yersinia, Pasteurella* and *Francisella* which was held in Malmö, Sweden 1972, the author proposed that *P. gallicida* be the proper name and synonym for *P. multocida* since this latter is only an occasionally and conventionally used name. On the other hand Frederiksen (1973) discussed the relationship between *Actinobacillus* (*A. lignieresii, A. equuli* and *A. suis*) and *Pasteurella* (*P. multocida, P. pneumotropica, P. haemolytica, P. gallinarum* and *P. ureae*) in regard to their biochemical properties. According to him, there is no obvious differentiation among these genera, the GC% of both genera falling within the range 40 to 42.

III. BIOLOGICAL AND BIOCHEMICAL CHARACTERISTICS

A. Biological properties

Pasteurella multocida is aerobic, has coccoid or short rods, $0.2-0.5 \times 0.5-1.0$ μm with capsules, Gram-negative, non-spore forming, non-motile, and shows bipolar staining.

The organisms rapidly dissociate after initial isolation when subcultured on artificial media. Since the capsular form exists in fresh cultures, the colony shows a distinctive fluorescent colour under oblique light (irridescent type). After subculturing, the capsule is lost and the colony becomes smaller, weaker, colourless and transparent (blue type). When the colony contains mucus, the fluorescent colours are weaker (mucoid type). The colony form, which is flat with notches around the margin, is known as the rough type (R type). The presence of the K antigen can be confirmed by the capsular swelling reaction when India ink and antiserum are added. The author succeeded in obtaining a purple colour by using Møller's method as is described later.

Carter and Bain (1960) tentatively stated that the blue colony type is the R type and designated it as R[S]. However, this type represents a K antigen loss variant and it is difficult to think of the somatic (O) antigen as varying into a rough antigen. Carter's description of colonial variation for *P. multocida* is based on that of *Diplococcus pneumoniae* as developed by

Griffith (1928). The author considers, however, that the so-called S–R variation of *P. multocida* would coincide more closely with the V–W variation of *Salmonella typhi* or other enteric bacteria.

Biological properties of *P. multocida* are shown in Table II.

TABLE II

**Morphological and cultural characteristics
of *Pasteurella multocida***

Cell-form	Short rods
Capsule	+
Flagella	−
Mucoid substance	+
Gram-stain	−
Bipolar stain	+
Pigment	−
Growth on:	
Blood agar	+ + +
Chocolate agar	+ + +
Nutrient agar	(+)*
SS agar	−
MacConkey agar	−
Growth at:	
10°C	−
25°C	(+)
35°C	+ +

* Weak growth.

B. Biochemical characteristics

In Tables III and IV, the biochemical characteristics are presented. Important properties for identification are the production of H_2S and indole, the non-haemolysis of sheep blood and sensitivity of Penicillin. Acid without gas is produced from glucose, galactose, fructose, mannose and sucrose when incubated at 37°C for 24 h. These sugar fermentations constitute the minimum definite requirements for the identification of the organisms. Cystine Tryptone Agar (CTA) medium (BBL) is the preferred medium for this test. Observation of indole and H_2S production are performed with Sulphide–Indole–Motility medium (SIM) medium (Difco).

The organism is inoculated into SIM medium in a test-tube, a slip of lead acetate paper is inserted with a rubber bung to fix it. After incubation at 37°C for 48 h, indole production is detected by adding 0·2 ml of Ehlrich's reagent (p-dimethylaminobenzaldehyde, 1 g; absolute ethanol,

TABLE III
Biochemical properties of *Pasteurella multocida*

Gelatin hydrolysis	−
Indole production*	+
H₂S production†	+
Nitrate reduction	+
VP reaction	−
MR reaction	−
Growth on KCN	+
ONPG§	d‡
Arginine decarboxylase	−
Lysine decarboxylase	−
Ornithine decarboxylase	+
Citrate utilization	−
Gluconate oxidation	−
Malonate utilization	−
Urease production	−
Catalase	+
Kovac's oxidase	+
Haemolysis	−
Sensitivity to Penicillin	+ + +

* SIM medium was used.
† Lead acetate paper.
‡ Different reactions by different strains.
§ O-nitrophenyl-β-D-galactosidase.

TABLE IV
Sugar fermentations* of 27 strains of *Pasteurella multocida*

Glucose	27 + †	
Xylose	26 +	1 −
Arabinose	20 +	7 −
Fructose	27 +	
Galactose	27 +	
Mannose	27 +	
Sucrose	27 +	
Maltose	14 +	13 −
Lactose	7 days‡	20 −
Trehalose	13 +	14 −
Mannitol	24 +	3 −
Sorbitol	16 +	11 −
Inositol	3 +	24 −
Dulcitol		27 −
Salicin	7 +	20 −

* Using CTA medium (BBL).
† Fermented within 24 h.
‡ Delayed fermentation.

95 ml; concentrated HCl, 20 ml) on the surface of the medium. A red colour of the reagent layer indicates a positive reaction. The production of a black colour on the bottom edge of lead acetate paper indicates H₂S formation.

To observe the sugar fermentations, cultures are inoculated into CTA medium in test-tubes fitted with rubber plugs and incubated at 37°C for 14 days. The organisms produce weak acid without gas and the colour of the medium changes from red to yellow.

According to Frederiksen (1973), the values for GC% of *P. multocida* fall

TABLE V

Reference strains of *Pasteurella multocida*

Strain no.	Serotype	Source	Country	Remarks
3397(A)	1 : A	Bovine pneumonia	U.S.A.	Several O-subgroups are pres-
Kobe 5	1 : A	Swine pneumonia	Japan	ent among the strains be-
M 4	1 : A	Sheep pneumonia	France	longing to O-group 1 (*Cornell Vet.* **51**, 522, 1961).
Kobe 6	2 : D	Swine pneumonia	Japan	
P 27	2 : D	Swine pneumonia	France	
P 8	3 : A	Swine pneumonia	France	
M 17	4 : D	Sheep pneumonia	France	
TS 8	5 : A	Fowl cholera in chicken	Formosa	
VA 3	5 : A	Fowl cholera in chicken	Viet Nam	
R 473	6 : B	Haemorrhagic septicaemia in cattle	Egypt	Several O-subgroups are pressent within this group.
PM	7 : A	Sepsis in cattle	Philippines	O-group 7 has antigenic relationship to O-group 5.
147	8 : − *†	Local wound in man	U.S.A.	O-group 8 has antigenic relationship to O-group 9.
P 1059	8 : A‡	Fowl cholera in turkeys	U.S.A.	
Liver	9 : A	Fowl cholera in turkeys	U.S.A.	
TS 9	10 : D	Swine pneumonia	Formosa	
Bunia II (2415)	6 : E	Haemorrhagic septicaemia in cattle	Zaire	
989	11 : B	Local wound in cattle	Australia	

* Blue type; † 8a, 8b; ‡ 8a.

into a relatively wide range, i.e. from 37 to 43. However, no conclusive research has been carried out on the relationship between GC% and the antigenic formula of the organisms.

As is shown in Table IV, differences in sugar fermentation are seen among the cultures studied. For the methods of determining the biochemical characteristics, except sugar fermentation, indole and H_2S production, see Cowan (1974).

IV. MEDIA COMPOSITION

A. Medium for initial isolation

For the initial isolation of *P. multocida*, blood agar is recommended. Trypticase Soy Agar (BBL) is used as a basal medium and to this 5–10% of defibrinated blood of horse or sheep is added.

B. Media for subculture and for production of antigen

Colonies supposed to be *P. multocida* are streaked on the Yeast extract–Proteose peptone–Cystine agar (YPC) or YPC agar with peptic blood (BYP) media detailed below to study colonial dissociation, to handle subcultures, to harvest packed cells for antigen production and to test for biochemical properties.

1. *YPC agar*

After several trials in order to obtain a copious growth of *P. multocida*, the author (1961a) developed a solid medium which is well suited for demonstrating colonial morphology and for accelerating growth. The composition of the medium is as follows.

Yeast extract (Difco)	5·0 g
Proteose peptone No. 3 (Difco)	15·0 g
L-Cystine	0·5 g
Glucose	2·0 g
Sucrose	2·5 g
Sodium sulphite	0·2 g
Potassium diphosphate	4·0 g
Powdered agar (Difco)	15·0 g
Distilled water	1000·0 ml

pH 7·2

It is autoclaved at 110°C (10 lb) for 15 min. After autoclaving, the agar is poured into a Petri dish or distributed into tubes for agar slant.

2. *BYP agar* (*Murata, Horiuchi and Namioka*, 1964)

(a) Preparation of a modified solution of peptic sheep blood (Fildes, 1920): To 50 ml of defibrinated sheep blood, 150 ml of saline, 6 ml of concentrated hydrochloric acid and 10 g of pepsin (Difco; 1 : 10,000 peptic powder) are added. The solution is kept in a water bath at 50°C for 20 h and occasionally shaken. After that, 12 ml or more of 20% NaOH are added to adjust the pH to 7·6. Finally, chlorofrom to make 0·25% (v/v) is added and the preparation is kept in an ice box (4°C) with a rubber plug. This solution is transparent and can be stored for more than one year.

(b) Preparation of BYP agar: The peptic sheep blood is added aseptically to autoclaved YPC agar in a proportion of 1 : 20 and kept at 50°C. This mixture is poured into a Petri dish or distributed into tubes for agar slant. More abundant growth can be obtained and the viability of sub-cultures is prolonged by using BYP agar instead of YPC agar.

3. *CTA medium for sugar fermentation*

The preferred medium for sugar fermentation of *P. multocida* is CTA medium (BBL). The composition of the medium is as follows.

Trypticase (BBL)	20·0 g
L-Cystine	0·5 g
NaCl	5·0 g
Sodium sulphite	0·5 g
Phenol red (or Bromothymol blue)	0·017 g
Powdered agar	3·5 g
Distilled water	1000·0 ml

pH 7·2

To the medium each carbohydrate is added in a concentration of 1% and dissolved thoroughly by heating. Two ml of the medium are then distributed into test-tubes of about 90 × 110 mm. The tubes are auto-claved at 110°C for 10 min.

4. *Stock cultures*

The culture is inoculated on to YPC or BYP agar slant and incubated at 37°C for 8–12 h when the cotton plug should be changed to a rubber one and the culture kept in an ice box (4°C). Subcultures are made every two or three weeks.

5. *Lyophilization*

It is inconvenient to keep cultures alive for a long time on artificial media and, in addition, colonial dissociation might easily appear with frequent subculture. As a result, cultures lose their virulence and anti-genicity. The best way to keep cultures in good condition for a long period is by lyophilization. The composition of the suspending medium for lyophilization is as follows.

Sucrose	1·0 g
Sodium glutamate	1·0 g
Distilled water	80·0 ml

After mixing, the solution is autoclaved at 115°C for 15 min and then horse serum is added aseptically in the proportion of 1 : 5. Ten mg of the organisms are suspended in 1 ml of the above medium and then freeze dried. Cells remain viable for 5–10 years at 4°C.

V. CAPSULAR STAINING

Though there are several methods for capsular staining of *P. multocida*, that of Møller (1951) gives the best results. The procedure is as follows.

(i) Rabbit serum	1·0 ml
20% solution of glucose	0·75 ml
Saline	3·25 ml

These are mixed and then kept in a refrigerator.

(ii) A loopful of the bacterial suspension and of the above solution are mixed on a glass slide and the mixture is extended gradually with a loop to cover a circle of diameter ca. 15 mm. The preparation is then dried at room temperature (without flame fixation).

(iii) After drying, the slide is held in a slightly inclined position and the fixing reagent is poured on for 15 sec. The formula of the reagent is as follows.

40% Formalin	10·0 ml
Lead acetate	4·5 g
Distilled water	140·0 ml

The surface of the slide is then blotted dry with filter paper. The slide should not be washed with water.

(iv) The slide is then stained with the following reagent for 2 to 3 min.

5% Crystal violet	10·0 ml
Distilled water	90·0 ml

(v) After staining, the slide is rapidly washed with a saturated solution of copper sulphate for 5 to 10 sec and then dried with filter paper. Again there should be no washing with water. Finally the preparation is observed microscopically. The whole capsule is stained a clear purple red with a pink background.

VI. SEROLOGY OF *PASTEURELLA MULTOCIDA*

Serological studies of *P. multocida* were first carried out in order to correlate serotypes with the host specificities of the organisms (Lignières, 1900). In 1947, Roberts studied 37 *Pasteurella* cultures and classified them into 4 types, I to IV, by cross-protection experiments on mice. He emphasized the presence of type I in cultures isolated from haemorrhagic septicaemia of cattle. After Roberts' classification was established, Carter (1952) reported that the capsular antigen of *P. multocida* could be divided into four serological groups, A, B, C and D, by means of precipitation tests. Subsequently, he (Carter, 1955) described the more sensitive haemagglutination test in which capsular substance is absorbed by the erythrocytes. From his studies it was shown that types I, II, and IV of Roberts were identical with groups B, A, C and D of Carter, respectively. Lately, Carter has excluded his group C since that reference strain had become rough. Namioka and Murata (1961b, c) studied O antigenic analysis and found 11 O groups among the organisms. With the combination of Carter's capsular groups and O groups, more than 14 serotypes have been established (Namioka and Bruner, 1963).

In Fig. 1, a scheme of the antigenic characteristics of the organisms is shown.

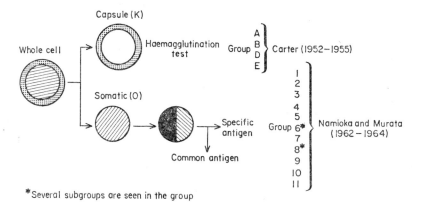

*Several subgroups are seen in the group

FIG. 1. Antigenic characteristics of *Pasteurella multocida*.

A. Capsular serotyping

Capsular serotyping may be carried out using Carter's method (1955).

1. *Reference strains*

There are 4 capsular groups, A, B, D and E against which antisera are prepared. The strain number and sources of the reference strains are as follows.

Capsular group	Strain No.	Source	Country
A	3397	Bovine pneumonia	U.S.A.
B	R473	Haemorrhagic septicaemia in cattle	Egypt
D	Kobe 6	Swine pneumonia	Japan
E	Bunia II	Haemorrhagic septicaemia in water buffalo	Zaire

Reference strains for the serotyping of *P. multocida* are available from the National Institute of Animal Health, Kodaira-city, Tokyo, 187 Japan.

2. *Preparation of antigen and antisera*

For the preparation of capsular antigen, selection of colonies is important: only the irridescent type of colony should be used. To select a suitable colony, the culture is streaked on to a YPC agar plate and in the earlier stages of cultivation a typical irridescent colony is selected.

Two loopfuls of culture are then inoculated on to either YPC or BYP agar plates (in this case, blood agar may also be used). A short incubation time is best for producing sufficient capsular antigen. Active culture is inoculated on to the media in the morning and incubated at 37°C. It is recommended that the cells be harvested in the evening (overnight incubation should be avoided). The growth on each plate is washed off in saline and then suspended in 0·3% formolized buffered saline ($Na_2HPO_4.12H_2O$, 1·9 g; KH_2PO_4, 1·1 g; NaCl, 4 g; formalin 3 ml; distilled water, 1000 ml) to produce a turbidity corresponding to tube No. 4 of McFarland's nephelometric series. This suspension may be used for the preparation of antisera and for preparing the extract for the haemagglutination test. Rabbits weighing about 2 kg receive 15 or more intravenous injections in amounts of 0·5, 1, 2, 4, 6, 6, ... ml, respectively, at five-day intervals. Antisera should have a titre of 1:320 or more in the haemagglutination test. Care is necessary for keeping antigen. If the antigens are kept in a refrigerator (4°C) for more than two weeks, some parts of the capsular antigens may dissolve in the buffered saline and become haptens. If antigen is used in this condition active antisera are not produced. Consequently, each of the antigen preparation to be inoculated should be distributed in small tubes and stored in a deep freezer ($-20\,°\mathrm{C}$) until the time of injection.

3. *Sensitization of erythrocytes with extracted antigen*

Though Carter reported (1955) that human O type erythrocytes are recommended for sensitization, sheep erythrocytes may also be used if the titre of the antisera is high (up to 1 : 320).

Overnight or short period growth is removed from agar plates with 4 ml of buffered saline. Then it is heated at $56\,°\mathrm{C}$ for 30 min to assist the removal of the capsular antigen. The heated bacterial suspension is centrifuged and the supernatant transferred to another tube. This constitutes the bacterial extract. To each 3 ml of extract is added 0·2 ml of packed erythrocytes which have been twice washed in saline. After thorough mixing, the extracts and red cells are placed in an incubator at $37\,°\mathrm{C}$ for 2 h. The red cells are then separated by centrifugation and washed once with 10 ml of buffered saline. Buffered saline is added to give a 1% suspension.

4. *The haemagglutination test*

Two-fold serial dilutions of each antiserum are made in buffered saline in approximately 10×110 mm tubes. The dilutions used should start from 1 : 10. Usually, 0·4 ml of a 1% suspension of treated erythrocytes are added to the tubes containing 0·4 ml of the diluted sera. Control tubes contain: (1) 0·4 ml of 1% suspension of treated cells and (2) 0·4 ml of 1 : 5 dilution of the serum used plus 0·4 ml of 1% suspension of red cells. The tubes are shaken vigorously, then left at room temperature for approximately 2 h, after which time a first reading is taken. The tubes are then placed in a refrigerator ($4\,°\mathrm{C}$) and a second reading is made the following morning. If the organisms possess little capsular substance a lower titre or no agglutination will be seen. A positive reaction consists of marked agglutination of the red cells while a negative test shows no significant clumping. The second reading is made after shaking the tubes lightly to dislodge the cells. The cells are then allowed to settle and a reading is made over a well-lighted mirror. All of the capsule groups are type specific. However, there is a slight antigenic relationship between groups B and E (Carter, 1963; Namioka and Murata, 1964; Penn and Nagy, 1974).

B. Serotyping of somatic (O) antigen

Granular agglutination characteristic of somatic antigens is obtained when the surface substance is destroyed by 1N HCl. Even after heating at a temperature of $121\,°\mathrm{C}$, agglutination is obtained but it is floccular and lacks the stability of O agglutination (Namioka and Murata, 1961b). If the organisms employed are not the R type, it should be possible to obtain clear specific O agglutination with 1N HC1 treatment regardless of the process of colonial variation. Absorption tests have confirmed that the O antigens of *P. multocida* are of two kinds; common and specific (Fig. 1).

When organisms with a capsule and those treated with HC1 were examined under an electron microscope, both showed a spherical shape but the latter (Fig. 3) characteristically had been reduced to about one-third the size of the former (Fig. 2). Since a considerable amount of nucleic acid and saccharide is included in the supernatant treated with HC1, surface and intracellular substances are solubilized during treatment. However, the antigen O remains as cell wall substance.

1. *Reference strains for O serotyping*

The strain number, source, and country for origin of reference strains are shown in Table V.

FIG. 2. *P. multocida* strain 3397 (1 : A), × 5000. Whole cell.

FIG. 3. *P. multocida* strain 3397 (1 : A), × 5000. Treated with 1N HCl.

2. *Preparation of antiserum*

Each culture is seeded on to a YPC or BYP agar plate and incubated at 37°C for 8 to 12 h. The growth on each plate is harvested with buffered saline and suspended in sufficient 0·3% formolized buffered saline to produce a turbidity corresponding to tube No. 4 of McFarlend's nephelometric series. This suspension is used for anti-serum production.

Rabbits weighing about 2 kg are given 15 or more intravenous injections of this suspension in amounts of 0·5, 1, 2, 4, 6, 6, . . . ml at five-day intervals. When the titre of the serum has reached 1 : 3,200 or more with 1N HCl-treated antigen, whole blood is collected and the serum separated.

3. *Preparation of antigen for agglutination test*

1N HCl-treated antigen is used. Packed cells obtained by seeding an 8–12 h-old culture (50 mg in wet weight) on to a YPC plate are suspended in 10 ml of 1N HCl saline and incubated in a plugged tube at 37°C overnight. After incubation the suspension is centrifuged and the sedimented organisms washed three times or more with buffered saline and then adjusted to pH 7·2. A sudden shift in pH from strong acid to base alters the surface electron charge of the organisms and the cells become autoagglutinable in buffered saline in a manner similar to that shown by rough (R) antigen. Therefore the pH should be adjusted very gradually while the organisms are washed with buffered saline.

4. *Preparation of O group factor sera*

O group factor sera, with which O group typing is carried out, are made by absorption with 1N HCl-treated antigen. Strains and antisera used for absorption are shown in Table VI. For absorption of agglutinin, serum diluted to 1 : 10 is mixed with packed cells harvested after 1N HCl treatment. After 2 h of incubation at 37°C the mixture is centrifuged and the resulting supernatant titrated. Sometimes better results are obtained following double absorption.

5. *Agglutination tests*

The tube agglutination test is carried out with factor sera of O groups and antigen treated with 1N HCl, adjusted to the turbidity of tube No. 1 of MacFarland's nephelometric series. Serum dilutions should start from 1 : 20 in a tube of about 90 mm × 110 and the amount of each dilution is 0·2 ml. After adding the same amount of antigen, the tubes are shaken and incubated at 37°C for 18 h and then the results read.

O antigens of these organisms contain several sub-factors and the organization of the O group resembles that of *Escherichia coli*. Therefore it is

TABLE VI

Strains and antisera used for preparation of factor sera

O-group	Antisera (ml)	Strain used for absorption	No. of YPC plates	Dilution with saline
1	3397 (0·5); Kobe 5 (0·3); M 4 (0·2)	P 8	15	1 : 10
2	P 27 (0·6); Kobe 6 (0·4)	Kobe 5	15	1 : 10
3	P 8 (1·0)	M 17	15	1 : 10
4	M 17 (0·6); M 11 (0·4)	M 4	15	1 : 10
5	TS 8 (0·5); VA 3 (0·5)	Kobe 6	10	1 : 10
6	R 479 (1·0)	Kobe 6	10	1 : 10
7	PM (1·0)	TS 8	15	1 : 10
8	147 (1·0)	Kobe 5	10	1 : 10
9	Liver	P 8	10	1 : 10
10	TS 9 (1·0)	P 27	10	1 : 10
11	989 (1·0)	R 479	10	1 : 10

suggested that the somatic antigen of *P. multocida* be called "O group" rather than the "O type". Even among strains of the same O group, there is not complete antigenic agreement. For example, it is known that in O groups 1 and 6, there are several O sub-groups and a reciprocal antigenic relationship is seen between O group 8 and 9.

In about 150 strains collected from various sources, 11 O groups have been demonstrated and by combination with capsular antigen the strains have been divided into more than 14 serotypes. These results are shown in Tables VII and VIII.

From the tables, it can be seen that six O groups are in Carter's group A, two O groups in group B, five O groups in group D and one O group in group E.

C. Pathogenicity and aetiology of *P. multocida* with special reference to haemorrhagic septicaemia and fowl cholera

When the serotype of the *Pasteurella* organisms is expressed as a combination of the O group and capsular antigen, the results may be used to examine the relationships between antigenic composition and the type of pasteurellosis caused in various animals. In the following paragraphs the problems connected with this will be discussed.

1. *Fowl*

Experimentally and in field cases, the only organisms capable of producing fowl cholera (haemorrhagic septicaemia in the fowl) are those with

TABLE VII

Relation between *Pasteurella* capsular and somatic serotypes and host animals

O-group	Capsule	Serotype	Process of disease	Animals	Strains examined
1	A	1 : A	Pneumonia	Swine	9
			Septicaemia	Mouse	2
	D	1 : D	Pneumonia	Swine	1
	—*	1 : —	Pneumonia	Swine	1
				Sheep	2
				Cattle	2
2	D	2 : D	Pneumonia	Swine	12
3	A	3 : A	Pneumonia	Swine	3
	D	3 : D	Pneumonia	Cat	1
4	D	4 : D	Pneumonia	Swine	2
			Pneumonia	Sheep	2
5	A	5 : A	Fowl cholera	Fowl	13
			Pneumonia	Swine	3
	—	5 : —	Fowl cholera	Fowl	21
			Pneumonia	Swine	1
			Local wound	Men	1
6	B	6 : B	Haem. sept.	Cattle	6
	E	6 : E	Haem. sept.	Cattle	1
	—	6 : —	Haem. sept.	Cattle	10
7	A	7 : A	Septicaemia	Cattle	5
	—	7 : —	Septicaemia	Cattle	2
8	A	8 : A	Fowl cholera	Fowl	1
9	A	9 : A	Fowl cholera	Fowl	7
10	D	10 : D	Pneumonia	Swine	1
11	B	11 : B	Local wound	Cattle	1
?	D	? : D†	Pneumonia	Cattle	3
			Sinusitis	Chicken	
			Bacteraemia	Turkey	

* No capsule present.
† O-group of the serotype is not determined yet.
Haem. sept.: Haemorrhagic septicaemia.

certain O groups among the organisms belonging to Carter's group A. These include 5: A, 8: A and 9: A. Experiments have shown that other types, i.e., 1: A, 3: A, 7: A, etc. have no pathogenicity in fowls and these types have not been found in field cases of fowl cholera.

In the United States, there is a disease that clearly differs from typical fowl cholera and from which 2: D and ?: D† have often been isolated; this

† This O group has not, as yet, been properly described or given a number.

TABLE VIII

Relation between Carter's capsule and O-group

Carter's capsule group	O-group
A	1
	3
	5*
	7
	8*
	9*
B	6†
	11
D	1
	2
	3
	4
	10
E	6†

* Pathogen of fowl cholera.
† Pathogen of haemorrhagic septicaemia.

is called "chronic fowl cholera". This has a very low mortality and patho-logical changes such as sinusitis are limited.

The important finding here is that since 5: A and 8: A are of the same capsular group and fowl cholera can be produced in the chicken with very few organisms, the 8: A vaccine will not protect against 5: A infection and conversely the 5: A vaccine will not protect against 8: A infection (Heddle-ston, 1962; Murata *et al.*, 1964). Therefore the capsule antigen is not sufficient to protect the host. The causal agents of fowl cholera are organisms of at least two serotypes and even if the chicken is immunized with one serotype, there will be no protection against fowl cholera infection caused by the other serotypes.

Murata, Horiuchi and Namioka (1964) have investigated the patho-genicity and protective ability of 1: A and 5: A of *P. multocida* in chickens and mice. They found that only 5: A was pathogenic in chickens and both types were pathogenic in mice. Naturally, chickens immunized with strains of 1 : A were not protected against a challenge from the strains of 5 : A and the converse was also true for mice.

When the irridescent and blue type of colony formation in certain strains are compared, the pathogenicity in the same host is stronger in the case of the former. This is explained in the same way that the virulence of *Salmonella typhi* containing Vi antigen possesses more pathogenicity compared with the Vi-loss variant of the same organism. It is evident that the presence of O groups cannot be overlooked when investigating the relation between the serotype and aetiology of *Pasteurella* organisms. As can be seen in Table VII, 5:A is often isolated in Taiwan from swine pneumonia. This organism causes fowl cholera in chickens but it will not produce haemorrhagic septicaemia in swine. This is very similar to the circumstance that *Salmonella enteritidis* causes typhoid in the mouse but in a human produces only enteritis.

2. *Cattle*

Both Carter's and our own results show that strains belonging to Carter's group B consist only of serotype 6: B when all of the group B strains were obtained from haemorrhagic septicaemia in cattle. However, Bain (1961) reported another type of organism which belonged to Carter's group B. He found that one *P. multocida* (Australian type) was isolated from a local wound in cattle in Australia. Although this was identified as belonging to Carter's group B, it did not cause haemorrhagic septicaemia experimentally in cattle and clearly differed in respect to pathogenicity from the group B (6: B), (Asian type) organism isolated in South East Asia which did so. When the capsular substance in both organisms was compared, it was found that there were no serological or biochemical differences. Bain and Knox (1961) and Knox and Bain (1960), however, made it clear that there was three times as much aldoheptose in the Asian type as in the Australian type. From the results, Bain and Knox concluded that the existing capsular type was inadequate to explain the relationship between epizootiology and serotype. The author also investigated Bain's Australian type (Strain 989) and confirmed that it had a new somatic antigen, O group 11, which bore no antigenic relation to that of O group 6 (Namioka and Murata, 1964).

Perreau (1962) and Carter (1963) investigated strains from haemorrhagic septicaemia of cattle in central Africa. They confirmed that these organisms had a capsule which differed from those of group B and designated these as a new group, group E. Subsequently the author found that organisms of Bain's group E belonged to O group 6 (Namioka and Murata, 1964). In a personal communication, Bain (1964) considered that 6: E and 6: B protected mice against their infection reciprocally. Therefore, even if the K antigen differs, there will be the same pathogenicity in certain hosts if the O group is the same. The findings mentioned above are summarized in Table IX.

3. *Other animals and men*

(a) *Horse and sheep:* Horse and sheep are very susceptible to the organisms

TABLE IX
Relationship between serotype and pasteurellosis

Carter's capsular group	O-group	Sero-type		Form of disease	Animals	Immunization
A	5	5 : A	Avi-	Fowl cholera	Chicken	Do not protect fowl
	8	8 : A	septica		Duck	or mouse with het-
	9	9 : A	group		Turkey	erologous strains
B	6*	6 : B	Bovi-	Haem. sept.	Cattle	Protect cattle† and
		6 : E	septica			mouse with hetero-
			group			logous strains
A	1‡	1 : A		Pneumonia,	Various	Do not protect mouse
	3	3 : A		local wound,	animals	with heterologous
	7	7 : A		secondary	and	strains
				infection	men	
B	11	11 : B				
D	1	1 : D				
	2	2 : D				
	3	3 : D				
	4	4 : D				
	10	10 : D				
		? : D				

* Subgroups present in O-group 6.

† Protection tests are not complete with some strains, i.e. various degrees of protection are seen in some O-subgroups in O-group 6.

‡ Subgroups present in O-group 1.

O-group 9 has a close antigenic relationship to O-group 8.

Haem. sept. = Haemorrhagic septicaemia.

which cause haemorrhagic septicaemia in cattle. Serotypes 6: B and 6: E, therefore, produce haemorrhagic septicaemia in horse and sheep especially in northern Africa.

(b) *Swine:* The disease which is customarily known as swine plague (Schweineseuche) has at present nothing which indicates that it is specifically a porcine disease. When *P. multocida* is isolated from swine pneumonia, it is tentatively called swine plague. In a report published in the 1930s, Ochi (1933) stated that inoculation of cattle, swine and sheep with a small amount of the pathogen caused similar haemorrhagic septicaemia experimentally in these animals. However, a swine disease which corresponds to haemorrhagic septicaemia of cattle is now very rare throughout the world.

Carter and Bain (1960) found that 10,000 times the normal dose of organisms which kill cattle was necessary to kill swine. When considering haemorrhagic septicaemia, it is doubtful whether there are host specific serotypes present in swine. Even if *Pasteurella* organisms are isolated from swine pneumonia, it will still not be possible to conclude definitely that they are the primary causal agent of shipping fever in cattle. When thinking about the aetiology of swine pneumonia, it is essential to give due consideration to *Haemophilus parasuis*, *Haemophilus parahaemolyticus*, *Mycoplasma suipneumoniae* and certain viruses.

(c) *Dog and cat:* Usually, all of the serotypes of *Pasteurella* organisms seem to be non-pathogenic in dogs and cats. The organisms are usually located in the oral cavity and respiratory canal of these animals.

(d) *Small laboratory animals:* Rabbits and mice are highly susceptible to inoculation with various serotypes, while guinea-pigs and rats are resistant. The pathogenicity of different strains for these animals varies: the irridescent type is usually strongly pathogenic while the blue type possesses low virulence. When small amounts ($10^3 - 10^4$) of the virulent strains are inoculated into mice by various routes, the animals are killed within a few days. All serotypes of the organisms are virulent to the same degree in mice.

(e) *Men:* There are no particular serotypes which cause haemorrhagic septicaemia in men. However, the organisms are often isolated in the adult or child suffering from a local wound. The wound may occur due to a cat scratching or biting and sometimes develops into bacteremia, which is why it is called "scratching fever". Any of the serotypes can produce such human infections.

In 1952 Olsen and Needham reviewed 21 cases of human pasteurellosis and added a series of 37 cases that they had examined at the Mayo Clinic. Reports compiled by 1970 (Hubbert and Rosen) list 316 cases in man. Where no animal contact can be found, a reservoir of *P. multocida* infection in man with interhuman transmission is postulated. Suppurative diseases of the respiratory tract were most common, but wound infections, meningitis, abscesses, and septicaemia were also observed. Many of the patients came from rural areas and most cases of wound infection resulted from animal bites.

VII. THE PROTECTIVE SUBSTANCE OF *PASTEURELLA MULTOCIDA*

The virulence of *P. multocida* is quickly decreased by subculturing it on artificial media, due to loss of capsular substance. Roberts (1947) reported the results of reciprocal protection tests by means of passive immunization of mice concluding that the capsular antigen is the main protective substance of *P. multocida*. Carter and Bain (1960) also stated that the vaccine alone from fresh culture insures protection. However, Bain (1954) had reported that a fresh culture of *P. multocida* 6:B which causes haemorrhagic septicaemia in cattle has a kind of masked antigen which differs from the capsule antigen of Carter, and he called it "phase I". When he made vaccine from organisms of 6:B which had lost phase I, the host was not given complete protection even when the capsule was present. However, at the present time, there is no serological proof for phase I.

In the work reported so far, it is considered that the somatic (O) antigen has considerable importance for the protective substance of these organisms when the O group differs even though the capsular group is the same. This is because there have been no results from reciprocal protection tests to indicate otherwise. However, Prince and Smith (1966a, b, c) treated 6: B organisms isolated from haemorrhagic septicaemia of cattle by various methods and found antigenic substances with about 20 different types of immunogenicity by means of Ouchterlony's gel-precipitation and by immuno-electrophoresis. They concluded that the most important antigens related to the serotype and protective agent were the β antigen in the capsule substance and the γ antigen (the O group of Namioka *et al.*) which can be considered as a somatic antigen and is the main component of the HC1-treated antigen. Thus the β (a part of the capsular substance) and the γ (somatic antigen) constitute the specific antigens which determine the serotype. The other substances are common to *P. multocida* and have almost no importance as protective agents. On the other hand, Penn and Nagy (1974) reported that the type specific antigen was shown between capsular type B and E while the endotoxins of the 2 serotype were common. However, the capsular antigen took part in protective immunity.

REFERENCES

Bain, R. V. S. (1954). *Bull. Off. Int. Epizoot.* **42**, 256–266.
Bain, R. V. S. and Knox, K. W. (1961). *Immunol.* **4**, 122–129.
Carter, G. R. (1952). *Can. J. Med. Sci.* **30**, 48–53.
Carter, G. R. (1955). *Am. J. Vet. Res.* **16**, 481–184.
Carter, G. R. (1963). *Can. Vet. J.* **4**, 61–63.
Carter, G. R. and Bain, R. V. S. (1960). *Vet. Rev. Annot.* **6**, 105–128.
Cowan, S. T. (1974). "Cowan and Steel's Manual for the Identification of Medical Bacteria". Cambridge University Press.
Griffith, F. (1928). *J. Hyg. (Camb).* **27**, 113–159.
Fildes, P. (1920). *Br. J. Exp. Pathol.* **1**, 129–130.
Frederiksen, W. (1973). *Contribut. Microbiol. Immunol.* **2**, 170–176.
Heddleston, K. L. (1962). *Avian Dis.* **6**, 315–321.
Hubbert, W. T. and Rosen, M. N. (1970). *Am. J. Publ. Health* **60**, 1103–1108.

Knox, K. W. and Bain, R. V. S. (1960). *Immunol.* **3**, 352–362.
Lignières, J. M. (1900). *Ann. Inst. Pasteur* **15**, 734–736.
Murata, M., Horiuchi, T. and Namioka, S. (1964). *Cornell Vet.* **54**, 293–307.
Møller, O. (1951). *Acta Path. Microbiol. Scand.* **28**, 127–131.
Namioka, S. and Murata, M. (1961a). *Cornell Vet.* **51**, 498–507.
Namioka, S. and Murata, M. (1961b). *Cornell Vet.* **51**, 507–521.
Namioka, S. and Murata, M. (1961c). *Cornell Vet.* **51**, 522–528.
Namioka, S. and Bruner, D. W. (1963). *Cornell Vet.* **53**, 41–53.
Namioka, S. and Murata, M. (1964). *Cornell Vet.* **54**, 520–534.
Ochi, Y. (1933). *J. Jap. Soc. Vet. Sci.* **12**, 185–197.
Olsen, A. M. and Needham, G. M. (1952). *Am. J. Med. Sci.* **224**, 77–81.
Penn, C. W. and Nagy, L. K. (1974). *Res. Vet. Sci.* **16**, 251–259.
Perreau, P. (1961). *Rev. Elev. Méd. Vét. Pays trop.* **14**, 245–247.
Prince, G. H. and Smith, J. E. (1966a). *J. Comp. Pathol.* **76**, 303–314.
Prince, G. H. and Smith, J. E. (1966b). *J. Comp. Pathol.* **76**, 314–320.
Prince, G. H. and Smith, J. E. (1966c). *J. Comp. Pathol.* **76**, 321–332.
Roberts, R. S. (1947). *J. Comp. Pathol. Therap.* **55**, 261–278.

CHAPTER XI

Serology of the Meningococcus

NEYLAN A. VEDROS

School of Public Health, University of California, Berkeley, California

I. INTRODUCTION

The natural habitat of *Neisseria meningitidis* is the nasopharynx of humans. It is estimated that approximately 5% of the population are carriers of meningococci during interepidemic periods and this rate may rise from 15 to 100% in closed populations, endemic zones, and during epidemics. Cerebrospinal meningitis (CSM) only occasionally develops, but the clinical results are dramatic, particularly in young children.

Serogroup A meningococci have always been associated with epidemic spread (Cheever, 1965), but recently a similar association has been observed with serogroup B (McCormick, *et al.*, 1974) and serogroup C

(Taunay *et al.*, 1974). However, the ratio of attack rate to carrier rate varies with Groups B and C (Devine and Hagerman, 1970) and possibly with some of the other recently recognized serogroups. All of the epidemiological studies would be greatly aided if it were possible to classify the meningococci accurately.

This Chapter will present the current status of serological classification of the meningococci and those techniques which are of practical importance in clinical and research laboratories. Biological parameters, such as virulence, will be noted where applicable.

II. TAXONOMY

Neisseria meningitidis is one of the species isolated from humans currently assigned to the genus *Neisseria*, family *Neisseriaceae* (Reyn, 1974). A set of minimum criteria for taxa of the family is being developed by the Subcommittee on Taxonomy of the *Neisseriaceae* and until this study is completed the meningococci are isolated and identified by standard techniques. They are Gram-negative, oxidase positive, and produce acid from glucose and maltose but not from other sugars (Catlin, 1974). Occasionally strains will vary in their sugar fermentation patterns (Hajek *et al.*, 1950; Catlin, 1973) but frequent passage on blood agar usually resolves this problem.

III. TECHNIQUES OF ISOLATION

The optimal procedure of isolation varies a little depending upon the specimen source.

A. Specimens from infected patients

Clinical specimens such as cerebrospinal fluid, blood, and less frequently petechial scrapings, are inoculated on Chocolate Blood Agar and incubated at 37°C under 10% CO_2 for 18–24 h. If the plates are pre-warmed at 37°C, meningococcal colonies may appear as early as 5 h after inoculation. Blood specimens should always be taken for culture, preferably inoculated at the bedside into pre-warmed infusion broth for primary isolation.

Typical meningococcus colonies are translucent and glistening. These are selected for Gram staining (Gram-negative diplococci). The oxidase reaction is carried out by adding one or two drops of a fresh solution of tetramethyl-*p*-phenylenediamine dihydrochloride (Steel, 1961) which changes an oxidase positive colony to purple then black. Since the reagent renders colonies non-viable and often spreads on moist plates, it is suggested that a small wedge of the agar containing sufficient growth be transferred to a separate Petri dish to conduct the oxidase test. The remaining colonies are picked with sterile, moist swabs and streaked on two Mueller–Hinton (MH, BBL) agar plates. One plate is used for antibiograms and the other for obtaining sufficient growth for serogrouping. The latter plate may also be used for sugar utilization tests if a sufficient number of isolated meningococcal colonies are not available on the original plate. The MH plates are incubated at 37°C in 10% CO_2 for 18–24 h.

TABLE I

Differentiation of the principal species of *Neisseria* from humans

| Species | Production of acid from | | | | |
	Glucose	Maltose	Sucrose	Lactose	Fructose
N. gonorrhoeae	+	−	−	−	−
N. meningitidis	+	+	−	−	−
N. lactamica	+	+	−	+	−
N. subflava†	+	+	−	−	−
N. sicca	+	+	+	−	+

† Differentiated from *N. meningitidis* by its yellow pigmented colonies.

Acid production from sugars is practical for most laboratories and, therefore, a useful test for differentiating *N. meningitidis* from other *Neisseria* species. The standard procedure involves removing meningococcal growth with a loop and inoculating tubes of approximately 1 ml of Cystine Trypticase Agar (CTA, BBL) containing respectively 1% final concentration of dextrose, maltose, fructose, saccharose, lactose and Phenol red as pH indicator. The tubes are incubated for 24–72 h and a positive test is indicated by the Phenol red changing from red to yellow. Mueller–Hinton Broth may be substituted for CTA (Beno *et al.*, 1968).

A rapid fermentation test (RFT) has recently been reported (Kellogg and Turner, 1973) and modified in our laboratory to give reproducible results within 30 min to 1 h. A heavy suspension of meningococci is made in Phosphate Buffered Saline (PBS) (pH 7·2) containing 0·01% Phenol red solution. Three drops of this suspension are added to 0·25 ml of PBS to which two drops of a 20% solution of the test carbohydrate has been previously added. The tubes are shaken well and incubated in a 35°C water bath. Colour change can be noted within 30 min to 1 h. The test measures pre-formed enzymes rather than actual growth with hydrolysis.

Initial tests with the RFT should be compared with the "usual" CTA test until experience is gained in interpreting the new test results.

B. Specimens from carriers

Specimens should be obtained from the posterior nasopharynx with sterile, moist swabs. Since the meningococci are intracellular (Sanborn and Vedros, 1966) the mucous membranes should be vigorously swabbed. The specimen is inoculated on to MH agar plates containing 3 μg/ml Vancomycin, 7·5 μg/ml Colistin and 12·5 units/ml Nystatin (BBL) (Thayer and Martin, 1966). To prevent digestion of the starch with amylase, only a corner of the plate is inoculated with the swab and the remainder of the plate with a sterile loop. The isolated colonies are then identified as described above for cases.

For carrier studies of large populations, two swabs can be used for the throat cultures. One swab is used to inoculate the standard TM plate while the other is used to inoculate TM containing 1 mg% Sulfadiazine. This permits the investigator to determine immediately the percentage of sulpharesistant strains in the population.

IV. SEROLOGY

A. Historical

Since the beginning of this century, serological differences among the meningococci have been noted and actively studied by many investigators. Based on the technique of agglutination and agglutinin absorption, the meningococci were divided into two large groups: meningococcus and parameningococcus (Dopter and Pauron, 1914). The high incidence of cerebrospinal fever and need for improved serum treatment during the First World War resulted in intense studies which culminated in further division of the meningococci into Types I, II, III and IV (Gordon and Murray, 1915). Not all workers agreed with this classification and the controversy continued. Branham (1942, 1953) added another type (Type IIα) which by agglutination and passive protection in mice appeared to be different from the classical Type II and the French Type C. In 1950 a Subcommittee of the Nomenclature Committee of the International Association of Microbiologists proposed a classification of the meningococcus into Groups A, B, C and D. The subcommittee followed Rule 7 Recommendation 8a of the International Code of Nomenclature which suggests that groups be designated by capital letters and types within the groups by arabic numerals (Table II). The designation of these serogroups as distinct and real was based on a number of technical developments necessary to reproduce serotyping among laboratories. Some of these developments

TABLE II

Major serogroups and specific antigens of *Neisseria meningitidis*

Usage prior to 1950 (Branham, 1953)	International Committee 1950 (Branham, 1953)	Group-specific antigen
I	A	N-acetyl-3-0-acetyl mannosamine phosphate (α 1–6) (Liu *et al.*, 1971)
II	B	N-acetyl Neuraminic acid (α 2–8) (Liu *et al.*, 1971)
II Alpha	C	N-acetyl, 0-acetyl neuraminic acid (Bhattacharjee *et al.*, 1975)
IV	D	Not known

were: recognition of the need for using fresh, smooth cultures (Rake, 1931), methods for keeping the isolates in a lyophilized state (Florsdorf and Mudd, 1935), use of "halo" formation and biological activity in the mouse-mucin test (Petrie, 1932; Miller, 1933) and improvements in the agglutination test (Noble, 1927) and capsular swelling technique (Milner and Shaffer, 1946). For a detailed discussion of studies on the serological relationships during the first 50 years of this century the reader is referred to reviews by Murray (1929) and Branham (1953).

B. Current serogroups and serotypes

1. *Serogroups*

Since the initial classification of meningococci in 1950 a number of ungroupable strains have appeared, particularly from carriers (Evans *et al.*, 1968; Hollis *et al.*, 1968). These strains did not agglutinate with highly specific antisera to Groups A, B, C, and D even after rapid passages on pre-warmed blood agar or intraperitoneally in mice. A number of investigators have examined these new strains and additional serogroups have been identified (Table III). Although these additional serogroups were originally detected by precipitation in gel, specific agglutinating sera have been prepared and are currently in use.

2. *Serotypes*

(a) *Group B*. It was first noted by Roberts (1967) that variation existed between strains of the same serogroup. The author noted that antisera to two Group B strains did not possess reciprocal opsonic or bactericidal activity. This was later confirmed by Frisch (1968). Frasch and Chapman (1972) extended these observations and by using the microbactericidal

12*

TABLE III

Additional serogroups of Neisseria meningitidis

Current terminology (Slaterus, 1961, 1963)	Other studies	Group-specific antigen
X	E (Hollis et al., 1968)	N-acetyl glucosamine phosphate (Bundle et al., 1973)
Y	Bo (Evans et al., 1968), E (Vedros, et al., 1968), F (Hollis et al., 1968)	N-acetyl neuraminic acid: glucose (Branche, 1970)
Z	G (Hollis et al., 1968)	Not known
Z'	29 E (Evans et al., 1968)	KDO (Bhattacharjee et al., 1974)
	W-135 (Evans et al., 1968)	Not known

technique were able to subdivide Group B into ten different serotypes (1–10). By using cross-absorption it was noted that many Group B strains shared a common serotype antigen (antigen 2). In a later study (Frasch and Chapman, 1972a) the authors demonstrated that the serotype antigens could be extracted with hot acid (0·0167N HCl) or saline and type specificity demonstrated by the use of the semi-quantitative capillary precipitin technique (Swift et al., 1943). The serotype antigens were found to be high molecular weight proteins (200,000 daltons) distinct from the group-specific polysaccharides (Liu et al., 1971) and closely related to the protein antigen previously reported (Jyssum, 1958). Further studies indicated that the serotype specific antigen of the group was a lipoprotein polysaccharide complex that was a constituent of the outer membrane of the cell envelope and could be extracted by either 0·2M LiCl or 0·2M CaCl₂ followed by gel filtration or centrifugation (Frasch and Gotschlich, 1974).

The use of typing was applied to Group B isolates from cases and carriers. It was found that 73% of case isolates contained the type-2 antigen compared with 27% in carriers (Frasch and Chapman, 1973).

(b) *Group C.* The macrobactericidal test and inhibition with defined poly-saccharide was employed (Gold and Wyle, 1970) to subdivide Group C into six serotypes (I–IV, 1 + IV, II + IV). Of 16 Group C strains examined nine contained a single serotype antigen and seven contained two antigens. These antigens appear to be proteins (Apicella, 1974) and different from subgroup antigens recently observed with Group C polysaccharide. In the latter study, in which haemagglutination (HA) and precipitation techniques were employed, the majority of Group C strains, designated C_1+ contain a neuraminidase-resistant component while a minority of strains, designated C_1- contain a neuraminidase-sensitive component.

C. Techniques

1. *Agglutination*

Agglutination and agglutinin absorption are still the most reliable procedures for routine serological classification of the meningococci. Occasionally, isolates from cases will not agglutinate in standard antiserum but this is so rare as to present no serious problem to the diagnostic laboratory. The problem is more acute with nasopharyngeal isolates from contacts and in epidemiological surveys. Rapid passage on blood agar or manipulation of the pH of the suspending fluid (as described below) usually resolves the problem.

Actively growing meningococcal cells are removed with a sterile swab and placed in 0·5 ml phosphate-buffered saline (PBS) (pH $7·2 \pm 0·1$) at room temperature. Because the pH of distilled water varies in different laboratories and NaCl has been found occasionally to be toxic for meningococci, PBS is recommended as the suspending fluid. A milky suspension of cells should be made and clumps allowed to settle for a minute. One drop is removed with a Pasteur pipette and placed in the well of a plastic tray or glass slide.

One drop of antiserum is added and the mixture rotated for 4 min at room temperature. The reaction is observed using indirect light (an inverted fluorescent lamp is satisfactory). High titre, specific antiserum with a heavy suspension of cells will usually produce a 4+ reaction in 1–2 min (see Fig. 1). Controls consist of a 1:0 dilution of normal horse or rabbit serum depending upon which animal was used to produce the grouping antiserum. A positive control test should be conducted occasionally to test the efficacy of the antiserum. If the isolate is ungroupable with known, specific antiserum then the cells should be suspended in PSB (pH 6·8) and the test conducted as described above.

A microagglutination technique has been developed for more objective interpretation of agglutination patterns (Vedros and Hill, 1966). The meningococci are grown in shaking culture (TSB; 37°C, air) and removed by centrifugation during mid-log phase (4–5 h). The cells are washed with saline and adjusted to a concentration of approximately 1×10^8 cells/ml in PBS. One millilitre of a 5% saline solution of 2,3,5-triphenyl tetrazolium chloride (TTC) is added to 30 ml of culture suspension and incubated at 37°C for 10–30 min. The TTC acting as a hydrogen acceptor is rapidly reduced intracellularly to the insoluble formazan, and confers a red coloration to the organisms. The cells can be stored at 4°C for several weeks and are used to test sera in microtitre plates (0·05 ml cell suspension to 0·05 ml heat inactivated sera). After 2 h incubation at 37°C and overnight in the refrigerator, agglutination patterns develop similar to haemagglutination. Controls consist of normal rabbit serum to determine spontaneous agglutination. Modifications of this technique and problems encountered with Group Z' are described by others (Devine and Hagerman, 1970).

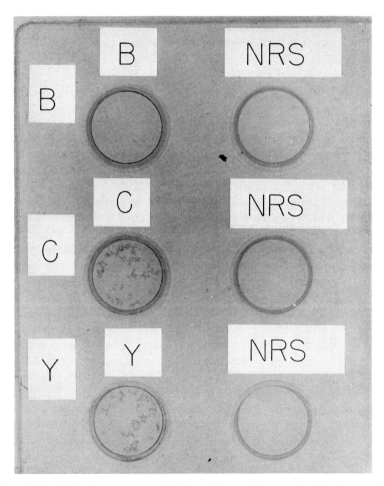

FIG. 1. Agglutination patterns in Dispo-Tray wells after 4 min shaking (room temperature). Top well on left (Group B) 1+ reaction; Bottom two wells on left (Group C, Y) 4+ reaction. Control rabbit serum on right.

2. Haemagglutination (HA)

The method of antigen sorbtion on red blood cells (RBC) has had widespread applications in serology (Stavitsky, 1954), but has been used little in meningococcal classification. The technique can measure as little as 0·0001 μg antibody nitrogen and this sensitivity, coupled with simplicity in procedures, makes haemagglutination a very attractive technique.

Jyssum (1956) coupled to RBC a nucleoprotein isolated by ethanol precipitation of an alkaline extract of several strains of meningococci. By absorption of various antisera with sensitized RBC and employing complement in a haemolytic modification of haemagglutination, the author was able to demonstrate a new subgroup of Group B. Edwards (1967) used similar extracts from Groups A, B, C, Y and Z and determined the optimum antigen concentration for sensitizing sheep RBC and the group-specificity of the reaction. As many as five different group-specific antigens could be attached to the RBC simultaneously and the reaction still retained its specificity and sensitivity.

Other studies have employed somatic antigens for detection of the antibody response in patients and carriers (Sanborn and Vedros, 1966), evaluation of the immunogenicity in rabbits af group-specific polysaccharides (Gotschlich et al., 1969) and host response in man to meningococcal cell antigens (Zollinger et al., 1974). Group-specific polysaccharides have been added to the HA reaction to cause inhibition and thereby demonstrate their group-specificity and indirectly the serogrouping of the meningococci.

Although HA is sensitive and easy to perform, it has disadvantages such as: lack of reproducibility, qualitative rather than quantitative nature, occasional non-specificity, and necessity for use of non-haemolytic reagents (Stavitsky, 1954). Many of these disadvantages can be overcome by the careful investigator, but HA is best used as an adjunct to other techniques for biophysical and chemical characterization of meningococcal antigens.

The following modification of the procedure of Edwards and Driscoll, (1967) has been found to be reliable for routine use:

(a) Meningococci are grown in TSB (shaking, air) and removed by centrifugation ($600 \times g$ during mid-log phase (4–5 h)). The cells are washed three times with cold saline and resuspended in 15 ml saline. The suspension is adjusted to pH 11·0 with 1N NaOH left at room temperature for 1 h, and readjusted to pH 6·5 with 1N HCl. Five volumes of absolute ethanol are added and the precipitate collected by centrifugation ($7000 \times g$ and resuspended in 20 ml saline. The insoluble residue is removed by centrifugation and the clear supernatant used to sensitize sheep red blood cells (SRBC).

(b) SRBC are sensitized by adding a washed 2% suspension of cells to an equal volume of antigen and incubating with occasional shaking for 1 h in a 37°C water bath. The SRBC are then sedimented by centrifugation (200 × g), washed once with saline, and resuspended to a 0·5% suspension in 0·01M phosphate-buffered saline (pH 7·2) containing normal rabbit serum at a final concentration of 1:200 (NRPBS). The rabbit serum has previously been adsorbed (0·1 ml packed washed SRBC/ml inactivated serum) to remove non-specific agglutinins.

(c) Serial two-fold dilutions of heat inactivated (56°C for 30 min) test serum are made in 0·025 ml of NRPBS diluent in Microtiter "V" plates (Cooke Engineering Co., Alexandria, Va.). One drop (0·025 ml) of sensitized SRBC is added to each well, carefully mixed and incubated at 37°C. The tests are read when the control cells (0·025 ml NRPBS plus 0·025 ml test cells) form a button after about 1 h. The antibody titre is considered to be the highest dilution of serum that agglutinates 75% or more of the SRBC. Serum controls containing serum plus non-sensitized SRBC should always be included and any serum which indicates non-specific haemagglutinins should be absorbed for 1 h at room temperature with an equal volume of a 50% suspension of SRBC.

(d) The optimum concentration of antigen for sensitizing the SRBC should be determined for each extract. Dilutions of antigen are added to SRBC and tested against dilutions of known, group-specific rabbit antiserum. The highest dilution of antigen causing agglutination of SRBC in the presence of one unit predetermined HA titre of homologous group antiserum is considered one unit of antigen. Two units of antigen are used in the final test described above.

3. *"Halo" precipitation*

The method of "halo" precipitation was first described by Petrie (1932) and essentially measures in immune serum agar plates, the production of soluble specific substances (SSS) by actively growing meningococci. It was suggested that the presence of a "halo" indicated the presence of capsular substances, smoothness, and virulence of the isolate as well as the presence of specific antibody in the immune serum. During the days of serum therapy, strains which produced a "halo" were chosen for production of antiserum and standardization of the sera in mice (Branham, 1953).

Approximately 0·1 ml of antiserum is added per 2 ml of MH agar and held at 42–45°C. The material is poured into a sterile Petri dish, allowed to gel, and spot inoculated with a fresh culture of the meningococci. After incubation overnight at 37°C (10% CO_2) the plates are examined for presence of "halos" around the colony. Six to eight isolates can be examined simultaneously on a regular 9 cm Petri plate.

Theoretically the technique is ideal for serological screening of a large number of isolates and this is currently under investigation (Robbins, personal communication). There are serious disadvantages, however, in definitive serological classification of meningococci with this method. For example, the "halos" are much more difficult to interpret than agglutination reactions; immune serum agar plates can only be stored for a few days at 4°C; sufficient quantities of high titre antiserum must be available since the amount required for one agar plate is equivalent to testing 20–22 isolates by macro-agglutination; and Group B, which has poorly defined surface polysaccharides, gives erratic results. It is hoped that many of these problems will be resolved because the procedure can be very useful for certain applications.

4. *Bactericidal assay*

The bactericidal assay procedure for meningococci is the only serological technique other than agglutination which does not require a purified antigen. For this reason and the fact that it measures antibodies which have been correlated with protection in man to meningococcal disease (Goldschneider *et al.*, 1969), the method requires careful consideration for its usefulness in serology of the meningococci.

There have been various modifications in the bactericidal assay and only general procedures will be presented below. The reader is referred to specific references for details (Tramont *et al.*, 1974; Frasch and Chapman, 1972).

(a) *Macromethod.* One-tenth millilitre of meningococcal suspension in Gey's Balanced Salt Solution (BSS) (Microbiological Associates, Bethesda) is added to 0·1 ml of serial two-fold diluted heat inactivated antisera plus 0·1 ml guinea-pig complement. Seven-tenths millilitre of Gey's BSS is added to give a final volume of 1·0 ml. After incubation in a water bath for 30 min, 0·1 ml aliquots are removed and inoculated on replicate plates of MH agar. Aliquots taken at time zero serve as the control as well as complement plus bacteria and inactivated complement (56°C, 30 min) plus bacteria and serum (1:10 dilution). Serum titres of bactericidal activity are recorded as the highest dilution which causes a 50% reduction in colony count from the control. The technique has been modified to provide quantitative evaluation of the bactericidal activity by incorporating in the growing culture ^{14}C sodium acetate (Kasper and Wyle, 1972). The author has found this technique to be quite reliable and reproducible providing the growing cells are removed at mid-log phase.

(b) *Micromethod.* The microbactericidal method has had wide application in evaluating the immune response to vaccines (Goldschneider *et al.*, 1969) and defining types within serogroups (Frasch and Chapman, 1972). The methods vary, but described below is one that has proved reliable:

(i) The test serum is pre-diluted 1 : 10 in Sørensen's phosphate buffered saline (pH 7·2) containing 0·001% Phenol red indicator. The serum is then diluted from 1:20 to 1:280 using 25 μl diluters (Cooke Engineering Company, Alexandria, Virginia) in U-well microtitration plates (Linbro Chemical Company, New Haven, Connecticut) containing 25 μl of the above buffer.

(ii) Rabbit complement, obtained by bleeding 3 Kg American Dutch rabbits by heart puncture, is added in 25 μl amounts per well. A dilution of complement in buffer (usually 1 : 3–1 : 4) is chosen at which the Neisser–Wechberg phenomenon of prozoning just fails to occur (Muschel et al., 1969).

(iii) Meningococci are harvested during the log phase of a shaking TSB culture and diluted in buffer plus 0·01% bovine serum albumin such that 10–20 bacterial cells result when 25 μl are added to each well.

(iv) The microtitre plates are incubated at 36°C for 30 min and the contents of the wells transferred with a Pasteur pipette to pre-dried 6% sheep blood agar plates. Colonies are counted after incubation at 36°C for 48 h in 10% CO_2 and compared with normal serum controls. The highest serum dilution causing a 50% or greater reduction in colony forming units is considered the bactericidal titre.

(c) *General comments.* The nature of the bactericidal reaction with the meningococci has been studied (Tramont et al., 1974) and the method has had important applications in defining subgroups. The method, however, has disadvantages in comparing results from laboratory to laboratory. For example, erratic and unreproducible results have been obtained with complement from guinea-pigs, humans, and adult rabbits. Furthermore, the micromethod employs only a few bacterial cells and therefore the media used for growth and method of evaluation of bactericidal activity must be carefully considered.

5. *Radioactive antibody binding assay (RABA)*

The isolation of highly purified, group-specific polysaccharides from meningococci (Gotschlich et al., 1969) and their use as vaccines has prompted several modifications of the quantitative radioactive binding test (Farr, 1958). One method (Gotschlich et al., 1972) involves the intrinsic labelling of Group A specific polysaccharides by growing the organisms in Frantz medium (Frantz, 1942) supplemented with 1 mCi of sodium acetate-1^{14}C and Group C polysaccharides in a similar medium supplemented with 25 mCi of tritium labelled sodium acetate. The polysaccharides are isolated by standard methods and added to the test serum. After overnight refrigeration the globulins are precipitated with 80% saturated (room temperature) ammonium sulphate. In a later report (Brandt et al., 1973), Group B and C polysaccharides were similarly labelled with sodium acetate-1^{14}C. The amount of antibodies can be expressed indirectly by the amount of antigen bound or directly by comparison to the antigen-binding capacity of dilutions of an antiserum with known precipitins. Both modifications measure antibodies without regard to immunoglobulin class but the tests could employ specific anti-immunoglobulin reagents to test for class-specific antibodies.

Another method employs the extrinsic labelling of the group-specific polysaccharide with ^{125}I (Gotschlich et al., 1972). In order to accomplish this, phenolic groups were inserted in the polysaccharide by activation with cyanogen bromide and reaction with tyramine. The antigen-binding assay was then carried out as described above. This technique has the disadvantage of having to modify the polysaccharide antigen for labelling, but distinct advantages in its sensitivity and comparison with previous data on antibody responses to pneumococcal polysaccharides.

The RABA test is technically demanding for the routine laboratory, but, it has been found to be the most accurate and sensitive for evaluating the antibody response in man following immunization with group-specific polysaccharides.

6. *Counterimmune electrophoresis (CIE)*

Counterimmune electrophoresis (CIE) is of particular importance because it is rapid, sensitive, very simple, and has been shown to be effective in the diagnosis of meningococcal infections (Greenwood et al., 1971). One procedure for CIE is detailed below (Edwards, 1970).

Microscopic or Kodak slides ($3\frac{1}{4} \times 4$ in. glass) are covered with 1% agarose in barbital buffer (0·1 ionic strength, pH 8·6). Parallel rows of wells, 3 mm in diameter are cut 1·5 mm apart. Antisera are placed in the wells on the anode side and test spinal fluid or antigen in the opposite wells. Filter paper is used as connecting wick. The electrode buffer is barbital-sodium acetate (0·5M, pH 8·6). Electrophoresis is carried out for 30 min using 20 mA/slide. The precipitin bands can be visualized using a viewer (Kaldestad Labs., Minneapolis, Minnisota) or a 7× hand lens. Positive controls should be included for every antigen and antiserum used.

7. *Miscellaneous*

In addition to the above techniques, other serological methods have been employed in studies with meningococci, e.g. complement fixation (Vedros et al., 1966), the immunodiffusion method (Outcherlony, 1962), precipitin test (Frasch and Chapman, 1972), fluorescent antibody (Metzger and Smith, 1960), bactericidal inhibition (Frasch and Chapman, 1973), bentonite flocculation (Wallace et al., 1970), and latex agglutination (Tramont and Artemstein, 1972).

V. BACTERIOPHAGES. BACTERIOCINS

In addition to the various serological procedures described above in Section IV for classifying the meningococci, the use of bacteriocinogeny and bacteriophage lysis has been considered by several investigators.

A. Bacteriophages

Bacteriophages have been isolated for the chromogenic *Neisseria* (Stone et al., 1956), and in one report for *N. meningitidis* (Cary and Hunter, 1967). Twelve Group B meningococci were grown in Eugon Broth (BBL, lot 406642) pH 7·7 at 37°C overnight. The supernatants were filtered through filters of 0·45 μm pore size and checked for lytic activity against homologous and heterologous Group B strains. Five phages were isolated and propagated to high titre (10^{-6}) using the semi-solid agar technique (Swanstrom and Adams, 1951). Preliminary electron microscopic studies of the phage indicated it consisted of a head-like structure with no tail. The phage was stable in storage at 5°C but inactivated at 51°C, and specific for *N. meningitidis*. Both Group B and C strains were susceptible to at least two of the five phages isolated. Strains from clinical disease appeared to be more susceptible to phage lysis than isolates from carriers.

The above report has not been confirmed and, indeed, many investigators have attempted without success to repeat the observations. This area of research, however, deserves serious attention.

B. Bacteriocins

Bacteriocins are antibacterial protein substances produced by a variety of bacteria which act on bacteria of the same or related species (Reeves, 1972). They often resemble bacteriophages in their mode of action (Nomura, 1963) and their synthesis is genetically determined (Jacob et al., 1960).

Bacteriocins from *N. meningitidis* were originally observed by Kingsbury (1966). Isolates passed *in vitro* only once or twice from the source were grown overnight in either TSB or MH broth on a reciprocal shaker (37°C) and high bacteriocin titres induced with Mitomycin C (1 μg/ml) or ultraviolet light. A number of Groups A, B and C strains were tested with six separately isolated bacteriocins (C_0-C_7). There was no correlation between serogroup classification by agglutination and bacteriocin susceptibility. For example, two Group B meningococci were susceptible to the same bacteriocins as two Group C and one Group A strain. The author further noted that it was not possible to correlate bacteriocin type with any other property such as virulence for the mouse, the source of the strain, or the geographical origin of the strain.

A more extensive study of the applicability of bacteriocin typing of meningococci to an epidemiological study was conducted by Counts *et al.* (1971). Using 14 indicator strains the authors subdivided Group C isolates into 11 patterns and Group B isolates into 32 patterns based upon their sensitivity to bacteriocins of *N. meningitidis*. Rather than classify strains by their ability to produce bacteriocins which inhibit sensitive indicator strains, the authors reversed the procedure by classifying isolates based on their sensitivity to meningocins produced by certain indicator strains. The technique involved the streaking of an overnight broth culture (MHB) on MH agar supplemented with Bacto-supplement B (Difco). After 48 h incubation, the growth was carefully removed and the remaining organisms killed with chloroform vapours. The test organisms were grown overnight in MHB and adjusted to an optical density of 0·03 at 550 nm. Approximately 0·01 ml was streaked with a calibrated loop in one direction across the line of the original growth. Controls consisted of a known sensitive and resistant strain. Triplicate plates were incubated at 37°C (5% CO_2) overnight and the degree of inhibition of growth assessed. Positive reactions ranged from slight but definite clearing to complete inhibition of growth. Although definitive subclassification of the meningococci was not possible by this technique, the authors were able to show that an outbreak of meningococcal disease was caused by a single bacteriocin type and that the "epidemic" type was able to colonize individuals and produce disease.

VI. GROUPING ANTISERUM

The production, use and availability of high titre, group-specific antisera for all of the distinct groups of the meningococci is obviously a critical matter. This problem was addressed in some detail by the W.H.O. Study Group on Cerebrospinal Meningitis Control.

A. Production

Meningococcal antisera have been produced in rabbits, horses, and burros. Individual methods of immunization should be obtained from the various institutes and companies listed in Section B. The following method has been used by the author since 1966 and the specificity of the sera has been confirmed by laboratories throughout the world:

The strains used for immunization were selected by their high virulence for mice, maintained in low passage from case material, and for Groups A, B, C and D, their homologous reaction with original prototypes proposed by Branham (1958). The designation and characteristics of these strains have been described previously (Vedros, 1972).

Stock cultures are lyophilized in TSB containing 6% lactose. The stocks are rehydrated with sterile 3 × distilled water and inoculated on MH agar plates. After incubation overnight at 37°C (10% CO_2) the cultures are placed in pre-warmed TSB broth (final conc. approx. 10^6 organisms/ml) and incubated at 37°C with shaking for 4 h. The cultures are then centrifuged (7000 × g 10 min, room temperature) and resuspended in Hanks Balanced Salt Solution (HBSS, pH 7·2). The suspension is adjusted to an optical density of 1·0 (520 nm) to give approx. 5×10^8 organisms/ml. Suitable aliquots are removed and stored immediately at −70°C until used. Working stocks can be stored at this temperature for up to three months with no detectable loss in viability or immunogenicity. The serogroups appear to be very stable under these conditions.

New Zealand white rabbits (2–3 kg) are pre-bled after two weeks quarantine and injected as follows:

Day 1–5—0·5 ml intravenously (i.v.)
Day 6–8—rest
Day 9–13—1·0 ml (i.v.)
Day 14–18—Rest
Day 19—trial bleeding and testing by agglutination
Day 20–21—bleed by cardiac puncture.

The above schedule, with the exception of Group B, has produced antisera that can be used satisfactorily at dilutions of 1:64–1:128. These are called "working dilutions" which will give a 4 + agglutination pattern with a positive control. Group B antisera are usually used at 1:2 or 1:4 dilution but higher, specific titres can be obtained by giving booster injections at day 23 and day 24 (1·5 ml i.v.) and bleeding on day 28.

The blood is allowed to clot at 4°C, aliquots removed aseptically, and stored either at −20°C or lyophilized. If the latter method is used, the vials should be stored in a refrigerator. Unless unavoidable, "working dilutions" of antisera should not be stored at −20°C or for periods longer than one month. A drop from 4 + to 1 + in agglutination patterns was noted particularly with Groups C and Y after one month's storage at −20°C.

If well-defined strains are maintained properly and the immunization schedule is controlled, high titred group-specific agglutinating sera can be obtained. Cross-absorption is not necessary to insure group-specificity. Occasional minor cross-reaction has been noted in Group B antisera with

Group D organisms but has not been a problem. A consistent observation has been that antisera to Group Z' react with both Groups Z and Z' whereas antisera to Group Z react only with Group Z. The common agglutinogens and their cross-reactions have been noted previously (Devine and Hagerman, 1970).

B. Availability

Grouping sera are available from Difco (Difco, Mich.), Borroughs-Wellcome Co. (Research Triangle Park, N.C.), National Communicable Disease Center (Atlanta, Ga.), Institut Pasteur (Paris, France), W.H.O. Collaborating Center for Reference and Research on Meningococci (Parc du Pharo, Marseille, France), and the *Neisseria* Repository (School of Public Health, University of California, Berkeley). The individual Institute or company should be contacted for further details.

VII. PATHOGENICITY

Meningococci are pathogenic only for humans and are not known to cause symptomatic or asymptomatic disease in any other animal species. It has generally been accepted that Group A is the "epidemic" strain while Group B is prevalent during interepidemic periods. These are vague terms, as noted earlier, since Group B and particularly Group C have been responsible in recent years for explosive outbreaks and for all practical purposes are "epidemic".

For decades, investigators have attempted to develop a suitable laboratory animal model in which to study virulence parameters of the meningococci. Mice, guinea-pigs, rabbits and primates have all been injected by various routes with varying and inconclusive results. For review see Branham (1940).

Although there has been no definitive correlation between serogroup, source of isolate (case or carrier) and nature of the infection in these artificial animal models, two of these models have been used recently to further characterize meningococcal isolates. As chemical and biological characteristics of serogroups and serotypes of meningococci are further refined, perhaps, these animal models will become more useful.

A. Mouse-mucin model

The use of mucin to enhance the infectivity of meningococci for mice was first described by Miller (1933) and later analysed in detail (Miller and Castle 1936). It is postulated that the mucin interferes with the hosts' local defence mechanism thereby permitting multiplication and invasion of the vascular system (Smith *et al.*, 1951). Recent studies by Calver *et al.*

(1976) indicate that iron is the major factor in mucin which enhances the establishment of infection in mice with meningococci. Mortality increased from 0 to 100% when mice were injected intraperitoneally with 800 μg/ml Fe^{2+} cations as ferrous sulphate 24 h before i.p. injection of 10^2 meningococci suspended in defined medium. Further, the iron chelating agent, deferoxamine mesylate was mixed with 5% hog gastric mucin for 24 h at room temperature and 1·0 ml of an equal volume of bacteria and mucin-chelate solution injected i.p. into mice. Mortality decreased from 100 to 7% with $1·7 \times 10^2$ Group A meningococci and 20 mg/ml of the iron chelator. These studies open the way for possible substitution of mucin with for example iron dextran for virulence titration of meningococci in mice. The majority of experience however has been with granular mucin and in these studies the test isolates are suspended in 5% hog gastric granular mucin, injected intraperitoneally into mice weighing 18–20 g, and death recorded over a 96 h period. An LD_{50} of less than ten meningococci can be obtained with some strains of Groups A, B and C but higher numbers ($> 10^2$) are required for Group Y. Of all the *Neisseria* only *N. meningitidis* is virulent for the mouse by this method. The test was extended for use in characterizing sera for therapy by Branham and Pittman (1940) but has not been satisfactory for evaluating protective antibody in the sera of humans following immunization with Groups A or C polysaccharide vaccines. The most useful application of the test recently has been for screening isolates for production of grouping antisera to Groups A, B, C and Y (Vedros, 1972) and for evaluating the immunogenicity of meningococcal cellular components (Cheng *et al.*, 1975).

B. Chick-embryo model

Injection of embryonated hen's eggs with Group A meningococci was first reported by Budding and Polk (1939). This extensive study demonstrated that the chick embryo was susceptible to meningococcal infection depending on its state of development. Following the inoculation of the chorio-allantois, body wall, or amniotic fluid of 12 day old embryos, invasion of the blood stream by meningococci occurred with widespread haemorrhagic lesions. Older embryos (14–15 days) responded with an inflammatory reaction which tended to localize the micro-organisms at the site of inoculation.

The chick embryo model is limited as a tool for evaluation of virulence parameters of the meningococci and as such has received little attention. Attempts were made to correlate serogroup and source of strains with virulence for the chick embryo. It was found that if 12 day old embryos were inoculated via the chorioallantoic cavity and deaths scored in 24 h, a satisfactory correlation between mortality and numbers of organisms could be obtained (Vedros, unpublished observations). For statistical significance, however, the test required a minimum of 25 embryos per dilution point and there was no difference noted between serogroups and source of the isolate. Recently it has been shown that 12 day old embryos inoculated intravenously were satisfactory for evaluating seroprotein (Veda et al., 1969). The author further noted that death was due primarily to infection and not due to released endotoxin (Veda et al., 1969).

VIII. VACCINES

The most practical and useful application of definitive serogrouping of the meningococci and establishment of a standard serological classification system is in the development and successful use of a vaccine for CSM. Since the turn of the century many vaccine trials have been conducted without success in Africa with Group A meningococci. These vaccines consisted of inactivated cultures of locally isolated strains and produced toxic side reactions. Studies by Gotschlich et al., (1969) and others resulted in the isolation of group-specific polysaccharides from Groups A and C. These polysaccharides are group-specific and have been shown effective as protective antigens in humans of certain age groups. The evidence is less clear with specific polysaccharides from the other serogroups including Group B. Attempts to isolate a protective antigen common to all the serogroups have been successful when tested in the mouse-mucin model (Cheng et al., 1975; Jennings et al., 1972). For a complete review of the preparation, characterization, and application of the Group A and C polysaccharide vaccines see the report of the W.H.O. study group on Cerebrospinal Meningitis Control, Technical Report Series 588, 1976.

Since a protective inducing antigen common to all the serogroups is not yet a reality, it is critical that accurate serological classification of the meningococci be made early in an epidemic and in limited carrier surveillance. If several serogroups are present in the population, a group-specific vaccine may result in replacement and increase by another serogroup. Since attack rates vary among the serogroups and only Groups A and C vaccines are available, effective control of an epidemic or outbreak relies heavily on accurate serological classification.

IX. SUMMARY

This Chapter attempts to bring together some of the latest techniques employed to characterize the meningococci. Only those procedures which have been used successfully in research and hospital laboratories are considered in detail. Agglutination is still the most reliable and routinely used technique. However, the antigenic variability of the meningococci and gradual appearance of new serogroups during the last decade makes it incumbent upon microbiologists to use a combination of techniques to meet their objectives. For example, a hospital laboratory may require CIE to detect the presence of meningococcal antigens in a spinal fluid sample which was culture negative. In a less-equipped laboratory in the field, agglutination with specific, high-titre antisera may be sufficient.

Effective control of meningococcal meningitis will require more knowledge of the biology of these bacteria. We know very little about the dynamics of airborne transmission of the meningococci in closed and semi-closed environments nor do we know very much about the nature of virulence of these micro-organisms. The Group B meningococci apparently share antigens with other enteric Gram-negative bacteria such as *Escherichia coli*. What role this plays in the difficulty in defining the protective antigen of the Group B and man's natural immunity to CSM remains to be defined. There are many complex problems concerning the meningococci which require resolution but accurate serological classification will greatly aid in the eventual control and understanding of CSM.

REFERENCES

Apicella, M. A. (1974). *J. infect. Dis.*, **129**, 147–153.
Beno, D. W., Devine, L. F., and Larson, G. L. (1968). *J. Bact.*, **96**, 563.
Bhattacharjee, A. K., Jennings, H. J., and Kenney, C. P. (1974). *Biochem. biophys. Res. Commun.*, **61**, 489–493.
Bhattacharjee, A. K., Jennings, H. J., Kenney, C. P., Martin, A., and Smith, I. C. P. (1975). *J. biol. Chem.*, **250**, 1926–1932.
Branche, W. C., Jr (1970). Doctoral Dissertation, Catholic University, Washington, D.C.
Brandt, B. L., Wyle, F. A., and Artenstein, M. S. (1972). *J. Immun.*, **108**, 913–920.
Brandt, B. L., Artenstein, M. S., and Smith, C. D. (1973). *Infect. Immun.*, **8**, 590–596.
Branham, S. E. (1940). *Bact. Rev.*, **40**, 59–96.
Branham, S. E., and Pittman, M. (1940). *Publ. Hlth Rep.*, **55**, 2340–2346.
Branham, S. E., and Carlin, S. A. (1942). *Proc. Soc. Exp. Biol. Med.*, **49**, 141–144.
Branham, S. E. (1945). *Am. J. Publ. Hlth*, **35**, 233–238.
Branham, S. E. (1953). *Bact. Rev.*, **17**, 175–188.
Branham, S. E., and Wormald, M. F. (1953). *J. Bact.*, **66**, 487–491.
Branham, S. E. (1958). *Int. Bull. bact. Nomencl. Taxon.*, **8**, 1–15.
Budding, G. J., and Polk, A. D. (1939). *J. Exp. Med.*, **70**, 499–512.
Bundle, D. R., Jennings, H. J., and Kenny, C. P. (1973). *Carbohyd. Res.*, **26**, 268–270.
Calver, G. A. Kenny, C. P., and Lavergne, G. (1976). *Can. J. Microbiol.*, **22**, 832–838.
Cary, S. G., and Hunter, D. H. (1967). *J. Virol.*, **1**, 538–542.
Catlin, B. W. (1973). *J. infect. Dis.*, **128**, 300–320.
Catlin, B. W. (1974). *In* "Manual of Clinical Microbiology", 2nd edn, pp. 116–123. American Society for Microbiology.

Cheever, F. S. (1965). The meningococci. *In* "Bacterial and Mycotic Infections of Man" (Ed. R. J. Dubos and J. G. Hirsch), 4th edn, pp. 448–449. J. B. Lippin-cott Co., Philadelphia.

Cheng, W. C., Webb, E., Vedros, N., and Ng, J. (1975). *J. Immun.*, **114**, 1497–1505.

Counts, G. W., Seeley, L., and Beaty, H. N. (1971). *J. infect. Dis.*, **124**, 26–32.

Devine, L. F., and Hagerman, C. R. (1970). *Infect. Immun*, **1**, 226–231.

Dopter, C. H., and Pauron, (1914). *C. r. Seanc Soc. Biol.*, **77**, 231–233.

Edwards, E. A., and Driscoll, W. S. (1967). *Proc. Soc. exp. Biol. Med.*, **126**, 876–879.

Edwards, E. A. (1970). *J. Immun.*, **106**, 314–317.

Edwards, E. A., Muehl, P. M., and Peckinpaugh, R. O. (1972). *J. Lab. clin. Med.*, **80**, 449–454.

Evans, J. R., Artenstein, M. S., and Hunter, D. H. (1968). *Am. J. Epidemiol.*, **87**, 643–646.

Farr, R. S. (1958). *J. infect. Dis.*, **103**, 239–245.

Florsdorf, E. W., and Mudd, S. (1935). *J. Immun.*, **29**, 389–425.

Frantz, I. D. (1942). *J. Bact.*, **43**, 757–761.

Frasch, C. E., and Chapman, S. S. (1972). *Infect. Immun.*, **5**, 98–102.

Frasch, C. E., and Chapman, S. S. (1972a). *Infect. Immun.*, **6**, 127–133.

Frasch, C. E., and Chapman, S. S. (1973). *J. infect. Dis.*, **127**, 149–154.

Frasch, C. E., and Gotschlich, E. C. (1974). *J. exp. Med.*, **140**, 87–104.

Frisch, A. W. (1968). *Am. J. clin. Pathol.*, **50**, 221–228.

Gold, R., and Wyle, F. A. (1970). *Infect. Immun.*, **1**, 479–484.

Goldschneider, I., Gotschlich, E. C., and Artenstein, M. S. (1969). *J. exp. Med.* **129**, 1307–1326.

Gordon, M. H., and Murray, E. G. D. (1915). *J. R. Army Med. Corps.* **25**, 411–423.

Gotschlich, E. C., Liu, T. Y., and Artenstein, M. S. (1969). *J. exp. Med.*, **129**, 1349–1365.

Gotschlich, E. C., Rey, M., Triau, R., and Sparks, K. J. (1972). *J. clin. Invest.*, **51**, 89–96.

Greenwood, B. M., Whittle, H. C., and Dominic-Rajkovic, O. (1971). *Lancet*, **2**, 519–521.

Hajek, J. P., Pelczar, M. J., Jr, and Faber, J. E., Jr (1950). *Am. J. clin. Pathol.*, **20**, 630–636.

Hollis, D. G., Wiggins, G. L., and Schubert, J. H. (1968). *J. Bact.*, **95**, 1–4.

Jacob, F., Schaeffer, P., and Wollman, E. L. (1960). *Symp. Soc. gen. Microbiol.*, **10**, 67–91.

Jennings, H. J., Martin, A., Kenny, C. P., and Diena, B. B. (1972). *Infect. Immun.*, **5**, 547–551.

Jyssum, K. (1956). *J. Immun.*, **76** (6), 433–440.

Jyssum, K. (1958). *Acta path. microbiol. scand.*, **42**, 216–227.

Kasper, D. L., and Wyle, F. A. (1972). *Proc. Soc. exp. Biol. Med.*, **139** (4), 1175–1180.

Kellogg, D. S., and Turner, E. M. (1973). *Appl. Microb.*, **25**, 550–552.

Kingsbury, D. T. (1966). *J. Bact.*, **9**, 1696–1699.

Liu, T. Y., Gotschlich, E. C., Dunn, F. T., and Jonnson, E. K. (1971). *J. biol. Chem.*, **246**, 4703–4712.

Liu, T. Y., Gotschlich, E. C., Jonnson, E. K., and Wysocki, J. R. (1971a). *J. biol. Chem.*, **246**, 2849–2858.

MacPherson, J. N., and Gillies, R. R. (1969). *J. med. Microbiol.* **2**, 161–165.

314 N. A. VEDROS

McCormick, J. B., Weaver, R. E., Thornsberry, C., and Feldman, R. A. (1974). *J. infect. Dis.*, **130**, 212–214.
Metzger, J. F., and Smith, C. W. (1960). *Armed Forces Med. J.*, **11**, 1185–1189.
Miller, C. P. (1933). *Science*, **78**, 340–341.
Miller, C. P., and Castle, R. (1936). *J. infect. Dis.*, **58**, 263–279.
Milner, K. C., and Shaffer, M. F. (1946). *Proc. Soc. exp. Biol. Med.*, **62**, 48–49.
Murray, E. G. D. (1929). *Med. Res. Council, Br. Special Rep.* Series No. 124.
Muschel, L. H., Gustafson, H. L., and Larsen, L. J. (1969). *Immunology*, **17**, 525–533.
Noble, A. (1927). *J. Bact.*, **14**, 287–300.
Nomura, M. (1963). *Cold Springs Harb. Symp. quant. Biol.*, **28**, 315–324.
Outcherlony, O. (1962). *Prog. Allergy*, **6**, 30–154.
Petrie, G. F. (1932). *Br. J. exp. Path.*, **13**, 380–394.
Rake, G. (1931). *Proc. Soc. exp. Biol. Med.*, **29**, 287–289.
Reeves, P. (1972). "The Bacteriocins". Springer-Verlag Publishing Co., New York.
Reyn, A. (1974). *In* "Bergey's Manual of Determinative Bacteriology", 8th edn.
Roberts, R. B. (1967). *J. exp. Med.*, **126**, 795–819.
Roberts, R. B. (1970). *J. exp. Med.*, **131**, 499–519.
Sanborn, W., and Vedros, N. A. (1966). *Hlth Lab. Sci.*, **3**, 111–117.
Slaterus, K. W. (1961). *Antonie van Leeuwenhoek J. Microbiol. Serol.*, **27**, 305–315.
Slaterus, K. W., Ruys, A. C., and Sieberg, I. G. (1963). *Antonie van Leeuwenhoek J. Microbiol. Serol.*, **29**, 265–271.
Smith, H., Harris-Smith, P. W., and Stanley, J. L. (1951). *Biochem. J.*, **50**, 211–215.
Stavitsky, A. B. (1954). *J. Immun.*, **72**, 360–375.
Stavitsky, A. B. (1964). *In* "Immunological Methods", pp. 363–396. F. A. Davis Co., Philadelphia.
Steel, K. J. (1961). *J. gen. Microbiol.*, **25**, 297–306.
Stone, R. L., Culbertson, C. G., and Powell, H. M. (1956). *J. Bact.*, **71**, 516–520.
Swanstrom, N., and Adams, M. H. (1951). *Proc. Soc. exp. Biol. Med.*, **78**, 372–378.
Swift, H. F., Wilson, A. T., and Lancefield, R. C. (1943). *J. exp. Med.*, **78**, 127–133.
Taunay, A. De E. (1974). *Pediat. Res.*, **8**, 429/155.
Thayer, J. D., and Martin, J. E. Jr. (1966). *Publ. Hlth Rep.*, **81**, 559–562.
Tramont, E. C., and Artenstein, M. S. (1972). *Infect. Immun.*, **5**, 346–351.
Tramont, E. C., Sadoff, J. C., and Artenstein, M. S. (1974). *J. infect. Dis.*, **130**, 240–247.
Veda, K., Diena, B. B., and Greenberg, L. (1969). *Bull. Wld Hlth Org.*, **40**, 235–240.
Veda, K., Diena, B. B., and Greenberg, L. (1969). *Bull. Wld Hlth Org.*, **40**, 241–244.
Vedros, N. A., and Hill, P. R. (1966). *J. Bact.*, **91**, 900–901.
Vedros, N. A., Hunter, D. H., and Rust, J. H. Jr. (1966). *Milit. Med.*, **131**, 1413–1417.
Vedros, N. A., Ng, J., and Culver, G. (1968). *J. Bact.*, **95**, 1300–1304.
Vedros, N. A. (1972). *Prog. Immunbiol. Stand.*, **5**, 472–477.
Wallace, R., Diena, B. B., Yugi, H., and Greenberg, L. (1970). *Can. J. Microbiol.*, **16**, 655–659.
Zollinger, W. D., Pennington, C. L., and Artenstein, M. S. (1974). *Infect. Immun.*, **10**, 975–984.

CHAPTER XII

Serotyping and Antigenic Studies of *Neisseria gonorrhoeae*†

DAN DANIELSSON AND JOHAN MAELAND

The Department of Clinical Bacteriology and Immunology, Central County Hospital, S-701 85 Örebro, Sweden, and The Department of Medical Microbiology, University of Trondheim, 7000 Trondheim, Norway

I. INTRODUCTION

As early as the first two decades of this century microbiologists had found serotyping of pathogenic bacteria to be of great importance from diagnostic, epidemiologic and therapeutic points of views. At the end of the third and the beginning of the fourth decades we thus had well-established and accepted serotyping schemes for various genera of bacteria such as *Salmonella*, *Shigella*, *Escherichia coli*, meningococci, streptococci, and pneumococci.

At the beginning of this century, serious attempts were also made to find serotypes among *Neisseria gonorrhoeae*, responsible for one of the venereal bacterial infections. These early studies were not only of academic interest, their main objectives were to find means for epidemiological

† This work has been supported in part by grants from the Swedish Medical Research Council, project No. 4778.

studies of gonorrhoea, to find representative gonococcal serotypes to be used in diagnostic serologic tests, and to determine the most representative strains with marked antibody stimulating qualities for use in stock vaccines and also in the application of selected strains for the production of curative sera. Most of these objectives are still valid, but so far all the attempts made during the last 70 years to define an accepted pattern of serotypes among gonococci have failed. However, the various immunological techniques that have been used for this purpose—agglutination, co-agglutination, complement fixation, agar gel precipitation, passive haemagglutination, radioimmune assay—have made it clear that besides common antigens, distinct type antigens also exist. Unfortunately, different investigations have never been co-ordinated and only exceptionally have research workers used gonococcal strains from other laboratories for comparative studies.

After 70 years of failure to establish an accepted serotyping pattern for gonococci, some basic discoveries of the cell biology of the gonococcus and new immunological techniques have now given new hopes of finding ways for antigenic characterization of the gonococcus and subsequently means for serotyping.

In this Chapter we will briefly report the results of some of the more important previous investigations which all give evidence of antigenic similarities and differences among various gonococcal strains. Particular attention will be paid to the immunological techniques that have been used to study the antigenic properties of whole gonococcal cells or fractions of cells.

II. SEROTYPING AND ANTIGENIC STUDIES OF WHOLE CELLS

A. Agglutination studies

At the beginning of this century Bruckner and Christeanu (1906), Torrey (1906), and Vannod (1906) reported that gonococci (GC) were agglutinated by anti-GC antiserum from immunized animals (horses and rabbits). The anti-GC antiserum used by Bruckner and Christeanu also agglutinated meningococci (MC). One year later, Torrey (1907) and Vannod (1907) reported continued studies and claimed that it was possible to differentiate GC from MC and other so-called apathogenic *Neisseria* with the agglutination tests. Torrey (1907) in his investigation studied ten strains among which three types were recognized. However, only six of the ten strains could be referred to the three groups. He then concluded that the gonococcus formed a heterogeneous group from an antigenic point of view.

The antigenic relationship between the strains studied was complex and various intermediate forms and variations existed.

During the following years many efforts were made by several investigators to separate GC into serotypes but without obvious results. Thus, Warren reported in 1921 a complete failure to differentiate gonococci with agglutination tests. Hermanies, on the other hand, in the same year stated that he had managed using absorbed sera to differentiate various gonococcal strains with agglutination tests. His technique of absorbing sera, however, was far from standardized.

In 1922, Torrey and Buckell gave a thorough report of an extensive study to separate GC strains into serotypes by tube agglutination. They gave a detailed description of the technique. Gonococci were cultured on ascitic agar medium and grown at 36–37°C for 24–48 h. (Whether increased CO_2-tension was used was not stated.)

The gonococcal strains used represented a wide clinical range of GC-infections—acute and chronic urethritis, arthritis, septicaemia, eye infection and vulvovaginitis infections in children. The strains were isolated from patients from different parts of U.S.A. and from patients who came to New York from widely separated countries.

Antigonococcal antisera were produced in rabbits by immunizing by the intravenous route with living or heat exposed (45–50°C for 15 min) gonococci once or thrice weekly, the latter procedure as a rule giving higher titres. Gonococci treated with tricresol (0·25%), acetone, or chloroform were inferior in this respect. The dosage and amount of organisms injected was not standardized, but were regulated entirely by the condition of the animal. Sera were preserved with 0·1% phenol. Freshly prepared suspensions of gonococci, approximately 3×10^9 cells/ml were used in the tube agglutination tests. Ordinary serological tubes (8 mm inside diameter) were used and to 0·5 ml of serum dilution was added 0·5 ml of the gonococcal suspension. The agglutination reactions were read after incubation of the tubes in a water bath at 50–55°C for 2 h and then overnight in the refrigerator.

Agglutination tests with 47 strains against eight monovalent sera gave various types of agglutination patterns without indications of an antigenic pattern. Some strains agglutinated poorly with their homologous antisera, but some of the sera gave much higher agglutination titres with certain heterologous strains. Poorly agglutinating GC strains were frequently encountered. Among 63 recently isolated strains 26 were inagglutinable with the test sera used. They stated that this might be due to the absence of group agglutinins, but this is contradicted since some of the strains became agglutinable after subculture. On the other hand, they never encountered strains which became inagglutinable after subculture. Similar observations were noted by Wilson (1954) and the probable background to this phenomenon will be discussed below.

Since Torrey and Buckell could not *separate* any gonococcal strains *into particular serotypes* by agglutination, they carried out extensive studies with a group of antigonococcal antisera each absorbed with 77 GC strains. The absorbing technique used was as follows: 0·2 ml of rather loosely packed live organisms were mixed with 4·8 ml of properly diluted serum. They did not state exactly how much the serum was diluted, but say that it was approximately the lowest dilution at which the homologous strain, in the dosage used, completely absorbed its agglutinins. Absorption was carried out for 2 h at 45–50°C. The absorbed serum was then tested against the absorbing strain and against the homologous strain of the anti-serum. Results from a series of 77 strains against one antiserum showed negative agglutination for each of the absorbing strains at a dilution of 1 : 500 of the antiserum. The titres with the homologous strains were un-affected, lowered, or absent at 1 : 500. These absorption–agglutination experiments were extended to 50 GC strains with 9 anti-GC antisera. No clearcut serotyping scheme was obtained. The strains were, however, placed in three groups with regard to their absorbing capacity. The major-ity, 39 of the strains, absorbed 75–100% of the agglutinins and was hence called the *main* or *regular* group. They did not claim that these strains were antigenically identical, but closely related and representative of a consider-able part of the gonococcus group. Bordering on this *regular* group, they encountered 16 strains with an absorbing capacity of approximately 50% of the agglutinins. These strains showed a close relationship to the regular group and were designated *"intermediate"*. Finally they encountered 19 strains which were more definitely separated from the regular group. These strains were designated *"irregular"*. It should be noted that Torrey and Buckell strongly emphasized that the three groups were not well separated from each other. Many of the strains could be placed into any of the three groups depending upon the serum used.

Torrey and Buckell also reported observations on antigenic lability dur-ing cultivation. Thus, some freshly isolated strains were primarily similar to members of the "irregular" group, but after some subcultivations developed affinities similar to members of the "regular" group. Strains primarily similar to members of the "intermediate" group behaved simi-larly. Further, they encountered inagglutinable strains. Ten out of 11 strains from patients with complications (ophthalmia, chronic prostatitis, epididymitis, arthritis, septicaemia) were of the regular or intermediate type.

All these very extensive investigations were thus rather disappointing. It was concluded that the gonococcus was very complex from an antigenic point of view and that there was no justification for the formulation of distinct serogroups for the gonococcus as had been done for meningococci.

Wilson (1954) reported more than four years of attempts at serotyping gonococci with the use of agglutination tests. His findings and observations are also of interest and merit a detailed description.

Wilson prepared anti-GC antisera by intravenously inoculating rabbits with GC isolated on Difco chocolate agar plates supplemented with yeast and glutamine. Four inoculations (0·5, 0·5, 1·0 and 1·0 ml) were given at intervals of four days with suspensions containing approximately 10^9 organisms/ml, the first two injections with organisms heated at 50°C for 30 min, the last with living organisms. The rabbits were bled four days after the last inoculation. Agglutination tests were performed at 50°C. For absorption of agglutinins, GC were suspended in a minimal volume of saline. This was mixed with an equal volume of serum and kept at 50°C for 4 h before centrifuging. Wilson did not state the wet or dry weight of the organisms used for absorption. We have found it crucial to use at least 100 mg (dry weight) organisms/0·1 ml serum.

Wilson gave a thorough description of the ability of GC strains to undergo "smooth↔rough" variation which differed from culture to culture. His description also illustrates all the difficulties investigators have met with when they have used agglutination tests for serotyping GC. Suspensions from "smooth" strains were usually stable and formed uniform suspensions, but some strains caused a lot of trouble which to some extent was independent of colony appearance. Thus, some strains with smooth colonies agglutinated in salt solution and in normal serum. Such strains were referred to as "*auto-agglutinable*". Certain other strains were stable in saline, but agglutinated to abnormally high titres with homologous antisera, absorbed agglutinins poorly, were less specific in their reactions with antisera, and were agglutinated by normal rabbit sera which did not agglutinate more stable suspensions of the same strain. Such strains were called "*hyperagglutinable*". Still other strains were agglutinable to higher titres than usual by specific antisera without being hyperagglutinable. These were called "*hypersensitive*". The autoagglutinable, hyperagglutinable, and hypersensitive states appeared to be progressive or reversible variations which a strain could undergo upon subculture. These states also gave different agglutination titres. Thus, the titre of an antiserum might be lower for its normally agglutinable homologous strain than for a hypersensitive or hyperagglutinable heterologous strain. These circumstances influenced the tests so that false results were obtained. However, Wilson circumvented these problems by rejecting hyperagglutinable or hypersensitive suspensions as untypable.

Wilson also encountered GC strains that changed from inagglutinable, to agglutinable after several subcultures. Similar reversible inagglutinability also developed in some cultures stored on agar slopes, and in strains passed through mice. Partially inagglutinable strains which were agglutinated by certain antisera, but not by others were also encountered. However, the problems with inagglutinable and partially inagglutinable strains were overcome by heating the suspension at 100°C for 30 min. In view of these findings Wilson carried out all the agglutination tests with heated suspensions. Suspensions for rabbit inoculation and agglutinin-absorption were not, however, heated since both inagglutinable and agglutinable subcultures of a strain stimulated the production of the same agglutinins in rabbits and absorbed the same agglutinins from specific antisera.

After these methodological studies, Wilson found it possible to serotype strains of *N. gonorrhoeae* with the use of agglutinin-absorption tests. At first, consistent results were not obtained regularly due to variation in the "smooth" gonococcal antigen. Cross absorptions and cross agglutination tests were carried out with strains relatively stable in their agglutinability. In this way he arrived at antigenic formulae for a group of strains based on eight antigens, four of which were group antigens, the other four type-specific antigens. The group antigens were labelled A, B_1, B_2, and C, the type specific antigens D, E, F, and G. A particular strain always contained from two to four group antigens and as a rule one type-specific antigen as well.

A collection of 148 strains was examined by agglutination tests with an antiserum containing antibodies for antigens A, B_1, and B_2, and with single-factor antisera for antigens C, D, E, F, and G. The results were as follows: 33 strains contained group antigens A, B_1, and B_2 only, 33 group antigens A, B_1, B_2, and C. Fifty-nine strains contained group antigens and one of the antigens D, E, F or G. Twenty-three strains (15%) were auto- or hyperagglutinable and were accordingly not classified.

Wilson found, however, that *N. gonorrhoeae* was capable of losing or gaining an antigen on subculture, irrespective of any temporary state of inagglutinability, hyperagglutinability or hypersensitivity of the strain. Thus, the antigenic formula of a particular strain during subculture could be: A, B_1, B_2; A, B_1, B_2, C; A, B_1, B_2, C, E. For another strain A, B_1, B_2; B_1, B_2, G; A, B_1, B_2, G; A, B_1, B_2, C; A, B_1, B_2, C, G. The liability of strains to vary in this way differed considerably. Some strains lost or gained antigens after only a few daily subcultures, others remained stable although subcultured daily for many months.

General comments on agglutination studies of the gonococcus

In retrospect the variability of agglutinogenic properties of various GC strains observed and reported by Torrey and Buckell (1922) and by Wilson

(1954) can be explained with our present knowledge of gonococcal colonial morphology types originally described by Kellogg *et al.* (1963). Four types with characteristic appearance (designated T1, T2, T3, and T4) are recognized on a special translucent agar under a stereomicroscope at a magnification of 10–20 ×. The colony types T1 and T2 are found in fresh isolates and are associated with virulence while types T3 and T4 are avirulent. Jephcott and Reyn (1971) and Swanson *et al.* (1971) independently of one another described the occurrence of fimbriae in the organisms of T1 and T2 but not in those of T3 and T4. Fresh isolates of GC are prone to auto-agglutination or clumping in saline or serum. These physical characteristics were carefully studied by Swanson *et al.* (1971) who demonstrated various degrees of clumping among the different types. The GC of T1 displayed slight or moderate clumping, T2 marked clumping, T3 moderate clumping and T4 no clumping at all. This behaviour was not correlated with fimbriation but mediated by what Swanson *et al.* (1971) referred to as "zones of adhesion".

By selective cultivation of certain colonial types, the variability of the agglutinogenic properties can be demonstrated. These physical qualities in one and the same strain of varying colony morphology certainly influence the agglutination reactions. Both Torrey and Buckell (1922) and Wilson (1954) (and several others) pointed out the poor ability of some strains to absorb agglutinins and they discussed the possibility that this might be due to the spontaneous clumping or aggregation of a particular strain. Our own data support this. It is also our experience that there are differences between strains of the same colony morphology with regard to their physical behaviour. All this can contribute to the observed antigenic differences, and particularly to the antigenic variation with time noted by Wilson. This means that antigenic differences could be of a quantitative instead of a qualitative nature. The amount of GC organisms used for absorptions has not always been standardized and it should be pointed out that all the absorptions were carried out with whole organisms. We have found that absorption with whole cells can give different results from absorption with disrupted cells. (See below under immunofluorescence, agar gel diffusion, and co-agglutination tests.)

B. Complement fixation

At the beginning of this century, Bruck (1906) and Mueller and Oppenheimer (1906) showed that the complement fixation (CF) test could be used to demonstrate GC antibodies in patients with disseminated gonococcal infection. Very soon this diagnostic test became widespread and was used in many laboratories as a diagnostic aid. There was much discussion about which strains should be used to cover those antigens concerned in the immune response. During the first two decades of this century a collection of ten gonococcal strains was used in some laboratories under the label of "Torrey strains", and these strains were supposed to represent different GC serotypes. This widespread impression was, however, contradicted by Torrey and Buckell (1922).

Torrey and Buckell (1922) in their very thorough serological study gave a detailed description of the CF test. Against their results from agglutination and agglutinin absorption tests they compared the antigenic potency of a group of GC strains in CF tests. Strain variations were found, but no cross absorption tests were carried out for serogrouping. However, their so-called regular strains, which had a broad antigenic spectrum and contained common GC antigens according to results by agglutination tests, were also shown to have the broadest antigenic spectrum in CF tests. They therefore recommended the use of GC antigen from one or two such ("regular") strains in the CF tests instead of a mixture of "regular" and "irregular" strains. This would only contribute to a dilution of the type specific antigens of the "irregular" strains. If antigens from "irregular" strains were to be included, they should be used separately from the antigen prepared from one or two regular strains. The CF test is still in use and we feel that these observations should be revived. In some laboratories, antigens from a wide collection of GC strains, 30–35 strains are used; in others from only a few selected strains. It was recently shown by Danielsson et al. (1972) and by Sandström and Danielsson (1977) that the number of positive diagnoses depends upon the antigens used in CF tests. This variation is more pronounced in patients with uncomplicated GC infections.

In 1943, Uroma demonstrated type-specific polysaccharide CF antigens which were prepared by extensive and repeated precipitations with alcohol. Later investigators have had difficulties in repeating Uroma's results or the preparative yield of antigen has been too small to allow characterization.

A new approach to serotyping GC by CF tests was made by Reyn during the 1940s. She initially used rabbit antisera which were rendered type specific, but because of more or less anticomplementarity of these sera and of normally occurring crossreacting antibodies with *Pasteurella* species, she switched to antisera prepared in guinea-pigs, (Reyn 1949a, b, c). The guinea-pigs were inoculated intravenously with formalin-treated and thoroughly washed organisms twice weekly over a period of four weeks. A total of 7×10^9 organisms grown on McLeod medium with ascitic fluid were inoculated per dose.

The complement fixation (CF) test used was that developed by Kristensen (1930) and used routinely at the State Serum Institute, Copenhagen, at the time of the investigation. Absorption was carried out with formalin-treated organisms. Five to ten millilitres of packed organisms were mixed with 10 ml of undiluted guinea-pig anti-GC antiserum. The mixture was refrigerated over-night and then centrifuged. Reyn pointed out that this absorption might equally well have been carried out at 37°C for 30 min. While absorption of rabbit sera resulted in anticomplementarity, this seldom occurred with guinea-pig sera.

Non-absorbed anti-GC antisera reacted with all GC strains tested. Reyn considered this to be due to a common antigen. Later experiments showed this antigen to be thermostable. In order to demonstrate type specific antigens, anti-GC sera were cross absorbed with selected GC strains. In this way so-called factor sera were produced. The term "factor" was applied by Reyn to the antibody contents of antisera. Examination of a GC strain with a series of factor-determining sera was described as "factor determination" or determination of the "factor formula" for that strain. Four factor sera, designated III, V, VI, and IX were prepared and used for such determinations. Factor formula for GC strains could be as follows:

GC strain	III	V	VI	IX	No. of strains
A	+	−	−	−	23 (8%)
B	−	−	−	+	41 (15%)
C	+	−	+	−	87 (32%)
D	−	+	−	+	52 (19%)
E	−	−	−	−	35 (13%)

In a series of 275 GC strains, 238 (85%) were typable, strains with formulae III–VI being the most frequent. Reyn also carried out an epidemiological study with 75 strains from 61 patients, corresponding to 30 chain infections. A fairly good agreement between the "types" within individual chains was seen. Twenty-eight out of 30 consisted of identical or nearly identical strains and only two chain infections showed divergence of "types". Reyn noted, however, that there were some deviations that could signify a certain variability of the gonococci. For instance, strains from one chain infection were found to have the same formula, thus belonging to the same type. Yet they were not able to exhaust each other's sera upon absorption. She concluded that two such strains contained a partial antigen lacking in the other strain. She also considered that this could possibly be due to mixed infection with other gonococcus strains, or to some change in the strain arising from mutation or from a changing of phase. Reyn presented no proof for either of these speculations. It might have been due to quantitative and not qualitative differences since she used whole GC cells to absorb antisera.

Reyn carried out a series of cross-absorption tests with strains of different types and thus arrived at an antigenic formula of such strains. She now also included a fifth factor serum designated XII. However, these cross-absorption experiments with strains of different types led only to the establishment of preliminary and rather uncertain antigenic formulae. Partial antigens corresponding to factor sera III and VI were thermostable while those corresponding to factor sera V and IX were thermolabile. The fact that the antigenic fixing capacity in some cases was stronger when the antigen was first heated at 100°C, was attributed to the possibility that a thermolabile antigen inhibited the attachment of antibody to a thermostable antigen. A disturbing observation was the fact that factor sera V, IX, and XII were unstable when stored at 4°C whereas factor sera III and VI could be kept for months at that temperature. Storage of factor sera in the refrigerator also often resulted in gelatinization. The reason for all this was not further investigated, but from a practical point of view it made it difficult to do antigenic factor examinations of GC strains.

General comments on CF studies

Reyn in her CF studies showed that the genococcus has thermostable common antigen(s) and type- or strain-specific antigens that are thermolabile or thermostable. These findings confirm the observations made by Torrey and Buckell in 1922 and they were also reconfirmed by Wilson in 1954. Reyn also showed that it was possible to serotype most GC strains with the use of factor sera in CF tests. This technique was, however, greatly hampered by the fact that these absorbed factor sera were unstable and gelified on storage. In other words, she also failed to develop a CF technique for serotyping GC organisms.

C. Immunofluorescence and agar gel diffusion studies

Deacon and his co-workers (1959) were the first to apply the immunoflorescence (IF) technique for the serologic demonstration and study of *N. gonorrhoeae*. Antigonococcal antisera were produced in rabbits injected subcutaneously with 5 ml of formalin-treated GC (3% formalin in saline for 1 h, then washed three times) in complete Freund's adjuvant followed four weeks later by four intravenous injections every third or fourth day with doses increasing from 0·5 to 2·0 ml. This intravenous series was repeated once 10–14 days later. Similar prolonged immunizations were also performed with GC treated by heat at 100 and 120°C respectively.

Deacon and his co-workers reported that they also met with inagglutinable GC strains in slide agglutination tests in the same way as did Wilson (1954) with tube agglutinations. They also supposed that this was due to K-like labile surface antigens. However, the prolonged immunization with formalin-treated organisms produced antiserum (anti-GC-F) that agglutinated both live and formalin-treated GC cells. The K antigen of the gonococcus was possibly demonstrated by this prolonged immunization. The results obtained after absorption of such an antiserum with GC cells treated at 120°C gave further support to the theory that the supposed K antigen had similar physical characteristics to the Vi antigen of *S. typhi* (Deacon *et al.*, 1959).

Deacon and his co-workers labelled the globulin portion of anti-GC-F with fluorescein isothiocyanate (FITC). Smears were prepared, stained and examined in the fluorescence microscope according to standard procedures (see Walker *et al.*, this series, Vol. 5A). Such conjugates stained GC brilliantly, especially those in urethral smears from males with acute gonorrhoea. GC in such smears often appeared with a solid stain which Deacon and his co-workers considered to be due to the supposed heat-labile K antigen. They believed that this was fully developed in acute gonorrhoeal infections and that there was a considerable loss of it in prolonged culture.

The anti-GC conjugates cross reacted with meningococci, but by absorption with these organisms the conjugates were made specific for *N. gonor-rhoeae*. Deacon and his co-workers showed that such conjugates could be successfully used for diagnostic purposes (Deacon *et al.*, 1959, 1960; Harris *et al.*, 1961). Several other investigators confirmed this and the IF technique is now routinely used in many laboratories as an aid in the laboratory diagnosis of gonorrhoea. It is not within the scope of this Chapter to review these studies (the reader is referred to papers by Danielsson (1965c), Danielsson and Forsum (1975) and Lind (1975)) but instead serologic investigations of *N. gonorrhoeae* with the IF method will be discussed.

Deacon and his co-workers were of the opinion that the supposed K antigen was of main importance for the IF staining of GC. They also thought this antigen to be related to virulence. They did not, however, further isolate or characterize this K antigen. In retrospect Kellogg and Thayer (1969) thought that the "surface component" observed in IF stained smears was very likely to be internal antigenic components leached to the outside of the cells.

Danielsson (1965a) reported further serological studies of *N. gonorrhoeae* with the IF technique in combination with the agar gel diffusion (AGD) method and the results he arrived at will be discussed below.

Danielsson first prepared a series of anti-GC antisera against a selected

13

GC strain and rabbits were immunized with the following antigenic preparations:

(a) organisms treated with formalin (3% in saline for 1 h followed by three washings)
(b) organisms disrupted with sonication
(c) the supernatant of disrupted cells
(d) the sediment of such disrupted cells (obtained by centrifugation at 30–40,000 × g for 30 min)
(e) organisms heated at 100°C for 1 h
(f) organisms heated at 120°C for 1 h.

The antigenic preparations (equivalent to 10^9 cells/ml) in Freund's complete adjuvant were injected subcutaneously or intramuscularly, 1·5 ml being given in each hind leg and 1·0 ml in each shoulder. Intravenous injections were given four to five weeks later every third to fourth day for two weeks with doses increasing from 0·5 to 2·0 ml. Ten days later this procedure was repeated and the animals were bled seven days after the last injection.

Antisera were assayed by tube agglutination (whole cells treated with formalin or heat at 100 and 120°C as antigen), complement fixation (whole cells treated with heat at 100°C as antigen), and agar gel diffusion with the micromodification of the Ouchterlony technique (cells disrupted by sonication as antigen) (see Oakley, this Series, Vol. 5A). The globulin portion of each antiserum was labelled with FITC and the IF reactions with untreated or formalin-treated cells, and cells treated by heat (100 and 120°C) were examined, the reference GC strain being used for preparation of the antigens.

Antisera obtained by immunization with formalin-treated whole cells, or cells disrupted by sonication, showed the highest immunological activity with all the four serological assay systems used. An antiserum obtained after immunization with formalin-treated whole cells was therefore selected for further IF studies and AGD tests.

The FITC-labelled globulin portion of this antiserum gave a 3–4+ bright or moderately bright peripheral staining of equal quality with untreated as well as with formalin-treated cells at dilutions of the conjugate of up to 1:256. Heating the cells at 60°C had no appreciable effect. After heating the cells to 100°C, the peripheral staining was less bright than in untreated or formalin-treated cells, and the gonococci also appeared smaller. Heating the cells to 120°C enhanced these effects and the IF titre with these cells was 2, two-fold, dilution steps lower. Absorption of the conjugate with formalin-treated whole cells (100 mg wet weight/0·1 ml conjugate) or cells disrupted by sonication eliminated the staining reactions with the reference GC strain completely. After corresponding absorptions with whole cells, treated by heat at 100 or 120°C, 3–4+ reactions were now obtained with untreated or formalin treated cells but the IF titre was reduced 3 to 5, two-fold, dilution steps respectively. Thus the presence of a K-like labile "surface antigen", as proposed by Deacon et al. (1959), is not decisive for the IF staining reactions; both heat-labile and heat-stable antigens participate.

AGD studies performed in parallel with the reference system also gave some interesting findings which deserve comment. GC cells disrupted by sonication were used as antigen in the AGD tests since that antigen gave more consistent and clear-cut results than diffusion with whole cells. A concentration of disrupted cells, corresponding to a wet weight of 100 mg/ml, was found optimal and used throughout the work. Approximately 15 precipitation lines were obtained. From a practical point of view they were placed in four groups, A, B, C, and D, since it was hard to decide which of them represented separate antigen–antibody entities and which of the lines were duplicates of one and the same antigen–antibody system. Both heat-labile and heat-stable antigens were found in these four groups which means that at least eight antigen–antibody systems were involved.

Absorption of the anti-GC reference serum with disrupted cells eliminated all the precipitins and no precipitation lines were formed. It should be observed that absorption of the anti-GC reference conjugate also eliminated the IF staining reactions. However, after absorption of the reference serum with whole cells, the precipitins responsible for the lines in group A, B, and D were removed while those responsible for most of the heavy lines in group C were left. It should also be observed that absorption of the reference conjugate with whole cells removed the IF staining reactions. The results thus showed that some antigens, liberated by disrupting the GC cells and demonstrated in AGD tests, do not primarily participate in the IF staining reaction.

Danielsson (1965a) also carried out comparative IF tests with 20, randomly selected, GC strains using the reference conjugate before and after this was absorbed with whole or disrupted GC cells. Corresponding comparative AGD tests were also performed with these 20 GC strains and the results obtained will be briefly discussed.

Using the reference conjugate, the IF titres were one or two dilution steps lower with the heterologous strains as compared with the homologous one. The reference conjugate was then absorbed with each of the heterologous strains as well as with the reference strain and subsequently tested against the absorbing strain as well as the others. Absorptions were performed with disrupted cells or formalin-treated whole cells with identical results.

The reference strain, subcultured 4, 27, or 102 times, absorbed all the antibodies responsible for the staining reactions of the heterologous strains. None of these were, however, able to absorb all the antibodies responsible for the staining of the reference strain but the IF titre was reduced 3 to 5, two-fold dilution steps (from 1:256 down to 1:32–1:8). Absorbing strains also removed IF staining antibodies from some of the other heterologous strains. Thus, the absorbing capacity was the same for two groups of the tested strains, 12 and 4 strains respectively, and differed only slightly in four other strains.

Although only one reference system was used, the findings with the IF technique demonstrated both common and type- or strain-specific GC antigens participating in the IF staining. These findings thus confirmed the results of other investigators.

The AGD studies performed in parallel with the IF tests were also of interest. The 20 heterologous GC strains gave reactions of identity with 13–14 out of 15 precipitation lines of the reference system. The one or two precipitation lines that were not formed belonged to the D group, i.e. those that were formed close to the antigen well. When the reference anti-GC antiserum was absorbed with disrupted cells no precipitation lines were formed with antigens of the absorbing strain. On the other hand, when the reference serum, absorbed with disrupted heterologous cells, was tested against its homologous strain, one or two precipitation lines belonging to group D were again formed.

D. Co-agglutination studies

Kronvall (1973) described the principles for serotyping pneumococci with the use of protein A-containing staphylococci coated with specific antibodies. Kronvall called this technique "co-agglutination" (in the following abbreviated COA) and pointed out its potential use for serological typing and identification of bacteria. It was based on the fact that protein A-containing staphylococci react with the Fc piece of the IgG molecule (Forsgren and Sjöquist, 1967).

The COA method has the advantage over standard slide agglutination tests of not being influenced by autoagglutinating bacterial strains. Kronvall's group (Christensen et al., 1973) took advantage of this property for serological grouping of streptococci and Juhlin and Winblad (1973) described its use for serotyping mycobacteria.

Danielsson and Kronvall (1974) successfully adopted the COA method for the rapid identification of N. gonorrhoeae organisms primarily detected as oxidase-positive colonies in gonococcal cultures. It has also a potential use for serotyping studies of gonococci (Danielsson and Sandström, 1977).

The procedures described below can be followed for the preparation of reagent staphylococci and coating them with antigonococcal antibodies.

1. *Preparation of protein A-containing staphylococci*

The Cowan I strain of *S. aureus* (NCTC 8530) is grown at 37°C for 16–18 h in CCY broth (Arvidsson *et al.*, 1971). For small-scale production 250 ml of broth in a so-called trypsinizing bottle is seeded with 2–4 ml of a 4–6 h broth culture of Cowan I staphylococci. The bottle is placed on a shaker to promote good aeration. The staphylococci are harvested by centrifugation at $2000 \times g$ for 20 min, washed three times in 0·01M phosphate buffered saline, pH 7·4 (PBS), then treated as a 10% suspension for 3 h with 0·5% formaldehyde in PBS, washed twice and finally exposed to 80°C for 4 min as described by Kronvall (1973). The heat treatment will stabilize the staphylococci and can be accomplished by passing the suspension with the aid of a continuous pump through a glass coil emersed in an 80°C water bath. After 2 additional washings in PBS the staphylococci are suspended to 10% (v/v) in PBS containing 0·1% sodium azide and stored at 4°C. A culture of 1 litre of broth will give a yield of approximately 60–70 ml 10% staphylococci, and according to our experience they will be stable for three or four months or longer.

2. *Production of antigonococcal antisera*

Antigonococcal antisera are obtained from rabbits immunized with formalin-treated whole gonococci (Danielsson, 1965a). Since we do not yet have defined serotypes we have used randomly selected gonococcal strains for production of diagnostic antisera. Organisms from a pool of six such strains and at a concentration of approximately 10^9 organisms/ml in sterile saline are used as antigens. We start the immunization by intramuscular injections of antigens with complete Freund's adjuvant, 1–1·5 ml in each of the hind and fore legs. Five weeks later a series of four intravenous injections is given three to four days apart with doses increasing from 0·25 to 2·0 ml. The rabbits are bled seven to ten days after the last injection.

This immunization procedure will usually give antisera of high immunological activity but some rabbits will be lost during the series of i.v. injections because of anaphylaxis. Antisera of corresponding quality will also be obtained by two series of i.v. injections, each series two weeks apart. The rabbits tolerate this immunization procedure better.

3. *Absorptions of antisera*

The polyvalent antigonococcal antibodies will give strong cross-reactions with various serogroups of meningococci and sometimes also with non-pathogenic *Neisseria* (Danielsson, 1965b). Antisera to be used for coating of protein A-containing staphylococci with IgG antibodies must therefore be absorbed appropriately as follows: one volume of antigonococcal anti-serum is mixed with one volume of formalin-treated meningococcal, or other organisms, packed by centrifugation at $2000 \times g$ for 20 min. The mixture is incubated at 37°C for 4 h and overnight at 4°C. The absorbed antiserum is recovered by centrifugation twice at $2000 \times g$ for 20 min.

4. *Coating of Cowan I staphylococci with antibodies*

For coating of the protein A-containing staphylococci, 1 ml of the 10% suspension is added to 0·1 ml of unabsorbed or absorbed rabbit anti-gonococcal antiserum. After mixing the suspension for 5 min the staphylococci are centrifuged at $2000 \times g$ for 10 min, washed twice in PBS and finally suspended to 1% in PBS containing 0·1% sodium azide. Control reagent staphylococci are coated in the same way with gammaglobulin from non-immunized rabbits. The reagents are stored in the refrigerator ($+4$°C) and will be stable for at least three to four months.

5. *Performance of co-agglutination tests*

The COA tests are performed on glass slides by emulsifying one or more bacterial colonies in two drops of the 1% suspension of reagent staphylococci coated with antigonococcal antibodies. Alternatively, bacterial colonies to be tested are emulsified in PBS to a concentration of approximately 1% and one drop of this suspension is mixed with one drop of the antibody-coated staphylococci. The slide is then tilted about once a second for 1–2 min while being observed with the naked eye in oblique light against a dark background. Control tests with protein A-containing staphylococci coated with gammaglobulin from non-immunized rabbits are always run in parallel.

In a positive reaction granular agglutinates are formed while in a negative reaction the suspensions of bacteria and reagent staphylococci will remain homogeneous or "milky". We grade the co-agglutinations as weak ($+$), moderate ($+ +$), strong ($+ + +$) or as very strong ($+ + + +$) reactions. The $+ + +$ and $+ + + +$ reactions usually start to appear after 20–30 tilts of the slide and as a rule they are fully developed within 1 min. The $+$ and $+ +$ reactions develop more slowly and require tilting of the slide for 2 min. In a positive reaction the control test must be negative.

According to our experience various COA patterns will appear with various GC strains. Some strains will give heavy agglutinates while some other strains give finely granular agglutination patterns. The reactions are also dependent upon the colony morphology types of the GC strains. T1 or T2 colonies give consistent and reproducible results while T3 or T4 colonies sometimes can be inagglutinable. On a few occasions we have met with GC strains that have given a false positive reaction ("pseudo-reaction") with the control reagent. These reactions have been eliminated by emulsifying the organisms in PBS or distilled water containing 1 mg trypsin/ml.

6. *Application of the COA test for* Neisseria *species identification*

In the report by Danielsson and Kronvall (1974) COA tests with reagent staphylococci coated with unabsorbed polyvalent antigonococcal antibodies gave strong cross reactions with various serogroups of meningococci and occasionally also with some *Moraxella* and *Haemophilus* strains. However, these cross reactions were eliminated by absorptions of the antigonococcal antisera with appropriate organisms. Reagent staphylococci coated with such absorbed antigonococcal antibodies specifically discriminated gonococci from meningococci and also from other oxidase positive Gram-negative bacteria. Such COA tests were found to be an excellent adjunct to the immunofluorescent and biochemical tests for a rapid identification of *N. gonorrhoeae* organisms primarily detected as oxidase positive colonies on GC agar plates (Danielsson and Kronvall, 1974). Recently Olcén, Danielsson and Kjellander (1975) showed that the COA method had several advantages over slide agglutination for serotyping *N. meningitidis*. Many meningococcal strains autoagglutinable by standard slide agglutination were serogrouped by the COA technique. We have also found the combined use of reagent staphylococci coated with antibodies specific for gonococci, or with antibodies specific for meningococci, to be excellent adjuncts to biochemical tests to discriminate *N. gonorrhoeae* from *N. meningitidis* or vice versa. This is especially true for the diagnosis of pharyngeal gonorrhoea but also for the identification of *N. meningitidis* in specimens from the genitourinary tract and the anal canal. Findings of meningococci in urogenital and rectal specimens doubtless present diagnostic problems both from the bacteriologic and the clinical points of views and an increase of such isolates was recently reported (Faur, Weisburd and Wilson, 1975). In such instances the combined use of biochemical and serological tests seems to give the most accurate diagnosis (Danielsson *et al.*, 1977).

7. *Possible use of COA tests for serotyping* Neisseria gonorrhoeae

The COA method offers two advantages: first, it is not influenced by autoagglutinating bacterial cells which is an inherent physical property of GC cells of the colony morphology types T1, T2, and T3 and makes the use of standard agglutination techniques nearly impossible. Secondly, GC antisera absorbed with whole or disrupted GC cells will inevitably contain considerable amounts of bacterial components of various chemical types (enzymes, toxins, nucleic acids, etc.) that will, as discussed above, interfere with the antigen–antibody reactions in the immunological techniques used. The COA method offers a particular advantage from this point of view since only the antibody molecules are adsorbed to protein A-containing staphylococci while the rest of the bacterial components in an absorbed serum as well as other serum constituents are washed away.

We have used these advantages of the COA method for a new approach to antigenic and serotyping studies of *N. gonorrhoeae*. Our preliminary results look promising for a better understanding of the mosaic of the antigenic patterns GC cells can exhibit (Danielsson and Sandström, 1977) and some of our findings will therefore be reported briefly.

Selected GC strains of colony morphology types T1 and T2 were used to produce "monovalent" anti-GC antisera in rabbits using various types of immunization techniques. Protein A-containing staphylococci were prepared and coated as described above with antibodies from these sera undiluted or two-fold diluted with an initial dilution of 1:5. With this procedure the homologous COA titres of the antisera were usually 1:20–1:40. The heterologous titres were equal or 1 to 4 two-fold dilution steps lower. In this respect our results with COA tests are in contrast to what other authors have reported with standard agglutination techniques applied for serologic studies of GC. Both Torrey and Buckell (1922) and Wilson (1954) reported that they sometimes achieved higher titres with heterologous GC cells than with homologous cells. This has not occurred with the COA technique. Wilson (1954) and Deacon *et al.* (1959) also reported that some GC strains were inagglutinable in some sera. We have also met with inagglutinable GC strains in COA studies but this property has been restricted to GC colonies of T3 and T4 colony morphology types and has been antiserum dependent. This inagglutinability disappeared after boiling the GC suspension which is in agreement with the observation made by Wilson (1952).

In absorption studies with both homologous and heterologous GC cells we have found that disrupted cells in proper concentrations (minimum 1 g wet weight/ml antiserum) have to be used for complete absorption. Thus, if whole cells instead of disrupted cells are used for the absorption, positive COA reactions can be obtained with organisms of the absorbing strain, especially when they have been kept in suspension for a couple of days.

In a series of cross-absorption studies with a selected group of anti-GC antisera using organisms from heterologous strains specific antigens were demonstrated. Serotyping patterns tentatively named 1, 2, 3, 4, etc., have been identified. Some factors are common, whilst others are demonstrated irregularly. Our findings with the COA technique indicate that immunogenic, absorbing and agglutinating properties of a particular GC strain have to be considered. We believe that this is also true for other immuno-logic techniques and may well explain the divergent results reported previously. It is also of interest to note that some antigenic factors are only demonstrated after the GC suspension is boiled.

Our conclusion is that the COA technique is an excellent tool for sero-typing studies of *N. gonorrhoeae*. Investigations are now under way to combine this technique with other immunochemical techniques for further characterization of the various GC antigens and their relation to other *Neisseria* species.

III. SEROTYPING AND ANTIGENIC STUDIES USING ANTIGEN-CONTAINING FRACTIONS FROM *N. GONORRHOEAE*

The challenge of defining serotypes among gonococci has also been approached by studying antigen-containing extracts of the bacterium. Some of the earlier investigators in this field claimed that type-specific antigens could be demonstrated in extracts from gonococci (Caspar, 1930, 1937; Uroma, 1943). In spite of considerable effort, however, no generally accepted serological classification of gonococci was attained.

During later years, a number of different techniques have been adopted for the study of antigen-containing fractions from *N. gonorrhoeae* including passive haemolysis, agglutination tests, and precipitation in agar gels. Studies which have shown different antigen specificities from various gonococcal isolates, will be discussed.

A. Passive agglutination or haemolysis

By passive agglutination we mean the antibody-mediated agglutination of erythrocytes or inert particles sensitized with antigen from the bacterium. Passive haemolysis denotes the measurement of antibody through its capa-city to cause lysis of antigen-sensitized erythrocytes in the presence of complement.

Thomas and Mennie (1950) and later Chanarin (1954) used the passive haemolysis test for the detection of antibodies against gonococcal antigens in serum from man or immunized rabbits. The antigen used was prepared by treatment of *N. gonorrhoeae* cells with alkali. Chanarin (1954) demon-strated two serotypes among strains of GC when using erythrocytes sensitized with the alkali extract. Out of 67 strains examined, 59 belonged to type I, 8 to type II.

Studies on antigens prepared from GC by treatment of whole cells with NaOH were extended by Maeland (1966). Antigen to be used for sensitization of erythrocytes was prepared from various strains isolated from patients with gonorrhoea and human or rabbit antibody detected by the passive haemolysis or haemagglutination test (Maeland, 1966, 1967). Using the strain 8551, it was shown that antibody against the erythrocyte-sensitizing antigen contained in the alkali extract could be inhibited by any of the extracts prepared from the bacterium with aqueous ether, trichloroacetic acid or heat treatment (Maeland, 1968). It was thus concluded that the antigen carried by erythrocytes exposed to the alkali extract was also present in the other extracts examined. The antigen resisted oxidation with periodate, but was destroyed by digestion with papain or pronase. It was assumed that the antigen, designated determinant b, was of protein nature.

Tauber and Garson reported in 1959 that endotoxic lipopolysaccharide could be extracted from gonococci by the phenol–water procedure described by Westphal et al. (1952). The gonococcal lipopolysaccharide was recovered from the water phase as with members of the Enterobacteriaceae. The same technique was used for the preparation of lipopolysaccharide from strain 8551 and the preparation was purified by repeated washings and ultra-centrifugation (Maeland, 1968). When tested untreated, the lipopoly-saccharide did not sensitize erythrocytes for agglutination by antiserum to strain 8551, but was able to do so after treatment of the preparation with NaOH similar to lipopolysaccharides from intestinal bacilli (Neter et al., 1956). The antigen carried by the sensitized erythrocytes was called deter-minant a. Haemagglutination inhibition experiments showed that deter-minant a was also present in the extracts prepared from strain 8551 with aqueous ether, trichloroacetic acid, or by heat treatment (Maeland, 1968). Accordingly, these latter preparations contained both the determinants a and b. On the other hand, the lipopolysaccharide prepared with phenol–water did not contain determinant b, only determinant a. It was assumed that determinant a was of carbohydrate nature since its activity was de-stroyed by oxidation with periodate, but was resistant to treatment with proteolytic enzymes (Maeland, 1968).

Experiments were performed to study the relationship between a and b in the preparation obtained from strain 8551 with aqueous ether (Maeland, 1969a). Separation of the determinants or alteration of the proportionate activity of a and b was not achieved by centrifugation of the preparation, treatment with aqueous phenol, electrophoresis, or gel filtration. Further-more, both a and b were present in the immunoprecipitate which formed when antiserum containing antibody against only one of the determinants was added to the antigen preparation. The results indicate that both a and b are present as constituent parts of the endotoxin complex, a belonging to its carbohydrate and b to its protein component (Maeland, 1969a). This suggestion accords with the results of chemical analysis (Maeland, 1969b, d;

TABLE I

Chemical composition (percentage of dry weight) of aqueous ether and phenol–water extracted endotoxins from N. gonorrhoeae strains 8551, V and VII (Maeland and Kristoffersen, 1971)

Source of endotoxin	Preparation method	Protein	Neutral sugars	Hexosamine	KDO†	Lipid	N	P
Strain 8551	Aqueous ether	88	1·8	1·1	..	3·0	14·1	0·3
	Phenol–water	11	12·8	7·0	8·5	34·4	4·4	1·3
Strain V	Aqueous ether	82	2·1	1·0	..	2·6	12·6	0·3
	Phenol–water	12	13·3	11·2	11·1	37·3	..	0·6
Strain VII	Aqueous ether	83	1·4	0·7	..	6·3	12·9	0·4
	Phenol–water	14	13·5	6·8	4·8	37·1	..	1·2

.. = Not performed.
† = 2-Keto-3 deoxyoctonate.

Maeland and Kristoffersen, 1971). As seen from Table I the aqueous ether endotoxin from strain 8551 as well as that from the "Copenhagen strains" V and VII contained lipid, carbohydrate and protein, the latter being the dominating component. On the other hand, lipid and carbohydrate were the major components of the lipopolysaccharides prepared from the same strains by the phenol–water method.

Methods for the detection by passive haemagglutination of antibodies against each of the determinants a and b were developed (Maeland, 1969c). Thus antibodies against determinant a were determined as follows: endotoxin was prepared by extraction of gonococci with aqueous ether or phenol–water and the preparation was partly purified by digestion with DNAase, ultracentrifugation and washing with distilled water. The preparation was then treated with alkali, 0.04N NaOH, $37°$C, 18 h, neutralized and digested with pronase to destroy determinant b. Erythrocytes sensitized with the final preparation were used in the test. Antibody against determinant b was measured by passive haemagglutination using erythrocytes sensitized with aqueous ether endotoxin that had been pretreated with alkali and oxidized with periodate (Maeland, 1969c).

This latter test system was used to examine the specificity and distribution among strains of gonococci and other bacteria of the protein determinant b. The results obtained indicate that the b determinant is a group-reactive antigen common to gonococci and meningococci (Maeland, 1969d).

Similar experiments were performed using the a determinant from the strains 8551, V and VII (Maeland, 1969d; Maeland et al., 1971). Antiserum against each of these strains showed activity both against erythrocytes sensitized with the homologous a determinant and against those sensitized with any of the heterologous determinants. The antisera were re-examined after absorption with whole bacterial cells, or the corresponding endotoxin preparations. Representative results of these experiments are shown in Table II. Absorption of the homologous antiserum removed all the antibodies to determinant a. Absorption of heterologous antiserum removed those antibodies showing cross-reactivity with the a determinant used for absorption but a determinant antibodies of other specificities were left unabsorbed. It would appear that the results, corroborated by haemagglutination inhibition experiments (Maeland, 1969; Maeland et al., 1971), accord with the assumption that several distinct antigenic specificities (a factors) are carried by the a determinant preparation from each of the three strains. Altogether six a factors were identified by the experiments performed and designated $a_1 \ldots a_6$. The antigenic formulae proposed for the strains 8551, V and VII, were $a_{1,5,6}$, $a_{1,2,3,6}$, and $a_{1,3,4}$ respectively.

The various a factors detected in each preparation may belong to one and the same molecular complex. On the addition to endotoxin from strain

8551 of antiserum containing antibody only against one of its *a* factors (a_1), the precipitate which formed contained all the factors carried by the 8551 preparation (Maeland *et al.*, 1971). These results support the notion that the *a* factors belonging to each antigen preparation are harboured by one and the same molecular complex analogous to the O factors of entero-bacterial lipopolysaccharides (Lüderitz *et al.*, 1966). Presumably, all the *a* factors are carried by the carbohydrate moiety. This is indicated by the finding that all the factors described resisted treatment with proteolytic

TABLE II

Titres in indirect haemagglutination test of rabbit antisera to
N. *gonorrhoeae* strains 8551, V and VII, before and after
absorption with endotoxin (Maeland, 1969b)

Antiserum	Absorbed with	Erythrocytes sensitized with determinant *a* of endotoxin		
		8851	V	VII
Anti-Gc-8551	None	1023	512	128
	Endotoxin 8551	< 16	< 16	< 16
	Endotoxin V	256	< 16	< 16
	Endotoxin VII	512	512	< 16
Anti-Gc-V	None	512	2048	256
	Endotoxin 8551	< 16	1024	< 16
	Endotoxin V	< 16	< 16	< 16
	Endotoxin VII	256	1024	< 16
Anti-Gc-VII	None	512	1024	1024
	Endotoxin 8551	< 16	512	256
	Endotoxin V	< 16	< 16	128
	Endotoxin VII	< 16	< 16	< 16

enzymes but were destroyed by periodate oxidation (Maeland *et al.*, 1971). Furthermore, the activity of antibody to some of the *a* factors could be inhibited by galactose or lactose (Maeland *et al.*, 1971).

In endotoxin prepared from the strains 8551, V, and VII, the sugar constituents detected were glucose, galactose, glucosamine, heptose and keto-deoxyoctonate (Maeland, 1969; Maeland and Kristoffersen, 1971). Accordingly, the preparations belong to the same chemotype in spite of the differences observed in serological specificity. It is interesting to note that the same monosaccharides detected in endotoxin from GC are ubi-quitous as constituents of the core region of *Salmonella* O antigens (Lüderitz *et al.*, 1966). Consequently, these sugar components make up all of the carbohydrate moiety of O antigens from members of the R II serogroup of *Salmonella* R forms devoid of their O-specific side chains (Lüderitz *et al.*, 1966). It is tempting to speculate whether the overall structure of the carbohydrate moiety of lipopolysaccharides from GC is similar to that of the O antigens of the *Salmonella* R II serogroup. On the other hand, some of the monosaccharides detected in gonococcal lipopolysaccharides may both be present in a backbone structure and in side chains carrying the *a* factors, in particular the glucose and galactose residues (Maeland *et al.*, 1971). Whatever the situation, the difference in specificity according to strain origin of the endotoxin preparations can be explained by assuming dissimilarity in sequence or other structural arrangements of some of the sugar constituents.

The *a* factors were found to be present in various combinations in all of 24 other gonococcal isolates examined (Maeland, 1969d). From this observation, it would appear that GC can be classified into different serological groups according to the *a* factors carried by the strains. However, the potential contribution of such serogrouping to the clinical and epidemiological study of gonorrhoea has not yet been fully evaluated. The question of whether the *a* factors, as demonstrated by indirect haemagglutination, can be detected by other techniques, such as immunofluorescence, bacterial agglutination or co-agglutination methods, also remains a topic for investigation. Conceivably, other *a* factors may be present in gonococci in addition to those described. The overall structure of endotoxin from GC as well as the fine structure and localization of the various *a* factors also awaits clarification.

The majority of the experiments were performed using rabbit antisera to GC. However, human serum antibodies against lipopolysaccharide from GC have been examined. In these studies, sera from patients with gonorrhoea have been tested against inert particles (Watt *et al.*, 1971) or red cells (Fletcher *et al.*, 1973; Maeland and Larsen, 1971, 1975; Ward *et al.*, 1972) coated with the lipopolysaccharide and the results compared with those obtained using serum from healthy individuals. Apparently, human sera may exhibit antibody activity against lipopolysaccharides from different gonococcal isolates, but not to the same degree (Maeland and Larsen, 1975; Ward *et al.*, 1972; Watt *et al.*, 1971). Recently, Maeland and Matre (1975) showed that sera from patients with gonorrhoea may contain antibodies of multiple specificities reacting with the carbohydrate determinant *a* from gonococci. Serotyping of GC has not been the object of these studies. Nevertheless, some of the results reported have confirmed the notion that multiple antigenic sites are carried by the lipopolysaccharide from *N. gonorrhoeae*.

B. Immunoprecipitation

Immunoprecipitation with antisera has enabled the detection of type-specific antigens in extracts from GC as reported by earlier workers (Caspar, 1930, 1937; Uroma, 1943). During later years much of the work on GC antigens has been based on double diffusion in agar gels and immunoelectrophoresis techniques. Whole GC cells, disintegrated cells or antigen-containing fractions prepared by various extraction methods have been examined. It has been convincingly demonstrated that gonococci contain many antigens giving rise to precipitation lines with rabbit antisera (Danielsson, 1965a, b; Danielsson *et al.*, 1969; Maeland, 1967; Reising and Kellog, 1965). Some of the antigens form precipitation lines with selected human sera (Danielsson *et al.*, 1972). Also, close antigenic relationship between gonococci, meningococci and certain apathogenic *Neisseria* strains has been established (Danielsson, 1965b).

Experiments utilizing immunoprecipitation have provided considerable evidence for the existence in GC of antigens that show strain specificity and thus may provide the basis necessary for serotyping of the bacterium. The more recent studies will be discussed below.

Danielsson (1965a) was the first to report the application of the micro-modification of the Ouchterlony technique for antigenic studies of *N. gonorrhoeae*. These investigations were combined with immunofluorescent antibody studies of the gonococcus. The details of the experimental results obtained in these studies are described on pages 324–328 to which the reader is referred. We would like to stress again, however, the different results obtained when absorptions were performed with whole or disrupted GC cells. Thus, absorption of the reference antiserum with disrupted homologous GC organisms emptied the reference antiserum of all antibodies. After absorption with whole cells it was of interest to note that several antibodies were left and these antibodies did not seem to participate in the immunofluorescent staining reaction of whole cells. Further experiments with other *Neisseria* (Danielsson, 1965b) gave evidence that absorption with whole organisms left antibodies reactive with protoplasmic antigens. It should also be mentioned that Danielsson (1965a) in his studies also demonstrated the presence of specific antigens in the homologous GC strain after the reference antiserum was absorbed with disrupted heterologous GC organisms. In retrospect these antigenic factors might well correspond to those recently described by Apicella (1974) discussed below.

Apicella (1974) prepared antigen from gonococci by phenol–water extraction and examined the alkali-digested water phase material. Among several antigens giving rise to precipitation lines with rabbit antiserum, one was selected for further studies including purification by DEAE-cellulose chromatography. Immunochemical analysis showed that the purified antigen was an acidic polysaccharide. Using rabbit antisera to gono-cocci, immunodiffusion experiments revealed one antigenic determinant common to different gonococcal isolates. In addition, the antigen showed activity which permitted the identification of two serologically distinct populations of N. gonorrhoeae, designated Gc_1 and Gc_2. Also, some evidence was provided that a third antigenically distinct population of gono-cocci may exist. Apicella in his studies used the same starting material as Maeland (1968), i.e. the water phase of the phenol–water extract. Therefore, the common and population-specific determinants detected by Apicella by immunoprecipitation may be identical to some of the a factors of gono-coccal endotoxin demonstrated by passive haemagglutination (Maeland et al., 1971). The relation of these antigen determinants to those described by Danielsson (1965a) were discussed above. However, at the present time only circumstantial evidence suggests such identity. Thus it is possible that the antigen isolated by Apicella has no relationship whatsoever to the endotoxin complex. Conversely, the antigen may represent an alkali-stable split product released from the lipopolysaccharide by alkali digestion. Hence, comparison of results must await further experiments.

The acid extraction method of Lancefield (1933), commonly included in the procedure used for serogrouping of streptococci, was applied to strains of N. gonorrhoeae by Hutchinson (1970). Out of 181 N. gonorrhoeae strains examined 143 could be classified into one or other of five serological groups by an immunoprecipitation test using rabbit antisera.

Pierce et al. (1975) examined acid and formamide extracts prepared from the virulent T1/T2 and avirulent T3/T4 variants (Kellogg et al., 1968) of the N. gonorrhoeae strain F-62. Testing of the extracts in gel immuno-diffusion reactions against rabbit antisera showed that neither of these extracts contained antigen that enabled the virulent to be differentiated from the avirulent variants. However, extract obtained by ultrasonication of the F-62 strain contained an antigen that was associated only with the virulent T1/T2 variants. The antigen was distinguishable from the endo-toxin and appeared not to be associated with the fimbriae of gonococci. The antigen, being susceptible to digestion with pronase or trypsin, was detected only in extracts from the F-26 strain, not in extracts prepared from corresponding colonial variants of other gonococcal isolates. The antigen described was thought to be intimately connected with virulence of the bacterium.

All of the above mentioned authors have demonstrated type- or popula-tion-specific antigens in the extracts examined. Mostly, different techniques were used for the preparation of the extracts. The various groups may have been working on different antigens. The implications of this would be that gonococci possess a variety of type-specific antigens. At the present time this possibility cannot be denied. However, it seems more likely that the same antigen(s) can be released from the bacterial cells by different techniques. The results reported may eventually affect the taxonomy and classification of gonococci. No doubt this will require further studies which, among others, should include attempts to reproduce the results reported and thorough comparison of the various techniques employed.

C. Other methods

Kellogg *et al.* (1963, 1968) pointed out the relationship between colony morphology and virulence of *N. gonorrhoeae* and defined four colony morphology types T1, T2, T3, and T4. Only the T1/T2 variants were linked with virulence of the bacterium. Later other investigators (Jephcott *et al.*, 1971; Swanson *et al.*, 1971) showed the T1/T2 cells were associated with surface fimbriae, not the T3/T4 cells. Buchanan *et al.* (1973) reported a technique for isolation and purification of gonococcal fimbriae. Antibody, raised against the fimbrial antigen, could be detected by immunofluorescent staining using fimbriated gonococci, but not when bacteria devoid of fimbriae were used. Conjugated antiserum stained the T1/T2 variants of different gonococcal isolates to the same extent. Buchanan *et al.* (1973) suggested that the fimbrial antigen(s) was common to all gonococci, but a divergent opinion was recently reported by Novotny and Turner (1975). Thus, it is still an open question whether fimbrial antigen is suitable for serotyping of gonococci. ^{125}I-labelled fimbrial antigen was used by Buchanan *et al.* (1973) in tests designed to measure antibodies in human sera. The results showed that in persons suffering from gonorrhoea antibody activity was significantly higher than in healthy controls. Thus, the fimbrial antigen may be an important immunogen during infection with gonococci.

Lymphocyte blastogenesis responses to gonococcal antigens have been studied to some extent. Blood lymphocytes from males with repeated infections by gonococci responded with greater blastogenesis to ultrasonicates of *N. gonorrhoeae* than those from normal subjects (Kearns *et al.* 1973; Kraus *et al.*, 1970). Rosenthal (1975) reported similar findings but she also found a lower lymphocyte transformation to GC antigen in patients with disseminated GC infection than in controls. Esquenazi and Streitfeld (1973) showed that the crude sonicate from gonococci contained various fractions stimulating blood lymphocytes from rabbits immunized with *N. gonorrhoeae* and that fractions from *N. catarrhalis* exhibited cross-reactivity. It is evident that further studies on gonococcal antigens involved in the cellular immune response are required.

IV. GENERAL SUMMARY AND CONCLUSIONS

Studies on gonococcal antigens have evoked interest among scientists in research centres in many parts of the world. Doubtless, the work performed during later years has greatly added to the knowledge of antigens produced by gonococci, humoral and, to a lesser extent, the cellular immune responses to these antigens. In spite of this, neither a generally accepted system for serogrouping of gonococci nor a test system useful in the serodiagnosis of gonorrhoea has evolved. No doubt a system for serogrouping of the bacterium would offer considerable potentialities to those studying the epidemiology of gonorrhoea. Furthermore, this would help in the selection of strains that could be used in a diagnostic test. It is our opinion that work aimed at the detection of serotypes among gonococci should continue.

Many of the authors referred to in this review have described antigens showing strain specificity. Thus antigenic heterogeneity that, theoretically, could offer the basis necessary for serotyping of gonococci, seems to be well documented. However, it is a most conspicuous feature that many of the research groups working on the serology of *N. gonorrhoeae* have described a possible grouping system that seems to be different from that described by the others. A variety of immunological methods, antigen preparations, and immunization schedules have been employed. Some of the investigators have used established laboratory strains, others freshly isolated strains, many times without regard to the effect that subculture may have on antigens produced by gonococci. To some extent this may explain the confusion. However, the failure to establish a serogrouping system probably also reflects the complexity of gonococcal antigens and the difficulties encountered by investigators in this field.

It is our opinion, that research on the serology of gonococci would benefit from the following measures:

1. Laboratory gonococcal strains should be established and made available to investigators.
2. Defined media that can easily be prepared in different laboratories should be used for culture of the bacterium.
3. Immunization schedules standardized as far as possible should be used by different investigators.
4. For the preparation of antigens, techniques that have proved useful in the past, should be re-examined, possibly by other research groups, in order to test the reproducibility of results already reported.
5. Designations should be established for the major antigens in gonococci and used for reference in the literature.
6. Particular emphasis should be put on increased communication

between people engaged in research on the gonococcus, including regular conferences.

7. The co-ordination of research, possibly under the auspices of a W.H.O. committee, should be considered.

REFERENCES

Apicella, M. A. (1974). *J. infect. Dis.*, **130**, 619–625.
Bruck, C. (1906). *D. med. Wschr.*, **32**, 1368–1369.
Bruckner, J., and Christéanu, C. R. (1906). *Soc. de Biologie*, Nos. 18–19.
Buchanan, T. M., Swanson, J., Holmes, K. K., Kraus, S. J., and Gotschlich, E. C. (1973). *J. clin. Invest.*, **52**, 2896–2909.
Caspar, W. A. (1930). *Klin. Wschr.* **9**, 2154–2158.
Caspar, W. A. (1937). *J. Immun.*, **32**, 421–439.
Chanarin, I. (1954). *J. Hyg. (Lond.)*, **52**, 425–443.
Christensen, P., Kahlmeter, G., Jonsson, S., and Kronvall, G. (1973). *Infect. Immun.*, **7**, 881–885.
Danielsson, D. (1965a). *Acta path. microbiol. scand.*, **64**, 243–266.
Danielsson, D. (1965b). *Acta path. microbiol. scand.*, **64**, 267–276.
Danielsson, D. (1965c). *Acta Univ. Upsaliensis*, **24**, 1–14.
Danielsson, D. G., Schmale, J. D., Peacock, W. L., Jr, and Thayer, J. D. (1969). *J. Bact.*, **97**, 1012–1017.
Danielsson, D., Thyresson, N., Falk, V., and Barr, J. (1972). *Acta derm.-venereol. (Stockh.)*, **52**, 467–475.
Danielsson, D., and Kronvall, G. (1974). *Appl. Microbiol.*, **27**, 368–374.
Danielsson, D., and Forsum, U. (1975). *Ann. N.Y. Acad. Sci.*, **254**, 334–349.
Danielsson, D., Olcén, P., and Sandstróm, E. (1977). FEMS Symposium on Gonorrhoea, London, Nov. 1976. In press.
Danielsson, D., and Sandstróm, E. (1977). (To be published.)
Deacon, W. E., Peacock, W. L., Freeman, E. M., and Harris, A. (1959). *Proc. Soc. exp. Biol. Med.*, **101**, 322–326.
Deacon, W. E., Peacock, W. L., Freeman, E. M., Harris, A., and Bunch, W. L. (1960) *Publ. Hlth Rep.*, **75**, 125–129.
Esquenazi, V., and Streitfeld, M. M. (1973). *Can. J. Microbiol.*, **19**, 1099–1102.
Faur, Y. C., Weisburd, M. H., and Wilson, M. E. (1975). *J. clin. Microbiol.*, **2**, 178–182.
Fletcher, S., Miller, R., and Nicol, C. S. (1973). *Br. J. vener. Dis.*, **49**, 508–510.
Forsgren, A., and Sjöquist, J. (1967). *J. Immun.*, **99**, 19–24.
Harris, A., Deacon, W. E., Tiedemann, J., and Peacock, W. L. (1961). *Publ. Hlth Rep.*, **76**, 93–97.
Hermanies, J. (1921). *J. inf. Dis.*, **28**, 133–142.
Hutchinson, R. I. (1970). *Br. med. J.*, **3**, 107.
Jephcott, A. E., Reyn, A., and Birch-Andersen, A. (1971). *Acta path. microbiol. scand.*, Section B, **79**, 437.
Juhlin, I. and Winblad, S. (1973). *Acta path. microbiol. scand.*, Section B, **81**, 179–180.
Kellogg, D. S., Jr, Peacock, W. L., Deacon, W. E., Brown, L., and Pirkle, C. I. (1963). *J. Bact.*, **85**, 1274–1279.
Kellogg, D. S., Jr, Cohen, I. R., Norins, L. C., Schroeter, A. L., and Reising, G. (1968). *J. Bact.*, **96**, 596–605.
Kellogg, D. S., Jr, and Thayer, J. D. (1969). *Ann. Rev. Med.*, **20**, 323–328.

Kearns, D. H., Seibert, G. B., O'Reilly, R., Lee, L., and Logan, L. (1973). *New Engl. J. Med.*, **289**, 1170–1174.

Kraus, S. J., Perkins, G. H., and Geller, R. C. (1970). *Infect. Immun.*, **2**, 655–658.

Kronvall, G. (1973). *J. med. Microbiol.*, **6**, 187–190.

Lancefield, R. C. (1933). *J. exp. Med.*, **57**, 571–595.

Ling, I. (1975). *Ann. N.Y. Acad. Sci.*, **254**, 400–406.

Lüderitz, O., Staub, A. M., and Westphal, O. (1966). *Bact. Rev.*, **30**, 192–255.

Maeland, J. A. (1966). *Acta path. microbiol. scand.*, **67**, 102–110.

Maeland, J. A. (1967). *Acta path. microbiol. scand.*, **69**, 145–155.

Marland, J. A. (1968). *Acta path. microbiol. scand.*, **73**, 413–422.

Maeland, J. A. (1969a). *Acta path. microbiol. scand.*, **76**, 475–483

Maeland, J. A. (1969b). *Acta path. microbiol. scand.*, **76**, 484–492.

Maeland, J. A. (1969c). *Acta path. microbiol. scand.*, **77**, 495–504.

Maeland, J. A. (1969d). *Acta path. microbiol. scand.*, **77**, 505–507.

Maeland, J. A., and Kristoffersen, T. (1971). *Acta path. microbiol. scand.*, Section B, **79**, 226–232.

Maeland, J. A., Kristoffersen, T., and Hofstad, T. (1971). *Acta path. microbiol. scand.*, Section B, **79**, 233–238.

Maeland, J. A. and Larsen, B. (1971). *Br. J. vener. Dis.*, **47**, 269–272.

Maeland, J. A. and Larsen, B., (1971). *Br. J. vener. Dis.*, **51**, 92–96.

Maeland, J. A. and Matre, R. (1975). *Br. J. vener. Dis.*, **51**, 176–178.

Mueller, R., and Oppenheimer, M. (1906). *Wien. Klin. Wschr.*, **19**, 894–898.

Neter, E., Westphal, Ol., Lüderitz, Ol., Sorzynski, E. A., and Eichenberger, E. (1956). *J. Immun.*, **75**, 377–385.

Novotny, P., and Turner, W. H. (1975). *J. gen. Microbiol.*, **89**, 87–92.

Olcén, P., Danielsson, D., and Kjellander, J. (1975). *Acta pathol. microbiol. scand.*, Section B, **83**, 387–396.

Pierce, W. A., Jr, Leong, J. K., and Hough, D. M. (1975). *Infect. Immun.*, **11**, 898–903.

Reising, G., and Kellogg, D. S. (1965). *Proc. Soc. exp. Biol. (N.Y.)*, **120**, 660–663.

Reyn, A. (1949a). *Acta pathol. microbiol. scand.*, **26**, 51–70.

Reyn, A. (1949b). *Acta pathol. microbiol. scand.*, **26**, 234–251.

Reyn, A. (1949c). *Acta pathol. microbiol. scand.*, **26**, 252–268.

Rosenthal, L. (1975). *In* "Genital Infections and Their Complications" (Ed. Danielsson, Juhlin and Mårdh), pp. 261–270. Almquist and Wiksell International, Stockholm.

Sandstrom, E., and Danielsson, D. (1977). *Acta derm.-venereal. (Stockh.)*, in press.

Swanson, J., Kraus, S. J., and Gotschlich, E. C. (1971). *J. exp. Med.*, **134**, 886–906.

Tauber, H., and Garson, W. (1959). *J. biol. Chem.*, **234**, 1391–1393.

Thomas, J. C., and Mennie, A. T. (1950). *Lancet*, **11**, 745–746.

Torrey, J. C. (1906). *J.A.M.A.* Jan., 20.

Torrey, J. C. (1907). *J. med. Res.*, **16**, 329–358.

Torrey, J. C., and Buckell, G. T. (1922). *J. Immun.*, **7**, 305–359.

Uroma, E. (1943). *Acta derm.-venereol. (Stockh.)*, Suppl. 9, 1–74.

Vannod, Th. (1906). *Dt. med. Wschr.*, **32**, 1984–1985.

Vannod, Th. (1907). *Zentbl. Baktl. ParasitKde.*, **44**, 10–11.

Warren, S. H. (1921). *J. Path. Bact.*, **24**, 424–438.

Ward, M. E., and Glynn, A. A. (1972). *J. clin. Path.*, **25**, 56–59.

Watt, P. J., Ward, M. E., and Glynn, A. A. (1971). *Br. J. vener. Dis.*, **47**, 448–451.

Westphal, O., Lüderitz, O., and Bister, F., (1952). *Z. Naturf.*, 7b, 148–155.

Wilson, J. F. (1954). *J. Path. Bact.*, **68**, 495–514.

CHAPTER XIII

Characteristics and Auxotyping of *Neisseria gonorrhoeae*

B. WESLEY CATLIN

Department of Microbiology, Medical College of Wisconsin, Milwaukee, Wisconsin

I. *NEISSERIA* SPECIES

Gonorrhoea has become practically epidemic in spite of antibiotic therapy. The lack of an adequate method to distinguish between strains of *N. gonorrhoeae* for epidemiological studies encouraged the development of a system of typing based on nutritional requirements. Auxotyping subdivides gonococci according to their ability to grow on standard chemically defined agar media which contain or lack certain compounds. The complete medium, NEDA (*Neisseria* defined agar), supports the growth of about 99% of the gonococci isolated from patient material. However, NEDA medium also promotes the growth of most other species of *Neisseria* and many other bacteria. Therefore, it is essential to identify an isolate as *N. gonorrhoeae* before typing it.

A. Infections

The site from which a strain is isolated is not necessarily indicative of
the species of *Neisseria* (Catlin, 1973). *N. meningitidis*, an inhabitant of
the nasopharynx, is a primary cause of septicaemia and meningitis, but has
occasionally been implicated in urogenital infections (Beck *et al.*, 1974).
Although gonorrhoea usually is associated with the urogenital tract, an
appreciable fraction of *N. gonorrhoeae* infections may involve the pharynx
(Wiesner *et al.*, 1973; Stolz and Schuller, 1974) and rectum (Kilpatrick,
1972). Infections of these sites may be symptomatic but are often asymptomatic (Pariser, 1972; Handsfield *et al.*, 1974). Detection of *N. meningitidis*
and *N. gonorrhoeae* in patient specimens which are likely to contain a mixture of other micro-organisms is facilitated by the use of culture media
made selective by the addition of appropriate antibiotics (Thayer and
Martin, 1966; Reyn, 1969).

Complications of gonorrhoea may arise by local extension of infection,
causing epididymitis in men and salpingitis, peritonitis, and perihepatitis
in women. Blood-borne infections may develop in patients with either
symptomatic or asymptomatic gonorrhoea. *N. gonorrhoeae* may be disseminated to many tissues, including the skin, joints, heart, liver, and
meninges (Holmes, 1974).

Disease may be caused occasionally by representatives of various species
which are regarded as non-pathogenic. These include *N. lactamica*, *N.
sicca*, *N. mucosa*, *N. subflava* and related chromogenic neisseriae, and
Branhamella (formerly *Neisseria*) *catarrhalis* (references cited in Catlin,
1974a).

B. Identification

N. gonorrhoeae and members of the species of *Neisseria* listed in Table I
are non-motile, Gram-negative cocci which commonly occur as pairs of
cells with their abutting sides flattened. Species of *Moraxella* and *Acinetobacter*, and some other Gram-negative rod-shaped isolates may grow as
coccoid cells that are easily confused with diplococci (Catlin, 1975). However, bacilli undergo cellular division in one plane only whereas these
neisseriae typically divide in two planes; the second division occurs at a
right angle to the first, resulting in the transient formation of tetrads.
Furthermore, in the presence of low concentrations of penicillins and some
other antibacterial agents which tend to block cross-wall formation, coccobacilli usually elongate and thus reveal their true bacillary form. These
agents do not cause elongation of the coccal neisseriae (Catlin, 1975).

Members of the genus *Neisseria* grow well on complex medium enriched
with heated-blood (chocolate agar) when incubated at 37°C in an atmo-

sphere of air with an increased content of carbon dioxide. After 18–24 h colonies of *N. gonorrhoeae* are smooth, greyish, and relatively small. On further incubation they increase in size and develop roughened surfaces with crenated margins, and their consistency tends to become viscid owing to cellular lysis. Close observation of colonies, especially those which have been subcultured repeatedly and are growing on transparent medium, may reveal four morphological types of colonies (T1–T4) (Kellogg *et al.*, 1963, 1968). Recently isolated cultures contain T1 and T2 colonies which are small (diameters about 0·5 mm in 20 h), glistening, opaque, and have high convex elevations. T3 and T4 colonies are not commonly represented in primary cultures, but appear in subcultures; they are larger (about 1 mm in 20 h) flatter, and less glistening as compared with T1 and T2 colonies (Fig. 1), and T4 is transparent.

(a)   (b)

Fig. 1. Colonies of *N. gonorrhoeae* on NEDA medium; 20 h cultures of strains (a) *SS* 7764/45 (auxotype 22), and (b) *MHD* 787 (auxotype 24) showing smaller T2 and larger T4 colonies, × 10.

All species of *Neisseria* oxidize a solution of 1% (w/v) tetramethyl-*p*-phenylenediamine dihydrochloride, resulting in the development of a dark purple coloration within 10 sec. The species are identified by their reactions in the media indicated in Table I. Strains of *N. gonorrhoeae* typically form acid (without gas) from 1% glucose. Maltose and the other carbohydrates are not attacked, and *o*-nitrophenyl-*β*-D-galactopyranoside (ONPG) is not cleaved. Hydrolysis of ONPG and production of acid from lactose are reactions which differentiate *N. lactamica* from *N. meningitidis*,

TABLE I

Typical characteristics of *Neisseria* species isolated from humans

Species	Colonies		Production of acid from					Synthesis of poly-saccharide from sucrose†
	Yellow pigmentation	Appearance and consistency	Glucose	Maltose	Sucrose	Lactose	Fructose	
N. gonorrhoeae	0	Smooth, small	+	0	0	0	0	0
N. meningitidis	0	Smooth, transparent, butyrous	+	+	0	0	0	0
N. lactamica	+	Smooth, transparent, butyrous	+	+	0	+	0	0
N. sicca	D	Wrinkled, dry, adherent	+	+	+	0	+	+
N. subflava	+	Smooth, transparent or opaque, often adherent	+	+	D‡	0	D‡	D
N. mucosa	D	Mucoid, often adherent	+	+	+	0	+	+
N. flavescens	+	Smooth, opaque	0	0	0	0	0	+
N. (Branhamella) catarrhalis	0	Smooth, opaque, often granular	0	0	0	0	0	0

Reactions: +, positive; 0, negative; D, different, either + or 0.

† Determined by dropping iodine solution (1:5 aqueous dilution of Burke's modification of Gram's iodine) on colonies that have grown for two to three days on an agar medium containing 1–2% (w/v) sucrose; + reaction indicated by rapid development of blue-black colour.

‡ Strains formerly designated *N. perflava* are +.

both of which may be isolated on Thayer–Martin selective medium. *N. gonorrhoeae* and *N. meningitidis* do not initiate growth from small inocula on (i) NaCl-free nutrient agar incubated at 37°C, or (ii) an enriched medium incubated at 22°C in an aerobic atmosphere, or at 37°C in a strictly anaerobic atmosphere. Further information on the various reactions of *Neisseria* is given by Reyn (1965, 1969, 1974) and Catlin (1974a).

Typical *Neisseria* are identified without difficulty. However, some isolates fail to produce acid in media containing 1% (w/v) glucose or some of the other carbohydrates listed in Table I (Reyn, 1965; Catlin, 1973). In some instances, this is due to production of metabolic products which are sufficiently alkaline to neutralize the weak acidity that normally results from the oxidation of glucose. Acid production by these bacteria can often be detected within a few hours when growth from a 20 h culture on "chocolate" agar is suspended (about 10^{10} cells/ml) in a lightly buffered salts solution with 10% glucose (or 10% maltose) together with a pH indicator (Catlin, 1974a). A few strains of *N. gonorrhoeae* or *N. meningitidis* apparently do not attack carbohydrates under any conditions. Their typical reactions on defined agar may aid identification. *N. meningitidis* has relatively few nutritional requirements; strains will grow on an agar medium containing mineral salts, lactate, and a few amino-acids (Catlin, 1973). On NEDA medium, their colonies are much larger than those of *N. gonorrhoeae*. Cystine (or cysteine) is required for growth of all strains (> 1000 tested) of *N. gonorrhoeae*, but of only 10% of *N. meningitidis* strains (50 tested). Therefore, the finding of equivalent amounts of growth on complete NEDA medium and on cystine-free NEDA medium (described in Section III.A) is presumptive evidence that a strain is not *N. gonorrhoeae*.

II. CHARACTERISTICS OF *N. GONORRHOEAE* POTENTIALLY USEFUL FOR TYPING

A. Structural components as antigens

For 70 years investigators have sought a reliable method for separating clinical isolates of *N. gonorrhoeae* into antigenically distinct types. Many different procedures have been used, but in general it is necessary to (i) obtain a gonococcal antigen preparation from each of a number of strains, (ii) prepare antisera by injection of experimental animals with the antigen preparations, (iii) absorb the antisera with selected antigens to remove cross-reacting antibodies, and (iv) detect reactions of the test antigen preparations with antibodies in one or more of the antisera. The techniques used for these assays have included agglutination, complement fixation, precipitation (Hutchinson, 1970), complement-mediated bactericidal action (Glynn and Ward, 1970; Tramont *et al.*, 1974), immunodiffusion (Apicella,

1974), indirect haemagglutination and haemagglutination inhibition (Maeland, 1969; Maeland *et al.*, 1971; Apicella and Allen, 1973), radioimmuno-
assay (Buchanan, 1975), or immune electron microscopy (Novotny and
Turner, 1975).

Wilson and Miles (1964) summarized the findings of 50 years of serological research with *N. gonorrhoeae* as indicating that probably there are
two main types having different degrees of antigenic complexity, together
with a number of intermediate types which contain one or more antigens
common to both main types. The Lancefield precipitin technique developed
for the classification of haemolytic streptococci was used by Hutchinson
(1970) for a study of the reactions of 181 strains of *N. gonorrhoeae* in five
absorbed antisera. One hundred strains were differentiated into five serotypes, whereas the remaining strains either gave no reaction in these sera
(38 strains) or reacted in two or more sera (43 strains), substantiating the
antigenic complexity of the gonococci. Many of the other recent investigations cited above have been directed primarily toward isolating and characterizing various gonococcal antigens which might serve as a basis for the
development of serotyping systems.

As viewed by electron microscopy, the cellular envelope of *N. gonorrhoeae* consists of multiple layers: the inner cytoplasmic membrane, a
dense lamina (the peptidoglycan layer), and the convoluted trilaminar
outer membrane (Swanson *et al.*, 1971; Novotny *et al.*, 1975). Some
preparations show portions of the outer membrane budded off or pulled
away from underlying layers, leaving the cell largely intact. Some of the
peeled-off material is considered to be endotoxin (Novotny *et al.*, 1975;
Stead *et al.*, 1975). Long, thin structures (fimbriae or pili), arise from the
cellular surface (Jephcott *et al.*, 1971; Swanson *et al.*, 1971). These fimbriae
are often numerous on cultured gonococci that form T1 and T2 colonies
and possess virulence for humans (Kellogg *et al.*, 1963, 1968). Gonococci
observed in urethral exudates from men with acute gonorrhoea exhibit
smoother surfaces and only a few fimbriae compared to gonococci grown
in culture media (Novotny *et al.*, 1975). The fimbriae produced by different
gonococcal strains are antigenically heterogeneous (Buchanan, 1975; Novotny and Turner, 1975). During multiplication in laboratory cultures, gonococci that produce T1 and T2 colonies undergo frequent genetic changes
leading to the appearance of variants which produce T3 and T4 colonies
and lack virulence (Kellogg *et al.*, 1963, 1968). Since the initial observations
of gonococcal fimbriae, investigators have been in agreement that T3 and
T4 variants lack definable fimbriae. Genetic instability of fimbriation
might imply that a system of typing based on antigens borne exclusively
by fimbriae would yield a substantial fraction of untypable strains. However, gonococci lacking fimbriae might remain typable if fimbrial antigen(s)

also are present in membranes of T3 cells, as is suggested by the immune electron microscopy observations of Novotny and Turner (1975).

Endotoxin preparations extracted from gonococci consist of protein with smaller amounts of lipid and carbohydrate. Antigenic determinants are associated with the carbohydrate component (determinant *a*) and with the protein component (determinant *b*) (Maeland, 1969; Apicella, 1974; Apicella and Allen, 1973). The *a* determinants exhibit six different antigenic specificities, and promise to be useful for serotyping (Maeland 1969; Maeland *et al.*, 1971). The protein determinant *b* obtained from three strains does not differ serologically, and is thought to be a group-reactive antigen common to both *N. gonorrhoeae* and *N. meningitidis* (Maeland, 1969).

A different approach to the preparation of envelope antigens was employed by Johnston and Gotschlich (1974). They isolated the envelope from gonococcal spheroplasts and separated it into cytoplasmic and outer membrane fractions. Analysis of the outer membrane by sodium dodecyl sulphate-polyacrylamide disc gel electrophoresis showed a relatively simple protein spectrum. One of the peaks accounted for 66% of the protein. Antigenic differences between the principal protein of outer membrane preparations from different gonococci are being investigated. Thus far Johnston *et al.* (1976) have discriminated 16 distinct serotypes.

B. Susceptibilities to inhibitory agents

Phages, bacteriocins, antibiotics, and a variety of chemical compounds have been used successfully to distinguish types within some bacterial species. Thus far no one has reported the isolation of bacterial viruses capable of lysing *N. gonorrhoeae*. Bacteriocins are antibacterial agents produced by bacteria which typically are (i) more active against other members of the same or closely related species than against the producer strain itself, (ii) protein in composition, and (iii) evoked by ultraviolet irradiation, Mitomycin C, or other inducing agents. A note by Flynn and McEntegart (1972) reported that bacteriocins produced by *N. gonorrhoeae* were useful for typing 75% of 100 isolates on the basis of characteristic patterns of growth-inhibition. Walstad *et al.* (1974) and Knapp *et al.* (1975) confirmed that *N. gonorrhoeae* produces growth-inhibitory substances, but concluded that the inhibitors were not typical bacteriocins. The antibacterial compounds were active against the producer strains as well as against other gonococci, were resistant to inactivation by heat, alkali, and proteolytic enzymes, and the concentrations produced were not increased by inducing agents. Differences between strains with respect to the amount of inhibitor produced or sensitivity to inhibition were found, but were considered to be insufficient for use in routine typing of gonocccci (Walstad *et al.*, 1974; Knapp *et al.*, 1975).

The antigonococcal action of the inhibitor described by Flynn and McEntegart (1972) was weak and inconsistent on "chocolate" blood agar. Also, 1% soluble starch or 2% (w/v) bovine serum albumin (Walstad *et al.*, 1974) or 10% inactivated horse serum (Knapp *et al.*, 1975) reduced or annulled the activity of this inhibitor. Starch and blood have long been recognized as agents which biologically neutralize toxic compounds present in culture media (Gould *et al.*, 1944; Evans and Smith, 1974). A compound which inhibited growth of about 50% of gonococci was isolated by Ley and Mueller (1946) from agar by continuous methanol extraction. The compound appeared to be a fatty acid, and corresponding inhibitory activities were exhibited by low concentrations of oleic and stearic acids.

A growth inhibitor produced by seven different strains of *N. gonorrhoeae* was isolated by Walstad *et al*, (1974) from chloroform–methanol extracts of washed whole cells. Antigonococcal activity was found in both the free (unesterified) fatty acid and the phospholipid fractions of the gonococcal lipids. Also, certain purified free fatty acids (myristic, palmitic, oleic, *cis*-vaccinic, palmitoleic, and ricinoleic) at concentrations of 0·001M inhibited the growth of *N. gonorrhoeae* strain FA5. Phosphatidylethanolamine (PE) was ineffective, but monoacyl PE at a concentration of 0·01M was inhibitory. Walstad, Reitz and Sparling (1974) postulated that the inhibitor found in cultures of gonococci results from the degradation of PE to inhibitory long-chain free fatty acids and monoacyl PE.

Growth of *N. gonorrhoeae* is also inhibited by a factor produced by practically all strains of *Candida albicans* (Hipp *et al.*, 1974, 1975). The inhibitory activity was originally investigated because the recovery of gonococci appeared to be impaired by the presence of this species of yeast which contained some cervical specimens transported to the laboratory on the Transgrow medium of Martin and Lester (1971). The technique for demonstrating the inhibitor involved streaking strains of *C. albicans* as 2 cm lanes across the surface of GC medium base (Difco) supplemented with Isovitalex (BBL) and incubating the culture at 37°C for 18–24 h. The agar was then loosened and inverted into the lid of the Petri dish; gonococci were streaked on the unused surface of the agar perpendicular to the yeast streaks, and the dish was incubated (37°C, 18–24 h). Gonococcal growth on areas of the medium distant from the *C. albicans* and absence of growth close to the yeast indicated sensitivity to the inhibitor. A grouping of gonococci was based on the responses to (a) inhibitor produced by five reference strains of *C. albicans* selected for potent inhibitor activity, and (b) inhibitor produced by the particular *C. albicans* strain isolated together with the gonococcus from a given transport medium specimen. Hipp *et al.*

(1975) divided 27 gonococcal isolates into three groups: (i) nine strains resistant to (a) and (b), (ii) 12 strains resistant to (b) and sensitive to (a), and (iii) six strains sensitive to (a) and (b).

Tests of other strains under different conditions (Catlin, unpublished observations) confirm the finding of Hipp *et al.* (1974) that a compound is produced by *C. albicans* which may inhibit the growth of gonococci (Fig. 2). A modified two-stage technique was used. For the first stage, a suspension of *C. albicans* was spread in a lane 1·0 cm-wide across the middle of a sterile nitrocellulose membrane (Millipore, type HA, 47 mm diameter) that had been centrally placed on the surface of supplemented GC medium

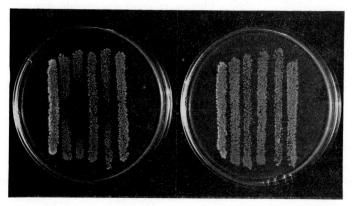

FIG. 2. Response of *N. gonorrheoae* to an inhibitory agent produced by *Candida albicans*. Second stage of procedure described in text showing (*a*) test, and (b) control cultures of six gonococcal isolates streaked in the following order: 762 (at left), 714, 667, 703, 661, and 741 (at right).

base agar in a 100 mm Petri dish. Corresponding preparations were incubated at 36°C for one and two days and at 24°C for two to four days. Dishes of medium with uninoculated membranes were incubated in parallel as controls. For the second stage, the membrane with its yeast growth was lifted off and discarded. The surface of the sterile underlying medium was streaked with up to six gonococcal isolates perpendicular to the lane containing inhibitor, and then the Petri dish was incubated at 36°C for 24 h. The differences between the responses of *MHD* 714, 667, 703, and 661 observed in Fig. 2a were only quantitative, and were minimized by incubation of the *C. albicans* culture for longer than the 42 h at 24°C used here. Therefore, it was not surprising that the differences found for these and other gonococci were difficult to reproduce in various tests with ten strains of *C. albicans*. The *N. gonorrhoeae* isolates *MHD* 762 and 741 were unaffected in tests with nine *C. albicans* strains, but were moderately inhibited by another *C. albicans* strain which produced wide zones of inhibition of most *N. gonorrhoeae* isolates. In spite of such differences of susceptibility, I concluded that the *C. albicans* inhibitor was not likely to be useful in routine typing of *N. gonorrhoeae* unless it could be purified and used as a sterile solution of known concentration.

Differences of gonococcal susceptibility to Penicillin, Streptomycin, and one or more other antibiotics have been used by various investigators as an aid in distinguishing treatment failure from reinfection (for example, Reyn and Bentzon, 1963; Silver and Darling, 1971; Schofield *et al.*, 1971), and in differentiating between false and true sources of a patient's infection (Schmidt and Larsen, 1962). The tendency of susceptible strains to become increasingly resistant to antibiotics, possibly even during treatment of a given patient, and the difficulty of obtaining reproducible resistance patterns with simple disc tests have been deterrents to the use of antibiotic susceptibility as a means of typing *N. gonorrhoeae* (Phillips *et al.*, 1970; Sparling, 1972; Holmes, 1974). However, when used to differentiate strains of one of the common auxotypes, antibiotic susceptibility patterns are useful. This will be described in Section IV.

C. Nutritional requirements

Strains of *N. gonorrhoeae* isolated from patients are cultivated on complex media enriched with components of blood. Studies of the nutritional requirements of gonococci isolated during 1942–45 from patients in Texas (Lankford and Skaggs, 1946) revealed that, although a proteose peptone–haemoglobin medium supported growth of the majority of strains, up to 25% had an additional requirement for glutamine. Some other isolates required thiamine pyrophosphate (THPP) for growth. The requirements for these compounds could be detected because they were lacking in autoclaved media. Subsequently, when chemically defined media were developed, many other compounds were identified as essential for growth of gonococci isolated from patients (Catlin, 1973; Carifo and Catlin, 1973; LaScolea and Young, 1974).

A requirement for cysteine (or cystine) is typical of all representatives of *N. gonorrhoeae*. In addition, some strains have specific requirements for one or more compounds which may include proline, methionine, histidine, lysine, arginine, hypoxanthine, uracil, and THPP. Furthermore, isoleucine, leucine, valine, and serine may be either stimulatory or required for growth of some gonococci. Some isolates will grow on a defined medium containing cysteine, but lacking all of the other compounds listed, whereas other gonococci will grow only if the medium is supplemented with some or most of the compounds. Recognition of this nutritional heterogeneity led to the development of auxotyping, a practical method for typing *N. gonorrhoeae*.

Each nutritional requirement indicates that the bacteria (which are called auxotrophic) are unable to perform an essential enzyme-catalysed step in the biosynthesis of a particular metabolite. These auxotrophic gonococci possess hereditary defects many of which are repairable by genetic transformation using deoxyribonucleic acid (DNA) isolated from a strain of *N. gonorrhoeae* that possesses the corresponding biosynthetic function (Catlin, 1974b). Transformation thus provides a rigorous means of verifying the hereditary basis of the nutritional requirements of gonococci, and also of analysing the various biosynthetic pathways. Nutritional requirements for proline, methionine, histidine, lysine, arginine, hypoxanthine, uracil, or THPP may be eliminated by genetic transformation (Catlin, 1974b, and unpublished observations).†

The requirement for THPP provides an example of a biosynthetic pathway of clinical isolates which has been analysed genetically. The growth requirement of some gonococci (here designated Thi) is satisfied either by thiamine or by THPP, whereas the requirement of Thp strains is satisfied only by THPP. Preparations of purified DNA from Thp strains repair the defect of Thi recipient bacteria, with the result that transformed bacteria require neither thiamine nor THPP. In reciprocal experiments treatment of Thp recipient gonococci with DNA from Thi bacteria eliminates the requirement for THPP, enabling the transformants to form colonies on medium lacking either THPP or thiamine. The sequence of these biosynthetic reactions is revealed by results of syntrophism tests, as follows. Thi and Thp gonococci are streaked on neighbouring areas of a defined medium which lacks THPP and thiamine (Fig. 3). Thp cells undergo limited growth and produce a compound biologically equivalent to thiamine which they are unable to use. This product diffuses some distance into the medium and "feeds" Thi cells, promoting the development of macrocolonies. The Thi bacteria do not form a compound which "feeds" Thp gonococci. This evidence indicates that the genetic block of Thi strains precedes that of Thp strains.

An auxotype is defined by a distinctive pattern of nutritional traits determined by tests of the ability of gonococci to grow on the standard defined media. Tests of 333 gonococcal isolates using the set of defined

† According to normal genetic usage, a strain which possesses a specific nutritional requirement for THPP would be designated Thp⁻. However, in this Chapter the designation Thp will be used. Similarly, for all other auxotropic traits the superscript mark will be omitted. This convention will simplify the abbreviations of the phenotypes determined by auxotyping.

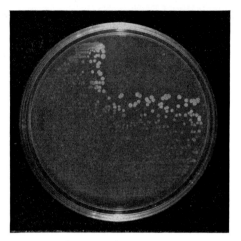

FIG. 3. Growth responses of two strains of *N. gonorrhoeae* which are defective in different steps of thiamine pyrophosphate biosynthesis. Macrocolonies are formed by the Thi strain "fed" by a thiamine-like compound produced by Thp gonococci (upper right area of medium) growing as microcolonies on a medium lacking thiamine pyrophosphate.

NEDA media described by Carifo and Catlin (1973) yielded examples of 22 different auxotypes. These were based upon the growth-responses to proline, arginine, ornithine, methionine, hypoxanthine, uracil, THPP, and thiamine. An abridged set of NEDA media was used for auxotyping a group of gonococci investigated by Knapp and Holmes (1975). The set of media described in Section III, which additionally tests requirements for histidine, lysine, and leucine, has detected 13 new auxotypes thus far (Catlin, unpublished results). In preparation for genetic studies, LaScolea and Young (1974) reduced the number of components in the NEDA medium and employed their medium (designated GGM) to demonstrate requirements for proline, arginine, isoleucine, and serine. Morello, Lerner and Bohnhoff (1976) modified the GGM medium and, using additional differential compounds, subdivided 216 gonococci into 20 types. These several studies clearly establish that strains of *N. gonorrhoeae* can be differentiated on the basis of their patterns of nutritional requirements.

III. TECHNICAL PROCEDURES FOR AUXOTYPING

A. Chemically defined culture media

The procedures and equipment required for gonococcal auxotyping are familiar and readily accessible to most bacteriologists. The main task involves preparing chemically defined culture media satisfactorily for growth of the biosynthetically diverse gonococci. The components must be of the highest purity—free of growth-inhibitory contaminants and of unwanted amino-acids or vitamins.

1. *Complete NEDA medium*

All components of the complete medium are listed in Table II. Most of the stock solutions are prepared in advance and stored at 4–6°C. Glass-distilled water is used for all solutions. Glassware must be scrupulously clean. The containers in which solutions are autoclaved or stored are preferably Pyrex glass, screw-top bottles and tubes (or equivalent) closed with caps fitted with nontoxic plastic liners. Solutions 1, 3, 5, 6, $CaCl_2$, and agar are sterilized by autoclaving at 121°C for 15–20 min depending on volume. Other solutions (with a few exceptions to be specified) are sterilized by filtration through sterile nitrocellulose membranes with 0·22–0·45 μm apertures. The preparation of each solution is described below.

Solution 1 is made in two steps. First, add 13·0 g of L-glutamic acid, 5·0 g of L-aspartic acid, and 37·0 mg of disodium ethylenediaminetetra-acetate (EDTA) to 900 ml of water in a beaker held at 50°C in a water bath. These compounds dissolve during the slow addition of NaOH sufficient to give a final pH of 7·2. The total volume of 5N NaOH (approximately 25 ml) is added in aliquots over a period of about 20 min with frequent stirring. The pH is determined at intervals with Bromothymol blue indicator. Solution 1 is completed by addition of: NaCl, 58·0 g; K_2SO_4, 10·0 g; $MgCl_2 \cdot 6H_2O$, 4·1 g; NH_4Cl, 2·2 g; and water sufficient to give a total volume of 1·0 litre.

To prepare 200 ml of **solution 3**, weigh 10·0 g of sodium lactate (60% syrup) and admix with 150 ml of water. Add 36·8 g of glycerol (glycerin) and 200·0 mg of polyvinyl alcohol (Matheson, Coleman, and Bell); dissolve by heating in a water bath at 100°C for 15–30 min with frequent stirring. Cool, add NaOH to bring the pH to 7·3 (Bromothymol blue indicator), add water sufficient to give a final volume of 195 ml, and sterilize (121°C, 15 min). Then add 5·0 ml of a 20% (v/v) solution of neutralized, sterile (121°C, 15 min) Tween 80 (polyoxyethylene sorbitan monoleate).

Solution 5 contains 34·8 g of K_2HPO_4 and 27·2 g of KH_2PO_4 in water sufficient to make 2 litres. Calcium chloride solution contains $CaCl_2 \cdot 2H_2O$, 3·68 g in 100 ml of water.

Solution 2a contains in 200 ml of water: L-arginine·HCl, 3·0 g; glycine, 500·0 mg; L-serine, 1·0 g. **Solution 2b** contains in 200 ml of water: L-leucine, 1·8 g; L-isoleucine, 600 mg; L-valine, 1·2 g. **Solution 8** contains in 200 ml of water: L-tryptophan, 1·6 g (dissolved at 50°C); L-threonine, 1·0 g; L-alanine, 2·0 g; L-lysine·HCl, 1·0 g; L-proline, 1·0 g. **Solution 9**

contains 1·0 g of L-phenylalanine and 1·0 g of L-asparagine·H$_2$O dissolved in 200·0 ml of water at 50°C.

The following seven solutions are separately prepared with the single compounds dissolved in water sufficient to give final volumes of 100 ml:

TABLE II

Components of complete defined medium (NEDA)†

Solution	Volume (ml) for 1 litre
Solution 1: L-glutamic acid, L-aspartic acid, disodium ethylenediaminetetraacetate, NaCl, K$_2$SO$_4$, MgCl$_2$·6H$_2$O, NH$_4$Cl	100·0
Solution 2a: L-arginine hydrochloride, glycine, L-serine	10·0
Solution 2b: L-leucine, L-isoleucine, L-valine	10·0
Solution 3: sodium lactate, glycerol, polyvinyl alcohol, Tween 80	5·0
Solution 4a: uracil, 17·8mM	4·0
Solution 4b: hypoxanthine, 5·88mM	4·0
Solution 5: K$_2$HPO$_4$, KH$_2$PO$_4$	200·0
L-Tyrosine, 0·05 M solution	6·0
L-Cysteine·HCl·H$_2$O, 0·1M solution	3·5
L-Cystine, 0·05M solution	3·0
cis-Oxaloacetic acid, 15·2mM solution	100·0
NaOH, 5N solution sufficient to give pH 7·1	
Solution 8: L-tryptophan, L-threonine, L-alanine, L-lysine hydrochloride, L-proline	10·0
Solution 9: L-phenylalanine, L-asparagine monohydrate	5·0
L-Glutamine, 0·068M solution	5·0
L-Histidine, 0·05M solution	2·0
L-Methionine, 0·1M solution	1·0
Spermine tetrahydrochloride, 0·05M solution	5·0
Sodium bicarbonate, 1·0M solution	0·5
Dextrose, 20·0% solution	25·0
Sodium acetate, 2·5M solution	10·0
Solution 6: haemin, L-histidine, 2,2′,2″-nitrilotriethanol	2·0
Solution 7: nicotinamide adenine dinucleotide, thiamine hydrochloride, calcium pantothenate	0·2
Solution 10: choline chloride, myo-inositol	0·2
(+) Biotin solution	1·0
Thiamine pyrophosphate chloride, 0·01M solution	0·1
NaOH, 1N solution sufficient to give pH 7·4±0·05	
Molten agar, 2%	500·0
CaCl$_2$·2H$_2$O, 0·25M solution	1·0
Fe(NO$_3$)$_3$·9H$_2$O, 0·01M solution	1·0

† Given in order of addition of sterile solutions; preparation of solutions is described in text.

(i) L-glutamine, 1·0 g; (ii) L-histidine, 776 mg; (iii) L-methionine, 1·49 g; (iv) spermine tetrahydrochloride, 1·74 g, (v) $NaHCO_3$, 8·4g; (vi) dextrose (glucose), 20 g; (vii) sodium acetate ($NaC_2H_3O_2 \cdot 3H_2O$), 34.0 g.

Solution 4a contains 200·0 mg of uracil dissolved in 2·0 ml of 5N NaOH and diluted with 98 ml of water. **Solution 4b** contains 80·0 mg of hypoxanthine dissolved in 10·0 ml of 1N HCl followed by addition of 90 ml of water. $Fe(NO_3)_3 \cdot 9H_2O$, 101·0 mg, is dissolved in 25·0 ml of water.

Solution 7 contains in 50·0 ml of water: nicotinamide adenine dinucleotide, 500·0 mg; thiamine hydrochloride, 250·0 mg; calcium pantothenate, 500·0 mg. THPP solution contains 115·0 mg of thiamine pyrophosphate chloride in 25·0 ml of water. Each solution is filter-sterilized, and volumes convenient for a single use are aseptically dispensed into sterile vials with tight closures for storage at −15 to −20°C.

Solution 6 contains 100·0 mg of haemin dissolved in 4·0 ml of 2,2',2"-nitrilotriethanol; then 96 ml of water and 100·0 mg of L-histidine are added. Solution 6, tubed in single-use volumes, is sterilized (121°C, 15 min), and stored at −20°C. **Solution 10** contains choline chloride, 349·0 mg, and myo-inositol, 90·0 mg, dissolved in 50 ml of water, and filter-sterilized.

(+) Biotin is a saturated solution in 50% (v/v) ethanol slightly acidified (pH 3–5) with HCl; it is not sterilized, but is stored at 4°C.

The following solutions are not stored, but are prepared in appropriate quantities on the day that the medium is made. The final preparations usually are sterile when made in sterile glassware and with sterile water. L-Tyrosine, 181·2 mg, is dissolved in 5·0 ml of 1N HCl and diluted with 15·0 ml of water. L-Cysteine·HCl·H_2O, 350·2 mg, is dissolved in 4·0 ml of 1N HCl and diluted with 16·0 ml of water. L-Cystine, 240·3 mg, is dissolved in 5·0 ml of 1N HCl and diluted with 15·0 ml of water. *cis*-Oxaloacetic acid, 200 mg, is dissolved in 100 ml of water.

The agar must be a highly purified product of high gel strength and low fatty acid content, which has been appropriately washed (see Section III.F). It is convenient to make up the agar (10·0 g in 500 ml of water) and sterilize it on the same day that the preparation is to be used in the medium. The hot agar is well mixed and held in a water bath at 50°C until added to the remainder of the medium.

The fluid portion of the NEDA medium is made up aseptically by admixing the sterile stock solutions in the volumes and order given in Table II. After adding the oxaloacetic acid, the medium is neutralized (pH 7·1) with 5N NaOH (drops of the medium being tested with Bromothymol blue indicator in a spot plate). Following addition of the last vitamin solution, 1N NaOH is added to adjust the pH to 7·4 ± 0·05. During this procedure use a pH meter to test small volumes of the medium (aseptically removed and then discarded); an irreversible precipitate develops above pH 7·5.

(Instead of mixing the solutions aseptically, this portion of the medium may be sterilized by filtration after adjustment of the pH.) Warm the medium to 50°C, combine it with the molten agar, and add the solutions of calcium and iron. The completed medium is dispensed in 25 ml volumes into flat-bottom (100 × 15 mm) Petri dishes. Leave the dishes at 20–24°C for about 20 h to reduce surface moisture; then place them in an inverted position (bottom up) in sterile plastic bags for storage at 4–6°C. Under these conditions the medium remains satisfactory for use for longer than four months.

The complete medium contains L-amino acids in the following final concentrations (mM): alanine, 1·12; arginine·HCl, 0·71; asparagine·H₂O, 0·17; aspartic acid, 3·76; cysteine·HCl·H₂O, 0·35; cystine, 0·15; glutamic acid, 8·83; glutamine, 0·34, glycine, 0·33; histidine (including that of solution 6), 0·113; isoleucine, 0·23; leucine, 0·69; lysine·HCl, 0·27; methionine, 0·10; phenylalanine, 0·15; proline, 0·434; serine, 0·48; threonine, 0·42; tryptophan, 0·39; tyrosine, 0·30; valine, 0·51. Other final concentrations (mM) are: spermine·4HCl, 0·25; haemin, 0·003; hypoxanthine, 0·024; uracil, 0·071; biotin, approximately 0·003; calcium pantothenate, 0·004; choline chloride, 0·010; myo-inositol, 0·002; nicotinamide adenine dinucleotide, 0·003; thiamine·HCl, 0·003; thiamine pyrophosphate chloride, 0·001.

2. *Other auxotyping media*

Table III lists the other defined media which comprise the auxotyping set recommended at the present time. These media differ from the complete NEDA medium only with respect to the differential compounds omitted or added. Solution 2a lacking L-arginine hydrochloride, solution 2b lacking L-leucine, and solution 8 lacking L-lysine hydrochloride and L-proline are needed, together with two other solutions. L-Ornithine hydrochlororide, 16·9 mg/ml (0·1M) 7·0 ml is used/litre of –ARG + ORN medium. A solution of thiamine hydrochloride 3·37 mg/ml (0·01M) 0·6 ml is added/litre of −V + THI medium.

Some workers will prefer to dispense the −V, −V + THI, and −V + THPP media into containers smaller than the 100 × 15 mm Petri dishes for economical inoculation of single cultures (see Section III.E, 2).

B. Non-defined culture media

Any routine laboratory medium which promotes satisfactory growth of *N. gonorrhoeae* may be used for preliminary subcultures.

GC medium base (Difco) is prepared single strength (36·0 g of dry medium/litre), autoclaved (121°C, 20 min), and supplemented with 10·0 ml of the solution described by White and Kellogg (1965). This supplement

TABLE III

Standard set of 14 defined media for gonococcal auxotyping

Designation	Component omitted from NEDA	Component added to medium (final concn)
Complete NEDA	None	None
–CYS	L-Cysteine·HCl·H$_2$O, L-cystine	None
–PRO	L-Proline	None
–ARG	L-Arginine·HCl	None
–MET	L-Methionine	None
–HIS	L-Histidine, solution 6	None
–LYS	L-Lysine·HCl	None
–LEU	L-Leucine	None
–HYX	Hypoxanthine	None
–URA	Uracil	None
–V	V mixture†	None
–V+THI	V mixture	Thiamine·HCl (0·006mM)
–V+THPP	V mixture	Thiamine pyrophosphate chloride (0·001mM)
–ARG+ORN	L-Arginine·HCl	L-Ornithine·HCl (0·7mM)

† Thiamine pyrophosphate chloride, biotin, and solutions 6, 7, and 10 (Table II).

contains glucose, 40·0 g; L-glutamine, 1·0 g; Fe(NO$_3$)$_3$·9H$_2$O, 50·0 mg; thiamine pyrophosphate chloride, 0·44 ml of the solution used for NEDA medium (Table II); water, sufficient to make a final volume of 100·0 ml. The supplement is sterilized by filtration, and is stored at −15°C.

C. Buffered salts solution

The solution used for preparing gonococcal suspensions is a portion of a defined fluid medium for meningococci (Catlin, 1973). The complete buffered salts solution is prepared by mixing 35 ml of solution A, 5 ml of solution B, 0·1 ml of 0·25M CaCl$_2$·2H$_2$O (as used in NEDA), 0·8 ml of glycerol, and 59 ml of distilled water. The final pH is adjusted to 7·4 by addition of 1N NaOH. **Solution A** contains: NaCl, 5·85 g; KCl, 0·186 g; NH$_4$Cl, 0·401 g; Na$_2$HPO$_4$, 1·065 g; KH$_2$PO$_4$, 0·170 g; Na$_3$C$_6$H$_5$O$_7$·2H$_2$O (sodium citrate), 0·647 g, in 350 ml of distilled water. **Solution B** contains 0·616 g of MgSO$_4$·7H$_2$O and 0·05 ml of a 0·15M solution of MnSO$_4$·H$_2$O in 50 ml of distilled water. The solutions are separately sterilized at 121°C for 15 min.

D. Reference bacteria

Strains needed for testing the adequacy of the auxotyping media are

TABLE IV

Reference strains of *Neisseria gonorrhoeae*

			Accession no.	
Strain	Auxotype	Phenotype	ATCC†	NCTC‡
ODH 2915	1	Zero	27628	10928
MHD 340	5	Thi	27629	10929
MHD 361	9	Pro, Hyx	27630	10930
SS 7764/45	22	Pro, Met, Thp	27631	10931
MCH 3317/70	12	Arg, Met	27632	10932
MHD 446	16	Arg°, Hyx, Ura	27633	10933

† American Type Culture Collection.
‡ National Collection of Type Cultures.

listed in Table IV. Preservation of these and other gonococci at $-60°$ to $-90°C$ is satisfactory and convenient. Cultures on a good non-defined medium incubated for 15–18 h are suspended at a high density (approximately 10^{10} bacteria) in 1 ml of trypticase soy broth (BBL) supplemented with 0·3% (w/v) yeast extract (Difco) and 15% (v/v) glycerol. Multiple vials are prepared, tightly sealed, and frozen without delay. Upon need, the bacteria are thawed at about 24°C, and a heavy inoculum is streaked on a non-defined medium. After incubation of this culture, a mixture of 10–20 typical colonies should be subcultured for use. A strain may be subcultured daily for not longer than a week; the culture is then discarded and a new one established from a frozen stock. The practice of repeated subculturing of single colonies should be avoided because of the risk of selecting mutant gonococci with differing characteristics.

E. Performance of tests

1. *Preparation of bacterial inocula*

Primary cultures isolated from one specimen occasionally represent a mixed infection with two strains of *N. gonorrhoeae* (Catlin and Pace, manuscript in preparation). Therefore, cultures to be typed are subjected to a single "purification" by selection of one typical colony which is subcultured on antibiotic-free non-defined medium. Inocula for all subsequent cultures are taken from multiple typical colonies.

Physiologically active gonococci are needed for auxotyping. In general, a culture on supplemented GC medium base incubated at 36°C for 14–17 h is satisfactory. Older cultures or those held at room temperature for longer than 15–30 min should not be used. The bacterial growth from an appropriate area, preferably some distance from the original site of inoculation, is gently removed with a platinum loop. A smooth suspension is made in 1 ml of sterile buffered salts solution (in an optically clear tube, 1·3 cm in dia.) by rubbing the loop with its mass of bacteria against the moistened inside surface of the tube. The suspension is agitated vigorously using a Vortex mixer and is adjusted to the "standard" density.

"Standard" density corresponds to approximately 1×10^8 colony-forming units (CFU)/ml. Such a suspension when examined in a Spectronic 20 colorimeter gives a reading of 0·100 absorbance at 600 nm. This approximately matches the turbidity of the McFarland barium sulphate standard number 1 (prepared by mixing 0·1 ml of 1% barium chloride aqueous solution with 9·9 ml of 1% H_2SO_4). In addition, if the Steers inocula-replicating apparatus is to be used, two serial dilutions of this standard gonococcal suspension are prepared in buffered salts solution. The first, a 1:10 dilution (to give 10^7 CFU/ml), is slightly turbid when examined in strong indirectly transmitted light and viewed against a dark background. The second dilution, which may be made using a calibrated 0·01 ml platinum loop, yields 10^5 CFU/ml, or less if the gonococci tend to remain in clusters. An experienced worker rapidly prepares the initial suspensions and adjusts their density to that of the McFarland standard. A second person working concurrently makes the subsequent dilutions in order to minimize the time between suspension and inoculation of the gonococci.

2. Inoculation of media

Primary auxotyping requires inoculation of the first 11 media listed in Table III, together with supplemented GC medium base inoculated last as a control. The −ARG + ORN medium is needed only for strains that fail to grow on −ARG medium. Similarly, −V + THI and −V + THPP media are used only for strains that fail to grow on −V medium. Media which were stored at 4°C should be allowed to warm to 20–25°C. Surface moisture which may be visible on the agar is allowed to evaporate by brief exposure of the open dish at 36°C. Medium so dry as to have a slightly wrinkled surface is unsatisfactory for inoculation by streaking, but may be used for inocula-replicating. The plates should be appropriately labelled before preparing the inocula.

Two inoculation procedures are satisfactory. The method originally described (Carifo and Catlin, 1973), which is suitable for processing small numbers of cultures, involves streaking quadrants of each medium (except −V) with a platinum loop (2 mm internal diameter, 24 gauge). The loop is filled with the standard suspension (10^8 CFU/ml), tapped in a uniform way against the inside of the tube to reduce the volume of contained inoculum and streaked lightly over the allotted surface in a manner designed to give isolated colonies. Advantages of this method are that only one suspension is needed, and it can be streaked on the media immediately.

A mechanical device for simultaneous application of inocula is used when the number of cultures to be typed exceeds 16 a day, or when additional media are to be inoculated for antibiotic resistance subtyping. Satisfactory results are obtained with the inocula-replicating apparatus described by Steers *et al.* (1959). This apparatus is available (from Melrose Machine Shop, Woodlyn, Pennsylvania 19094, U.S.A.) in two models. One has an aluminium head carrying 32 equally spaced inoculating rods for use with 100 mm round Petri dishes. The second model carries 36 rods for use with 100 mm square dishes. The aluminium seed plates contain corresponding numbers of reservoirs. The two dilutions (10^7 and 10^5 CFU/ml) of each suspension are pipetted in volumes of 0·5 ml into wells of the seed plate. When all dilutions have been added, the inoculating rods are dipped into the suspensions and the inocula are transferred gently to the surface of the medium. Each plate is inspected to ascertain that all inocula were deposited. If one is missing, apply it with a loop rather than restamping all inocula. Up to 100 plates of media have been sequentially inoculated starting with the defined media and continuing with antibiotic-containing media (preceded and followed by antibiotic-free supplemented GC medium base to determine the constancy of the inocula). The rods deposit approximately 0·002 ml volumes on the agar surface. (Corrosion of the aluminium rods is minimized by careful rinsing to remove the salts solution prior to decontamination by autoclaving.) Other types of replicating devices can be used if corresponding numbers of bacteria are inoculated.

Each strain should be tested separately on –V medium in order to avoid false-positive results due to syntrophy. Medium in a small dish or tube (a slope) is streaked with a scant loopful of the standard suspension. At the same time this suspension is streaked on supplemented GC medium base for possible use the following day as inoculum for –ARG+ORN, –V+THI, or –V+THPP media.

3. *Incubation*

As soon as the drops of inoculum have dried, plates are incubated at 36°C in an atmosphere of air with high humidity and 8–10% carbon dioxide. If a CO_2 incubator is not available, the CO_2 may be generated chemically [$2NaHCO_3 + H_2SO_4 = Na_2SO_4 + 2H_2O + 2CO_2$] in a closed container of known capacity (Reyn, 1965). For example, for plates in a 4·5 litre jar, use 1·5 g of $NaHCO_3$ (placed in a deep Petri dish) with 7 ml of $1N$ H_2SO_4 (contained in a shallow plastic weighing boat taped securely inside the dish). After closing the cover, tilt the jar to mix the acid and base and place the unit in a regular incubator.

4. *Reading and recording of results*

Plates are normally screened after incubation for 18–24 h. Strains which have not produced visible growth on –ARG medium or on –V medium are retested by streaking a standard suspension on complete NEDA and on the one or two appropriate subset media (– ARG + ORN, – V + THI, –V + THPP). All plates are promptly reincubated at 36°C in 8% CO_2. The final reading is made after a total incubation of 48 h. Plates are examined by indirectly transmitted light against a dark background with the aid of a × 5 hand-lens. Attention is given also to the presence of microcolonies visible in light reflected from the agar surface.

A standard suspension streaked on a quadrant of complete NEDA medium normally produces confluent growth at the site streaked with the initial inoculum and semi-confluent growth or discrete colonies on the progressively more distant regions. Different densities of growth due to dilution by streaking correspond, in principle, to the differences obtained with two appropriate dilutions of the suspension deposited by the Steers inoculating rods (Fig. 4a). Results are equally satisfactory with the two inoculation procedures. However, use of the Steers replicator is more efficient and economical.

In reading the results obtained with a given strain, the first step is to compare the amounts of growth on complete NEDA medium and on GC medium base (inoculated after inoculation of all defined media). The quantities of growth on these two media are expected to be similar if the lot of NEDA medium is satisfactory (Fig. 4a, b). The reference strains of *N. gonorrhoeae* (Table IV) are used to determine the growth-promoting qualities of complete NEDA, as well as to ascertain that the growth responses obtained on the differential media are typical. Reading next requires a careful comparison of the growth of the two inocula on complete NEDA with that on each of the other auxotyping media. In addition, the optical characteristics and the sizes of discrete colonies should be noted. Microcolonies, which represent limited cellular multiplication on a medium lacking a compound required for sustained growth, are produced by some gonococci. For example, Thi or Thp strains which have been grown previously on a complete medium store a supply of the required growth factor sufficient for subsequent growth of minute colonies on –V medium.

The following is a suggested system for recording the growth observed at each inoculation site.

+ + = confluent growth.
+ = semi-confluent growth, or > 10 discrete colonies.
± = ≤ 10 colonies: record the number.
0 = no growth.

0m = minute colonies (≤ 0.2 mm diameter), or slight haze with not more than one macrocolony.

sm = colonies smaller than normal, but readily visible (≥ 0.3 mm).

tg = growth is transparent, greyish; opaque, whitish growth is typical and is not recorded.

After the results obtained with a given strain have been recorded for both inoculum densities on the entire set of auxotyping media, the worker is able to decide whether growth on each medium is positive (+ + or + at the heavy inoculum site), negative (0 or 0m at both sites), or doubtful (for example, ± for both inocula or ± and 0). A strain should be retested if a doubtful growth-response is found on any auxotyping medium. A doubtful response often converts to a definite positive response upon additional careful testing of physiologically active cells from a GC medium base culture. The problem of sparse growth on the complete NEDA medium is discussed in Section III.F.

5. *Assignment of auxotypes*

The pattern of growth-responses on auxotyping media is unequivocal for most gonococci. Typical strains of *N. gonorrhoeae* do not grow on –CYS medium. A strain which exhibits growth on all other media is a member of auxotype 1 (Table V). Members of auxotype 2 grow on all media except –CYS and –PRO. Gonococci that fail to grow on medium lacking arginine (–ARG) may be subdivided into two groups (Arg and Arg°) according to their response to ornithine. Strains designated Arg are able to grow on the –ARG + ORN medium. For Arg° strains, on the other hand, ornithine does not substitute for arginine; thus, growth does not occur on –ARG + ORN medium.

Figure 4 illustrates various auxotypes. Results on –V and –LEU media required for establishing auxotypes 5, 22, and 31 are not shown. The paired inocula of each gonococcal isolate were deposited in horizontal rows; their identification numbers and auxotypes are as follows:

Row 1: 756, type 1; 763, type 1
Row 2: 741, type 2; 762, type 3; 703, type 2
Row 3: 249, type 7; 661, type 7; 554, type 5
Row 4: 667, type 1; 928, type 31; *SS*7764/45, reference, type 22
Row 5: 922, type 31; 714, type 9; 584, type 1
Row 6: 776, type 1; 799, type 1

Independent cultures of these gonococci grown on GC medium base have been tested repeatedly because of their particular interest (described in Section V). However, in routine work only strain 714 would be retyped.

The colonies observed here on –MET medium (Fig. 4f) were sparse at both inoculum densities (recorded as ± 9, ± 12, sm, tg). Such a response was not likely to be due to a high frequency of mutation to methionine-nondependence, since the number of spontaneous mutants is expected to be proportional to the number of cells inoculated. In other tests nearly confluent growth was obtained on –MET medium verifying that strain 714 does not require methionine.

F. Precautions and difficulties

Much remains to be learned about the growth responses of gonococci on defined media. Some problems encountered in auxotyping relate to biological differences between particular strains of *N. gonorrhoeae*. For example, the inability of a strain to grow on any one or on all of the NEDA media may be due to the presence of one or more compounds in inappropriate concentrations or, possibly, to the absence of a compound required for growth. Such difficulties are not easily dealt with in routine work. Other problems may be resolved by use of pure compounds or modified methods, as suggested below.

1. *Contamination of media*

Unwanted chemicals introduced inadvertently into the medium may lead to false-positive results due to stimulation of gonococcal growth or to false-negative results if the added chemical alters the pH of the medium or is toxic. The following are examples of some potential sources of contamination.

(a) *Products elaborated by microbial contaminants.* Microbial contamination of the agar media usually is obvious and is remedied by appropriate sterilization of the components. A potential difficulty which is less obvious involves microbial contamination of the water or of a solution which will later be sterilized. *Pseudomonas* and various other organisms are able to multiply in distilled water which has been collected and held in a "clean" container. Such water, although not visibly turbid when used for preparing solutions may introduce metabolic products (e.g. thiamine) in quantities sufficient to promote growth of auxotrophic gonococci (Carifo and Catlin, 1973).

If demineralized by passage through ion exchange resins, the water should be distilled thereafter to remove traces of resin.

Water for all components of the defined media is preferably twice-distilled. Water that will not be used soon after distillation must be sterilized before storage.

TABLE V

Gonococcal auxotypes: growth response patterns on the standard set of defined media†

Auxotype	Phenotype‡	-PRO	-ARG	-MET	-HIS	-LYS	-LEU	-HYX	-URA	-V	-V +THI	-V +THPP	-ARG +ORN
1	Zero	+	+	+	+	+	+	+	+	+	ND§	ND	ND
2	Pro	0	+	+	+	+	+	+	+	+	ND	ND	ND
3	Arg	+	0	+	+	+	+	+	+	+	ND	ND	+
4	Met	+	+	0	+	+	+	+	+	+	ND	ND	ND
5	Thi	+	+	+	+	+	+	+	+	0	+	+	ND
6	Thp	+	+	+	+	+	+	+	+	0	0	+	ND
7	Pro, Arg	0	0	+	+	+	+	+	+	+	ND	ND	+
8	Pro, Met	0	+	0	+	+	+	+	+	+	ND	ND	ND
9	Pro, Hyx	0	+	+	+	+	+	0	+	+	ND	ND	ND
10	Pro, Hyx, Thi	0	+	+	+	+	+	0	+	0	+	+	ND
11	Pro, Arg, Hyx, Ura	0	0	+	+	+	+	0	0	+	ND	ND	+
12	Arg, Met	+	0	0	+	+	+	+	+	+	ND	ND	+
13	Arg, Hyx	+	0	+	+	+	+	0	+	+	ND	ND	+
14	Arg, Hyx, Ura	+	0	+	+	+	+	0	0	+	ND	ND	+
15	Arg, Met, Hyx, Ura	+	0	0	+	+	+	0	0	+	ND	ND	+
16	Arg°, Hyx, Ura	+	0	+	+	+	+	0	0	+	ND	ND	0
17	Arg°, Met, Hyx, Ura	+	0	0	+	+	+	0	0	+	ND	ND	0
18	Arg°, Hyx, Ura, Thp	+	0	+	+	+	+	0	0	0	0	+	0

	Phenotype											
19	Arg, Hyx, Ura, Thp	+	+	+	+	0	0	0	0	0	+	+	+
20	Arg, Hyx, Ura, Thi	+	0	+	+	0	0	0	+	+	0	+	+
21	Pro, Thp	0	+	+	0	+	+	+	0	+	0	+	ND
22	Pro, Met, Thp	0	+	+	+	+	+	+	0	+	0	+	ND
23	Pro, Thi	+	0	+	+	+	+	+	0	+	0	+	ND
24	Arg, Thi	+	+	+	+	+	+	+	0	+	+	+	+
25	Lys	+	+	+	0	+	+	+	+	+	+	+	ND
26	His	+	+	+	0	0	+	+	+	+	ND	ND	ND
27	Arg, His	+	+	+	0	0	+	+	+	+	ND	ND	ND
28	Arg, His, Hyx, Ura	+	+	+	0	+	+	+	0	+	ND	ND	+
29	Arg°, His, Hyx, Ura	+	+	+	0	0	0	0	0	+	ND	ND	+
30	Arg, Leu, Hyx, Ura	+	+	+	+	0	0	0	0	+	ND	ND	0
31	Arg°, Leu, Hyx, Ura	+	+	+	+	0	0	0	0	+	ND	ND	+
32	Arg°, Leu, Hyx, Ura, Thp	+	+	+	+	0	0	0	0	0	+	+	0
33	Pro, Arg°, Met, Hyx, Ura	0	0	0	+	0	0	0	+	+	0	+	0
34	Pro, Arg°, Met, Leu, Hyx, Ura	0	0	+	+	0	0	0	+	+	ND	ND	+
35	Pro, Arg, Hyx, Ura, Thp	0	0	+	+	0	0	0	+	+	0	+	+

† All typable strains of *N. gonorrhoeae* display growth (+) on complete NEDA medium, and absence of growth (0) on –CYS medium.

‡ Phenotypic abbreviations used in auxotyping are simplified by omission of customary superscript marks.

§ ND, test not done.

(b) *Amino acids.* Supposedly pure preparations may contain substantial concentrations of other compounds. Thus, methionine sufficient for growth of a methionine auxotroph was present in a preparation of glutamic acid (Catlin, unpublished) and in a "chromatographically pure" homocystine (Catlin, 1967). Also, a "chromatographically pure" L-leucine was contaminated with both methionine and cystine (Demain, 1965).

(c) *Agar.* This natural product may contain various growth factors (Davis and Mingioli, 1950). To eliminate thiamine and other water-soluble contaminants, the powdered agar is washed by suspending 25 g in 500 ml of distilled water, sedimenting the well-mixed agar by centrifugation, and discarding the supernatant. The sediment is washed twice more with water, followed by two washes with 95% ethanol, and is finally dried thoroughly.

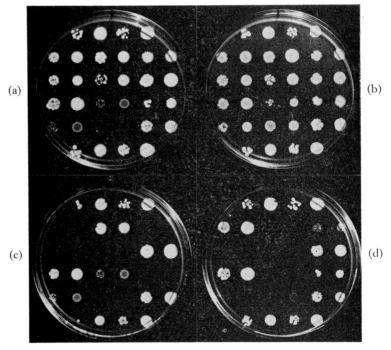

Fig. 4. Growth responses of 16 gonococcal isolates on representative auxotyping media (given in Table III): (a) complete NEDA; (b) supplemented GC medium base; (c) –PRO; (d) –ARG; (e) –ARG+ORN; (f) –MET; (g) –HYX; (h) –URA. Pairs of bacterial suspensions were deposited by Steers inoculating rods at corresponding sites on each medium (diluted inoculum at left, 100-fold higher density at right); cultures were incubated at 36°C for 48 h in air + 8% CO_2

This purification is recommended as a standard procedure for all agar to be incorporated in NEDA media.

Agar also may contain free fatty acids which are toxic for gonococci (Section II.B). Fatty acids are not removed by washing with ethanol but only by more rigorous extraction (Ley and Mueller, 1946). Personal experience with agar (Purified grade, Difco) incorporated in NEDA medium has shown that some lots are essentially free of inhibitory activity; other lots of agar exert antigonococcal activities ranging from slight (partial inhibition of some strains) to complete (absence of growth of all strains of *N. gonorrhoeae*). Other investigators have also encountered difficulty with toxic agar (Knapp and Holmes, 1975). Slight inhibitory activity is annulled by soluble starch. Some workers may choose to add 0·1% starch routinely, as was done for the defined medium of LaScolea and Young (1974). In this case, 1·0 g of reagent grade starch is added to 500 ml of agar in water and both dissolved with frequent stirring while heated in a boiling water bath.

Since starch may be contaminated, the use of Dowex-1 anionic exchange resin in the medium has also been studied (Catlin, unpublished experi-

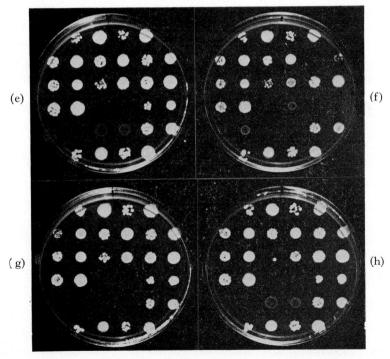

(e)

(f)

(g)

(h)

Fig. 4 (e–h)

ments). This satisfactorily replaced blood or starch in a liquid culture medium for *Bordetella pertussis* (Sutherland and Wilkinson, 1961). Like starch, Dowex-1 (Bio-Rad analytical grade AG1-X8) exhibits detoxifying effects when incorporated in NEDA medium. Before use, the resin is treated with 1N NaOH, washed exhaustively with distilled water, and dried. The resin, added 2·0 g/litre of agar, is present during autoclaving, and is discarded after decanting the agar. Fresh resin (previously autoclaved in water) is added, 1·0 g to a litre of NEDA medium which is then frequently mixed to prevent settling of the resin as the medium is poured into Petri dishes.

(d) *Tween 80*. This mixture of polyoxyethylene ethers of mixed partial oleic esters of sorbitol anhydrides is useful, presumably reducing the toxicity of fatty acids by complexing them in micellar form. However, some preparations of Tween 80 may contain free fatty acids. If necessary, these can be extracted with a mixture of isopropyl alcohol, heptane, and H_2SO_4 by the method of Dole (1956), or can be separated chromatographically (Wisnieski *et al.*, 1973).

(e) *Other potential sources of contamination*. Glassware requires special attention. After normal washing, it is soaked in strong acid (HNO_3 or H_2SO_4) and thoroughly rinsed in tap water followed by distilled water. Special precautions are taken to avoid the carry-over of thiamine and other stable compounds. Cotton plugs and caps with porous liners should not be used. Nitrocellulose membrane filters for sterilization are preferred to filters composed of asbestos (Seitz), porcelain, or sintered glass. Some commercially available membranes have been treated with a detergent (to facilitate wetting) which may need to be rinsed off.

Another possible source of difficulty relates to the growth-inhibitory effect of a toxic residue from the gaseous agent used for sterilizing plastic Petri dishes. On one occasion this explanation for unsatisfactory growth was found by dispensing a preparation of defined medium into glass Petri dishes and into the suspect plastic dishes; quantitative assays of gonococci revealed gross differences between the average numbers of colonies recovered on the media in the two sets of dishes.

2. *Problems relating to bacteria*

(a) *Inocula*. Bacteria taken from a medium rich in preformed nutrients must be physiologically active in order to convert to growth on a synthetic medium composed of low molecular weight biosynthetic precursors. The practice of suspending the gonococci in buffered salts solution is hazardous because compounds required for initiating growth from small inocula may leak from the cells. Furthermore, autolysis may occur. Thus, cellular suspensions should be prepared from fresh cultures using high quality suspending fluid, and the typing media should be promptly inoculated. Strains with multiple nutritional requirements are especially sensitive to deleterious environmental conditions.

If on the defined media gonococcal growth is deficient, leaving the auxotype in doubt, the test should be repeated. Two modifications of the routine procedure may improve the retest results. (i) Inoculum cells may be physiologically "adapted" to growth on defined media. For this, bacteria taken from a 14–17 h culture on supplemented GC medium base are streaked directly on complete NEDA. Growth of numerous colonies on the complete medium indicates that the majority of cells of the population initiated growth and, therefore, that they are unlikely to be progeny of rare mutants. Accordingly, the nutritional characteristics of the bacteria growing on this NEDA subculture should be genetically unchanged, but biosynthetic enzymes needed for prompt growth on NEDA will have become operative. (ii) The undiluted cellular suspension, as soon as it is prepared from a 16–18 h NEDA culture, is streaked with a loop on to a quadrant or one-half of the surface of each auxotyping medium, thereby reducing the time of exposure to the buffered salts solution.

(b) *"Fastidious" strains.* An additional problem is presented by some strains which do not grow well even on a heated blood agar. Possibly they are unusually sensitive to toxic free fatty acids, either pre-existing in the medium or produced by the gonococci themselves (Section II.B). The presence of starch or anionic exchange resin in NEDA media improves the growth of some of these gonococci. However, the growth of a few other strains on complete NEDA medium may be unsatisfactory in spite of the use of large inocula. Irregular patches of confluent growth seen after incubation for 18–24 h may indicate that the bacteria are unable to initiate growth upon subculture. However, careful inspection using low power ($\times 10$–$\times 25$) magnification and transmitted light may reveal small glistening colonies at the margins of the non-glistening patches. By picking and subculturing the small colonies, being careful to avoid carry-over of masses of lysing bacteria, it may be possible to select bacteria (presumably genetic variants) that are capable of relatively normal growth on complete NEDA medium. Subcultures of multiple independent variants selected in this way usually show the same auxotype; such evidence is needed to validate auxotyping results obtained with any problem strain of this kind.

(c) *Syntrophy.* Various interactions occur between strains growing near to one another. Bacteria may excrete quantities of vitamins or amino-acids sufficient to promote growth of auxotrophic gonococci. A widely diffusing thiamine-like compound, produced by Thp strains and other gonococci, "feeds" Thi strains inoculated on –V medium (Fig. 3). Thi strains will not be detected unless inocula are separated by a distance of about 4 cm or preferably are streaked on –V medium in separate dishes. Most bacteria do not "feed" Thp strains. Another conspicuous example of syntrophy is the "feeding" of *N. gonorrhoeae* by *N. meningitidis* when both are inoculated on –CYS medium. Contaminant bacteria also liberate compounds which may stimulate gonococci; thus, it is essential to work with pure cultures of *N. gonorrhoeae*.

3. *Incubation*

Standardization is important also for incubation. Because of genetic and physiological variations, gonococci may respond differently to environmental variations. The importance of maintaining a uniformly high content of CO_2 in the atmosphere was illustrated by results obtained in a study of 74 strains (Catlin, 1973). All were able to grow on complete NEDA medium incubated in air plus 8% CO_2, and 75% multiplied in normal air although usually at a slower rate. Methionine was required for growth of eight strains irrespective of the atmospheric CO_2 concentration. Three other strains exhibited a conditional requirement for methionine which was related to CO_2 concentration. Growth did not occur on –MET medium when cultures were incubated in air; however, growth was satisfactory in air supplemented by 8% CO_2. Growth was sparse or equivocal on –MET medium incubated in the atmosphere obtained by burning a candle to extinction in a closed jar nearly filled with Petri dishes (probably less than 3% CO_2). In addition to providing an adequate atmosphere, care is needed to assure that entry of CO_2 into the Petri dish is not prevented by a moisture seal.

IV. SUBTYPING BASED ON DRUG RESISTANCE

The practical disadvantage of auxotyping as a means of subdividing *N. gonorrhoeae* lies in the prevalence of strains with only a few nutritional requirements. The majority of isolates comprise auxotypes 1, 2, and 3. However, large differences of response to antibacterial agents are found among these types making it feasible to distinguish between members of an auxotype on the basis of their profiles of resistance to 10–15 different compounds. Where auxotyping is done with an inocula-replicating device, the same gonococcal suspensions are efficiently inoculated on to the additional media needed for quantitative tests of resistance.

Appropriate concentrations of each antibacterial agent are incorporated in agar medium. Supplemented GC medium base is satisfactory for this purpose although its contents of starch (which may absorb compounds) and glucose (which reduces the pH) may influence some test results. Other media favourable for growth of gonococci may be used. For tests employing GC medium base, the following ranges of concentrations have been used: Bacitracin, 0·05–1·5; Chloramphenicol, 0·1–4·0; Erythromycin, 0·02–2·0; Lincomycin, 3·0–50·0; Nalidixic acid, 0·2–2·0; Oxacillin, 0·1–30·0; benzyl Penicillin, 0·005–1·5; Rifampicin, 0·02–1·0; Streptomycin, 2·0–20·0 and 1000; Sulfadiazine, 1·0–150·0; Tetracycline, 0·05–2·0; Vancomycin, 3·0–40·0. Four concentrations of Streptomycin (2, 10, 20, 1000 μg/ml) are sufficient, but between six and nine different concentrations are used for each of the other drugs. These concentrations span the ranges of resistance expected for >98% of strains isolated (in 1975) from venereal disease clinic patients in the mid-continental United States. Rare variant strains are encountered which may be either more sensitive or more resistant to a particular drug; these are retested using additional concentrations.

Standard drug solutions and rigid controls are needed to assure test reproducibility. When the media have been stored at 4°C, the antigonococcal activities of the drugs remain satisfactory for five to six days. Deterioration of the drugs and variations of the medium or of incubation conditions which may affect the responses of gonococci are monitored by two or more standard strains of *N. gonorrhoeae* of differing resistance. Inoculation and incubation of these media is the same as for those of the auxotyping set.

The results are read after incubation for 48 h. Resistance is, in our laboratory, determined as the highest concentration of drug allowing development of ≥ 5 colonies of the larger inoculum. This concentration is normally one dilution step below the minimal inhibitory concentration (MIC, read as complete growth inhibition). Although the assigned value may be too low, it is free of the uncertainty of the MIC end-point which may be 100% too high if a two-fold series of concentrations is used. In practice, the concentrations of each drug used for subtyping are selected on the basis of the anticipated degree of resistance of the gonococci under investigation. Two-fold differences of resistance are usually reproducible for each of the drugs listed, except Lincomycin and Vancomycin. Tests of resistance to these two antibiotics show greater variation. Therefore, the responses of two strains to Vancomycin or Lincomycin should be regarded as significantly different only where the difference is three-fold (e.g. 10 and 30 μg/ml) or where smaller differences are confirmed by further tests.

V. PRESENT AND FUTURE OF AUXOTYPING

N. gonorrhoeae thus far has been subdivided into 35 auxotypes (Table V). Auxotypes 1, 2, 3, and 14 are most commonly encountered. However, the percentages of each differ according to the place of residence of the patients and the nature of their infections. Thus, in a study of strains isolated from patients with uncomplicated gonorrhoea (UG), Knapp and Holmes (1975) found that representatives of auxotypes 1 and 2 accounted for 59 and 38%, respectively, of 91 strains obtained in the Philippines and Taiwan. In Seattle, Washington, representatives of auxotype 1 accounted for only 28% and auxotype 2 for 19% of 72 UG strains, whereas 10% of the strains were auxotype 3 and 36% were auxotype 14 or 16. A different distribution of auxotypes was found among strains causing disseminated gonococcal infections of 42 patients in Seattle. Representatives of auxotypes 14 and 16 were responsible for 79% and auxotype 11 for 10% of these disseminated infections. Multiple requirements which included arginine, hypoxanthine, and uracil were identified in 42% of 36 strains isolated from patients with disseminated infections investigated in Chicago (Morello, Lerner and Bohnhoff, 1976). A study in Milwaukee of 251 isolates from urogenital and rectal sites demonstrated that 18% of these gonococci were Arg, Hyx, Ura types, and most of the remaining strains were members of auxotypes 1 (26%), 2 (34%), and 3 (18%) (Carifo and Catlin, 1973). This distribution of auxotypes differed significantly from that found for 67 oropharyngeal isolates from 49 Milwaukee patients (Catlin and Pace, unpublished observations). Representatives of auxotypes 1 (33%), 2 (37%), and 3 (24%) were responsible for throat infections of 46 patients; the other three involved the auxotypes 4, 24, and 31.

The data obtained in the studies cited above suggest that strains requiring arginine, hypoxanthine, and uracil are more likely to cause disseminated infections, and less likely to colonize the oropharynx. A marked susceptibility to benzyl Penicillin and most other antibiotics is another outstanding feature of these strains which has been noted in all of these studies. The Arg, Hyx, Ura strains examined by Knapp and Holmes (1975) were sensitive to 0·015 μg/ml benzyl Penicillin. In addition, most Arg, Hyx, Ura strains are (i) highly susceptible to the toxic effects of certain compounds (e.g. free fatty acids) present in agar and in some extracts of animal tissues used in culture media, a sensitivity which may account in part for the familiar "delicate" growth; (ii) likely to be inhibited by an imbalance of branched amino acids (Dr Josephine Morello, personal communication); and (iii) likely to show equivocal reactions in glucose-containing differential media used for confirming the identity of *N. gonorrhoeae*. Although one or more of these attributes may be exhibited also by gonococci with simpler growth requirements, in general representatives of auxotypes 1, 2, and 3 are less sensitive to deleterious environmental influences, are more likely to develop resistance to antibiotics, and are physiologically more active than strains with multiple nutritional requirements. Additional epidemiological, metabolic, and genetic studies of representatives of various auxotypes are needed to elucidate the biological importance of the nutritional traits and their bearing on antibiotic resistance and on the potential of gonococci for infecting various tissues.

The value of auxotyping as an epidemiological tool depends on the genetic stability of the auxotrophic traits in the infected host. This aspect of auxotyping was investigated for gonococci isolated at one time from two or more anatomic sites of each of 76 persons (Catlin and Pace, manuscript in preparation). The auxotype was the same for the paired or multiple isolates from 73 of these patients, whereas cervical and rectal specimens from three women yielded different auxotypes. These differing pairs of isolates were 741 and 762, 703 and 714, and 661 and 667; the results of representative tests are illustrated in Figs. 2, 4, and 5. No significant differences were found between strains 703 and 714 with respect to resistances to the 12 antibacterial agents listed in Section IV or to the compound produced by *Candida albicans*. The similarities suggest that strain 703 may have lost a requirement for hypoxanthine during multiplication either in the patient or on laboratory media, thereby changing the auxotype from 9 to 2 without affecting the resistance traits. (An absolute requirement for hypoxanthine exhibited initially by two other strains also was lost during repeated subcultures.) The other unmatched pairs of gonococci differed with respect to relative resistances as well as auxotype. Strains 741 (Pro) and 762 (Arg) exhibited two-fold or greater differences of resistance to four drugs. Strains 661 (Pro, Arg) and 667 (Zero phenotype) were differentiated on the basis of their responses to six agents, including Oxacillin (661 resistant to $1 \cdot 0$ $\mu g/ml$ and 667 to $0 \cdot 1$ $\mu g/ml$) Chloramphenicol ($1 \cdot 5$ and $0 \cdot 5$ $\mu g/ml$), Erythromycin ($0 \cdot 5$ and $0 \cdot 05$ $\mu g/ml$), and Sulfadiazine ($10 \cdot 0$ and $50 \cdot 0$ $\mu g/ml$). Thus, auxotyping when combined with resistance subtyping detected simultaneous dual infection of two patients. Furthermore, the results with gonococci from 73 patients verify that autotrophic traits are relatively stable during infection.

Although typing cannot establish that two strains of *N. gonorrhoeae* are the same, differences are detected such that the source of an infection may be identified. Treatment failure may thereby be differentiated from reinfection. The persistence of gonorrhoea in spite of therapy with benzyl Penicillin is exemplified by four auxotype 1 isolates obtained from the same patient; 756 and 763 were isolated from cervical and rectal specimens taken at one time, and 776 and 799 were from specimens taken six days

(a)

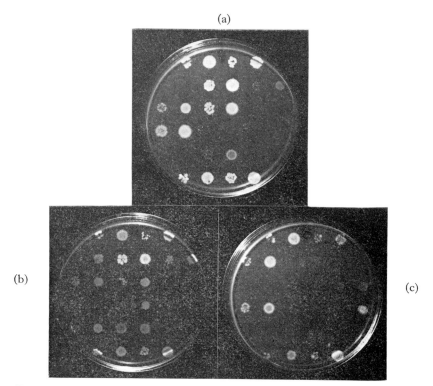

FIG. 5. Differing resistances of *N. gonorrhoeae* to drugs incorporated in supplemented GC medium base: (a) 0·5 μg/ml of Chloramphenicol; (b) 0·2 μg/ml of
Erythromycin; (c) 20 μg/ml of Sulfadiazine. These media were inoculated immediately following inoculation of the auxotyping media shown in Fig. 4, using the
same suspensions of 16 gonococcal isolates.

and 18 days thereafter. These isolates (Fig. 4, 5) were all highly resistant
to penicillins (minimal inhibitory concentrations, 1·0 units/ml benzyl
Penicillin, determined by a method different from that given in Section
IV). Also, they were resistant to 1000 μg/ml of Streptomycin, 3·0 μg/ml of
Chloramphenicol, 1·0 μg/ml of Erythromycin, and 150 μg/ml of Sulfadiazine. This patient was treated successfully with Tetracycline, as shown
by a subsequent negative culture. On the other hand, differing pre- and
post-treatment isolates indicate reinfection. This is illustrated by strain
584 (auxotype 1) which was isolated from a test-of-cure culture taken 11
days after benzyl Penicillin treatment of the patient from whom strain 554
(auxotype 5) had been isolated. The minimal inhibitory concentrations of
benzyl Penicillin were 0·05 units/ml for strain 554 and 0·1 units/ml for

584. The two strains were differentiated also by their responses to Oxacillin (resistance to 0·2 and 1·0 μg/ml), Sulfadiazine (35·0 and 10·0 μg/ml), and Vancomycin (5·0 and 15·0 μg/ml); both were susceptible to Streptomycin.

Distinction between auxotype 1, 2, and 3 strains is based upon susceptibility differences to 12 antigonococcal agents (Fig. 5). This combined approach is a reliable way to type gonococci. In the future when methods for serotyping have been perfected, auxotyping and serotyping may complement one another.

REFERENCES

Apicella, M. A. (1974). *J. infect. Dis.*, **130**, 619–625.
Apicella, M. A., and Allen, J. C. (1973). *Infect. Immun.*, **7**, 315–321.
Beck, A., Fluker, J. L., and Platt, D. J. (1974). *Br. J. Vener. Dis.*, **50**, 367–369.
Buchanan, T. M. (1975). *J. exp. Med.*, **141**, 1470–1475.
Carifo, K., and Catlin, B. W. (1973). *Appl. Microbiol.*, **26**, 223–230.
Catlin, B. W. (1967). *J. Bact.*, **94**, 719–733.
Catlin, B. W. (1973). *J. infect. Dis.*, **128**, 178–194.
Catlin, B. W. (1974a). *In* "Manual of Clinical Microbiology" (Ed. E. H. Lennette, E. H. Spaulding and J. P. Truant), pp. 116–123. American Society for Microbiology, Washington, D.C.
Catlin, B. W. (1974b). *J. Bact.*, **120**, 203–209.
Catlin, B. W. (1975). *J. clin. Microbiol.*, **1**, 102–105.
Davis, B. D., and Mingioli, E. S. (1950). *J. Bact.*, **60**, 17–28.
Demain, A. L. (1965). *J. Bact.*, **89**, 1162.
Dole, V. P. (1956). *J. clin. Invest.*, **35**, 150–154.
Evans, N. M., and Smith, D. D. (1974). *J. med. Microbiol.*, **7**, 305–310.
Flynn, J., and McEntegart, M. G. (1972). *J. clin. Path.*, **25**, 60–61.
Glynn, A. A., and Ward, M. E. (1970). *Infect. Immun.*, **2**, 162–168.
Gould, R. G., Kane, L. W., and Mueller, J. H. (1944). *J. Bact.*, **47**, 287–292.
Handsfield, H. H., Lipman, T. O., Harnisch, J. P., Tronca, E., and Holmes, K. K. (1974). *New Engl. J. Med.*, **290**, 117–123.
Hipp, S. S., Lawton, W. D., Chen, N. C., and Gaafar, H. A. (1974). *Appl. Microbiol.*, **27**, 192–196.
Hipp, S. S., Lawton, W. D., Savage, M., and Gaafar, H. A. (1975). *J. clin. Microbiol.*, **1**, 476–477.
Holmes, K. K. (1974). *Adv. Internal Med.*, **19**, 259–285.
Hutchinson, R. I. (1970). *Br. med. J.*, **3**, 107.
Jephcott, A. E., Reyn, A., and Birch-Andersen, A. (1971). *Acta path. microbiol. scand.*, Section B, **79**, 437–439.
Johnston, K. H., and Gotschlich, E. C. (1974). *J. Bact.*, **119**, 250–257.
Johnston, K. H., Holmes, K. K., and Gotschlich, E. C. (1976). *J. exp. Med.*, **143**, 741–758.
Kellogg, D. S., Jr, Peacock, W. L., Jr, Deacon, W. E., Brown, L., and Pirkle, C. I. (1963). *J. Bact.*, **85**, 1274–1279.
Kellogg, D. S., Jr, Cohen, I. R., Norins, L. C., Schroeter, A. L., and Reising, G. (1968). *J. Bact.*, **96**, 596–605.
Kilpatrick, Z. M. (1972). *New Engl. J. Med.*, **287**, 967–969.

Knapp, J. S., Falkow, S., and Holmes, K. K. (1975). *J. clin. Path.*, **28**, 274–278.

Knapp, J. S., and Holmes, K. K. (1975). *J. infect. Dis.*, **132**, 204–208.

Lankford, C. E., and Skaggs, P. K. (1946). *Archs. Biochem.*, **9**, 265–283.

LaScolea, L. J., Jr, and Young, F. E. (1974). *Appl. Microbiol.*, **28**, 70–76.

Ley, H. L., Jr, and Mueller, J. H. (1946). *J. Bact.*, **52**, 453–460.

Maeland, J. A. (1969). *Acta path. microbiol. scand.*, **77**, 505–517.

Maeland, J. A., Kristoffersen, T., and Hofstad, T. (1971). *Acta path. microbiol. scand.*, Section B, **79**, 233–238.

Martin, J. E., Jr, and Lester, A. (1971). *Hlth Serv. Mental Hlth Admin. Hlth Rep.*, **86**, 30–33.

Morello, J. A., Lerner, S. A., and Bohnhoff, M. (1976). *Infect. Immun.*, **13**, 1510–1516.

Novotny, P., Short, J. A., and Walker, P. D. (1975). *J. med. Microbiol.*, **8**, 413–427.

Novotny, P., and Turner, W. H. (1975). *J. gen. Microbiol.*, **89**, 87–92.

Pariser, H. (1972). *Med. Clins N. Am.*, **56**, 1127–1132.

Phillips, I., Rimmer, D., Ridley, M., Lynn, R., and Warren, C. (1970). *Lancet*, **1**, 263–265.

Reyn, A. (1965). *Bull. Wld Hlth Org.*, **32**, 449–469.

Reyn, A. (1969). *Bull. Wld Hlth Org.*, **40**, 245–255.

Reyn, A. (1974). *In* "Bergey's Manual of Determinative Bacteriology" (Ed. R. E. Buchanan and N. E. Gibbons), pp. 427–433. Williams and Wilkins Co., Baltimore.

Reyn, A., and Bentzon, M. W. (1963). *Acta derm.-venereol*, **43**, 394–398.

Schmidt, H., and Larsen, S. O. (1962). *Acta derm.-venereol.*, **42**, 294–304.

Schofield, C. B. S., Masterton, G., Moffett, M., and McGill, M. I. (1971). *J. infect. Dis.*, **124**, 533–538.

Silver, P. S., and Darling, W. M. (1971). *Br. J. Vener. Dis.*, **47**, 367–372.

Sparling, P. F. (1972). *Med. Clins N. Am.*, **56**, 1133–1144.

Stead, A., Main, J. S., Ward, M. E., and Watt, P. J. (1975). *J. gen. Microbiol.*, **88**, 123–131.

Steers, E., Foltz, E. L., and Graves, B. S. (1959). *Antibiot. Chemother.*, **9**, 307–311.

Stolz, E., and Schuller, J. (1974). *Br. J. Vener. Dis.*, **50**, 104–108.

Sutherland, I. W., and Wilkinson, J. F. (1961). *J. Path. Bact.*, **82**, 431–438.

Swanson, J., Kraus, S. J., and Gotschlich, E. C. (1971). *J. exp. Med.*, **134**, 886–906.

Thayer, J. D., and Martin, J. E., Jr. (1966). *Publ. Hlth Rep.*, **81**, 559–562.

Tramont, E. C., Sadoff, J. C., and Artenstein, M. S. (1974). *J. infect. Dis.*, **130**, 240–247.

Walstad, D. L., Reitz, R. C., and Sparling, P. F. (1974). *Infect. Immun.*, **10**, 481–488.

White, L. A., and Kellogg, D. S., Jr. (1965). *Appl. Microbiol.*, **13**, 171–174.

Wiesner, P. J., Tronca, E., Bonin, P., Pedersen, A. H. B., and Holmes, K. K. (1973). *New Engl. J. Med.*, **288**, 181–185.

Wilson, G. S., and Miles, A. A. (1964). "Topley and Wilson's Principles of Bacteriology and Immunity". Williams and Wilkins Co., Baltimore.

Wisnieski, B. J., Williams, R. E., and Fox, C. F. (1973). *Proc. natn. Acad. Sci. (U.S.A.)*, **70**, 3669–3673.

Subject Index

A

Actinobacillus, 253, 273
  characteristics of, 254
A. equuli, 273
A. lignieresii, 273
A. suis, 273
Acinetobacter, 346
Antibiogram, typing by, 24

B

Bacteriocin typing, 18–22
Bacterium tularense, 227
Biochemical typing, 23–24
Branhamella catarrhalis, 346
Brucella
  A antigen of, 211
  bacteriophage typing of, 214–218
  differential reactions of,
    biotypes, 208
    species, 208
  dissociation in, 205
  epidemiological markers for, 220
  identification of, 201–222
  inhibition of, by dyes, 209
  M antigen of, 211
  metabolic patterns of, 212
  reference cultures of, 222
  serological typing of, 211–214
B. abortus, 202–222
  carbon dioxide requirement of, 207
B. canis, 202–222
B. melitensis, 202–222
B. ovis, 202–222
B. suis, 203–222
"Brucella agar", 206
Brucellas
  characterization of, 205–218
  distribution, 218
Brucellergen test, 220
Brucellosis, epidemiology of, 219

C

Candida albicans, 353
Cerebrospinal meningitis, 293

"Chicken cholera", 272
Communicable diseases, 2
Corynebacterium diphtheriae
  bacteriocin typing of, 21
  phage typing of, 3–17
C. ovis, phage typing of, 10
C. ulcerans, phage typing of, 10

E

Enterobacteriaceae, 253
  relationship between O-antigens of
    Pseudomonas aeruginosa and O-
    antigens of 111
Epidemic foci, 4
Epidemic outbreaks, role of carriers in, 5
Epidemiological typing methods, com-
    bined use of, 25
Escherichia coli
  bacteriocin typing of, 21
  biochemical typing of, 24
  infections by, 48
  phage typing of, 3–17

F

Fowl cholera, 285
Francisella, 273
F. novicida, 227–233
F. tularensis, 227–233
  agglutination in, 231
  Ascoli test for, 231
  bacteriological examination for, 229
  identification of, 227–233
  immunofluorescent technique to de-
    tect, 232
  precipitin test for, 231
  serological techniques in identifica-
    tion of, 230–233
  specimens for isolation of, 228
F. tularensis holearctica, 228

G

Genetic mechanisms, modification of
  phage types by, 13

radioactive antibody binding assay of, 304
serology of, 296
serogroups of, 297, 298
serotypes of, 297
specific antigens of, 297
taxonomy, 294
vaccines for, 311
N. mucosa, 346, 348
N. sicca, 295, 346, 348
Neisseria species, 345
Neisseriaceae, 294
N. subflava, 295, 346, 348
Nosocomial infections, 1–28
    application of typing methods to, 39–59

P

Pasteurella, 253–269, 273
    characteristics of, 254
    definition of, 253
    serotypes of, capsular and somatic, 286
P. gallicida, 273
P. gallinarum, 273
P. haemolytica, 254, 271, 273
    biotypes of, 258
        A, 255
        T, 255
        relation to serotypes, 263
    biotyping of, 253–269
    indirect haemagglutination (IHA) test for, 260
    serotypes of, 261
        relation to biotypes, 263
    serotyping of, 253–269
    subtypes of, 256
    types of, distribution and prevalence of, 264
    typing of, 255, 266
        procedures for, 256
        serological, 260
P. multocida, 254, 271–292
    capsular serotyping of, 281
    capsular staining of, 279
    characteristics of, 274
        antigenic, 280
        biochemical, 271–292
        biological, 273

factor sera of, 285
haemagglutination test for, 282
nomenclature of, 272
O serotyping of, 283
pathogenicity of, 285
protective substance of, 290
reference strains of, 276
serology of, 280
serotype of, relationship between pasteurellosis and, 289
serotypes of, 271–292
somatic (O) antigen of, 282
taxonomy of, 272
P. pneumotropica, 254, 273
P. ureae, 254, 273
Phage typing, 2–17
    applications of, 3
    limitations of, 10
    methodology of, 16
    usefulness of, 3
Pseudomonas, infections, 94
P. aeruginosa
    agglutinability of, 99, 116
    antibody in patient sera, detection of, 140
    antigenic scheme of, 118
    antigenic structure of, 98
    antigens of,
        immunoelectrophoretic characteristics of, 131
        methods of examining, 123–140
    autoplaques, 172
    classification by O-antigens, 101
    cross-reaction between other bacterial species and, 115
    enzyme antigens of, detection of, 137
    epidemiological types of, 153
    fimbriae of, 122
    haemagglutination for the detection of antibodies of, 130
    H-agglutination of, 135
    H-antigen variation in, 118
    H-antigens of,
        characteristics of, 114–120
        classification by, 117
        determination of, 134–135
        immunogenicity of, 116
    H-antisera of, preparation of, 134
    heat-stable antigens of, detection of, 136